Taste of Home's
Light&Tasty
Annual Recipes 2005

PICTURED ABOVE AND ON FRONT COVER: Lime Honeydew Sorbet (page 218) and Steak with Three Peppers (page 118).

Annual Recipes 2005

Editor: Julie Schnittka
Senior Art Director: Linda Dzik
Senior Editor/Books: Heidi Reuter Lloyd
Associate Editor: Jean Steiner
Associate Art Director: Maribeth Greinke
Graphic Art Associates: Ellen Lloyd, Catherine Fletcher
Editorial Assistant: Barb Czysz
Food Editor: Janaan Cunningham
Food Photographers: Rob Hagen, Dan Roberts
Senior Food Photography Artist: Stephanie Marchese
Food Photography Artists: Julie Ferron, Sue Myers

Executive Editor: Kathy Pohl
Food Editor: Janaan Cunningham
Associate Food Editor: Diane Werner RD
Managing Editor: Julie Kastello
Art Director: Julie Wagner
Associate Editors: Mark Hagen, Sharon Selz, Barbara Schuetz, Ann Kaiser
Proofreader: Jean Steiner
Recipe Editor: Janet Briggs
Test Kitchen Director: Mark Morgan RD
Assistant Food Editor: Karen Wright
Senior Home Economist: Peggy Fleming RD
Home Economists: Wendy Stenman, Nancy Fridirici,
Pat Schmeling, Amy Welk-Thieding RD
Test Kitchen Assistants: Suzanne Kern, Sue Megonigle
Editorial Assistants: Ursula Maurer, Joanne Weid, Barb Czysz, Mark Ann Koebernik
Food Photographers: Rob Hagen, Dan Roberts
Senior Food Photography Artist: Stephanie Marchese
Food Photography Artist: Julie Ferron
Photo Studio Manager: Anne Schimmel
Graphic Art Associates: Ellen Lloyd, Catherine Fletcher
Senior Vice President, Editor in Chief: Catherine Cassidy
President: Barbara Newton
Chairman and Founder: Roy Reiman

Taste of Home Books
© 2005 Reiman Media Group, Inc.
5400 S. 60th Street, Greendale WI 53129

International Standard Book Number: 0-89821-443-2
International Standard Serial Number: 1537-3134

To order additional copies of this book, write: *Taste of Home* Books,
P.O. Box 908, Greendale WI 53129; call toll-free 1-800/344-2560 to order
with a credit card. Or visit our Web site at **www.reimanpub.com**.

Contents

502 Low-in-Fat, Flavorful Favorites

MOST FOLKS these days keep an eye on what they eat. They strive to prepare well-balanced meals that are lean on fat and calories but that are full of enough flavor to please and satisfy a family.

So it's no wonder *Light & Tasty* has become the sole source of good-tasting, good-for-you meals in many homes.

You see, unlike most other food magazines, *Light & Tasty* takes a *common sense* approach to calorie-wise eating. It's not a diet magazine, so it doesn't lecture or urge diet and exercise but instead suggests simple options with lighter ingredient choices.

The recipes in *Light & Tasty* are lean on fat and calories. But most important, they're full of flavor. So getting your family to eat healthy meals is easy. It's no wonder that folks who are lightening up their menus have come to rely on *Light & Tasty*, even when they're cooking for finicky eaters.

And now all 502 light-done-right recipes from the fourth year of *Light & Tasty* magazine are at your fingertips in this timeless cookbook, *2005 Light & Tasty Annual Recipes*.

Many of the dishes are family-favorites of our readers, so they're guaranteed to offer great, home-style flavor. The taste is still there…these recipes have just been lightened up a bit with less fat, calories, cholesterol, etc.

Yet, these dishes won't leave you hungry. You'll find lots of great-tasting comfort foods, like Hearty Beef Vegetable Stew, Crispy Oven-Baked Chicken, Creamy Skillet Potatoes, Cinnamon Buns, Cherry Chocolate Cake and much more. Each of these mouth-watering dishes is leaner on fat, calories or sodium…but not leaner on flavor.

In addition, every recipe has been reviewed by a Registered Dietitian and includes Nutritional Analysis, plus Diabetic Exchanges where appropriate.

With *2005 Light & Tasty Annual Recipes*, healthy eating for the whole family has never been easier…or more enjoyable!

Diane Werner, R.D.

Associate Food Editor, *Light & Tasty*

What's Inside These Recipe-Packed Pages?

AS IF 502 great-tasting recipes aren't enough reasons to love *2005 Light & Tasty Annual Recipes*, the following helpful features will certainly make this big book a valued reference in your kitchen for years to come.

Here's What's New! If you are on a special diet—or someone you cook for is—finding suitable recipes is even easier!

That's because low-carb, low-fat, low-sodium and meatless dishes are now clearly labeled right below the recipe title. Turn the page for an explanation of these special diet indicators.

User-Friendly Chapters. To assist in your menu planning, we've compiled all 502 recipes into 15 convenient chapters, such as Light Bites & Beverages, Beefed-Up Main Dishes, Chicken & Turkey Entrees, Meatless Main Dishes, Side Dishes & Condiments and Dazzling Desserts. (For a complete listing of chapters, turn back to page 3.)

Mouth-Watering Meals. You'll find 15 complete meals (including pictures!), which are perfect for either weekend entertaining (page 237) or weekday family dining (page 250).

De-Light-Ful Dinner Planner. In addition to the meal chapters mentioned above, we've created 27 menu plans. (See the De-Light-Ful Dinner Planner on page 7.) Each meal features recipes found inside the book, as well as suggestions for "appealing partners" (side dishes, desserts or beverages) and meal-preparation pointers.

Hundreds of Color Photos. *More than half* of the 502 recipes in this timeless collection are shown in full color. So you can be sure these full-flavored foods not only taste terrific but are eye-appealing as well.

Easy-to-Use Indexes. Finding all 502 recipes is a snap with two simple-to-use indexes. The general index lists every recipe by food category, major ingredient and/or cooking technique. The alphabetical recipe listing is perfect for folks looking for a specific family favorite.

There's also a reference index that directs you to the many helpful kitchen tips and healthy-eating hints throughout the book. (The indexes begin on page 272.)

Nutritional Analysis Nuggets

Our Nutritional Guidelines

EVERY RECIPE in *2005 Light & Tasty Annual Recipes* fits the lifestyle of health-conscious cooks. The recipes present a variety of foods that will easily fit into a meal plan that is within the standards of the USDA's Daily Nutrition Guide (see box below). The target nutritional content of recipes, on a per serving basis, is:

- 400 calories (or less)
- 12 grams of fat (or less)
- 1,000 mg sodium (or less)
- 100 mg cholesterol (or less)

How we calculated the Nutritional Analysis

- Whenever a choice of ingredients is given in a recipe (such as 1/3 cup of sour cream or plain yogurt), the first ingredient listed is the one calculated in the Nutritional Analysis.
- When a range is given for an ingredient (such as 2 to 3 teaspoons), we calculate the first amount given.
- Only the amount of marinade absorbed during preparation is calculated.
- Garnishes listed in recipes are generally included in our calculations.

Diabetic Exchanges

ALL recipes in this book have been reviewed by a Registered Dietitian. Diabetic Exchanges are assigned to recipes in accordance with guidelines from the American Diabetic and American Dietetic Associations. The majority of recipes in *2005 Light & Tasty Annual Recipes* are suitable for diabetics.

Special Diet Indicators

TO HELP folks on restricted diets easily find dishes to suit their needs, we clearly indicate recipes that are low in carbohydrates, fat or sodium or that contain no meat. You'll find these colored special diet indicators after the recipe title where appropriate:

Low-carb (One serving contains 15 grams or less of carbohydrates)
Low-fat (One serving contains 3 grams or less of fat)
Low-sodium (One serving contains 140 milligrams or less of sodium)
Meatless (Appetizers, salads, breads, side dishes and entrees that contain no meat)

Your Serving Size Guide

Grains Group

1 bread slice, pancake or waffle

Half of an average bagel (the size of a hockey puck)

1 cup dry cereal

1/2 cup cooked cereal, rice or pasta

Vegetable Group

1 cup raw leafy greens

1/2 cup of any chopped vegetable, raw or cooked

6-ounce glass of vegetable juice

1 small potato

Fruit Group

1 medium piece of fruit

1/2 cup sliced fruit

6-ounce glass of orange juice or any 100% fruit juice

Milk Group

8-ounce container of yogurt

1 cup cottage cheese

2 ounces soft cheese (mozzarella)

1-1/2 ounces hard cheese (cheddar) (size of two dominoes)

8-ounce glass of milk

Meat and Beans Group

3 ounces cooked lean meat, poultry or fish (size of a deck of cards)

2 tablespoons peanut butter

1/2 cup beans

Daily Nutrition Guide

	Women 25-50	Women over 50	Men over 24
Calories	2,200	1,900 or less	2,900
Fat	73 g or less	63 g	96 g or less
Saturated Fat	24 g or less	21 g or less	32 g or less
Cholesterol	300 mg or less	300 mg or less	300 mg or less
Sodium	2,400 mg or less	2,400 mg or less	2,400 mg or less
Carbohydrates	335 g	283 g	446 g
Fiber	20-30 g	20-30 g	20-30 g
Protein	50 g	50 g or less	63 g

This chart is only a guide. Calorie requirements vary, depending on size, weight and amount of activity. Children's calorie and protein needs vary as they grow.

De-Light-ful Dinner Planner

To make meal planning easy,
turn to these 27 tasty menu suggestions
featuring recipes from this book, "appealing
partners" to round out the dinners and
meal-preparation pointers.

Texas Chops and Rice (page 16)

Hearty Gumbo

For a warming meal that has plenty of flavor but not too much spice, try **Quick Shrimp Gumbo** (p. 34) from Mrs. Leo Merchant of Jackson, Mississippi. Her savory specialty is chock-full of good stuff, including sliced kielbasa, shrimp and green pepper.

For an easy accompaniment, bake a batch of **Green Onion Biscuits** (p. 190). Our Test Kitchen stirred up this simple recipe that comes together in no time.

Appealing Partners

♦ Macaroni salad
♦ Cut vegetables with dip

Practical Tips

🍎 You'll need half a package of kielbasa to make the gumbo. Wrap the remaining half tightly in plastic wrap and store it in the refrigerator to make Oven Cassoulet (p. 150).

🍎 If you have leftover cooked rice on hand, you can use 1 cup of it in place of the 1/2 cup of quick-cooking rice called for in the gumbo.

🍎 For a change of pace, use garlic powder instead of onion powder in the biscuit recipe.

A Taste of The Orient

Get a head start on tonight's dinner by marinating **Teriyaki Flank Steak** (p. 121) the night before. Nancy Fairless of Clifton, New Jersey creates a robust blend that seasons and tenderizes the meat.

Asian Coleslaw (p. 46), which calls for Chinese cabbage, has a "fluffier" texture than regular coleslaw. Alta Goodman of Canton, South Dakota dresses the mixture with white wine vinegar, sesame oil and a touch of sugar.

Appealing Partners

♦ Sesame Green Beans 'n' Water Chestnuts (recipe on p. 76)
♦ Fresh orange wedges

Practical Tips

🍎 For the most tender results, our Test Kitchen recommends slicing the flank steak thinly across the grain.

🍎 When making the coleslaw, the type of sesame oil you choose will dictate its flavor. Light-colored sesame oil is milder while darker Oriental sesame oil has a bolder taste.

🍎 Alta suggests adding shredded turkey or chicken to the coleslaw and serving it as a light main dish.

Turkey and Taters

Loretta Paulus of Venice, Florida relies on an oven bag to help keep the moistness in **Braised Turkey Thighs** (p. 125). She serves them with a thick gravy flecked with bits of carrot, celery and onion.

The gravy is especially good over **Light 'n' Creamy Mashed Potatoes** (p. 76) from our Test Kitchen. They have less fat than traditional mashed potatoes, but they taste so good that your family will never guess they're lighter.

Appealing Partners

♦ Steamed broccoli
♦ Cranberry sauce

Practical Tips

🍎 Using an oven bag for cooking the turkey helps retain moisture and makes cleanup easier. Look for boxes of oven bags near the aluminum foil and plastic wrap at most grocery stores.

🍎 If you like a smooth gravy, cool the vegetables and gravy slightly before pureeing in the blender.

🍎 When preparing the mashed potatoes, use russet (Idaho) potatoes for best results.

Filling Family Fare

For a stick-to-your-ribs supper, try **Oven Cassoulet** (p. 150) from Diane Molberg of Emerald Park, Saskatchewan. A golden bread crumb topping completes this full-flavored meal-in-one that's loaded with fiber-rich beans.

Amber Kimmich of Powhatan, Virginia rounds out the meal with **Chive-Mushroom Spinach Salad** (p. 47). A warm dressing made with sauteed mushrooms, onion and garlic is a light change from heavier bacon dressings.

Appealing Partners

♦ Vegetable soup
♦ Angel food cake with berry sauce

Practical Tips

👌 Instead of great northern beans, you can use other white beans, such as white kidney or cannellini beans.

👌 To make soft bread crumbs for the casserole's topping, tear three slices of white bread into pieces. Use a blender or food processor to process them into crumbs to yield 1-1/2 cups.

👌 If you don't have balsamic vinegar on hand for the salad dressing, try red wine vinegar instead.

A Plate with Pizzazz

A sprinkling of oregano and basil provides the pleasant Italian flavor you'll find in **Pork Chops with Pizza Sauce** (p. 154). Joanna Iovino of Commack, New York serves them with noodles.

When a guiltless dessert is in order, Anissa DeGrasse of Mountain Home Air Force Base, Idaho turns to **Pudding Grahamwiches** (p. 18). The fun frosty snacks are a snap to assemble with graham crackers, sugar-free instant pudding and reduced-fat whipped topping.

Appealing Partners

♦ Green peas
♦ Cucumber salad

Practical Tips

👌 The pork chop recipe calls for 2 cups hot cooked noodles, so you'll need to boil 4 ounces uncooked noodles (about 3 cups).

👌 When making the dessert, Anissa says you can press the edges of the sandwiches in grated chocolate or M&M miniature baking bits instead of mini chocolate chips.

👌 For variety, substitute chocolate or cinnamon-topped graham crackers.

Mexican Main Dish

Tired of the typical tacos and burritos? Try this zippy casserole from Judy Munger of Warren, Minnesota. **Taco Noodle Dish** (p. 127) has satisfying southwestern flavor, plus lots of tasty toppings.

Cool your palate with **Bottoms-Up Cherry Limeade** (p. 20) from Awynne Thurstenson of Siloam Springs, Arkansas. The sweet lime beverage gets its pretty color from cherry juice.

Appealing Partners

♦ Honeydew melon wedges
♦ Orange sherbet

Practical Tips

👌 Judy's entree recipe includes the fresh vegetables that she uses most often, but the casserole is equally delicious when topped with diced green onions, green pepper, green olives and even shredded zucchini.

👌 When making the main dish, you can replace the noodles with another pasta, such as small bow ties or spirals.

👌 Awynne says she often uses plain water in her beverage instead of sparkling water as a nice change from sodas and other carbonated drinks.

Flavorful Fillets

Stew and Salad Supper

Grilled Goodness

Elizabeth Harrer of Lockport, New York dresses up tender fish with sour cream and sauteed peppers and onions to make **Onion Peppered Roughy** (p. 162). The elegant entree is quick and easy enough for weeknights.

For an aromatic accompaniment, stir up **Minty Orzo and Peas** (p. 79), a swift stovetop side dish from Kristen Dunphy of Haverhill, Massachusetts.

For a meal that'll stick to your ribs and not your waistline, try **Hearty Beef Vegetable Stew** (p. 116) from Angela Nelson of Ruther Glen, Virginia. It simply simmers in the slow cooker all afternoon.

Hickory barbecue sauce and a little Liquid Smoke lend distinctive flavor to the thick salad dressing shared by Betty McConoughey of Loves Park, Illinois. **Smoky Thousand Island Salad Dressing** (p. 51) is delicious dolloped over tossed greens.

Chili sauce provides the tasty flavor on **Grilled Turkey Kabobs** (p.131) from Marilyn Rodriguez of Fairbanks, Alaska. Moist chunks of turkey alternate with crisp-tender zucchini, pepper, mushrooms and cherry tomatoes.

Skip the after-dinner coffee and enjoy a dish of **Coffee Mousse** (p. 206) instead. Vernette Dechaine of Pittsfield, Maine shares the recipe for this fluffy finale to the meal.

Appealing Partners

♦ Honey Lime Fruit Toss (recipe on p. 53)
♦ Cut asparagus

Appealing Partners

♦ Corn muffins
♦ Assorted citrus segments

Appealing Partners

♦ Wild rice blend
♦ Three-bean salad

Practical Tips

👃 When grating the lemon peel for the side dish, grate all the peel. Place any extra in a heavy-duty resealable plastic bag and freeze for future use.

👃 Feel free to use long grain rice instead of orzo in the side dish if your family prefers it. The taste will still be delicious!

Practical Tips

👃 When she doesn't have enough time to use her slow cooker, Angela assembles the stew ingredients in a Dutch oven, covers it and bakes it for 2-1/2 hours at 350°.

👃 Toss in your family's favorite vegetables when preparing the green salad for Smoky Thousand Island Salad Dressing.

Practical Tips

👃 You can also broil the kabobs in your oven instead. Broil the skewers 4-6 inches from the heat for 3-4 minutes on each side or until the juices run clear.

👃 These savory skewers would also taste great with chicken, pork or beef.

👃 For a change of pace, give the dessert a mocha taste. Instead of using frozen whipped topping, Vernette suggests preparing an envelope of whipped topping mix with low-fat chocolate milk.

Easy Italian Entree

Fresh garlic, basil and caraway seeds nicely season **Italian Sausage 'n' Peppers Supper** (p. 138) from Teresa Puszkar of Colorado Springs, Colorado.

Round out the menu with slices of make-ahead **Lemon Yogurt Cream Pie** (p. 211). The light airy dessert from Susan Kostecke of St. Louis, Missouri is a snap to whip together and pop in the fridge the night before.

Appealing Partners

- Spinach salad
- Italian bread

Practical Tips

- In a hurry? Substitute 1-1/2 teaspoons of Italian seasoning for the basil, oregano and thyme called for in the main dish.

- If your family likes dishes with some kick, add crushed red pepper flakes or cayenne pepper to the pasta toss.

- Feel free to experiment with other flavors of yogurt when making the dessert. When using a citrus yogurt, add the corresponding citrus peel. When using other yogurt flavors, omit the peel altogether.

Fast Flounder

It doesn't take long for Michelle Smith of Sykesville, Maryland to bake **Breaded Flounder Fillets** (p. 166) in the oven. A light coating, which has a mild cornmeal flavor, helps the delicate fish stay moist.

To accompany it, our Test Kitchen created **Stir-Fry Sesame Green Beans** (p. 84). Dried apricots are an unusual addition to the swift stovetop side dish, which adds color to most any meal.

Appealing Partners

- Cucumber salad
- Sliced strawberries and bananas

Practical Tips

- The breading also would be good on other types of fish, such as orange roughy, grouper or sole.

- Don't have fresh gingerroot for the side dish? In a pinch, you can use 1/2 teaspoon ground ginger in place of the 2 teaspoons minced fresh gingerroot called for in the recipe.

- It's easy to toast sesame seeds on the stovetop. Place them in a dry skillet over medium heat. Cook them, stirring occasionally, just until golden brown.

Sizzling Steak

Whip up the marinade for **Grilled Citrus Steak** (p. 113) this morning and you're well on your way to getting dinner on the table tonight. Joan Whyte-Elliott of Fenelon Falls, Ontario shares the recipe.

Round out the meal with **Onion-Basil Grilled Vegetables** (p. 85) from Jan Oeffler of Danbury, Wisconsin. Onion soup mix flavors the tasty medley of fresh veggies grilled in a foil packet.

Appealing Partners

- Blackberry Frozen Yogurt (recipe on p. 216)
- Herbal iced tea

Practical Tips

- "Do not overcook the steak," Joan urges. "It is excellent when done medium-rare to medium." For the most tender results, slice the meat thinly across the grain.

- For potlucks, Joan says she serves the sliced beef on Italian buns. "It's always the first to go," she notes.

- When assembling the Onion-Basil Grilled Vegetables, feel free to add any produce your family prefers, such as mushrooms, zucchini or parsnips.

Fiesta of Flavor

Spice up suppertime with **Tangy Turkey Tostadas** (p. 142) from Julie Lee of Memphis, Tennessee. This family-pleasing main dish calls for good-for-you ingredients like ground turkey, fiber-rich beans and a variety of vegetables.

Lisa Castillo of Bourbonnais, Illinois sends in her recipe for **Refreshing Lemon-Lime Drink** (p. 27). The cool beverage is not too tart and not too sweet.

Appealing Partners

♦ Seasoned rice
♦ Watermelon wedges

Practical Tips

👆 When shopping for ingredients for the main dish, you'll most likely find packages of corn tostadas near the hard-shell tacos in the Mexican food section.

👆 The turkey mixture also can be served taco-style in soft flour or corn tortillas.

👆 If you're not watching your sodium, Lisa recommends serving the beverage like a traditional margarita. "Rub a lime wedge on the rim of each glass and then dip it in salt before pouring each serving," she suggests.

Meatless Mainstay

Feta cheese adds the finishing touch to **Bell Peppers and Pasta** (p. 181) from Sharon Csuhta of Wadsworth, Ohio. The speedy stovetop entree is so delicious, you won't miss the meat.

Looking for a change of pace from typical store-bought dressings? Try **Mixed Greens Salad with Tarragon Dressing** (p. 60) from Janice Mitchell of Aurora, Colorado. The homemade dressing gets its unique flavor from tarragon vinegar.

Appealing Partners

♦ Minestrone soup
♦ Crunchy breadsticks

Practical Tips

👆 If you have a family of confirmed meat lovers, feel free to add slices of leftover grilled steak or strips of cooked chicken to the pasta toss.

👆 Spiral or medium shell pasta can be used in place of the penne pasta.

👆 For the herb dressing, Janice uses fresh tarragon from her garden to make the flavored vinegar. But you should be able to find prepared tarragon vinegar in the vinegar section at your supermarket.

Casual Dining

You'll have dinner well in hand when you serve **Cajun Chicken Sandwiches** (p. 138) from Amber Peterson of Oakes, North Dakota. She rubs a robust combination of seasonings on the chicken breasts before cooking them on the grill.

For dessert, try **Candy Chip Bar Cookies** (p. 222) from Wendy Budlong. The Acton, Massachusetts baker stirs colorful mini baking bits into a quick batter that's mildly flavored with peanut butter.

Appealing Partners

♦ Vegetable sticks with dip
♦ Potato salad

Practical Tips

👆 When preparing the Cajun Chicken Sandwiches, Amber sometimes makes a very large batch of seasoning and uses it on a variety of items besides chicken. Try it on pork, fish or even beef.

👆 If the weather isn't conducive to grilling, broil the chicken breasts in your oven instead. Broil 4-6 inches from the heat for 3-4 minutes on each side or until the juices run clear.

👆 When making the bar cookies, use chips instead of baking bits.

The Best Burgers

A short ingredient list makes **Hearty Backyard Burgers** (p. 120) a winner on busy evenings. Paula LeFevre of Garden, Michigan boosts the grilled flavor with beer, garlic, onion and Worcestershire sauce.

Looking for a change from regular coleslaw? Try refreshing **Broccoli Slaw** (p. 74) from Betty Kleberger of Florissant, Missouri, who suggests assembling the salad ahead of time. "I like to let it sit in the refrigerator for a couple of hours so the flavors blend," she explains.

Appealing Partners

♦ Fruity Rainbow Salad (recipe on p. 68)
♦ Fat-free fudge pops

Practical Tips

🍎 Topping your burgers with lettuce and tomato is an easy way to add vegetables to your meal. Among the tomatoes on the grocery list are two for tonight's meal. Simply cut each one in six slices and serve two slices with each burger.

🍎 Don't have a can of Mexicorn for the slaw? Feel free to substitute 1-1/4 cups canned or frozen corn instead. The salad will have much the same flavor.

Effortless Entree

In Woodstock, Illinois, Alice Nulle uses a nicely seasoned coating to keep her **Crispy Oven-Baked Chicken** (p. 148) moist and juicy without frying.

To accompany the entree, toss together **Green Pepper Tomato Salad** (p. 53) from Lili Hill of Athens, Georgia. It makes the most of fresh seasonal veggies and offers color and crunch in every bite.

Appealing Partners

♦ Lemonade
♦ Baked beans

Practical Tips

🍎 The coating for the chicken calls for 1-1/4 cups of crushed cornflakes. To crush the cornflakes, start with 4-1/2 cups of cereal. Then process them in a blender or food processor. Or place them in a bowl and crush with the bottom of a heavy glass. Or place them in a plastic bag and crush them with a rolling pin.

🍎 When assembling the salad, feel free to substitute 3 cups cherry or grape tomatoes instead of tomato wedges.

Lovely Meat Loaf

Your family won't know they're eating ground turkey when they taste **Spinach Turkey Roll** (p. 146) shared by Delia Kennedy of Deer Park, Washington. The tender meat loaf has pretty spirals of spinach throughout and spaghetti sauce on top for a fast final touch.

To complement the meat loaf, fix **Creamy Skillet Potatoes** (p. 93). Denise Pritchard of Seminole, Oklahoma relies on her stovetop to prepare this yummy potato side dish.

Appealing Partners

♦ Tossed garden salad with low-fat dressing
♦ Green beans

Practical Tips

🍎 You'll need two slices of wheat bread to make a cup of soft bread crumbs for the Spinach Turkey Roll. Simple tear the bread into pieces and pulse in a blender or food processor to create soft crumbs.

🍎 We recommend using the red potatoes called for in the Creamy Skillet Potatoes recipe, because they retain their shape best when boiled.

From-the-Sea Favorite

Sherry West of New River, Arizona bastes **Glazed Salmon Fillet** (p. 171) with a lip-smacking sauce while grilling it. It's nice enough for company, yet quick enough for a weeknight.

Round out this mouth-watering meal with **Confetti Rice** (p. 90), a simple stovetop side dish that works well with any entree. Dorothy Bayes of Sardis, Ohio seasons the rice with oregano and fresh parsley.

Appealing Partners

- Honeydew melon balls
- Steamed carrots

Practical Tips

For a marvelous main-dish salad, Sherry suggests serving the grilled salmon over mixed baby greens tossed with a store-bought Asian-style dressing.

Salmon can be part of a healthy menu plan. While it's higher in total fat, it's low in saturated fat. Plus, salmon is high in omega-3 fatty acids, which help reduce the risk of heart disease.

Slow-Cooked Specialty

Steer clear of last-minute dinner-time details when you serve **Slow Cooker Beef Au Jus** (p. 108) from Carol Hille of Grand Junction, Colorado. It's easy to assemble the ingredients for this savory slow-cooked beef in the morning, then let it simmer all day.

Top off the meal with slices of delightful **Lemon Berry Pie** (p. 227). Ann Flores of Seneca, Kansas takes advantage of convenience items to create the layered treat.

Appealing Partners

- Boiled red potatoes
- Sauteed zucchini

Practical Tips

When serving the beef, Carol suggests thickening the juices to make a gravy.

For the pie, you need both grated lemon peel and lemon juice. First, use a grater to remove just the yellow part of the peel. Then cut the lemon in half to squeeze the juice. A large lemon yields more than enough peel and juice for the pie.

Make Manicotti!

Liven up your weeknights with hearty **Spinach Manicotti** (p. 186) from Mary Steiner of West Bend, Wisconsin. Mary gives this traditional favorite a tasty twist by adding chunky salsa to the tomato sauce.

A wedge of well-seasoned **Herb Focaccia Bread** (p. 198) makes the perfect accompaniment for the manicotti. Our Test Kitchen enhanced these fragrant "loaves" with onion, rosemary and thyme. Using a convenient hot roll mix speeds up preparation of this tender yeast bread.

Appealing Partners

- Minestrone soup
- Italian green beans

Practical Tips

Mary assembles the Spinach Manicotti the day before and refrigerates it overnight. If you do make the manicotti ahead, wait until just before baking to pour on the final layer of sauce.

To give Herb Focaccia Bread a different flavor, try other combinations of herbs such as basil and oregano instead of rosemary and thyme.

Prime Pork Roast

An ordinary weeknight meal becomes something special when you serve down-home **Cider Pork Roast** (p. 150) from Terry Danner of Rochelle, Illinois. The slow-cooked meat is moist and tender with a pleasant fruity taste.

For an attractive yet simple side dish, stir up **Sesame Seed Citrus Noodles** (p. 95). Trisha Kruse of Boise, Idaho dresses up the noodles with lemon peel, orange peel and basil for a burst of refreshing flavor...and color!

Appealing Partners

♦ Steamed broccoli
♦ Fresh fruit cups

Practical Tips

🍎 When preparing the pork roast, dried rosemary can be substituted for fresh. Put the rosemary in a tied cheesecloth bag and place the bag in the slow cooker with the roast.

🍎 Apple cider and apple juice can be used interchangeably in the Cider Pork Roast recipe.

Sandwich Supper

Turn on your slow cooker in the morning and let the fixin's for savory **Shredded Beef Sandwiches** (p. 112) cook all day. Marie Basinger of Connellsville, Pennsylvania flavors the tender meat with everything from cayenne to cola.

For a crunchy accompaniment or a before-dinner appetizer, arrange a variety of cut veggies on a platter and serve with well-seasoned **Dill Dip** (p. 28) from Judy Bartnik of Wausau, Wisconsin. This thick easy dip is so creamy, no one will guess it's light.

Appealing Partners

♦ Makeover Cherry Coconut Bars (recipe on p. 225)
♦ Coleslaw

Practical Tips

🍎 If you'd like your beef sandwiches with more "kick", increase the cayenne pepper and chili powder.

🍎 Avoid buying and cutting up whole vegetables to serve with the dip by purchasing precut celery, broccoli and other veggies from your grocery store's salad bar as well as baby carrots and cherry tomatoes.

Satisfying Stew

Your family will be all smiles when you rustle up **Texas Ranch-Style Stew** (p. 120) from Mrs. J.W. West of Alvord, Texas. Each hearty bowl is chock-full of nutritious beans, tomatoes, corn, ground beef and pasta seasoned to please.

Make sure everyone leaves room for **Chewy Coconut Macaroons** (p. 232), which you can make ahead and store in an airtight container. Peggy Key of Grant, Alabama enhances these yummy coconut chews with a hint of almond extract.

Appealing Partners

♦ Tossed salad
♦ Corn bread

Practical Tips

🍎 Add extra nutrition to Texas Ranch-Style Stew by stirring in leftover cooked veggies when you add the pasta. Cook and stir until the vegetables are heated through.

🍎 Baked beans will give the stew a slightly sweeter taste. Experiment with different canned varieties to find your family's favorites.

🍎 Vanilla extract can be substituted for the almond extract in the macaroons recipe.

Fabulous Fajitas

Dinner's on the table in no time when you serve **Turkey Fajitas** (p. 148) from Bonnie Basinger of Lees Summit, Missouri. The colorful sweet peppers and tender strips of turkey fold nicely into warm flour tortillas. Cilantro, cumin and cayenne add to the Mexican flavor of this fun main dish.

What better complement for fajitas than a serving of fast-to-fix **Spanish Rice** (p. 95) from Sharon Donat of Kalispell, Montana? The rice is moist and mildly seasoned.

Appealing Partners

♦ Fresh salsa
♦ Fruit juice popsicles

Practical Tips

🍎 For a change of pace, you can exchange chicken breast or sirloin steak with the turkey tenderloin in the fajitas.

🍎 You can use instant rice in place of the long grain rice in the Spanish Rice recipe. Instead of using 1 cup uncooked long grain rice, use 2 cups uncooked instant rice. Prepare it according to package directions using the same amount of broth called for in the recipe.

Texas Chops And Rice

It's a snap to put dinner on the table when you prepare **Texas-Flavored Pork Chops** (p. 160). The mildly seasoned chops from Andrea Keith of Kentwood, Michigan bake in half an hour or less.

While they're in the oven, fix **Lemony Herbed Rice** (p. 96). Canned green chilies and fresh herbs spice up this stovetop side dish shared by Connie Rank-Smith of Sherwood, Wisconsin.

Appealing Partners

♦ Steamed baby carrots
♦ Chilled grapefruit segments

Practical Tips

🍎 If you like your food with a bit more heat, add cayenne pepper to the coating for the pork chops.

🍎 To trim minutes from the side dish, replace the long grain rice with 3 cups instant rice (use the same amount of broth called for in the recipe). Simply add rice to the boiling broth and green chilies, cover and let it stand for 5 minutes before fluffing. There's no need to simmer.

🍎 Don't have time to grate the peel of a fresh lemon? Buy a jar of grated lemon peel available in the spice aisle.

Pot Roast And Potatoes

Spending a few minutes the night before will be time well spent when you serve **Sweet 'n' Tangy Pot Roast** (p. 114) from the slow cooker. Carol Mulligan of Honeoye Falls, New York jazzes up the flavor of the gravy with ketchup, Dijon mustard and Worcestershire sauce.

A perfect accompaniment to the roast is **Supreme Potato Casserole** (p. 96) from Joy Allen of Forsyth, Georgia. She takes advantage of reduced-fat and fat-free dairy products to give a creamy treatment to sliced potatoes.

Appealing Partners

♦ Torn romaine with low-fat vinaigrette
♦ Sauteed broccoli florets

Practical Tips

🍎 If you don't get the entree into the slow cooker in the morning, assemble it at lunchtime. Then simmer it in the slow cooker on high for 4-6 hours.

🍎 Don't have time to cook the potatoes before baking the casserole? Substitute 2-1/2 to 3 cups frozen hash browns that have been thawed …or use cooked sliced home fries available in packages in the dairy section of most grocery stores.

Light Bites & Beverages

The next time you're in the mood for a satisfying snack or a thirst-quenching beverage, try one of the tempting treats or refreshing drinks on the following pages. They're anything but lightweight in taste!

Ginger-Cinnamon Fruit Dip (page 22)

Pudding Grahamwiches

Low-fat

(Pictured below)

*My children love eating these sweet snacks,
and they love making them even more!
I love that they're very low in fat, yet so yummy.*
—Anissa DeGrasse
Mountain Home Air Force Base, Idaho

 1-1/2 cups cold fat-free milk
    1 package (1 ounce) sugar-free instant vanilla
      pudding mix
    1 carton (8 ounces) frozen reduced-fat whipped
      topping, thawed
    1 cup miniature marshmallows
   24 graham crackers (about 5 inches x 2-1/2 inches
      each), broken in half
    5 tablespoons miniature semisweet chocolate
      chips

In a large bowl, whisk milk and pudding mix for 2 minutes. Let stand for 2 minutes or until soft-set. Fold in whipped topping and marshmallows. Spread pudding mixture over half of graham crackers. Top with remaining crackers.

Place chocolate chips in a shallow dish. Press edges of sandwich into chips to coat. Wrap each sandwich in plastic wrap; place in an airtight container and freeze. Remove from the freezer about 5 minutes before serving. **Yield:** 2 dozen.

Nutritional Analysis: One sandwich equals 108 calories, 3 g fat (2 g saturated fat), trace cholesterol, 143 mg sodium, 18 g carbohydrate, 1 g fiber, 2 g protein.
Diabetic Exchanges: 1 starch, 1/2 fat.

Horseradish Mustard Dip

Low-carb *Low-fat* **Meatless**

A tongue-tingling blend of zesty flavors comes together in this versatile vegetable dip. It's also great on ham, turkey or roast beef sandwiches. I stir a little into my potato salad, egg salad and tuna salad, too. To suit more timid tastes, cut the horseradish back to 2 teaspoons.
—Shirley Glaab, Hattiesburg, Mississippi

    3/4 cup fat-free plain yogurt
      3 tablespoons minced chives
      2 tablespoons reduced-fat mayonnaise
      1 tablespoon snipped fresh dill *or* 1 teaspoon dill
        weed
      1 tablespoon prepared horseradish
      1 tablespoon Dijon mustard
    1/4 teaspoon salt
    1/8 teaspoon white pepper
Assorted cut vegetables

In a bowl, combine the first eight ingredients. Cover and refrigerate until serving. Serve with assorted vegetables. **Yield:** 1 cup.

Nutritional Analysis: One serving (1/4 cup dip, calculated without vegetables) equals 51 calories, 3 g fat (trace saturated fat), 4 mg cholesterol, 338 mg sodium, 5 g carbohydrate, trace fiber, 2 g protein.
Diabetic Exchanges: 1/2 starch, 1/2 fat.

Ruby Fruit Slush

Low-fat **Low-sodium**

Perfect for the holidays, this rosy refresher puts thirst on ice quite nicely. It's conveniently made ahead, so I'm sure to have some in the freezer for easy entertaining. My kids love this drink.
—Sarah Gingerich, Unionville, Missouri

      3 quarts tropical fruit punch
      1 can (46 ounces) unsweetened pineapple juice
      1 bottle (48 ounces) cranberry apple juice
 4-1/2 cups water
      1 can (12 ounces) frozen orange juice
        concentrate, thawed
      2 liters diet ginger ale *or* lemon-lime soda, chilled

In a very large bowl or bowls, combine the first five ingredients. Transfer to four 2-qt. freezer containers. Freeze, stirring several times to make slushy. Remove containers from freezer 1-2 hours before serving; stir until slushy. Stir a fourth of ginger ale into each container. **Yield:** 2 gallons.

Nutritional Analysis: One serving (1 cup) equals 108 calories, trace fat (0 saturated fat), 0 cholesterol, 30 mg sodium, 27 g carbohydrate, trace fiber, trace protein.
Diabetic Exchanges: 1 fruit, 1/2 starch.

Herb Cheese Spread

Low-carb Low-fat Meatless

I have a friend who runs a greenhouse and holds a spring tea showcasing herbs and recipes that use them. This cheese spread is a favorite. Spread the herbed mixture on assorted crackers and breads to make a crowd-pleasing appetizer.
—Josie Smith, Winamac, Indiana

1 package (8 ounces) fat-free cream cheese
1 tablespoon butter, softened
1 teaspoon *each* minced fresh basil, parsley and chives
1/2 teaspoon *each* chopped fresh oregano, dill and garlic
1/4 teaspoon salt
Assorted crackers *or* bread

In a mixing bowl, beat cream cheese, butter and herbs until smooth. Refrigerate for at least 1 hour to allow flavors to blend. Serve on crackers or bread. **Yield:** 1 cup.

Nutritional Analysis: One serving (2 tablespoons cheese spread, calculated without crackers) equals 41 calories, 2 g fat (1 g saturated fat), 6 mg cholesterol, 243 mg sodium, 2 g carbohydrate, trace fiber, 4 g protein.
Diabetic Exchange: 1 lean meat.

Black-Eyed Pea Salsa

Low-carb Low-fat Meatless

(Pictured above)

Whenever there's a family gathering, my sister-in-law brings this zesty bean dip, and it's a big hit. Since it keeps well in the refrigerator, it's great to have on hand for unexpected guests.
—Pamela Smith, Flushing, New York

1 can (15-1/2 ounces) black-eyed peas, rinsed and drained
1 can (15 ounces) black beans, rinsed and drained
1 can (11 ounces) shoepeg corn, drained
1-1/3 cups mild salsa
1 cup medium salsa
3/4 cup chopped green pepper
1/2 cup chopped green onions
1 can (2-1/4 ounces) chopped ripe olives, drained
1 jalapeno pepper, seeded and chopped
1 envelope Italian salad dressing mix
1 teaspoon ground cumin
1/2 teaspoon garlic powder
Tortilla chips

In a bowl, combine the first 12 ingredients. Serve with tortilla chips. **Yield:** 6 cups.

Editor's Note: When cutting or seeding hot peppers, use rubber or plastic gloves to protect your hands. Avoid touching your face.

Nutritional Analysis: One serving (1/4 cup salsa, calculated without chips) equals 58 calories, trace fat (trace saturated fat), 0 cholesterol, 411 mg sodium, 11 g carbohydrate, 2 g fiber, 2 g protein.
Diabetic Exchanges: 1 vegetable, 1/2 starch.

Tropical Fruit Drink

Low-fat Low-sodium

This yummy thirst-quencher with its smoothie-like texture stars strawberries, kiwifruit and mango. Pour your kids tall glasses—it's a good way to get them to eat fruit.
—Janet Eggers, Suring, Wisconsin

1-1/2 cups orange juice
1 cup halved strawberries
1 medium mango *or* 2 medium peaches, peeled, seeded and cut into chunks
2 kiwifruit, peeled and quartered
1 tablespoon honey
14 ice cubes
1/2 cup chilled club soda

Place the first five ingredients in a blender; cover and process until smooth. Add ice cubes; cover and process until smooth. Stir in soda. Serve immediately in chilled tall glasses. **Yield:** 4 servings.

Nutritional Analysis: One serving (1 cup) equals 130 calories, trace fat (trace saturated fat), 0 cholesterol, 4 mg sodium, 33 g carbohydrate, 3 g fiber, 1 g protein.
Diabetic Exchange: 2 fruit.

Bottoms-Up Cherry Limeade

Low-carb Low-fat *Low-sodium*

(Pictured above)

*My guests enjoy this refreshing cherry-topped
drink. It's just right on a hot southern
summer evening. And it's pretty, too.*
—Awynne Thurstenson, Siloam Springs, Arkansas

**3/4 cup lime juice
Sugar substitute equivalent to 1 cup sugar
  2 liters lime carbonated water, chilled
1/2 cup maraschino cherry juice
  8 maraschino cherries with stems
  8 lime slices**

In a bowl, combine lime juice and sugar substitute. Cover
and refrigerate. Just before serving, stir carbonated water
into lime juice mixture. For each serving, place 1 tablespoon
cherry juice in a glass. Add crushed ice and about 1 cup of
lime juice mixture. Garnish with a maraschino cherry and
a lime slice. **Yield:** 8 servings.

Editor's Note: This recipe was tested with Splenda No
Calorie Sweetener. Look for it in the baking aisle of your grocery store.

Nutritional Analysis: *One serving (1 cup) equals 52 calories, trace fat (trace saturated fat), 0 cholesterol, trace sodium, 14
g carbohydrate, trace fiber, trace protein.*
Diabetic Exchange: *1 fruit.*

Zesty Pita Chips

Low-carb Low-fat *Low-sodium* Meatless

*If you're trying to snack healthier these days, give this
recipe a try. Crispy pita wedges are a low-sodium
substitute for salty commercial chips, and their zippy
seasoning is a fun alternative to creamy dips.
I bake batches of these satisfying nibbles.*
—Katina Tanner, Benton Harbor, Michigan

**2 teaspoons Italian seasoning
2 teaspoons paprika
1 teaspoon garlic powder
4 pita breads (6 inches), split**

In a small bowl, combine the Italian seasoning, paprika and
garlic powder. Cut each pita half into six pieces; place on an
ungreased baking sheet. Spray both sides of wedges with
nonstick cooking spray; sprinkle wedges with seasoning
mixture. Bake at 350° for 10-12 minutes or until golden
brown, turning halfway through baking time. Cool on wire
racks. **Yield:** 16 servings.

Nutritional Analysis: *One serving (3 chips) equals 43 calories, trace fat (trace saturated fat), 0 cholesterol, 81 mg sodium,
9 g carbohydrate, trace fiber, 1 g protein.*
Diabetic Exchange: *1/2 starch.*

Sun-Dried
Tomato-Flavored Hummus

Meatless

*I didn't like the hummus I bought in a box mix or in
refrigerated tubs, so I made my own version using a
pesto sauce mix. My husband and I enjoy it in
sandwiches, but it's great on crackers, too. We like it so
much that we eat any leftovers with a spoon!*
—Kathleen Tribble, Buellton, California

**1 can (15 ounces) garbanzo beans *or* chickpeas,
    rinsed and drained
1/3 cup reduced-fat mayonnaise
  1 tablespoon sun-dried tomato pesto sauce mix
  1 teaspoon lemon juice
Assorted crackers**

In a food processor or blender, combine the beans, mayonnaise, sauce mix and lemon juice; cover and process until blended. Serve on crackers. Store leftovers in the refrigerator. **Yield:** 1-1/4 cups (5 servings).

Editor's Note: This recipe was tested with Knorr Sun-Dried Tomato Pesto Sauce.

Nutritional Analysis: One serving (1/4 cup hummus, calculated without crackers) equals 139 calories, 7 g fat (1 g saturated fat), 6 mg cholesterol, 363 mg sodium, 16 g carbohydrate, 3 g fiber, 4 g protein.
Diabetic Exchanges: 1 starch, 1 fat.

Broccoli Chicken Cups

Low-carb

(Pictured below)

Frozen puff pastry makes these rich and creamy appetizers a snap to prepare. Sometimes, instead of chopping the tomatoes, I put a slice on top of each cup before popping them in the oven.
—*Marty Kingery, Point Pleasant, West Virginia*

2-1/2 cups diced cooked chicken breast
  1 can (10-3/4 ounces) reduced-fat reduced-sodium condensed cream of chicken soup, undiluted
  1 cup frozen chopped broccoli, thawed and drained
  2 small plum tomatoes, seeded and chopped
  1 small carrot, grated
  1 tablespoon Dijon mustard
  1 garlic clove, minced
1/4 teaspoon pepper
  1 sheet frozen puff pastry, thawed
1/4 cup grated Parmesan cheese

In a large bowl, combine the first eight ingredients; set aside. On a lightly floured surface, roll pastry into a 12-in. x 9-in. rectangle. Cut lengthwise into four strips and widthwise into three strips. Gently press puff pastry squares into muffin cups coated with nonstick cooking spray. Spoon chicken mixture into pastry cups. Sprinkle with Parmesan cheese. Bake at 375° for 25-30 minutes or until golden brown. Serve warm. **Yield:** 1 dozen.

Nutritional Analysis: One filled cup equals 182 calories, 10 g fat (3 g saturated fat), 23 mg cholesterol, 310 mg sodium, 13 g carbohydrate, 1 g fiber, 10 g protein.
Diabetic Exchanges: 1 lean meat, 1 starch, 1 fat.

Fruity Dip

Low-sodium   Meatless

Your guests are sure to have fun guessing what's in this dip—it has such a variety of flavors. In addition to fruit, you can serve it with fresh veggies or herbed crackers.
—*Phyllis Shaughnessy, Livonia, New York*

  1 large grapefruit
1/4 cup 100% apricot fruit spread
1/4 cup reduced-sugar orange marmalade
1/4 to 3/4 teaspoon almond extract
  2 cups (16 ounces) reduced-fat lemon yogurt
1/2 cup sliced almonds, toasted, *divided*
Assorted fresh fruit

Cut grapefruit in half. With a sharp knife, slice between the membrane of each section and the peel. Remove sections and chop; discard juice. Remove membranes from grapefruit shells. Refrigerate shells until serving.

In a bowl, combine the fruit spread, marmalade, almond extract and chopped grapefruit. Stir in yogurt. Cover and refrigerate for at least 1 hour.

Set aside 1 tablespoon almonds. Chop remaining almonds. Just before serving, stir chopped almonds into dip. Spoon into reserved grapefruit shells. Sprinkle with sliced almonds. Serve with fruit. **Yield:** 2-3/4 cups.

Nutritional Analysis: One serving (1/4 cup dip, calculated without fruit) equals 114 calories, 4 g fat (1 g saturated fat), 2 mg cholesterol, 27 mg sodium, 17 g carbohydrate, 1 g fiber, 4 g protein.
Diabetic Exchanges: 1/2 fat-free milk, 1/2 fruit, 1/2 fat.

🍎 Fast Frozen Yogurt

FOR a cool, low-calorie treat, push a Popsicle stick through the foil cover of a small fat-free yogurt. (Be sure to remove the plastic lid first if there is one.)

Pop it in the freezer until it's frozen, then remove the plastic container and enjoy your frosty fruit pop!
—*Dianne Meyers, Lakemoor, Illinois*

Italian Ranch Chicken Strips

Low-fat

Zesty chicken strips pass the trim-and-tasty test I give most of my recipes. I prefer food that is low in fat but has lots of flavor. I made these chicken strips for supper one night...and they were a huge hit! They're simple to make, too.
—LaDonna Reed, Ponca City, Oklahoma

    2/3 cup cornflake crumbs
      1 teaspoon Italian seasoning
    1/2 teaspoon garlic powder
    1/3 cup reduced-fat ranch salad dressing
      1 teaspoon water
    1/2 pound boneless skinless chicken breasts, cut
        into strips

In a shallow bowl, combine the cornflake crumbs, Italian seasoning and garlic powder. In another shallow bowl, combine dressing and water. Dip chicken into dressing mixture, then coat with crumb mixture.

Arrange chicken on a baking sheet coated with nonstick cooking spray. Lightly spray top of chicken with nonstick cooking spray. Bake, uncovered, at 400° for 12-15 minutes or until juices run clear. **Yield:** 4 servings.

Nutritional Analysis: One serving equals 147 calories, 2 g fat (trace saturated fat), 33 mg cholesterol, 413 mg sodium, 17 g carbohydrate, trace fiber, 15 g protein.
Diabetic Exchanges: 2 very lean meat, 1 starch.

Hot Crab Dip

Low-carb Low-fat

I lightened up a recipe for traditional crab dip with reduced-fat and fat-free sour cream and cheeses. Feel free to experiment with different cheeses to suit your tastes. This is great for a party because you can make it a day ahead and refrigerate it.
—Cammy Brittingham, Cambridge, Maryland

      1 package (8 ounces) fat-free cream cheese
    1/2 cup fat-free sour cream
      2 tablespoons fat-free mayonnaise
      1 teaspoon Worcestershire sauce
    1/2 teaspoon seafood seasoning
    1/2 teaspoon spicy brown mustard
    1/2 teaspoon reduced-sodium soy sauce
    1/8 teaspoon garlic salt
      2 cans (6 ounces *each*) crabmeat, drained, flaked
        and cartilage removed *or* 1/2 pound imitation
        crabmeat, flaked
    1/3 cup plus 2 tablespoons shredded reduced-fat
        cheddar cheese, *divided*
    1/3 cup plus 2 tablespoons shredded part-skim
        mozzarella cheese, *divided*
Melba rounds

In a large mixing bowl, beat cream cheese until smooth. Add the sour cream, mayonnaise, Worcestershire sauce, seafood seasoning, mustard, soy sauce and garlic salt; mix

well. Stir in crab, 1/3 cup cheddar cheese and 1/3 cup mozzarella cheese.

Place in a shallow 1-qt. baking dish coated with nonstick cooking spray. Sprinkle the remaining cheese on top. Bake at 350° for 25-30 minutes or until mixture bubbles around the edges. Serve warm with melba rounds. **Yield:** 2-1/2 cups.

Nutritional Analysis: One serving (1/4 cup dip, calculated without melba rounds) equals 91 calories, 3 g fat (2 g saturated fat), 31 mg cholesterol, 320 mg sodium, 5 g carbohydrate, trace fiber, 12 g protein.
Diabetic Exchange: 2 lean meat.

Ginger-Cinnamon Fruit Dip

Low-carb Low-fat Low-sodium Meatless

(Pictured below and on page 17)

Keep your eyes peeled for "double dipping" when you put out this taste-tempting treat from our Test Kitchen! It makes a sensational snack or a "must" for any brunch. Ginger and cinnamon perk up the creamy dip that's terrific on apples, pears and bananas.

      1 carton (6 ounces) reduced-fat vanilla yogurt
    1/4 cup whipped reduced-fat cream cheese
      1 teaspoon ground ginger
    1/4 teaspoon ground cinnamon
Assorted fresh fruit

In a small bowl, combine the yogurt, cream cheese, ginger and cinnamon until blended. Cover and refrigerate for at least 1 hour. Serve with fruit. **Yield:** 3/4 cup.

Nutritional Analysis: One serving (2 tablespoons dip, calculated without fruit) equals 52 calories, 2 g fat (1 g saturated fat), 8 mg cholesterol, 57 mg sodium, 7 g carbohydrate, trace fiber, 2 g protein.
Diabetic Exchange: 1/2 starch.

Baked Sweet Potato Chips

Low-fat   Meatless

The next time you have the hungries, don't reach for high-fat junk food. Instead, spend a few minutes preparing these oven-baked sweet potato slices from our Test Kitchen.

2 medium sweet potatoes (about 10 ounces *each*)
1 teaspoon dried rosemary, crushed
1 teaspoon dried parsley flakes
3/4 teaspoon garlic salt
1/2 teaspoon paprika
1/4 teaspoon ground mustard
Dash white pepper

Cut potatoes into 1/8-in. slices; spray both sides of slices with nonstick cooking spray. In a bowl, combine seasonings. Add the potatoes; toss gently to coat. Place in a single layer in two 15-in. x 10-in. x 1-in. baking pans coated with nonstick cooking spray.

Bake, uncovered, at 400° for 20-25 minutes or until potatoes are golden brown and tender, turning several times. **Yield:** 5 dozen chips.

Nutritional Analysis: One serving (15 chips) equals 109 calories, trace fat (trace saturated fat), 0 cholesterol, 351 mg sodium, 25 g carbohydrate, 4 g fiber, 2 g protein.
Diabetic Exchange: 1-1/2 starch.

Hot Apple Cider

Low-fat   Low-sodium

(Pictured above right)

I really enjoy this hot cider because it has a citrus tang unlike other recipes I've tried. Not only do I like the flavor combination, but I love the aroma it adds to my home.
—Darlene Brenden, Salem, Oregon

1 quart unsweetened apple juice
1/2 cup water
1/2 cup orange juice
1/4 cup sugar
1/4 cup lemon juice
2 cinnamon sticks (3 inches)
1 tablespoon brown sugar
1-1/2 teaspoons whole cloves
Additional cinnamon sticks, optional

In a large saucepan, combine the first eight ingredients; bring to a boil. Reduce heat; simmer, uncovered, for 15 min-

utes. Strain, discarding cinnamon sticks and cloves. Serve warm; garnish with additional cinnamon sticks if desired. **Yield:** 5 cups.

Nutritional Analysis: One serving (1 cup) equals 157 calories, trace fat (trace saturated fat), 0 cholesterol, 7 mg sodium, 39 g carbo hydrate, trace fiber, trace protein.

Caramel Apple Dip

Low-carb   Low-sodium

Luscious caramel apples aren't forbidden fruit when you fix them this way. Folks will never know they're eating lighter when they dip apple slices into this warm, yummy caramel-flavored dip!
—Tami Escher, Dumont, Minnesota

1 package (8 ounces) reduced-fat cream cheese, cubed
1/2 cup caramel ice cream topping
1/2 cup marshmallow creme
Apple slices

In a microwave-safe mixing bowl, combine the cream cheese and ice cream topping until blended. Add the marshmallow creme; mix until blended.

Microwave, uncovered, on 50% power for 1 minute; stir. Microwave 30-60 seconds longer, stirring every 15 seconds or until warm. Transfer to a serving dish. Serve immediately with apple slices. **Yield:** 12 servings.

Editor's Note: This recipe was tested in a 1,100-watt microwave.

Nutritional Analysis: One serving (2 tablespoons dip, calculated without fruit) equals 102 calories, 4 g fat (3 g saturated fat), 14 mg cholesterol, 109 mg sodium, 13 g carbohydrate, 0 fiber, 3 g protein.
Diabetic Exchanges: 1 starch, 1 fat.

Warm Broccoli Cheese Spread

Low-carb Meatless

(Pictured below)

I cut this recipe out of a newspaper a year ago and decided to trim it down by substituting fat-free and reduced-fat ingredients. Whenever I make this for an occasion, I end up being asked for the recipe.
—Patricia Moore, Toledo, Ohio

- 1 package (8 ounces) fat-free cream cheese, cubed
- 1 cup (8 ounces) reduced-fat sour cream
- 1 envelope Italian salad dressing mix
- 1 package (10 ounces) frozen chopped broccoli, thawed, drained and patted dry
- 2 cups (8 ounces) shredded reduced-fat cheddar cheese, *divided*

Reduced-fat wheat snack crackers

In a large mixing bowl, beat the cream cheese, sour cream and salad dressing mix until blended. Fold in broccoli and 1-1/2 cups cheese. Spoon into a shallow 1-qt. baking dish coated with nonstick cooking spray. Bake, uncovered, at 350° for 20 minutes. Sprinkle with remaining cheese. Bake 5 minutes longer or until cheese is melted. Serve warm with crackers. **Yield:** 3-1/2 cups.

Nutritional Analysis: One serving (1/4 cup spread, calculated without crackers) equals 96 calories, 5 g fat (4 g saturated fat), 19 mg cholesterol, 287 mg sodium, 4 g carbohydrate, 1 g fiber, 8 g protein.
Diabetic Exchanges: 1 lean meat, 1/2 fat.

Frosty Fruit Pops

Low-carb Low-fat **Low-sodium**

Our Test Kitchen came up with these icy sugar-free treats that take just three ingredients and a blender to make. Kids —and adults—will enjoy cooling off with the two-layer pops that are full of fruit flavor.

- 1 cup unsweetened apple juice, *divided*
- 2 cups fresh strawberries
- 2 cups fresh blueberries

In a blender or food processor, combine 1/2 cup apple juice and strawberries; cover and process until blended. Fill 3-oz. paper or plastic cups half full. Cover each with foil; insert wooden sticks into cups. Freeze for at least 2 hours or until firm. Place blueberries and remaining apple juice into a blender or food processor; cover and process until blended. Fill cups with blueberry mixture. Cover and freeze for 3-4 hours or until firm. **Yield:** 11 pops.

Nutritional Analysis: One pop equals 33 calories, trace fat (trace saturated fat), 0 cholesterol, 4 mg sodium, 8 g carbohydrate, 1 g fiber, trace protein.
Diabetic Exchange: 1/2 fruit.

🍎 Cut Calories in Kettle Corn

I HAVE come up with a method to make a healthier version of kettle corn.

I pop the popcorn in an air popper. As I layer each batch in the bowl, I spritz the kernels with butter-flavored cooking spray and alternately sprinkle on light layers of Equal and Morton Lite Salt.
—*Linda Branum, Livingston, Texas*

Shrimp with Dipping Sauce

Low-carb Low-fat

(Pictured above right)

Our Test Kitchen crew let their imaginations go overboard to dream up this light and spicy shrimp party starter. The well-seasoned shrimp are delicious on their own...or coated with the dipping sauce that stars garlic and sesame oil.

- 1 tablespoon reduced-sodium soy sauce
- 2 teaspoons hot pepper sauce
- 1 teaspoon canola oil
- 1/4 teaspoon garlic powder
- 1/8 to 1/4 teaspoon cayenne pepper
- 1 pound uncooked medium shrimp, peeled and deveined
- 2 tablespoons chopped green onions

DIPPING SAUCE:
- 3 tablespoons reduced-sodium soy sauce
- 1 tablespoon rice vinegar
- 1 tablespoon orange juice

2 teaspoons sesame oil
2 teaspoons honey
1 garlic clove, minced
1-1/2 teaspoons minced fresh gingerroot

In a large nonstick skillet, heat the first five ingredients for 30 seconds, stirring constantly. Add shrimp and onions; stir-fry for 4-5 minutes or until shrimp turn pink. Combine sauce ingredients; serve with shrimp. **Yield:** 6 servings.

Nutritional Analysis: One serving (2 ounces cooked shrimp with 1 tablespoon sauce) equals 97 calories, 3 g fat (trace saturated fat), 112 mg cholesterol, 588 mg sodium, 4 g carbohydrate, trace fiber, 13 g protein.
Diabetic Exchange: 2 lean meat.

Gazpacho Shrimp Appetizer

Low-carb

(Pictured above)

Served in a footed glass, this refreshing appetizer is pretty enough for a formal dinner. To change it into a main dish, I combine the ingredients and serve them on a tortilla along with shredded lettuce and sour cream.
—Patricia Clark, Lake Forest, California

1/2 pound cooked medium shrimp, peeled and deveined
1 medium green pepper, chopped
1 medium tomato, seeded and chopped
1 can (5-1/2 ounces) spicy V8 juice
1/2 medium ripe avocado, peeled and cubed
3 green onions, sliced
2 tablespoons minced fresh cilantro
1 can (2-1/4 ounces) sliced ripe olives, drained
2 tablespoons lime juice
1/4 cup fat-free sour cream
1 medium lime, sliced
Cilantro leaves, optional

In a bowl, combine the first nine ingredients. Cover and refrigerate for 1 hour or until chilled. Using a slotted spoon, transfer to individual footed glasses. Dollop with sour cream. Garnish with lime slice and cilantro if desired. **Yield:** 4 servings.

Nutritional Analysis: One serving equals 156 calories, 6 g fat (1 g saturated fat), 111 mg cholesterol, 425 mg sodium, 11 g carbohydrate, 3 g fiber, 15 g protein.
Diabetic Exchanges: 2 very lean meat, 2 vegetable, 1 fat.

bowl; cover and let stand for 15-20 minutes. Peel off and discard charred skin; cut into julienne strips.

In a bowl, combine the olives, vinegar, oregano, basil, pepper and remaining oil; set aside.

Place crust on a 12-in. pizza pan. Spoon oil mixture over crust. Top with garlic, peppers, onion and cheeses. Bake at 350° for 15-20 minutes or until cheese is melted. **Yield:** 12 servings.

Nutritional Analysis: One slice equals 138 calories, 7 g fat (2 g saturated fat), 10 mg cholesterol, 321 mg sodium, 14 g carbohydrate, 1 g fiber, 5 g protein.
Diabetic Exchanges: 1 starch, 1 fat.

Roasted Garlic and Pepper Pizza

Low-carb   Meatless

(Pictured above)

Years ago, I found the recipe for this appealing appetizer, lightened it and added some of our favorite ingredients. It can be prepared ahead of time and put in the oven as your guests arrive. We occasionally use it as an easy Sunday evening meal, too.
—*Bonnie Matherly, Buckingham, Illinois*

1 large garlic bulb
1 teaspoon plus 2 tablespoons olive oil, *divided*
2 large sweet red peppers
1/2 cup sliced stuffed olives
2 tablespoons red wine vinegar
1 teaspoon dried oregano
1/2 teaspoon dried basil
1/8 teaspoon white pepper
1 prebaked thin crust Italian bread shell (10 ounces)
3/4 cup sweet onion slices
3/4 cup crumbled feta cheese
1/3 cup shredded Parmesan cheese

Remove papery outer skin from garlic (do not peel or separate cloves). Cut top off of garlic head. Brush with 1 teaspoon oil. Wrap bulb in heavy-duty foil. Bake at 425° for 20-25 minutes or until softened. Cool for 10-15 minutes; squeeze softened garlic out of skins. Cut garlic cloves into slices.

Cut peppers in half; remove and discard seeds. Broil peppers cut side down 4 in. from the heat until skins are blistered and blackened. Immediately place peppers in a

Peanut Shrimp Kabobs

Low-carb

Soy sauce and peanut butter are combined in a sauce that nicely glazes shrimp on the grill. I like to serve these kabobs as an appetizer when I'm entertaining.
—*Helen Gilden, Middletown, Delaware*

1/4 cup sugar
1/4 cup reduced-sodium soy sauce
1/4 cup reduced-fat creamy peanut butter
1 tablespoon water
1 tablespoon canola oil
3 garlic cloves, minced
1-1/2 pounds uncooked medium shrimp, peeled and deveined

In a small saucepan, combine the first six ingredients until smooth. Cook and stir over medium-low heat until blended and sugar is dissolved. Set aside 6 tablespoons sauce.

If grilling the kabobs, coat the grill rack with nonstick cooking spray before starting the grill. On eight metal or soaked wooden skewers, thread the shrimp. Brush with remaining peanut sauce. Grill kabobs, uncovered, over medium heat or broil 4 in. from the heat for 2-3 minutes on each side or until shrimp turn pink, turning once. Brush with reserved sauce before serving. **Yield:** 8 servings.

Nutritional Analysis: One kabob equals 151 calories, 5 g fat (1 g saturated fat), 126 mg cholesterol, 492 mg sodium, 10 g carbohydrate, 1 g fiber, 16 g protein.
Diabetic Exchanges: 2 lean meat, 1/2 starch.

Cream Cheese Chili Spread

Low-carb   Meatless

Looking for something wonderful to boost the flavor of your bagel? Spread on a tasty topper! Pepped up with a little chili powder, this pleasant spread adds punch to a warm toasted bagel at breakfast, brunch or snacktime.
—*Alice Guzman, Albuquerque, New Mexico*

1 package (8 ounces) reduced-fat cream cheese
1/2 cup diced green pepper

2 tablespoons finely chopped onion
1 teaspoon chili powder
1/4 teaspoon salt
1/4 teaspoon ground cumin
1/4 teaspoon garlic powder
1/8 teaspoon pepper

In a small mixing bowl, beat cream cheese until smooth. Add the green pepper, onion, chili powder, salt, cumin, garlic powder and pepper; mix well. **Yield:** 10 servings.

Nutritional Analysis: One serving (2 tablespoons) equals 63 calories, 5 g fat (3 g saturated fat), 17 mg cholesterol, 152 mg sodium, 2 g carbohydrate, trace fiber, 2 g protein.
Diabetic Exchange: *1 fat.*

Hot Mexican Dip

Low-carb

This hearty dip won't last long at your next gathering. Green chilies, taco sauce and chili powder add zip to the appetizing blend of ground turkey, refried beans, cheese and seasonings.
—*Heather O'Neill, Dudley, Massachusetts*

1 pound lean ground turkey
1-1/2 teaspoons chili powder
1 teaspoon onion powder
1/4 teaspoon salt
1 can (16 ounces) fat-free refried beans
1 can (4 ounces) chopped green chilies
3/4 cup taco sauce
2 cups (8 ounces) shredded reduced-fat Mexican cheese blend, *divided*
1 cup (8 ounces) fat-free sour cream
1/3 cup chopped green onions
Baked tortilla chips

Crumble turkey into a large nonstick skillet. Cook over medium heat until no longer pink; drain. Add the chili powder, onion powder and salt; set aside. In a 13-in. x 9-in. x 2-in. baking dish coated with nonstick cooking spray, layer the beans, turkey mixture, green chilies, taco sauce and 1-1/2 cups cheese.

Cover and bake at 400° for 25-30 minutes or until the

Better Beverages

I HAVE two tips for flavorful beverages. When serving punch for a party or get-together, cool it with an ice ring made from the punch instead of using regular ice cubes. Not only is this more decorative, but the large ring melts slower and prevents the punch's flavor from becoming diluted.

Also, when serving mugs of hot chocolate, place fresh or dried mint in the bottom of the cup for a refreshing taste.
—*Ruth Collins*
Prince George, Virginia

cheese is melted and bubbles around edges. Cool for 5 minutes. Spread the sour cream on top; sprinkle with the green onions and remaining cheese. Serve with tortilla chips. **Yield:** 15 servings.

Nutritional Analysis: One serving (calculated without tortilla chips) equals 133 calories, 5 g fat (2 g saturated fat), 32 mg cholesterol, 389 mg sodium, 9 g carbohydrate, 2 g fiber, 12 g protein.
Diabetic Exchanges: *2 lean meat, 1/2 starch.*

Refreshing Lemon-Lime Drink

Low-fat   Low-sodium

(Pictured below)

Here is a lighter version of the famous margarita—without the alcohol! It goes very well with Mexican dishes or as a cool summertime drink in the shade.
—*Lisa Castillo, Bourbonnais, Illinois*

1 can (12 ounces) frozen limeade concentrate, thawed
2/3 cup frozen lemonade concentrate, thawed
1 teaspoon orange extract
1-1/2 cups water
6 cups chilled diet lemon-lime soda
1 medium lemon, sliced
1 medium lime, sliced

In a large container, combine the limeade and lemonade concentrates and orange extract. Stir in water. Just before serving, stir in lemon-lime soda. Serve over ice. Garnish with lemon and lime slices. **Yield:** 3 quarts.

Nutritional Analysis: One serving (1 cup) equals 84 calories, trace fat (trace saturated fat), 0 cholesterol, 1 mg sodium, 22 g carbohydrate, trace fiber, trace protein.
Diabetic Exchange: *1-1/2 fruit.*

Walnut Balls

Meatless

Most of my family members don't eat meat, so I've made these appetizers for special occasions ever since a friend shared them with me. The moist bites and tangy sauce are always well received.
—Bonnie Young, Desert Hot Springs, California

- **2 eggs, beaten**
- **3 egg whites, beaten**
- **1 small onion, finely chopped**
- **3 tablespoons minced fresh parsley**
- **1-1/2 teaspoons poultry seasoning**
- **2 garlic cloves, minced**
- **1/2 teaspoon salt**
- **1-1/4 cups finely crushed reduced-sodium saltine crackers**
- **3/4 cup ground walnuts**
- **3/4 cup shredded reduced-fat cheddar cheese**
- **APRICOT BARBECUE SAUCE:**
- **3/4 cup 100% apricot spreadable fruit**
- **1/2 cup ketchup**
- **1/4 cup lemon juice**
- **2 tablespoons brown sugar**
- **2 tablespoons finely chopped onion**
- **1 tablespoon canola oil**
- **1/2 teaspoon salt**
- **1/2 teaspoon dried oregano**

In a bowl, combine the first seven ingredients. Add the crackers, walnuts and cheese; mix well. Coat hands with nonstick cooking spray; shape mixture into 1-in balls. Place in a 13-in. x 9-in. x 2-in. baking dish coated with nonstick cooking spray.

In a small saucepan, combine sauce ingredients. Bring to a boil. Pour over walnut balls. Bake, uncovered, at 350° for 25 minutes or until a meat thermometer reads 160°. **Yield:** 8 servings.

Nutritional Analysis: One serving (4 balls with sauce) equals 265 calories, 12 g fat (3 g saturated fat), 61 mg cholesterol, 585 mg sodium, 34 g carbohydrate, 1 g fiber, 8 g protein.
Diabetic Exchanges: 1-1/2 fat, 1 lean meat, 1 starch, 1 fruit.

Dill Dip

Low-carb Low-fat Meatless

My sister-in-law shared this creamy dip with me, and my family loves it. It's a great way to get everyone to eat their vegetables, too.
—Judy Bartnik, Wausau, Wisconsin

- **1 cup (8 ounces) reduced-fat sour cream**
- **1 cup fat-free mayonnaise**
- **1 tablespoon chopped onion**
- **1 tablespoon minced fresh parsley**
- **1 tablespoon dill weed**
- **3/4 teaspoon seasoned salt**
- **Assorted vegetables**

In a bowl, combine the first six ingredients. Cover and refrigerate for 1 hour or until chilled. Serve with vegetables. **Yield:** 2 cups.

Nutritional Analysis: One serving (2 tablespoons dip, calculated without vegetables) equals 32 calories, 2 g fat (1 g saturated fat), 7 mg cholesterol, 175 mg sodium, 3 g carbohydrate, trace fiber, 1 g protein.
Diabetic Exchange: 1/2 starch.

Salmon Canapes

Low-carb

(Pictured below)

My boyfriend's mother gave me the idea for this classy appetizer that I serve for Sunday brunch and special occasions like New Year's Eve. The textures and flavors of the dill, cream cheese and smoked salmon are scrumptious together. Spread on cocktail rye bread, it's sure to be the toast of your buffet!
—Tristin Crenshaw, Tucson, Arizona

- **1 package (8 ounces) reduced-fat cream cheese**
- **1 teaspoon snipped fresh dill *or* 1/4 teaspoon dill weed**
- **36 slices cocktail rye bread**
- **12 ounces sliced smoked salmon**
- **1 medium red onion, thinly sliced and separated into rings**
- **Fresh dill sprigs, optional**

In a small mixing bowl, combine cream cheese and dill. Spread on rye bread. Top with salmon and red onion. Garnish with dill sprigs if desired. **Yield:** 12 servings.

Nutritional Analysis: One serving (3 canapes) equals 155 calories, 7 g fat (3 g saturated fat), 21 mg cholesterol, 905 mg sodium, 15 g carbohydrate, 2 g fiber, 11 g protein.
Diabetic Exchanges: 1 starch, 1 lean meat, 1/2 fat.

Parmesan Yogurt Dip

*Low-carb Low-fat **Low-sodium** Meatless*

(Pictured above)

We like to eat raw vegetables a few times a week as a side dish for a meal...and this is a healthier alternative to ranch dressing for a veggie dip.
—Kathleen Tribble, Buellton, California

1 cup fat-free plain yogurt
1/4 cup grated Parmesan cheese
1/4 cup reduced-fat sour cream
3 tablespoons minced fresh parsley
1 green onion, thinly sliced
1 teaspoon prepared mustard
1 teaspoon onion powder
1/4 teaspoon salt
1/8 teaspoon pepper
Assorted vegetables

In a bowl, combine the yogurt, Parmesan cheese, sour cream, parsley, green onion, mustard, onion powder, salt and pepper. Cover and refrigerate for at least 2 hours. Serve with assorted vegetables. **Yield:** 1-1/4 cups.

Nutritional Analysis: One serving (2 tablespoons dip, calculated without vegetables) equals 30 calories, 1 g fat (1 g saturated fat), 4 mg cholesterol, 120 mg sodium, 3 g carbohydrate, trace fiber, 2 g protein.
Diabetic Exchange: 1/2 starch.

Party Vegetable Spread

Low-carb Low-fat Meatless

This chunky spread is a tasty treat for a party or any event featuring finger food.
—Martha Reese, Highlands, North Carolina

3/4 cup shredded carrot
1/4 cup chopped seeded cucumber
1/4 cup chopped celery
1/4 cup chopped green pepper
1/4 cup finely chopped onion
1 package (8 ounces) fat-free cream cheese
2 tablespoons reduced-fat mayonnaise
1 tablespoon lemon juice
1/4 teaspoon salt
1/8 teaspoon pepper
Snack rye bread

In a bowl, combine the carrot, cucumber, celery, green pepper and onion. Drain on paper towels for 30 minutes. In a small mixing bowl, combine the cream cheese, mayonnaise, lemon juice, salt and pepper. Stir in vegetables. Cover and refrigerate for at least 2 hours. Serve on bread. **Yield:** 1-3/4 cups.

Nutritional Analysis: One serving (1/4 cup spread, calculated without bread) equals 56 calories, 2 g fat (1 g saturated fat), 4 mg cholesterol, 303 mg sodium, 5 g carbohydrate, 1 g fiber, 5 g protein.
Diabetic Exchanges: 1 very lean meat, 1 vegetable.

🍎 Special Serving Dish

WHEN serving healthier appetizers, such as fresh vegetables with low-fat dip, I like to dress up the serving platter. So I cut the tops off red or green peppers and remove the seeds and membranes. Then I fill the pepper cups with the dip. This is a great way to add color to your buffet table.
—*Emma Knight, Claxton, Georgia*

Banana Berry Smoothies

Low-fat   Low-sodium

My family is fond of smoothies, and we are always trying something new. This is one fruity blend they always want more of. Feel free to experiment with other juices, sherbet flavors and frozen fruits. You'll be surprised and delighted with the number of tasty combinations you can come up with.
—Debbie Nelson, Sandy, Utah

2-1/2 cups orange juice
1 cup raspberry sherbet
1 large firm banana, sliced and frozen
1 cup frozen unsweetened strawberries
1 cup frozen blueberries

In a blender, combine all the ingredients in the order listed; cover and process for 30 seconds or until smooth. Stir if necessary. Pour into chilled glasses; serve immediately. **Yield:** 5 servings.

Nutritional Analysis: One serving (1 cup) equals 148 calories, 1 g fat (trace saturated fat), 2 mg cholesterol, 16 mg sodium, 35 g carbohydrate, 2 g fiber, 2 g protein.
Diabetic Exchange: 2 fruit.

Feta-Spinach Melts

Low-carb   Low-fat   Meatless

(Pictured at right)

Spinach and feta cheese top crisp slices of French bread in these festive-looking hors d'oeuvres. I've made them for parties, and everyone raves about them.
—Alina Abbott, Mesa, Arizona

3 packages (6 ounces *each*) fresh baby spinach, chopped
1 teaspoon water
1/2 cup crumbled feta cheese
1 plum tomato, seeded and chopped
1/4 cup finely chopped red onion
3 tablespoons fat-free mayonnaise

3 tablespoons fat-free sour cream
1 garlic clove, minced
1/2 teaspoon salt
1/2 teaspoon dill weed
20 slices French baguette (1/2 inch thick)

In a large microwave-safe bowl, combine spinach and water. Cover and microwave on high for 1-1/2 to 2 minutes or until spinach is wilted, stirring twice; drain and squeeze dry. Add the feta cheese, tomato, onion, mayonnaise, sour cream, garlic, salt and dill weed; set aside.

Arrange bread on a baking sheet. Broil 4 in. from the heat for 1-2 minutes or until lightly toasted. Spread each with about 1 tablespoonful spinach mixture. Broil 3-4 minutes longer or until heated through. **Yield:** 10 servings.

Editor's Note: This recipe was tested in a 1,100-watt microwave.

Nutritional Analysis: Two slices equals 100 calories, 3 g fat (1 g saturated fat), 8 mg cholesterol, 400 mg sodium, 15 g carbohydrate, 2 g fiber, 4 g protein.
Diabetic Exchanges: 1 starch, 1/2 fat.

Simmer Up a Souper Bowl!

Soups are naturally nutritious, oh-so flavorful
and sure to please in any season. Whether
it's a cool soup in summer or a steaming
pot of hearty chili on a winter's day,
soup is good for the body—and the spirit!

Tomato Chicken Rice Soup (page 40)

Meatball Alphabet Soup

(Pictured above)

Bite-size meatballs made from ground turkey perk up this fun alphabet soup. A variety of vegetables accents the rich tomato broth that is nicely seasoned with herbs. Our Test Kitchen staff came up with the recipe.

  1 egg, lightly beaten
  2 tablespoons quick-cooking oats
  2 tablespoons grated Parmesan cheese
1/4 teaspoon garlic powder
1/4 teaspoon Italian seasoning
1/2 pound lean ground turkey
  1 cup chopped onion
  1 cup chopped celery
  1 cup chopped carrots
  1 cup diced peeled potatoes
  1 tablespoon olive oil
  2 garlic cloves, minced
  4 cans (14-1/2 ounces *each*) reduced-sodium
     chicken broth
  1 can (28 ounces) diced tomatoes, undrained
  1 can (6 ounces) tomato paste
1/4 cup minced fresh parsley
  1 teaspoon dried basil
  1 teaspoon dried thyme
3/4 cup uncooked alphabet pasta

In a bowl, combine the first five ingredients. Crumble turkey over mixture and mix well. Shape into 1/2-in. balls. In a nonstick skillet, brown meatballs in small batches over medium heat until no longer pink. Remove from the heat; set aside.

In a large saucepan or Dutch oven, saute the onion, celery, carrots and potatoes in oil for 5 minutes or until crisp-tender. Add garlic; saute 1 minute longer. Add the broth, tomatoes, tomato paste, parsley, basil and thyme; bring to

a boil. Add pasta; cook for 5-6 minutes. Reduce heat; add meatballs. Simmer, uncovered, for 15-20 minutes or until vegetables are tender. **Yield:** 9 servings.

Nutritional Analysis: One serving (1-1/2 cups) equals 191 calories, 5 g fat (1 g saturated fat), 44 mg cholesterol, 679 mg sodium, 26 g carbohydrate, 4 g fiber, 12 g protein.
Diabetic Exchanges: 2 vegetable, 1 starch, 1 lean meat.

Lentil Sausage Soup

This recipe makes a very large pot of hearty soup, but it freezes and reheats well. It's a stand-alone meal at our house. Packed with lentils, long grain rice and cheese tortellini in a tomato broth, it's a tasty alternative to vegetable soup.
—*Melanee Van Ee-Mortensen, Fort Collins, Colorado*

  1 package (19-1/2 ounces) turkey Italian sausage
     links, casings removed
 13 cups water
  1 cup chopped carrots
1/2 cup chopped celery
  2 teaspoons onion powder
3/4 teaspoon dried oregano
1/2 teaspoon garlic powder
1/2 teaspoon dried basil
1/2 teaspoon seasoning salt
1/4 teaspoon pepper
  2 cups dry lentils, rinsed
1/2 cup uncooked long grain rice
  2 cans (one 15 ounces, one 8 ounces) tomato
     sauce
2-1/2 cups frozen cheese tortellini

Crumble sausage into a nonstick skillet. Cook over medium heat until no longer pink; drain. In a large saucepan or Dutch oven, combine the water, carrots, celery, onion powder, oregano, garlic powder, basil, seasoning salt and pepper. Add lentils and rice. Bring to a boil. Reduce heat; cover and simmer for 18-20 minutes or until lentils and rice are tender. Stir in tomato sauce; return to a boil. Add tortellini and sausage. Cook for 3-4 minutes or until tortellini are tender, stirring several times. **Yield:** 13 servings.

Nutritional Analysis: One serving (1-1/2 cups) equals 270 calories, 6 g fat (2 g saturated fat), 27 mg cholesterol, 651 mg sodium, 36 g carbohydrate, 11 g fiber, 20 g protein.
Diabetic Exchanges: 2 starch, 2 lean meat.

Simple Vegetable Stock

WHENEVER I cook fresh or frozen vegetables, I drain the liquid into a large plastic container that can be put in the freezer. I keep adding to it.

When I want to make a soup or stew, I thaw it and use it as the liquid to cook the meat and veggies in. It adds flavor and vitamins that would otherwise go down the drain. —*Betty Jo LaBahn*
El Reno, Oklahoma

Steak 'n' Vegetable Soup

(Pictured below)

This hearty soup calls for lots of fresh herbs to enhance the flavor of the other ingredients. The aroma while it is cooking is absolutely wonderful. I like to serve steaming bowls alongside a green salad and baking powder biscuits.
—Edie DeSpain, Logan, Utah

　1 pound boneless beef sirloin steak, cut
　　　into 1/2-inch cubes
　1 cup chopped onion
　2 teaspoons canola oil
　2 cups cubed red potatoes
　1 cup chopped carrots
　1 cup frozen peas
　1 can (14-1/2 ounces) beef broth
　1 cup water
　2 tablespoons balsamic vinegar
　1 tablespoon minced fresh parsley
　1 tablespoon minced chives
1-1/2 teaspoons minced fresh basil *or* 1/2 teaspoon
　　　dried basil
　1 teaspoon minced fresh thyme *or* 1/4 teaspoon
　　　dried thyme
　3/4 teaspoon salt
　1/4 teaspoon pepper

In a large saucepan, cook beef and onion in oil until meat is no longer pink; drain. Stir in the potatoes, carrots and peas. Add the broth, water, vinegar, parsley, chives, basil, thyme, salt and pepper. Bring to a boil. Reduce heat; cover and simmer for 20-30 minutes or until meat and vegetables are tender. **Yield:** 6 servings.

Nutritional Analysis: *One serving (1 cup) equals 212 calories, 7 g fat (2 g saturated fat), 51 mg cholesterol, 602 mg sodium, 17 g carbohydrate, 3 g fiber, 21 g protein.*
Diabetic Exchanges: *2 lean meat, 1 starch, 1 vegetable.*

Vegetarian Split Pea Soup

Low-fat　**Meatless**

Even the pickiest pea soup lover will request this version time and again. Thick and well-seasoned, it packs a nutritional punch, plus plenty of fiber and protein.
—Michele Doucette, Stephenville, Newfoundland

　6 cups vegetable broth
　2 cups dried green split peas, rinsed
　1 medium onion, chopped
　1 cup chopped carrots
　2 celery ribs with leaves, chopped
　2 garlic cloves, minced
1/2 teaspoon dried marjoram
1/2 teaspoon dried basil
1/4 teaspoon ground cumin
1/2 teaspoon salt
1/4 teaspoon pepper
　5 tablespoons shredded carrots

In a large saucepan, combine the first nine ingredients; bring to a boil. Reduce heat; cover and simmer for 1 hour or until peas are tender, stirring occasionally. Add salt and pepper; simmer 10 minutes longer. Cool slightly. In small batches, puree soup in a blender; return to the pan. Heat for 5 minutes. Garnish with shredded carrots. **Yield:** 7 servings.

Nutritional Analysis: *One serving (1 cup) equals 204 calories, 1 g fat (trace saturated fat), 0 cholesterol, 1,047 mg sodium, 37 g carbohydrate, 13 g fiber, 14 g protein.*
Diabetic Exchanges: *1-1/2 starch, 1 lean meat, 1 vegetable.*

Meatless Chili

Low-fat　**Meatless**

My husband is a big meat eater, so when he's out of town, I try to cut back on meat and make this hearty chili. It's very quick and easy.
—Eve Visser, South Bend, Indiana

　1 can (15-1/2 ounces) hot chili beans
　1 can (15 ounces) black beans, rinsed and
　　　drained
　1 can (14-1/2 ounces) Mexican stewed tomatoes,
　　　cut up
　1 cup frozen corn, thawed
1/2 cup chunky salsa
1/2 cup coarsely chopped green pepper
1/2 cup coarsely chopped sweet red pepper
　1 tablespoon ground cumin
　2 teaspoons chili powder
　4 tablespoons fat-free sour cream
　4 tablespoons shredded reduced-fat cheddar
　　　cheese

In a large saucepan, combine the first nine ingredients. Bring to a boil. Reduce heat; cover and simmer for 15 minutes or until vegetables are crisp-tender. Top each serving with sour cream and cheese. **Yield:** 4 servings.

Nutritional Analysis: *One serving (1-1/2 cups) equals 313 calories, 3 g fat (2 g saturated fat), 8 mg cholesterol, 1,049 mg sodium, 61 g carbohydrate, 15 g fiber, 17 g protein.*
Diabetic Exchanges: *3 vegetable, 2 starch, 2 lean meat.*

Cheddar Potato Chowder

I made this soup only occasionally because the original recipe was quite high in fat. I doctored it up a bit, using healthier ingredients, and now we eat this rich flavorful chowder more often.
—Ellie Rausch, Goodsoil, Saskatchewan

- 2 cups water
- 2 cups diced unpeeled red potatoes
- 1 cup diced carrots
- 1/2 cup diced celery
- 1/4 cup chopped onion
- 1 teaspoon salt
- 1/4 teaspoon pepper
- 1/4 cup all-purpose flour
- 2 cups 2% milk
- 2 cups (8 ounces) shredded reduced-fat cheddar cheese
- 1 cup cubed fully cooked lean ham

In a Dutch oven, combine the first seven ingredients. Bring to a boil. Reduce heat; cover and simmer for 10-12 minutes or until tender.

Meanwhile, place flour in a large saucepan; gradually whisk in milk. Bring to a boil over medium heat; cook and stir for 2 minutes or until thickened. Remove from the heat. Add cheese; stir until melted. Stir the ham and the cheese sauce into undrained vegetables; stir until combined. **Yield:** 7 servings.

Nutritional Analysis: One serving (1 cup) equals 212 calories, 9 g fat (5 g saturated fat), 29 mg cholesterol, 847 mg sodium, 18 g carbohydrate, 2 g fiber, 16 g protein.
Diabetic Exchanges: 1 starch, 1 lean meat, 1 fat, 1/2 fat-free milk.

Chicken Tortilla Soup

The fresh lime and cilantro in this zesty treat remind me of warmer climates—a nice bonus on chilly days here. I lightened up the original recipe by baking the tortilla strips rather than frying them.
—Marianne Morgan, Traverse City, Michigan

- 3 corn tortillas (6 inches), cut into 1/4-inch strips
- 4 teaspoons olive oil, *divided*
- 1/4 teaspoon salt
- 3/4 pound boneless skinless chicken breasts, cut into 1/2-inch chunks
- 1 large onion, chopped
- 5 cups reduced-sodium chicken broth
- 1 pound red potatoes, cut into 1/2-inch cubes
- 1 cup frozen corn
- 1 can (4-1/2 ounces) chopped green chilies
- 1/4 cup minced fresh cilantro
- 1/4 teaspoon pepper
- 3 tablespoons lime juice

In a large resealable plastic bag, combine tortilla strips, 1 teaspoon oil and salt. Seal bag and shake to coat. Arrange tortilla strips on an ungreased baking sheet. Bake at 400° for 8-10 minutes or until crisp, stirring once. Remove to paper towels to cool.

In a large saucepan, saute chicken in remaining oil until lightly browned. Add the onion. Cook and stir until onion is tender. Add broth and potatoes. Bring to a boil. Reduce heat; cover and simmer for 10 minutes. Add the corn, chilies, cilantro and pepper. Cook until heated through. Stir in lime juice. Top each serving with tortilla strips. **Yield:** 6 servings.

Nutritional Analysis: One serving (1-1/2 cups) equals 221 calories, 4 g fat (1 g saturated fat), 33 mg cholesterol, 757 mg sodium, 27 g carbohydrate, 4 g fiber, 19 g protein.
Diabetic Exchanges: 2 lean meat, 1-1/2 starch.

Quick Shrimp Gumbo

(Pictured below)

This hearty dish is one of our favorites. I've made it with all shrimp or with all turkey sausage, and it's just as good. I usually cook it in the microwave.
—Mrs. Leo Merchant, Jackson, Mississippi

- 1 cup finely chopped onion
- 3 garlic cloves, minced
- 1 teaspoon canola oil
- 1/2 pound reduced-fat fully cooked kielbasa *or* Polish sausage, halved and cut into 1/4-inch slices
- 1-1/2 cups chopped green pepper
- 1 can (14-1/2 ounces) diced tomatoes, undrained
- 1 cup reduced-sodium chicken broth
- 1 bay leaf
- 1 teaspoon Italian seasoning
- 1/2 teaspoon salt
- 1/2 teaspoon chili powder

1/4 teaspoon pepper
1/8 teaspoon hot pepper sauce
3/4 pound uncooked medium shrimp, peeled and deveined
1/2 cup uncooked instant rice
Lemon slices, optional

In a large saucepan, saute onion and garlic in oil for 2 minutes. Stir in sausage; cook and stir for 2 minutes or until sausage begins to brown. Add green pepper; cook and stir for 2 minutes. Stir in the tomatoes, broth, seasonings and hot pepper sauce.

Bring to a boil. Cook, uncovered, for 2 minutes. Stir in shrimp. Cook 3-4 minutes longer or until shrimp turn pink. Stir in rice. Remove from the heat. Cover and let stand for 5 minutes or until rice is tender. Discard bay leaf. Serve with lemon slices if desired. **Yield:** 4 servings.

Nutritional Analysis: One serving (1-1/4 cups) equals 246 calories, 5 g fat (1 g saturated fat), 146 mg cholesterol, 1,211 mg sodium, 27 g carbohydrate, 3 g fiber, 23 g protein.

Diabetic Exchanges: 3 very lean meat, 2 vegetable, 1 starch, 1/2 fat.

Tomato Basil Soup

Meatless

After just one taste of this slightly sweet tomato and herb soup, my family never went back to canned soup again! I adapted this recipe from one I had seen in an old cookbook.
—Chris Baker, South Lake Tahoe, California

4 medium carrots, peeled and finely chopped
1 large onion, finely chopped
1/4 cup butter
1 can (49 ounces) reduced-sodium chicken broth or 6 cups vegetable broth, *divided*
1 can (29 ounces) tomato puree
5 teaspoons dried basil
1-1/2 teaspoons sugar
1/2 teaspoon salt
1/2 teaspoon white pepper
1 can (12 ounces) fat-free evaporated milk

In a Dutch oven, cook carrots and onion in butter over medium-low heat for 30 minutes or until vegetables are tender, stirring occasionally. Remove from the heat and cool slightly.

In a blender or food processor, place 1/2 cup broth and the cooled vegetables; cover and process until blended. Return to the Dutch oven. Stir in the tomato puree, basil, sugar, salt, pepper and remaining broth. Bring to a boil. Reduce heat; simmer, uncovered, for 30 minutes. Reduce heat to low. Gradually stir in evaporated milk; heat through (do not boil). **Yield:** 6 servings (2-1/4 quarts).

Nutritional Analysis: One serving (1-1/2 cups) equals 201 calories, 8 g fat (5 g saturated fat), 23 mg cholesterol, 1,004 mg sodium, 24 g carbohydrate, 3 g fiber, 10 g protein.
Diabetic Exchanges: 3 vegetable, 1-1/2 fat, 1/2 fat-free milk.

Southwestern Broccoli Cheese Soup

Low-fat Meatless

(Pictured above)

A friend gave me the recipe for this chunky vegetable soup, which I've been making for years. Recently, I changed the ingredients to give it some southwestern flair—and my husband liked it even better!
—Peggy Hendrix, Richardson, Texas

4 cups water
4 reduced-sodium chicken bouillon cubes *or* vegetable bouillon cubes
4 cups fresh broccoli florets
3 cups frozen southern-style hash brown potatoes
1 cup chopped carrots
1 cup chopped celery
1/2 teaspoon *each* salt and pepper
3 tablespoons all-purpose flour
2 cups fat-free milk
6 ounces reduced-fat process cheese (Velveeta), cubed
1 cup chunky salsa

In a large saucepan, combine the water, bouillon cubes, vegetables, salt and pepper. Bring to a boil. Reduce heat; cover and simmer for 8-10 minutes or until the vegetables are tender. Combine the flour and milk until smooth; gradually stir into the soup. Bring to a boil; cook and stir for 2 minutes or until thickened. Reduce heat to low. Add the cheese; cook and stir until cheese is melted. Add the salsa; cook and stir until heated through. **Yield:** 9 servings (about 2 quarts).

Nutritional Analysis: One serving (1 cup) equals 160 calories, 3 g fat (1 g saturated fat), 9 mg cholesterol, 883 mg sodium, 27 g carbohydrate, 3 g fiber, 9 g protein.
Diabetic Exchanges: 1-1/2 starch, 1 vegetable.

Creamy Chicken Potato Soup

(Pictured below)

Any time I serve this thick comforting soup, I'm asked for the recipe. Because it is loaded with chunks of potatoes and chicken, no one suspects that it's low in fat.
—*Carla Reid, Charlottetown, Prince Edward Island*

- 1 medium onion, chopped
- 2 tablespoons butter
- 3 cups reduced-sodium chicken broth
- 1 pound potatoes (about 2 medium), cut into 1/2-inch cubes
- 1-1/2 cups diced cooked chicken breast
- 1/2 teaspoon salt
- 1/4 teaspoon pepper
- 1/4 cup all-purpose flour
- 1 cup fat-free milk
- 1 cup reduced-fat evaporated milk
- 1 teaspoon minced fresh parsley
- 1 teaspoon minced chives

In a large saucepan, saute onion in butter until tender. Stir in broth and potatoes. Bring to a boil. Reduce heat; cover and simmer for 10-15 minutes or until potatoes are tender. Stir in the chicken, salt and pepper. Combine flour and fat-free milk until smooth; stir into saucepan. Add evaporated milk. Bring to a boil; cook and stir for 2 minutes or until thickened. Sprinkle with parsley and chives. **Yield:** 6 servings.

Nutritional Analysis: One serving (1-1/3 cups) equals 232 calories, 5 g fat (3 g saturated fat), 43 mg cholesterol, 646 mg sodium, 27 g carbohydrate, 2 g fiber, 19 g protein.
Diabetic Exchanges: 2 very lean meat, 1-1/2 starch, 1/2 fat-free milk.

Tuscan Turkey Sausage Soup

While trying to reproduce my favorite soup from an Italian restaurant's menu, I hit upon this tasty combination of turkey sausage, broth and mushrooms. Fennel, caraway seeds and herb seasoning give the quick-to-fix soup plenty of flavor without adding salt. Serve it steaming hot alongside a crisp salad and bread for a well-rounded meal.
—*Thomas Licking, Green Lake, Wisconsin*

- 12 ounces turkey Italian sausage links
- 4 cups reduced-sodium chicken broth
- 1 can (10-3/4 ounces) reduced-fat reduced-sodium condensed cream of chicken soup, undiluted
- 1 can (8 ounces) mushroom stems and pieces, drained
- 1 small onion, chopped
- 1 tablespoon Italian seasoning
- 1/4 teaspoon salt-free garlic and herb seasoning
- 1/8 teaspoon caraway seeds
- 1/8 teaspoon fennel seed, crushed
- 1 can (15-1/2 ounces) great northern beans, rinsed and drained
- 1 small leek (white portion only), cut into 1-inch strips

In a nonstick skillet coated with nonstick cooking spray, cook sausage over medium heat until no longer pink; drain. Let cool and slice. In a large saucepan, whisk together the broth, soup, mushrooms, onion, Italian seasoning, garlic and herb seasoning, caraway seeds and fennel seed. Add sausage. Bring to a boil. Reduce heat; simmer, uncovered, for 5 minutes. Add beans and leek. Simmer 10 minutes longer or until vegetables are tender. **Yield:** 8 servings.

Nutritional Analysis: One serving (1 cup) equals 181 calories, 5 g fat (2 g saturated fat), 26 mg cholesterol, 978 mg sodium, 19 g carbohydrate, 4 g fiber, 14 g protein.
Diabetic Exchanges: 2 lean meat, 1 starch.

Hearty Turkey Vegetable Soup

(Pictured above right)

I found this recipe on the Internet, but it was too high in fat. After experimenting, I created a more nutritious version. I often double this chili-like soup to freeze or to share with friends.
—*Julie Anderson, Bloomington, Illinois*

1 pound lean ground turkey
1 medium onion, chopped
2 small zucchini, quartered lengthwise and sliced
1 large carrot, cut into 1-inch julienne strips
3 cans (14 ounces *each*) reduced-sodium beef broth
1 jar (26 ounces) garden-style pasta sauce *or* meatless spaghetti sauce
1 can (16 ounces) kidney beans, rinsed and drained
1 can (15-1/2 ounces) great northern beans, rinsed and drained
1 can (14-1/2 ounces) Italian diced tomatoes, undrained
1 tablespoon dried parsley flakes
2 teaspoons dried oregano
1 teaspoon pepper
1 teaspoon hot pepper sauce
1 cup uncooked small shell pasta

In a Dutch oven coated with nonstick cooking spray, cook turkey and onion over medium heat until meat is no longer pink; drain. Add zucchini and carrot; cook and stir 1 minute longer. Stir in the broth, pasta sauce, beans, tomatoes, parsley, oregano, pepper and hot pepper sauce.

Bring to a boil. Reduce heat; cover and simmer for 45 minutes. Meanwhile, cook pasta according to package directions. Just before serving, stir in pasta. **Yield:** 10 servings (3-3/4 quarts).

Nutritional Analysis: One serving (1-1/2 cups) equals 242 calories, 4 g fat (1 g saturated fat), 38 mg cholesterol, 888 mg sodium, 34 g carbohydrate, 7 g fiber, 17 g protein.
Diabetic Exchanges: 2 lean meat, 2 vegetable, 1-1/2 starch.

Quick Black Bean Soup

My mother is a native of Cuba and cooks the best black bean soup anywhere, but her recipe is complicated and takes 2 days to complete. I came up with this faster version, and I think the results are excellent!
—Ileana Sisson, Osteen, Florida

2 cans (15 ounces *each*) black beans, rinsed, drained and *divided*
1-1/2 cups water
1 cup chicken broth
1 medium green pepper, sliced
1/2 small onion, chopped
1 garlic clove, minced
2 tablespoons olive oil
2 teaspoons red wine *or* additional chicken broth
1/2 teaspoon salt
1/2 teaspoon pepper
1/4 teaspoon dried oregano
1/4 teaspoon paprika
1 bay leaf

In a small bowl, mash 1 can black beans until smooth; set aside. In a large saucepan, combine the remaining ingredients and remaining can of beans. Bring to a boil. Reduce heat; simmer, covered, for 10-15 minutes. Add mashed beans, stirring to combine. Discard bay leaf before serving. **Yield:** 4 servings.

Nutritional Analysis: One serving (1 cup) equals 257 calories, 7 g fat (1 g saturated fat), 0 cholesterol, 876 mg sodium, 36 g carbohydrate, 10 g fiber, 12 g protein.
Diabetic Exchanges: 2 starch, 1 very lean meat, 1 fat.

Slimming Down Soup Recipes

IT'S easy to bring smile-fetching soup to the front burner of a food-smart meal plan. Keep the following secrets in mind when you are lightening up your soup du jour:

- **Skip the Salt.** Set down the salt shaker and stir additional herbs or a salt-free seasoning blend into your soup instead. When recipes call for canned chicken broth, substitute the low-sodium variety.
- **Thin Thickeners.** Watching your weight doesn't mean writing off creamy soups. Puree a cooked peeled potato and reduced-fat milk or fat-free half-and-half to a creamy consistency. Slowly stir the mixture into boiling soup to thicken it. To thicken southwestern soups and chili, add pureed cooked beans.
- **Cut Back on Beef.** Try preparing the recipe with additional vegetables or pasta instead of beef. Or, consider replacing beef with cooked poultry now and again.

salt and pepper. Sprinkle with parsley. **Yield:** 10 servings (about 3-1/2 quarts).

Nutritional Analysis: One serving (1-1/2 cups) equals 136 calories, 2 g fat (trace saturated fat), 3 mg cholesterol, 416 mg sodium, 26 g carbohydrate, 6 g fiber, 6 g protein.
Diabetic Exchanges: 2 vegetable, 1 starch.

Oriental Shrimp Soup

Low-carb   Low-fat

I love this soup so much, I sometimes double the recipe.
In fact, I've nicknamed it the "House Specialty"!
If I have leftover chicken or pork, I sometimes
substitute it for the shrimp.
—*Michelle Smith, Sykesville, Maryland*

  1 ounce uncooked thin spaghetti, broken
    into 1-inch pieces
  3 cups plus 1 tablespoon water, *divided*
  3 packets reduced-sodium chicken bouillon and
    seasoning mix
1/2 teaspoon salt
1/2 cup sliced fresh mushrooms
1/2 cup fresh *or* frozen corn
  1 teaspoon cornstarch
1-1/2 teaspoons reduced-sodium teriyaki sauce
  1 cup thinly sliced romaine lettuce
  1 can (6 ounces) small shrimp, rinsed and
    drained
  2 tablespoons sliced green onion

Cook pasta according to package directions; drain. In a saucepan, combine 3 cups water, chicken bouillon and salt; bring to a boil. Stir in mushrooms and corn. Reduce heat; cook, uncovered, until vegetables are tender.

Combine cornstarch, teriyaki sauce and remaining water until smooth; stir into soup. Bring to a boil; cook and stir for 1-2 minutes or until slightly thickened. Reduce heat; add the lettuce, shrimp, green onion and spaghetti; heat through. **Yield:** 4 servings.

Editor's Note: This recipe was tested with Herb Ox Instant Broth & Seasoning Chicken Bouillon.

Nutritional Analysis: One serving (1 cup) equals 111 calories, 1 g fat (trace saturated fat), 74 mg cholesterol, 725 mg sodium, 13 g carbohydrate, 1 g fiber, 12 g protein.
Diabetic Exchanges: 1 starch, 1 very lean meat.

Savory Mushroom-Barley Soup

Low-fat   Meatless

(Pictured above)

Fresh mushrooms and barley star in this tasty soup.
Onions, celery and carrots make it a hearty
favorite throughout the year.
—*Christine Wright, Franklinton, North Carolina*

  4 cups water
3/4 cup uncooked medium pearl barley
  4 medium onions, chopped
  2 celery ribs, chopped
  1 tablespoon olive oil
1-1/2 pounds sliced fresh mushrooms
  6 cups reduced-sodium beef broth *or* vegetable
    broth
  2 cups sliced carrots
  1 can (6 ounces) tomato paste
1/2 teaspoon salt
1/4 teaspoon pepper
1/2 cup minced fresh parsley

In a large saucepan, bring water and barley to a boil. Reduce heat; cover and simmer for 30 minutes or until barley is partially cooked. (Do not drain.)

Meanwhile, in a soup kettle or Dutch oven, saute onions and celery in oil until tender. Add mushrooms; cook and stir for 5 minutes. Stir in the broth, carrots, tomato paste and barley mixture.

Bring to a boil over medium heat. Reduce heat; cover and simmer for 30 minutes, stirring occasionally. Stir in

Favorite Soup Made Lighter

FEW THINGS are more comforting on a cool night than a steaming bowl of rich, creamy homemade soup. "My mother has a recipe for Potato Cheese Soup, and it is delicious!" says Bethany Thayer of Troutville, Virginia. "But I know the calorie and fat content must be ridiculous, so I thought maybe you could help lighten it up."

Our Test Kitchen staff was eager to lend a hand. Since more than half of the fat in the original recipe came from mayonnaise, they replaced 1 cup mayonnaise with 1/3 cup reduced-fat mayonnaise.

They then replaced the full-fat cheeses with reduced-fat varieties and used a higher proportion of cheddar to Velveeta to keep the creamy texture while lowering the sodium content.

The sodium was cut even further by using reduced-sodium broth and low-sodium bouillon granules.

Makeover Potato Cheese Soup has about 40% fewer calories, two-thirds less fat, less than half the saturated fat, about half the cholesterol and a third less sodium of the original. Yet its comforting taste and creamy consistency will surely please the soup lovers in your family!

Potato Cheese Soup

Meatless

    4 cups water
2-1/2 cups chicken *or* vegetable broth
    5 cups diced peeled potatoes
    2 large carrots, finely chopped
    1 large onion, finely chopped
    1 tablespoon chicken bouillon granules *or* 3 vegetable bouillon cubes
    2 celery ribs, finely chopped
    1 large sweet red pepper, finely chopped
    1 cup mayonnaise
    8 ounces process cheese (Velveeta), cubed
    1 cup (4 ounces) shredded sharp cheddar cheese
  1/2 cup shredded Swiss cheese
  1/4 cup mashed potato flakes
  1/4 teaspoon pepper

In a Dutch oven, combine first six ingredients. Bring to a boil. Reduce heat; simmer, uncovered, for 8-10 minutes or until vegetables are tender. Stir in celery and red pepper; simmer for 6-8 minutes or until tender.

Reduce heat to low. Gradually stir in mayonnaise until blended. Add cheeses; stir until melted. Add potato flakes and pepper; mix well. Remove from heat; let stand for 15 minutes. **Yield:** 12 servings (3 quarts).

Nutritional Analysis: One serving (1 cup) equals 341 calories, 25 g fat (9 g saturated fat), 44 mg cholesterol, 749 mg sodium, 19 g carbohydrate, 2 g fiber, 10 g protein.

Makeover Potato Cheese Soup

Meatless

(Pictured below)

    4 cups water
2-1/2 cups reduced-sodium chicken *or* vegetable broth
    5 cups diced peeled potatoes
    2 large carrots, finely chopped
    1 large onion, finely chopped
    2 tablespoons low-sodium chicken bouillon granules *or* 6 vegetable bouillon cubes
    2 celery ribs, finely chopped
    1 large sweet red pepper, finely chopped
    4 ounces reduced-fat process cheese (Velveeta), cubed
  1/3 cup reduced-fat mayonnaise
    2 cups (8 ounces) shredded reduced-fat cheddar cheese
  1/2 cup reduced-fat Swiss cheese
  1/4 cup mashed potato flakes
  1/4 teaspoon pepper

In a Dutch oven, combine first six ingredients. Bring to a boil. Reduce heat; simmer, uncovered, for 10-15 minutes or until vegetables are tender. Stir in celery and red pepper; simmer for 10 minutes or until tender.

Reduce heat to low. Stir in process cheese and mayonnaise until blended. Add cheddar and Swiss cheeses; stir until melted. Stir in the potato flakes and pepper. Remove from the heat; let stand for 15 minutes. **Yield:** 12 servings (3 quarts).

Nutritional Analysis: One serving (1 cup) equals 195 calories, 9 g fat (4 g saturated fat), 23 mg cholesterol, 520 mg sodium, 21 g carbohydrate, 2 g fiber, 10 g protein.

Diabetic Exchanges: 1 starch, 1 vegetable, 1 lean meat, 1 fat.

Tomato Chicken Rice Soup

Low-fat

(Pictured on page 31)

This hearty soup is loaded with vegetables, chicken, rice and herbs. When friends come for lunch, I warm up some garlic toast and make a meal of it. It's a great way to cut back on calories and fat.
—Gwen Shawley, El Mirage, Arizona

1/4 cup all-purpose flour
1 large onion, chopped
1 large green pepper, chopped
2 celery ribs, chopped
3 green onions, chopped
3 garlic cloves, minced
2 teaspoons canola oil
2 cups water
2 cans (14-1/2 ounces *each*) reduced-sodium chicken broth
2 cups cooked brown rice
2 cups cubed cooked chicken breast
1 can (14-1/2 ounces) diced tomatoes
1 teaspoon dried oregano
1 teaspoon dried thyme
1 bay leaf
3/4 teaspoon salt

In a small nonstick skillet, brown flour over medium-high heat; set aside. In a Dutch oven or soup kettle, saute the onion, green pepper, celery, green onions and garlic in oil until tender; stir in flour until blended. Stir in the remaining ingredients; bring to a boil. Reduce heat; simmer, uncovered, for 15 minutes. Discard bay leaf. **Yield:** 7 servings.

Nutritional Analysis: One serving (1-1/2 cups) equals 197 calories, 3 g fat (1 g saturated fat), 34 mg cholesterol, 682 mg sodium, 25 g carbohydrate, 3 g fiber, 17 g protein.
Diabetic Exchanges: 2 very lean meat, 2 vegetable, 1 starch.

Crab Bisque

I decided to try my hand at making a light seafood soup after tasting one while dining out. I came up with this low-fat bisque and everyone loved it. It was even featured on a local TV show recently!
—Corney Welsh, Baton Rouge, Louisiana

2 cups chopped onions
1 cup chopped celery
1 cup chopped green pepper
4 garlic cloves, minced
1/4 cup reduced-fat margarine
4 cups diced peeled potatoes
2 cups fat-free milk
4 cups fat-free half-and-half
10 ounces reduced-fat process cheese (Velveeta), cut into 1-inch cubes
1 can (1 pound) crabmeat, drained, flaked and cartilage removed
3/4 teaspoon salt
1/4 teaspoon white pepper

In a soup kettle or Dutch oven, saute the onions, celery, green pepper and garlic in margarine until tender. Reduce heat to medium; add the potatoes and milk. Cook, uncovered, for 20 minutes or until potatoes are just tender, stirring occasionally.

Remove 1-1/2 cups of the potato mixture; mash and return to the pan. Reduce heat to low. Stir in half-and-half and process cheese. Cook and stir until cheese is melted. Add the crab, salt and pepper. Cook 10 minutes longer or until heated through. **Yield:** 12 servings (3 quarts).

Editor's Note: This recipe was tested with Parkay Light stick margarine.

Nutritional Analysis: One serving (1 cup) equals 237 calories, 5 g fat (2 g saturated fat), 44 mg cholesterol, 802 mg sodium, 27 g carbohydrate, 2 g fiber, 18 g protein.
Diabetic Exchanges: 1 fat-free milk, 1 lean meat, 1 vegetable, 1/2 starch, 1/2 fat.

Roasted Pepper Potato Soup

Meatless

(Pictured below)

I really enjoy potato soup, and this rich creamy version is different than most I've tried. I like its lemon and cilantro flavors, but you can adjust the ingredients to best suit your family's taste buds.
—Hollie Powell, St. Louis, Missouri

2 medium onions, chopped
2 tablespoons canola oil
1 jar (7-1/4 ounces) roasted red peppers, undrained, chopped
1 can (4-1/2 ounces) chopped green chilies, drained

2 teaspoons ground cumin
1 teaspoon salt
1 teaspoon ground coriander
3 cups diced peeled potatoes
3 cups vegetable broth
2 tablespoons minced fresh cilantro
1 tablespoon lemon juice
1/2 cup reduced-fat cream cheese, cubed

In a large saucepan, saute onions in oil until tender. Stir in the roasted peppers, chilies, cumin, salt and coriander. Cook and stir for 2 minutes. Stir in potatoes and broth; bring to a boil. Reduce heat; cover and simmer for 10-15 minutes or until potatoes are tender. Stir in cilantro and lemon juice. Cool slightly.

In a blender, process the cream cheese and half of the soup until smooth. Return all to pan and heat through. **Yield:** 6 servings.

Nutritional Analysis: *One serving (1 cup) equals 204 calories, 9 g fat (3 g saturated fat), 11 mg cholesterol, 1,154 mg sodium, 26 g carbohydrate, 4 g fiber, 6 g protein.*
Diabetic Exchanges: *2 vegetable, 1-1/2 fat, 1 starch.*

Hearty Beef Barley Soup

My entire family just loves this delicious and comforting soup. Loaded with chunks of tender beef, the rich broth also includes plenty of fresh mushrooms, sliced carrots and quick-cooking barley.
—Barbara Beattie, Glen Allen, Virginia

2 tablespoons all-purpose flour
1/2 teaspoon salt
1/4 teaspoon pepper, *divided*
1 pound lean boneless beef sirloin steak, cut into 1/2-inch cubes
1 tablespoon canola oil
2 cups sliced fresh mushrooms
2 cans (14-1/2 ounces *each*) reduced-sodium beef broth
2 medium carrots, sliced
1/4 teaspoon garlic powder
1/4 teaspoon dried thyme
1/2 cup quick-cooking barley

In a large resealable plastic bag, combine the flour, salt and 1/8 teaspoon pepper. Add beef and shake to coat. In a Dutch oven, brown beef in oil over medium heat. Remove beef and set aside.

In the same pan, saute mushrooms until tender. Add the broth, carrots, garlic powder, thyme and remaining pepper; bring to a boil. Add barley and beef. Reduce heat; cover and simmer over low heat for 20-25 minutes until the meat, vegetables and barley are tender. **Yield:** 4 servings.

Nutritional Analysis: *One serving (1-1/4 cups) equals 300 calories, 9 g fat (2 g saturated fat), 68 mg cholesterol, 782 mg sodium, 26 g carbohydrate, 5 g fiber, 28 g protein.*
Diabetic Exchanges: *3 lean meat, 2 vegetable, 1 starch.*

Chicken Corn Soup with Rivels

Low-fat

(Pictured above)

Traditional chicken soup gets an interesting twist from a dumpling-like broth-stretcher called rivels. This light-on-fat recipe is chock-full of chicken, vegetables and herbs. You won't be able to resist it.
—Elissa Armbruster, Medford, New Jersey

1 cup chopped carrots
1 celery rib, chopped
1 medium onion, chopped
2 teaspoons canola oil
2 cans (14-1/2 ounces *each*) reduced-sodium chicken broth
2 cups fresh *or* frozen corn
2 cups cubed cooked chicken breast
1/2 teaspoon minced fresh parsley
1/4 teaspoon salt
1/4 teaspoon dried tarragon
1/4 teaspoon pepper
1 egg, beaten
3/4 cup all-purpose flour

In a large saucepan, saute the carrots, celery and onion in oil until tender. Add the broth, corn, chicken and seasonings. Bring to a boil. Meanwhile, for rivels, cut egg into flour with a fork until crumbly. Drop dough by teaspoonfuls into boiling soup, stirring constantly. Cook and stir for 1-2 minutes or until rivels are cooked through. **Yield:** 7 servings.

Nutritional Analysis: *One serving (1 cup) equals 189 calories, 3 g fat (1 g saturated fat), 64 mg cholesterol, 456 mg sodium, 24 g carbohydrate, 3 g fiber, 18 g protein.*
Diabetic Exchanges: *2 very lean meat, 1-1/2 starch.*

Zippy Three-Bean Chili

(Pictured below)

Use convenient canned pinto, black and great northern
beans to speed up preparation of this hearty chili.
The one-dish meal has a stew-like consistency
and a peppy Tex-Mex flavor.
—*Agnes Hamilton, Scott Depot, West Virginia*

 1 pound lean ground beef
 1/2 cup chopped onion
 1 cup chopped fresh mushrooms
 1/2 cup chopped green pepper
 1/2 cup chopped sweet red pepper
 1 garlic clove, minced
 2 cups water
 1 can (14-1/2 ounces) diced tomatoes and green
 chilies, undrained
 1 envelope reduced-sodium taco seasoning
 1 can (15-1/2 ounces) great northern beans,
 rinsed and drained
 1 can (15 ounces) black beans, rinsed and
 drained
 1 can (15 ounces) pinto beans, rinsed and
 drained
 8 tablespoons shredded reduced-fat cheddar
 cheese, *divided*

In a large saucepan, cook beef and onion over medium heat
until meat is no longer pink; drain. Add the mushrooms, peppers and garlic; cook and stir 3 minutes longer or until vegetables are almost tender. Stir in the water, tomatoes and
taco seasoning. Bring to a boil. Reduce heat; simmer, uncovered, for 30 minutes. Add beans; simmer 30 minutes
longer. Sprinkle each serving with 1 tablespoon cheese.
Yield: 8 servings (2 quarts).

Nutritional Analysis: One serving (1 cup chili with 1 table-
spoon cheese) equals 269 calories, 6 g fat (3 g saturated fat), 33
mg cholesterol, 738 mg sodium, 32 g carbohydrate, 8 g fiber, 21
g protein.
Diabetic Exchanges: 2 lean meat, 1-1/2 starch, 1 vegetable.

El Paso Bean Soup

We have so few bad-weather days in New Mexico that
we like to celebrate cold rainy ones with bowls of hot
soup. My family likes this ham and bean variety
alongside green chili corn muffins.
—*Beverly Peacock, Santa Teresa, New Mexico*

 1 medium onion, chopped
 1 medium carrot, chopped
 2 garlic cloves, minced
 2 tablespoons olive oil
 4 cups reduced-sodium beef broth
 1 can (16 ounces) fat-free refried beans
 2 cans (15-1/2 ounces *each*) great northern
 beans, rinsed and drained
 1-1/3 cups cubed fully cooked lean ham
 1 teaspoon dried parsley flakes
 1 teaspoon ground cumin
 1 teaspoon chili powder
 1/4 teaspoon pepper
 2 medium tomatoes, chopped

In a large saucepan, saute the onion, carrot and garlic in oil
until tender. Stir in broth and refried beans; whisk until
smooth. Stir in the beans, ham, parsley, cumin, chili powder
and pepper. Bring to a boil. Reduce heat; cover and simmer
for 15 minutes. Stir in the tomatoes and heat through. **Yield:**
6 servings (2-1/4 quarts).

Nutritional Analysis: One serving (1-1/3 cups) equals 289
calories, 7 g fat (1 g saturated fat), 13 mg cholesterol, 1,145 mg
sodium, 37 g carbohydrate, 12 g fiber, 19 g protein.
Diabetic Exchanges: 2 starch, 2 lean meat, 1 vegetable.

🍎 Secrets for Soup in a Snap

WE NEED to watch our cholesterol, so I make a large
batch of low-cholesterol soup. I start with dry beans,
peas, barley and rice, and add several seasonal vegetables and seasonings.

I can keep the soup in a sealed container in the
refrigerator for 3 to 4 days. To serve, I just add
some cubed cooked chicken breast to a portion and
heat it up. —*Mary Ann Dischinger*
Minneapolis, Minnesota

cover and simmer for 30-40 minutes or until the vegetables are just tender.

Add corn and beans. Bring to a boil. Reduce heat; cover and simmer for 5-10 minutes or until vegetables are tender. **Yield:** 9 servings (about 3-1/4 quarts).

Nutritional Analysis: One serving (1-1/2 cups) equals 227 calories, 7 g fat (2 g saturated fat), 49 mg cholesterol, 584 mg sodium, 24 g carbohydrate, 4 g fiber, 19 g protein.
Diabetic Exchanges: 2 lean meat, 2 vegetable, 1 starch.

Seafood Soup

Low-carb

This tomato-based soup is loaded with tender chunks of salmon, shrimp and chopped veggies. Simply seasoned with basil, oregano and garlic, it makes a filling meal-in-a-bowl.
—Valerie Bradley, Beaverton, Oregon

1/2 cup chopped onion
1/2 cup chopped green pepper
  3 tablespoons minced fresh parsley
  1 tablespoon olive oil
  1 cup chopped carrots
  1 garlic clove, minced
  1 can (15 ounces) tomato sauce
  1 can (14-1/2 ounces) diced tomatoes
3/4 cup white wine *or* chicken broth
  1 bay leaf
1/2 teaspoon dried oregano
1/4 teaspoon dried basil
1/4 teaspoon pepper
3/4 pound salmon fillets, skinned and cut
    into 3/4-inch cubes
1/2 pound uncooked medium shrimp, peeled and
    deveined

In a large saucepan, saute the onion, green pepper and parsley in oil until tender. Add carrots and garlic; cook and stir for 3 minutes. Stir in the tomato sauce, tomatoes, wine or broth and seasonings. Bring to a boil. Reduce heat; cover and simmer for 30 minutes. Stir in salmon and shrimp. Cover and cook 7-10 minutes longer or until fish flakes easily with a fork and shrimp turn pink. Discard bay leaf. **Yield:** 6 servings.

Nutritional Analysis: One serving (1 cup) equals 212 calories, 9 g fat (2 g saturated fat), 87 mg cholesterol, 620 mg sodium, 13 g carbohydrate, 3 g fiber, 19 g protein.
Diabetic Exchanges: 3 lean meat, 2 vegetable.

Beefy Vegetable Soup

(Pictured above)

This chunky soup is loaded with tender beef stew meat, carrots, potatoes and green beans—and it sure is tasty! A little steak sauce and garlic powder season the broth perfectly.
—Jimmy Osmon, Upper Darby, Pennsylvania

1-1/2 pounds lean beef stew meat
  1 tablespoon canola oil
  2 cans (14-1/2 ounces *each*) reduced-sodium
    beef broth
1-1/2 cups water
  2 tablespoons reduced-sodium soy sauce
  3 medium potatoes, cubed (about 1 pound)
  3 medium carrots, cubed
  3 celery ribs, chopped
  2 tablespoons Worcestershire sauce
  2 tablespoons steak sauce
  1 tablespoon garlic powder
1/2 teaspoon salt
1/4 teaspoon dried oregano
1/8 teaspoon ground nutmeg
1/8 teaspoon pepper
  2 cups fresh *or* frozen corn
1-3/4 cups frozen cut green beans

In a large kettle or Dutch oven, brown beef over medium heat in oil. Add the broth, water and soy sauce. Bring to a boil. Reduce heat; cover and simmer for 1 hour.

Add the potatoes, carrots, celery, Worcestershire sauce, steak sauce and seasonings. Bring to a boil. Reduce heat;

Southwestern Chicken Black Bean Soup

This recipe was given to me by a good friend a couple of years ago, and I've been making it ever since. We love Mexican food, and bowls of this pack enough flavor to please even my husband.
—Emily Fast, Leavenworth, Kansas

- **1 pound boneless skinless chicken breasts, cubed**
- **1 tablespoon canola oil**
- **1/2 cup chopped onion**
- **1 jalapeno pepper, seeded and finely chopped**
- **3 garlic cloves, minced**
- **2 cans (14-1/2 ounces *each*) reduced-sodium chicken broth**
- **3 cups fresh *or* frozen corn**
- **1 can (15-1/2 ounces) black beans, rinsed and drained**
- **2 tablespoons lime juice**
- **1/2 teaspoon salt**
- **1/2 teaspoon hot pepper sauce**
- **1/4 teaspoon pepper**
- **1/2 cup minced fresh cilantro**
- **16 baked tortilla chips, crumbled**
- **1/2 cup shredded reduced-fat cheddar cheese**

In a large kettle or Dutch oven, saute chicken in oil until no longer pink. Remove with a slotted spoon and set aside. In the same pan, saute onion and jalapeno pepper until tender; add garlic and saute for 1 minute.

Stir in the broth, corn, beans, lime juice, salt, hot pepper sauce, pepper and reserved chicken; bring to a boil. Reduce heat; simmer, uncovered, for 30 minutes. Stir in cilantro. Top each serving with crumbled tortilla chips and cheese. **Yield:** 8 servings (2 quarts).

Editor's Note: When cutting or seeding hot peppers, use rubber or plastic gloves to protect your hands. Avoid touching your face.

Nutritional Analysis: *One serving (1 cup soup with 1 tablespoon cheese and 2 crumbled tortilla chips) equals 227 calories, 4 g fat (1 g saturated fat), 37 mg cholesterol, 647 mg sodium, 27 g carbohydrate, 4 g fiber, 21 g protein.*
Diabetic Exchanges: *2 lean meat, 1-1/2 starch, 1 vegetable.*

Potato Leek Soup

Low-fat

Soups featuring potatoes and leeks are popular in Scotland, where I first tasted this dish in a cozy pub. For variety, add a cup of cooked lentils.
—Laura Sebranek, Green Bay, Wisconsin

- **2 cups cubed peeled potatoes**
- **1 medium leek (white and 1 inch of green portion), thinly sliced**
- **1 medium turnip, peeled and cubed**
- **1 celery rib with leaves, chopped**
- **1/4 cup shredded carrot**
- **1/4 cup chopped onion**
- **1/4 cup diced fully cooked lean ham**
- **1 teaspoon reduced-sodium chicken bouillon granules**
- **1 tablespoon butter**
- **2 tablespoons cornstarch**
- **1/2 teaspoon salt**
- **1/8 teaspoon pepper**
- **1-1/4 cups fat-free milk**
- **3/4 cup fat-free evaporated milk**

In a large saucepan, combine first eight ingredients; add enough water just to cover. Bring to a boil. Cook, uncovered, over medium heat for 15-20 minutes or until tender.

Meanwhile, in a microwave-safe bowl, microwave butter until melted. Stir in cornstarch, salt and pepper until smooth. Gradually add milk and evaporated milk. Microwave, uncovered, on high for 8-10 minutes or until thickened and bubbly, stirring every 2 minutes. Stir into vegetable mixture. **Yield:** 5 servings.

Editor's Note: This recipe was tested in a 1,100-watt microwave.

Nutritional Analysis: *One serving (1-1/2 cups) equals 181 calories, 3 g fat (2 g saturated fat), 11 mg cholesterol, 548 mg sodium, 31 g carbohydrate, 3 g fiber, 9 g protein.*
Diabetic Exchanges: *1-1/2 starch, 1/2 fat-free milk, 1/2 fat.*

Strawberry Soup

Low-fat   Low-sodium   Meatless

I enjoyed a cool berry soup at a restaurant several years ago. The manager gave me some of the ingredients and none of the amounts, so I tinkered with what I had to get this refreshing rendition.
—Phyllis Hammes, Rochester, Minnesota

- **1 pound fresh strawberries**
- **1-1/4 cups reduced-fat vanilla yogurt, *divided***
- **3 tablespoons confectioners' sugar**
- **2 tablespoons orange juice concentrate**
- **1/8 teaspoon almond extract *or* 1/2 teaspoon lemon juice**

In a food processor or blender, combine the strawberries, 1 cup yogurt, confectioners' sugar, orange juice concentrate and extract; cover and process until smooth. Garnish each serving with a dollop of remaining yogurt. **Yield:** 3 servings.

Nutritional Analysis: *One serving (1 cup) equals 174 calories, 2 g fat (1 g saturated fat), 5 mg cholesterol, 69 mg sodium, 35 g carbohydrate, 3 g fiber, 6 g protein.*
Diabetic Exchanges: *1-1/2 fruit, 1/2 reduced-fat milk, 1/2 starch.*

Step Up to The Salad Bar

Whether you're looking for a standout side dish to accompany a main course, a tangy take-along for the neighborhood barbecue or an appealing addition to your lunchtime lineup, nothing beats garden-fresh salads!

Mediterranean Medley Salad (page 51)

meal, I suggest taking a walk after dinner with your loved ones. Pepperoncini gives the dish zip, and olive oil dressing adds Mediterranean flavor.
—Rosemary Morgan, Pacifica, California

3 cups cooked small shell pasta
1 cup halved cherry tomatoes
1 cup whole pitted ripe olives
1 cup pepperoncini, thinly sliced
3 tablespoons olive oil
3 tablespoons lemon juice
1 garlic clove, minced
1 teaspoon minced fresh oregano *or* 1/4 teaspoon dried oregano
1 teaspoon salt
1/4 teaspoon pepper

In a bowl, combine the pasta, tomatoes, olives and pepperoncini. In a small bowl, combine the oil, lemon juice, garlic, oregano, salt and pepper. Pour over pasta mixture and toss to coat evenly. Cover and refrigerate for at least 3 hours. **Yield:** 6 servings.

Nutritional Analysis: One serving (3/4 cup) equals 184 calories, 10 g fat (1 g saturated fat), 0 cholesterol, 936 mg sodium, 20 g carbohydrate, 1 g fiber, 3 g protein.
Diabetic Exchanges: 2 fat, 1 starch, 1 vegetable.

Asian Coleslaw

Low-carb Meatless

(Pictured above)

Here's a recipe for coleslaw without all the greasy mayonnaise. It's very well-liked by the people who've tried it. A bit of sugar mellows the tangy dressing.
—Alta Goodman, Canton, South Dakota

5 cups Chinese *or* napa cabbage (1-1/4 pounds), thinly sliced and ribs removed
3 medium carrots, shredded
2 green onions, thinly sliced
1/4 cup minced fresh cilantro
1/3 cup white wine vinegar
1 tablespoon canola oil
1 tablespoon sesame oil
1 teaspoon sugar
1/2 teaspoon salt

In a large bowl, combine the cabbage, carrots, green onions and cilantro. In a small bowl, whisk together the remaining ingredients. Pour over cabbage mixture and toss to coat. Cover and refrigerate for 1 hour or until chilled. **Yield:** 6 servings.

Nutritional Analysis: One serving (1 cup) equals 75 calories, 5 g fat (1 g saturated fat), 0 cholesterol, 223 mg sodium, 8 g carbohydrate, 3 g fiber, 1 g protein.
Diabetic Exchanges: 1 vegetable, 1 fat.

Pepperoncini Pasta Salad

Meatless

My family comes from a very hot part of Italy, so chilled pasta salads are always a big hit. To top off this light

Spring Salad

Low-carb Low-fat Meatless

Our family has been savoring this salad for more than 75 years. It goes back to my Bavarian grandmother. With a large family to raise, she turned to the garden for inexpensive ingredients. The lightly dressed tomatoes, cucumbers and radishes are still a hit at meals and potlucks today.
—Mari Malmquist, Muskego, Wisconsin

2 medium tomatoes, seeded and chopped
2 cups thinly sliced radishes
1 large cucumber, quartered, seeded and chopped
1/2 cup white vinegar
1/2 cup water
Sugar substitute equivalent to 1/2 cup sugar
1/2 teaspoon salt
1/4 teaspoon pepper

In a large bowl, combine the tomatoes, radishes and cucumber. In a small bowl, whisk together the vinegar, water, sugar substitute, salt and pepper until sugar substitute is dissolved (mixture will foam up slightly). Pour over vegetable mixture; toss to coat evenly. Cover and refrigerate for at least 1 hour. Serve with a slotted spoon. **Yield:** 6 servings.

Editor's Note: This recipe was tested with Splenda No Calorie Sweetener. Look for it in the baking aisle of your grocery store.

Nutritional Analysis: One serving (3/4 cup) equals 44 calories, trace fat (trace saturated fat), 0 cholesterol, 208 mg sodium, 10 g carbohydrate, 1 g fiber, 1 g protein.
Diabetic Exchange: 2 vegetable.

Easy Waldorf and Raisin Salad

Low-fat **Low-sodium** *Meatless*

This appealing recipe puts a healthy spin on classic Waldorf salad. Crunchy apples, celery and pecans, juicy pineapple and chewy raisins are dressed with reduced-fat mayonnaise and sour cream. I suggest serving the salad in a lettuce-lined bowl.
—Janice Smith, Cynthiana, Kentucky

    4 cups cubed apples
    1 cup unsweetened pineapple tidbits
    2 tablespoons chopped celery
    2 tablespoons chopped pecans
    2 tablespoons raisins
    1 cup (8 ounces) fat-free sour cream
    1 tablespoon reduced-fat mayonnaise
1-1/2 teaspoons sugar
1-1/2 teaspoons orange juice

In a large bowl, combine the first five ingredients. In a small bowl, combine the sour cream, mayonnaise, sugar and orange juice. Pour over apple mixture; toss to coat. Cover and refrigerate for 2 hours or until chilled. Toss just before serving. **Yield:** 6 servings.

Nutritional Analysis: *One serving (3/4 cup) equals 147 calories, 3 g fat (trace saturated fat), 7 mg cholesterol, 52 mg sodium, 28 g carbohydrate, 3 g fiber, 3 g protein.*
Diabetic Exchanges: *1 fruit, 1/2 fat-free milk, 1/2 fat.*

White Bean Tuna Salad

I adapted this recipe from one in my local newspaper. The zippy Dijon dressing adds interest to the beans, tuna, olives and onion. It makes a filling and healthy lunch that I like to take to work.
—Kathleen Law, Post Falls, Idaho

1/4 cup red wine vinegar
    3 garlic cloves, minced
    2 teaspoons Dijon mustard
    1 teaspoon sugar
1/2 teaspoon salt
1/4 teaspoon pepper
    2 tablespoons olive oil
    2 cans (15 ounces *each*) white kidney *or*
       cannellini beans, rinsed and drained
    2 cans (6 ounces *each*) light water-packed tuna,
       drained and flaked
3/4 cup sliced ripe olives
1/2 cup chopped red onion

In a small bowl, combine the first six ingredients; gradually whisk in oil. In a large bowl, combine the beans, tuna, olives and onion; add dressing and toss gently. Refrigerate until serving. **Yield:** 6 servings.

Nutritional Analysis: *One serving (3/4 cup) equals 247 calories, 7 g fat (1 g saturated fat), 17 mg cholesterol, 754 mg sodium, 23 g carbohydrate, 6 g fiber, 20 g protein.*
Diabetic Exchanges: *3 lean meat, 1 starch, 1 vegetable.*

Chive-Mushroom Spinach Salad

Low-carb *Meatless*

(Pictured below)

I'm always looking for ways to spice up salads. This one is a cross between two of our favorites. I usually make a double batch of the dressing and use leftovers for dipping bread.
—Amber Kimmich, Powhatan, Virginia

    8 cups fresh baby spinach
    2 cups sliced fresh mushrooms
    1 tablespoon chopped onion
    1 garlic clove, minced
    2 tablespoons olive oil
    3 tablespoons minced chives
    2 tablespoons lemon juice
    2 tablespoons balsamic vinegar
    1 teaspoon sugar
1-1/2 cups seasoned salad croutons
1/4 cup shredded Parmesan cheese

Place spinach in a large salad bowl; set aside. In a large skillet, saute the mushrooms, onion and garlic in oil for 2-4 minutes. In a small bowl, combine the chives, lemon juice, vinegar and sugar. Pour into the skillet. Cook and stir 1 minute longer or until mushrooms are tender. Add to spinach with croutons and Parmesan cheese; toss to coat. Serve immediately. **Yield:** 6 servings.

Nutritional Analysis: *One serving (1-1/3 cups) equals 117 calories, 6 g fat (1 g saturated fat), 2 mg cholesterol, 235 mg sodium, 11 g carbohydrate, 1 g fiber, 5 g protein.*
Diabetic Exchanges: *1 vegetable, 1 fat, 1/2 starch.*

Fat-Free Bean Salad

Low-fat   Meatless

I recently made this salad to serve at a turkey barbecue. It was just as big a hit as it was for our son's confirmation dinner some 40 years ago. My trim treatment of the timeless sweet-and-sour beans doesn't cut down on flavor one bit.
—Ruth Beitelspacher, Aberdeen, South Dakota

2 cans (14-1/2 ounces *each*) French-style green
  beans, drained
1 can (16 ounces) kidney beans, rinsed and
  drained
2 cups chopped sweet onions
1 cup sweet pickle relish
1/2 cup chopped green pepper
1/4 cup white vinegar
1/3 cup sugar

In a bowl, combine the green beans, kidney beans, onions, pickle relish and green pepper. In a small bowl, combine the vinegar and sugar; mix well. Pour over bean mixture; toss to coat evenly. Cover and refrigerate for at least 2 hours. Serve with a slotted spoon. **Yield:** 8 servings.

Nutritional Analysis: One serving (3/4 cup) equals 156 calories, trace fat (trace saturated fat), 0 cholesterol, 672 mg sodium, 36 g carbohydrate, 6 g fiber, 5 g protein.
Diabetic Exchanges: 2 vegetable, 1-1/2 starch.

Mango Chicken Salad

(Pictured at right)

Come summer, I like to pack this refreshing salad for a picnic lunch. Each of the ingredients can be stored in a separate container in a cooler and assembled at the picnic. It's always a hit.
—Carolyn Black, Richmond, British Columbia

8 cups torn red leaf lettuce
2 cups torn mixed salad greens
4 medium tomatoes, thinly sliced
1-1/2 cups thinly sliced cucumber
6 boneless skinless chicken breast halves
  (4 ounces *each*), grilled and thinly sliced
MANGO SALAD DRESSING:
2 large ripe mangos *or* 4 medium peaches,
  peeled and cut into chunks
1/4 cup lime juice
1/4 teaspoon salt
1/8 to 1/4 teaspoon cayenne pepper
1/4 cup sunflower kernels

Divide lettuce and salad greens among six plates. Top with the tomatoes, cucumber and chicken. In a blender, combine the mangos, lime juice, salt and cayenne; cover and process

until smooth. Serve with salad. Sprinkle with sunflower kernels. **Yield:** 6 servings.

Nutritional Analysis: One serving equals 221 calories, 6 g fat (1 g saturated fat), 63 mg cholesterol, 166 mg sodium, 18 g carbohydrate, 3 g fiber, 25 g protein.
Diabetic Exchanges: 3 lean meat, 1 vegetable, 1 fruit.

Warm Sausage Potato Salad

(Pictured at right)

No one will ever guess that this creamy potato salad is lightened up! It's hearty and satisfying, with plenty of sausage chunks mixed in with the red potatoes and green beans.
—Connie Staal, Greenbrier, Arkansas

6 cups cubed red potatoes
2 cups fresh green beans, halved and cut in half
  lengthwise
1 pound reduced-fat fully cooked smoked
  sausage, quartered and sliced
1 medium onion, diced
2 tablespoons butter
3 tablespoons all-purpose flour
3/4 teaspoon ground mustard
1/2 teaspoon salt
1/4 teaspoon pepper
1-1/2 cups fat-free milk
3/4 cup reduced-fat mayonnaise

Place potatoes in a saucepan and cover with water; bring to a boil. Reduce heat; cover and cook for 4 minutes. Add beans; cook 3-4 minutes longer or until vegetables are tender. Drain and place in a bowl. Add the sausage and onion.

In a saucepan, melt butter. Stir in the flour, mustard, salt and pepper until smooth; gradually add the milk. Bring to a boil; cook and stir for 1-2 minutes or until thickened. Remove from the heat. Stir in the mayonnaise; pour over vegetable mixture and toss to coat. Transfer to a 3-qt. baking dish coated with nonstick cooking spray. Cover and bake at 350° for 45-50 minutes or until heated through. **Yield:** 13 servings.

Nutritional Analysis: One serving (3/4 cup) equals 194 calories, 8 g fat (3 g saturated fat), 26 mg cholesterol, 533 mg sodium, 22 g carbohydrate, 2 g fiber, 8 g protein.
Diabetic Exchanges: 1-1/2 starch, 1 lean meat, 1/2 fat.

A Twist on Pasta Salad

Low-fat Meatless

I lightened up this recipe I found on the back of a pasta box many years ago. It's become a staple at our home and for family gatherings. Feel free to use whatever vegetables you have on hand.
—Pat Morris, Marlton, New Jersey

1-1/4 cups uncooked tricolor spiral pasta
1/4 cup reduced-sodium chicken *or* vegetable
   broth
3 tablespoons red wine vinegar
1 tablespoon canola oil
1 garlic clove, minced
1 teaspoon sugar
1 teaspoon dried basil
1/2 teaspoon salt
2 cups broccoli florets
1 cup halved cherry tomatoes
1 large sweet red pepper, julienned
1/4 cup grated Parmesan cheese

Cook pasta according to package directions; rinse under cold water. Drain. In a large bowl, whisk together the broth, vinegar, oil, garlic, sugar, basil and salt. Add the pasta, broccoli, tomatoes, pepper and Parmesan and toss to coat.
Yield: 8 servings.

Nutritional Analysis: One serving (3/4 cup) equals 104 calories, 3 g fat (1 g saturated fat), 2 mg cholesterol, 221 mg sodium, 16 g carbohydrate, 2 g fiber, 4 g protein.
Diabetic Exchanges: 1 vegetable, 1/2 starch, 1/2 fat.

Oriental Bulgur Rice Salad

Meatless

(Pictured at right)

Some people call me the "Queen of Wheat" because I'm always telling them how to use it in creative ways. This tasty salad was a hit with my family. I often add cooked chicken or seafood to turn it into a main dish.
—Brenda Tew, Shelley, Idaho

1/2 cup uncooked bulgur
1-1/2 cups boiling water
1-1/2 cups cooked long grain rice
1/2 cup thinly sliced celery

1/2 cup coarsely grated carrot
1/2 cup sliced green pepper
1/4 cup dried cranberries
SALAD DRESSING:
1/4 cup minced fresh parsley
1/4 cup rice vinegar
2 tablespoons olive oil
1 tablespoon finely chopped onion
1 tablespoon water
1 teaspoon *each* sesame oil and honey
1 garlic clove, minced
1/2 teaspoon *each* salt, ground mustard and
   Chinese five-spice powder
1/4 teaspoon pepper
9 cups torn mixed salad greens
1/4 cup sliced almonds, toasted

Place bulgur in a bowl. Stir in boiling water. Cover and let stand for 30 minutes or until most of the liquid is absorbed. Drain and squeeze dry.

In a bowl, combine the rice, celery, carrot, green pepper, cranberries and bulgur. In a jar with a tight-fitting lid, combine the parsley, vinegar, olive oil, onion, water, sesame oil, honey, garlic and seasonings; shake well. Pour over the rice mixture; toss gently to coat. Arrange the greens on salad plates. Top with the rice mixture; sprinkle with almonds.
Yield: 6 servings.

Editor's Note: Look for bulgur in the cereal, rice or organic food aisle of your grocery store.

Nutritional Analysis: One serving (2/3 cup rice mixture with 1-1/2 cups greens) equals 203 calories, 8 g fat (1 g saturated fat), 0 cholesterol, 227 mg sodium, 30 g carbohydrate, 5 g fiber, 5 g protein.
Diabetic Exchanges: 1-1/2 starch, 1-1/2 fat, 1 vegetable.

Mediterranean Medley Salad

(Pictured on page 45)

*This refreshing alternative to pasta salad is perfect
for casual summer luncheons. You can serve it
as a main dish with the tuna...or without it for
a nice rice side. Sometimes, I substitute reduced-fat
mayonnaise for the olive oil.*
—Merwyn Garbini, Tucson, Arizona

    2 cups cooked brown rice
    1 can (6 ounces) light water-packed tuna, drained
      and flaked
  1/2 cup sliced ripe olives
  1/2 cup sliced celery
  1/2 cup frozen peas, thawed
    1 medium tomato, diced
  1/2 cup chopped green pepper
  1/4 cup thinly sliced radishes
  1/4 cup sliced green onions
  1/4 cup grated carrot
LEMON HERB SALAD DRESSING:
    2 tablespoons olive oil
    2 tablespoons water
    2 tablespoons lemon juice
    1 tablespoon Italian seasoning
    1 teaspoon sugar
  1/2 teaspoon salt
    1 garlic clove, minced
  1/4 teaspoon lemon-pepper seasoning

In a large bowl, combine the first 10 ingredients. In a jar with
a tight-fitting lid, combine salad dressing ingredients; shake
well. Pour over salad and toss to coat. Cover and refrigerate for at least 1 hour. **Yield:** 4 servings.

*Nutritional Analysis: One serving (1-1/2 cups) equals 284
calories, 11 g fat (2 g saturated fat), 18 mg cholesterol, 669 mg
sodium, 33 g carbohydrate, 5 g fiber, 14 g protein.*
*Diabetic Exchanges: 2 very lean meat, 1-1/2 starch, 1-1/2 fat,
1 vegetable.*

Pistachio Fruit Salad

Low-fat **Low-sodium** *Meatless*

*My husband, a diabetic, always smiles when he finds
this fun and fluffy salad on the menu. I pair
pistachio pudding with pineapple, oranges and
other fruits for a tasty guilt-free treat.*
—Gail Bartlett, Hallowell, Maine

    1 can (20 ounces) crushed unsweetened
      pineapple
    1 package (1 ounce) sugar-free instant pistachio
      pudding mix
    1 can (15 ounces) unsweetened fruit cocktail,
      drained
    1 can (11 ounces) reduced-sugar mandarin
      oranges, drained
    1 cup reduced-fat whipped topping

Drain pineapple, reserving juice. In a bowl, whisk together
reserved juice and pudding mix for 2 minutes (mixture will

be thick). Stir in the pineapple, fruit cocktail and mandarin
oranges. Fold in whipped topping. Cover and refrigerate until serving. **Yield:** 6 servings.

*Nutritional Analysis: One serving (3/4 cup) equals 122 calo-
ries, 1 g fat (1 g saturated fat), 0 cholesterol, 62 mg sodium, 27 g
carbohydrate, 2 g fiber, 1 g protein.*
Diabetic Exchange: 2 fruit.

Smoky Thousand Island Salad Dressing

Low-carb *Low-fat* **Meatless**

(Pictured above)

*To be honest, I usually make this salad dressing with
a quick scoop of this, a dollop of that and a squirt or
shake of the other ingredients. But I carefully
measured everything for the recipe here.*
—Betty McConoughey, Loves Park, Illinois

  1/2 cup reduced-fat mayonnaise
    2 tablespoons sweet pickle relish
    2 tablespoons ketchup
    1 tablespoon hickory barbecue sauce
    1 teaspoon prepared horseradish
    1 teaspoon prepared mustard
    1 teaspoon Liquid Smoke, optional

In a small bowl, combine all the ingredients; stir until well-
blended. Store, covered, in the refrigerator. **Yield:** 14 tablespoons.

*Nutritional Analysis: One serving (2 tablespoons) equals 56
calories, 3 g fat (1 g saturated fat), 5 mg cholesterol, 278 mg
sodium, 6 g carbohydrate, trace fiber, trace protein.*
Diabetic Exchanges: 1/2 starch, 1/2 fat.

Italian Grilled Chicken Salad

(Pictured below)

Simple yet elegant, this entree salad is one of my husband's favorites. We love the juicy chicken, fresh greens and bread that's toasted over an open flame.
—Lisa Rawsk, Milwaukee, Wisconsin

  3 tablespoons balsamic vinegar
  3 tablespoons olive oil
  1 teaspoon dried rosemary, crushed
  1 garlic clove, minced
1/2 teaspoon salt
1/2 teaspoon coarsely ground pepper
  4 boneless skinless chicken breast halves
    (4 ounces *each*)
  4 ounces Italian bread, sliced
  4 cups torn romaine
  2 cups chopped seeded tomatoes
  1 cup white kidney *or* cannellini beans
1/3 cup minced fresh basil

In a jar with a tight-fitting lid, combine the first six ingredients; shake well. Remove 1 tablespoon vinegar mixture; brush over chicken. Cover and refrigerate for 30 minutes. Set aside remaining vinegar mixture.

Coat grill rack with nonstick cooking spray before starting grill. Grill chicken, covered, over medium heat for 4-6 minutes on each side or until juices run clear. Brush bread slices with 1 tablespoon reserved vinegar mixture. Grill bread, uncovered, over medium heat for 2 minutes on each side or until toasted. Slice chicken and cut bread into cubes; set aside.

In a large bowl, combine the romaine, tomatoes, beans, basil and bread cubes. Drizzle with remaining vinegar mixture; toss to coat. Arrange on salad plates. Top with chicken. Serve immediately. **Yield:** 4 servings.

Nutritional Analysis: One serving (1-1/2 cups dressed salad with chicken) equals 379 calories, 13 g fat (2 g saturated fat), 66 mg cholesterol, 632 mg sodium, 31 g carbohydrate, 5 g fiber, 33 g protein.
Diabetic Exchanges: 3 lean meat, 1-1/2 starch, 1-1/2 fat, 1 vegetable.

Fruit and Vegetable Salad

Low-carb   Meatless

Getting your family to eat fruits and veggies will be a snap, thanks to this tantalizing salad. A simple reduced-fat dressing coats a crunchy mix of peppers, celery, cabbage, apples and grapes. Not overpowering, it complements their flavors instead of hiding them.
—Vicky LaMance, Middletown, Ohio

  1 medium green pepper, chopped
  1 cup chopped celery
  1 cup shredded cabbage
3/4 cup chopped unpeeled red apple
1/2 cup seedless red grapes, halved
1/4 cup reduced-fat mayonnaise
1/4 teaspoon salt
Lettuce leaves

In a bowl, combine the first five ingredients. In a small bowl, combine the mayonnaise and salt. Stir into pepper mixture. Cover and refrigerate for at least 1 hour. Serve on lettuce leaves. **Yield:** 4 servings.

Nutritional Analysis: One serving (1 cup) equals 95 calories, 5 g fat (1 g saturated fat), 5 mg cholesterol, 298 mg sodium, 12 g carbohydrate, 2 g fiber, 1 g protein.
Diabetic Exchanges: 1 vegetable, 1/2 fat, 1/2 fruit.

Marinated Salad

Meatless

(Pictured at right)

This chilled pasta salad is pleasing to the eye and the palate. Serve it when sweet corn, tomatoes and zucchini are in season. This make-ahead favorite is lightly dressed with tarragon vinegar, olive oil and dill weed.
—Susan Branch, Kalamazoo, Michigan

3-1/4 cups fresh whole kernel corn, cooked and
    drained
  2 cups cherry tomatoes, halved
1-1/2 cups cooked rigatoni *or* large tube pasta
  1 medium zucchini, halved lengthwise and thinly
    sliced
1/2 cup pitted ripe olives
1/3 cup tarragon vinegar
  2 tablespoons olive oil
1-1/2 teaspoons dill weed
  1 teaspoon salt
1/2 teaspoon ground mustard
1/4 teaspoon garlic powder
1/4 teaspoon pepper

In a large bowl, combine the corn, tomatoes, rigatoni, zucchini and olives. In a small bowl, whisk together the vinegar, oil, dill, salt, mustard, garlic powder and pepper. Pour over corn mixture; toss to coat. Cover and refrigerate for at least 2 hours. **Yield:** 7 servings.

Nutritional Analysis: One serving (1 cup) equals 166 calories, 6 g fat (1 g saturated fat), 0 cholesterol, 429 mg sodium, 28 g carbohydrate, 4 g fiber, 4 g protein.
Diabetic Exchanges: 1-1/2 starch, 1 vegetable, 1 fat.

Honey Lime Fruit Toss

Low-fat **Low-sodium** *Meatless*

(Pictured above)

A tongue-tickling lime dressing complements the fruit in this refreshing and versatile medley. Serve it at breakfast or as a summery side dish.
—*Angela Oelschlaeger, Tonganoxie, Kansas*

1 can (20 ounces) unsweetened pineapple chunks
1 can (11 ounces) mandarin oranges, drained
2 cups sliced fresh strawberries
2 medium firm bananas, cut into 1/4-inch slices
2 kiwifruit, peeled, halved and sliced
2 tablespoons lime juice
1 tablespoon honey
1/4 teaspoon grated lime peel

Drain pineapple, reserving 1/4 cup juice; set juice aside. In a bowl, combine the pineapple, mandarin oranges, strawberries, bananas and kiwi. In a small bowl, combine the lime juice, honey, lime peel and reserved pineapple juice. Pour over fruit; gently toss to coat. **Yield:** 6 servings.

Nutritional Analysis: One serving (3/4 cup) equals 133 calories, 1 g fat (trace saturated fat), 0 cholesterol, 7 mg sodium, 33 g carbohydrate, 4 g fiber, 1 g protein.
Diabetic Exchange: *2 fruit.*

Green Pepper Tomato Salad

Low-carb *Low-fat* *Meatless*

My mother has made this tasty salad for as long as I can remember. It's no surprise that this recipe has worked its way into my hand-written "Most Used Recipes" book.
—*Lili Hill, Athens, Georgia*

3 medium tomatoes, seeded and chopped
1 medium green pepper, chopped
1 celery rib, thinly sliced
1/2 cup chopped red onion
2 tablespoons cider vinegar
1 tablespoon sugar
1/2 teaspoon salt
1/8 teaspoon pepper

In a large bowl, combine the tomatoes, green pepper, celery and onion. In a small bowl, combine the vinegar, sugar, salt and pepper. Stir into tomato mixture. Cover and refrigerate for at least 2 hours, stirring several times. Serve with a slotted spoon. **Yield:** 6 servings.

Nutritional Analysis: One serving (3/4 cup) equals 34 calories, trace fat (trace saturated fat), 0 cholesterol, 213 mg sodium, 8 g carbohydrate, 1 g fiber, 1 g protein.
Diabetic Exchanges: *1 vegetable.*

Couscous Salad

Meatless

While visiting my in-laws in the Canary Islands, we had a rooftop buffet for 20 people to celebrate our anniversaries. This was one of the dishes my mother-in-law prepared.
—Debbie Kangas, Victoria, British Columbia

1-2/3 cups water
1-1/4 cups uncooked couscous
   4 medium tomatoes, seeded and chopped
   1 large red onion, chopped
   2 tablespoons minced fresh parsley
   2 tablespoons minced fresh cilantro
   1 teaspoon minced fresh mint *or* 1/4 teaspoon dried mint
 1/3 cup lemon juice
   3 tablespoons olive oil
 1/2 teaspoon salt
 1/4 teaspoon pepper

In a saucepan, bring water to a boil. Stir in couscous; cover. Remove from heat; let stand 5 minutes. In a bowl, combine couscous, tomatoes, onion and herbs. Whisk together the lemon juice, oil, salt and pepper. Pour over couscous mixture; toss to coat. Chill overnight. **Yield:** 8 servings.

Nutritional Analysis: One serving (3/4 cup) equals 168 calories, 5 g fat (1 g saturated fat), 0 cholesterol, 156 mg sodium, 26 g carbohydrate, 2 g fiber, 4 g protein.
Diabetic Exchanges: 1-1/2 starch, 1 vegetable, 1 fat.

Springtime Tossed Salad

Low-carb Low-sodium Meatless

(Pictured at right)

I first sampled a version of this salad at a restaurant, then I experimented until I came up with a lightened-up dressing that tasted great. Raspberry juice gives a nice fruity flavor to the mixed greens. This is one of my family's favorite summer dishes, which I often serve with whole grain crusty rolls. The salad is extremely quick to toss together.
—Laura Kopp, Shiocton, Wisconsin

1/2 cup raspberry juice *or* cranberry-raspberry juice
   3 tablespoons white wine vinegar *or* cider vinegar
   1 tablespoon olive oil
   8 ounces spring mix salad greens
   2 cans (11 ounces *each*) mandarin oranges, drained
1/2 cup crumbled blue cheese
1/4 cup chopped pecans, toasted

In a small bowl, whisk together the raspberry juice, vinegar and oil. Cover and refrigerate. In a large bowl, combine the salad mix, mandarin oranges and blue cheese.

Pour dressing over salad mixture; toss to coat. Add pecans; toss to coat. Serve immediately. **Yield:** 6 servings.

Nutritional Analysis: One serving (1 cup) equals 94 calories, 7 g fat (2 g saturated fat), 6 mg cholesterol, 104 mg sodium, 8 g carbohydrate, 2 g fiber, 3 g protein.
Diabetic Exchanges: 1 fat, 1/2 fruit.

Sesame Shrimp Rice Salad

(Pictured at right)

Crispy snow peas, red pepper and onion, plus tender shrimp are combined in this refreshing salad. The light sesame dressing is mildly seasoned with ginger and soy.
—Sunshine Wall, Jacksonville, Florida

   5 cups water
   2 cups fresh snow peas
   1 pound cooked medium shrimp, peeled and deveined
   2 cups cooked brown rice
   1 medium red onion, diced
   1 medium sweet red pepper, diced
1/3 cup minced fresh parsley
   2 tablespoons lemon juice
   1 tablespoon reduced-sodium soy sauce
   1 tablespoon canola oil
   2 teaspoons sesame oil
1/2 teaspoon ground ginger *or* 1-1/2 teaspoons minced fresh gingerroot
   1 garlic clove, minced

In a saucepan, bring water to a boil. Add peas; cover and cook for 2 minutes. Drain and immediately place peas in ice water. Drain and pat dry.

In a large bowl, combine the shrimp, rice, onion, red pepper, parsley and snow peas. In a jar with a tight-fitting lid, combine the remaining ingredients; shake well. Pour over shrimp mixture; toss to coat. Serve immediately. **Yield:** 4 servings.

Nutritional Analysis: One serving (1-1/2 cups) equals 302 calories, 8 g fat (1 g saturated fat), 181 mg cholesterol, 372 mg sodium, 33 g carbohydrate, 5 g fiber, 26 g protein.
Diabetic Exchanges: 3 very lean meat, 2 vegetable, 1-1/2 starch, 1 fat.

● Create Crispy Lettuce

TO MAKE salad greens really crisp, I wash them, use a salad spinner to remove the water and then put them in the serving bowl. I place a wet paper towel over the top and pop the bowl in the fridge. The greens get nice and extra-crisp for dinner in just 15 minutes. *—Sandy Robben, Cocoa Beach, Florida*

Cranberry-Raspberry Gelatin Salad

Low-fat   Low-sodium

The festivities will start off on a "berry" flavorful note when this fruity salad is on the table. You can serve this as a colorful holiday dessert, too. To add a little crunch, sprinkle low-fat graham cracker crumbs over the top.
—Evelyn Joy, Alameda, California

2 packages (.3 ounce *each*) sugar-free raspberry gelatin
1-3/4 cups boiling reduced-calorie cranberry-raspberry juice, *divided*
1 can (16 ounces) whole-berry cranberry sauce
1 can (20 ounces) crushed pineapple, undrained
2-1/2 cups frozen unsweetened raspberries, thawed
1 cup (8 ounces) reduced-fat sour cream
2 tablespoons brown sugar
1 cup reduced-fat whipped topping

In a large bowl, dissolve gelatin in 1 cup boiling cranberry juice. Stir in cranberry sauce, breaking up mixture. Stir in remaining cranberry juice until blended. Cover and refrigerate until partially set, about 1-1/4 hours.

Fold in pineapple and raspberries. Transfer to an 11-in. x 7-in. x 2-in. dish coated with nonstick cooking spray. Refrigerate until firm. In a bowl, combine sour cream and brown sugar until blended. Fold in whipped topping. Spread over gelatin mixture. Serve immediately. **Yield:** 12 servings.

Nutritional Analysis: One piece equals 148 calories, 2 g fat (2 g saturated fat), 7 mg cholesterol, 28 mg sodium, 30 g carbohydrate, 2 g fiber, 2 g protein.
Diabetic Exchanges: 1 fruit, 1 starch.

Greek Tomato Salad

Low-carb   Meatless

(Pictured above)

My German father-in-law loves to vacation in Greece. After a stay on the sunny beaches of Rhodes, he gave me the recipe for this zesty salad, full of fresh tomatoes, red onion, green pepper, ripe olives and feta cheese. I like to serve it for a light lunch with sourdough, French or Italian bread.
—Jerry Lappin, Garden City, Kansas

1/4 cup red wine vinegar
2 tablespoons olive oil
1 garlic clove, minced
1/2 teaspoon dried oregano
1/4 teaspoon dried basil
1/8 teaspoon sugar
1/8 teaspoon salt
1/8 teaspoon pepper
1 cup thinly sliced red onion, separated into rings
1/2 cup coarsely chopped green pepper
4 medium tomatoes, *each* cut into 8 wedges
6 medium pitted whole ripe olives, halved
3 tablespoons crumbled feta cheese

In a bowl, whisk together the vinegar, oil, garlic, oregano, basil, sugar, salt and pepper. Add red onion and green pepper; toss to coat. Stir in the tomatoes, olives and cheese. Cover and refrigerate for at least 1 hour. Serve with a slotted spoon. **Yield:** 5 servings.

Nutritional Analysis: One serving (1 cup) equals 120 calories, 8 g fat (2 g saturated fat), 5 mg cholesterol, 179 mg sodium, 12 g carbohydrate, 2 g fiber, 2 g protein.
Diabetic Exchanges: 2 vegetable, 1-1/2 fat.

Corn and Red Pepper Barley Salad

Meatless

Here's a delicious way to present barley at its best. Instead of being lost in a sea of other ingredients in a soup or stew, that basic grain plays a starring role in the delicious chilled salad created by our Test Kitchen staff. Sweet corn and red pepper lend it a summery taste and color. Try taking a bowl to pass at your next picnic.

8 cups water
1-1/2 cups uncooked medium pearl barley
1-1/2 teaspoons salt
1 medium sweet red pepper
2 cups fresh *or* frozen corn, thawed
2/3 cup thinly sliced green onions, *divided*
1/3 cup grated Parmesan cheese
SALAD DRESSING:
1/4 cup balsamic vinegar
2 tablespoons water
2 tablespoons lemon juice
1 teaspoon sugar
1 teaspoon Italian seasoning

3/4 teaspoon garlic powder
1/4 teaspoon pepper
1/4 cup olive oil

In a saucepan, combine the water, barley and salt; bring to a boil. Reduce heat; cover and simmer for 15-18 minutes or until barley is just tender. Drain and set aside.

Meanwhile, halve pepper; remove stem and seeds. Broil pepper skin side up 4 in. from the heat until skin blisters and blackens, about 8-10 minutes. Immediately place pepper in a bowl; cover with plastic wrap and let stand for 15-20 minutes. Peel off and discard charred skin. Chop pepper.

In a bowl, combine corn, 1/2 cup onions, Parmesan, roasted pepper and barley. In another bowl, combine vinegar, water, lemon juice, sugar, Italian seasoning, garlic powder and pepper. Slowly whisk in oil. Pour over barley mixture; toss gently to coat. Sprinkle with remaining onions. **Yield:** 8 servings.

Nutritional Analysis: One serving (3/4 cup) equals 256 calories, 9 g fat (2 g saturated fat), 3 mg cholesterol, 509 mg sodium, 41 g carbohydrate, 8 g fiber, 7 g protein.
Diabetic Exchanges: 2-1/2 starch, 1-1/2 fat.

Cran-Blueberry Mold

Low-fat **Low-sodium**

I found this not-too-sweet recipe in our local newspaper many years ago. It's a family favorite—especially when fresh blueberries are in season.
—*Cindy Steffen, Cedarburg, Wisconsin*

2 envelopes unflavored gelatin
1-1/2 cups cold water
Sugar substitute equivalent to 1/4 cup sugar
2 cups reduced-calorie cranberry juice, chilled
2 cups fresh peaches, peeled and cut into chunks
1-1/2 cups fresh blueberries

In a saucepan, sprinkle gelatin over water; let stand for 1 minute. Add sugar substitute. Cook and stir until mixture is warm and gelatin and sugar substitute are dissolved (do not boil). Transfer to a bowl. Stir in cranberry juice. Cover and refrigerate until slightly thickened. Fold in peaches and blueberries. Transfer to a 7-cup mold or 2-qt. bowl coated with nonstick cooking spray. Refrigerate until firm. Unmold onto a plate or serving platter. **Yield:** 6 servings.

Editor's Note: This recipe was tested with Splenda No Calorie Sweetener. Look for it in the baking aisle of your grocery store.

Nutritional Analysis: One serving (1 cup) equals 71 calories, trace fat (trace saturated fat), 0 cholesterol, 9 mg sodium, 16 g carbohydrate, 2 g fiber, 3 g protein.
Diabetic Exchange: 1 fruit.

Curried Broccoli Salad

Meatless

(Pictured below)

We love this salad's crunch and color. It has just the right combination of spices and a hint of sweetness from coconut and dried cranberries. This is one of our favorite end-of-garden recipes.
—*Nancy Fleming, Rainier, Washington*

1/4 cup fat-free salad dressing *or* mayonnaise
2 tablespoons flaked coconut
1/4 teaspoon salt
1/4 teaspoon ground cumin
1/4 teaspoon ground turmeric
1/8 teaspoon ground allspice
1/8 teaspoon pepper
4 cups fresh broccoli florets
1/2 cup finely chopped red onion
1/2 cup dried cranberries
1/2 cup chopped walnuts, toasted

In a large bowl, combine the first seven ingredients; mix well. Add the broccoli, onion, cranberries and walnuts; toss to coat. Cover and refrigerate for at least 1 hour before serving. **Yield:** 5 servings.

Nutritional Analysis: One serving (1 cup) equals 161 calories, 9 g fat (2 g saturated fat), 1 mg cholesterol, 239 mg sodium, 19 g carbohydrate, 4 g fiber, 4 g protein.
Diabetic Exchanges: 2 fat, 1 vegetable, 1 fruit.

Herb Vegetable Orzo Salad

Meatless

The chilled salad our Test Kitchen tossed together is an ideal warm-weather refresher. Golden corn, grape tomatoes and fresh basil bring the very best of summer to the table. Subtly salty olives add an interesting contrast to the other sun-sweetened veggies.

   1 cup uncooked orzo pasta
   2 cups frozen corn, thawed
1/2 cup chopped sweet red pepper
1/2 cup halved grape *or* cherry tomatoes
1/2 cup pitted Greek olives, halved
1/4 cup chopped sweet onion
1/4 cup minced fresh basil *or* 4 teaspoons dried basil
   2 tablespoons minced fresh parsley
   3 tablespoons olive oil
   2 tablespoons balsamic vinegar
1/4 teaspoon salt
1/4 teaspoon pepper

Cook pasta according to package directions; drain and rinse in cold water. Place in a large serving bowl; add the corn, red pepper, tomatoes, olives, onion, basil and parsley. In a jar with a tight-fitting lid, combine the oil, vinegar, salt and pepper; shake well. Pour over salad and toss to coat. **Yield:** 8 servings.

Nutritional Analysis: One serving (3/4 cup) equals 192 calories, 7 g fat (1 g saturated fat), 0 cholesterol, 157 mg sodium, 29 g carbohydrate, 2 g fiber, 5 g protein.
Diabetic Exchanges: 2 starch, 1 fat.

Lemon Artichoke Romaine Salad

Low-carb   Meatless

(Pictured at right)

I created this dish when I was trying to duplicate a very lemony Caesar salad. I think my version is not only delicious but more healthful, too!
—Kathleen Law, Pullman, Washington

 10 cups torn romaine
   4 plum tomatoes, sliced
   1 can (14 ounces) water-packed artichoke hearts, rinsed, drained and quartered
   1 can (2-1/4 ounces) sliced ripe olives, drained
   3 tablespoons water
   3 tablespoons lemon juice

   3 tablespoons olive oil
   2 garlic cloves, minced
   1 teaspoon salt
   1 teaspoon coarsely ground pepper
1/3 cup shredded Parmesan cheese

In a bowl, combine first four ingredients. Combine water, lemon juice, oil, garlic, salt and pepper. Pour over salad; toss to coat. Sprinkle with cheese. **Yield:** 8 servings.

Nutritional Analysis: One serving (1-1/2 cups) equals 114 calories, 7 g fat (1 g saturated fat), 2 mg cholesterol, 730 mg sodium, 10 g carbohydrate, 4 g fiber, 5 g protein.
Diabetic Exchanges: 2 vegetable, 1 fat.

Tarragon Chicken Salad

(Pictured at right)

This attractive salad was a big hit at a summer party a few years ago. The addition of green beans and red potatoes is a tasty twist.
—Janet Holowczak, South Windsor, Connecticut

1/2 cup white wine *or* chicken broth
   2 tablespoons chopped onion
   1 garlic clove, minced
   4 teaspoons minced fresh tarragon *or* 1 teaspoon dried tarragon
3/4 teaspoon salt, *divided*
1/4 teaspoon pepper, *divided*
1/2 cup reduced-fat sour cream
1/4 cup reduced-fat plain yogurt
   2 tablespoons fat-free mayonnaise
   4 cups cubed cooked chicken breast
1/2 small red onion, cut into thin strips
   2 cups water
3/4 pound red potatoes, cut into 3/4-inch chunks
   1 pound fresh green beans, cut into 2-inch pieces
1-1/2 teaspoons olive oil

In a saucepan, bring wine or broth, onion, garlic, tarragon, 1/2 teaspoon salt and 1/8 teaspoon pepper to a boil. Boil and stir for 7-9 minutes or until liquid is evaporated.

In a bowl, combine sour cream, yogurt, mayonnaise and tarragon mixture. Add chicken and onion; toss to coat. Chill for at least 2 hours.

In a nonstick saucepan, bring the water to a boil. Add potatoes. Reduce heat; cover and simmer for 5 minutes. Add beans. Cover and simmer 6-9 minutes longer or until potatoes are tender. Drain and place in a bowl. Drizzle with oil and sprinkle with remaining salt and pepper; toss gently to coat. Chill for at least 2 hours.

Just before serving, spoon the chicken mixture onto the center of a serving plate. Arrange bean mixture around chicken mixture. **Yield:** 6 servings.

Nutritional Analysis: One serving (1-1/2 cups) equals 268 calories, 7 g fat (3 g saturated fat), 87 mg cholesterol, 428 mg sodium, 17 g carbohydrate, 4 g fiber, 33 g protein.
Diabetic Exchanges: 4 lean meat, 1 starch.

Mixed Greens Salad with Tarragon Dressing

Low-carb   Meatless

(Pictured above)

I use tarragon I grow in my garden to make the vinegar in this easy dressing. Since the dressing keeps well, I double the recipe most of the time and use half in this great-tasting salad.
—Janice Mitchell, Aurora, Colorado

    2 tablespoons tarragon vinegar
    2 tablespoons canola oil
    2 teaspoons sugar
    1 garlic clove, minced
  1/2 teaspoon salt
  1/4 teaspoon ground mustard
  1/4 teaspoon pepper
  1/4 teaspoon lemon juice
  1/4 teaspoon Worcestershire sauce
    6 cups torn mixed salad greens
    2 radishes, thinly sliced
    1 cup salad croutons
    2 tablespoons sesame seeds, toasted

In a small bowl, whisk together the first nine ingredients. In a large salad bowl, toss salad greens, radishes, croutons and sesame seeds. Drizzle with dressing; toss to coat. **Yield:** 4 servings.

Nutritional Analysis: One serving (1-1/2 cups) equals 147 calories, 10 g fat (1 g saturated fat), 0 cholesterol, 370 mg sodium, 11 g carbohydrate, 2 g fiber, 3 g protein.
Diabetic Exchanges: 2 fat, 1 vegetable, 1/2 starch.

Citrus Gelatin Salad

Low-fat   Low-sodium

With its sunny color and refreshing citrus flavor, this pretty salad is perfect for summer get-togethers.
—Cynthia Norris, Winnetka, California

    2 envelopes unflavored gelatin
  1/4 cup cold water
    1 cup sugar
1-3/4 cups boiling water
    3 tablespoons lemon juice
    1 drop yellow food coloring, optional
    1 can (20 ounces) unsweetened pineapple tidbits, drained
  1/2 cup sliced firm banana
1-1/2 cups miniature marshmallows
TOPPING:
  1/2 cup sugar
    3 tablespoons cornstarch
  2/3 cup orange juice
  1/4 cup lemon juice
1-1/2 cups reduced-fat whipped topping

In a bowl, combine gelatin and cold water; let stand for 1 minute. Add sugar and boiling water; stir until sugar and gelatin are dissolved. Stir in lemon juice and food coloring if desired; set aside. Layer pineapple, banana and marshmallows in a 13-in. x 9-in. x 2-in. dish. Pour gelatin mixture over top. Cover and refrigerate overnight.

In a saucepan, combine sugar and cornstarch. Gradually stir in juices until smooth. Bring to a boil; cook and stir for 2 minutes or until thickened. Remove from the heat; cool to room temperature. Transfer to a mixing bowl; add whipped topping. Beat until blended. Spread over gelatin layer. Cover and chill for 1 hour or until serving. Cut into squares. **Yield:** 16 servings.

Nutritional Analysis: One serving equals 132 calories, 1 g fat (1 g saturated fat), 0 cholesterol, 5 mg sodium, 31 g carbohydrate, trace fiber, 1 g protein.
Diabetic Exchange: 2 fruit.

Ranch Broccoli Pasta Salad

Here's an easy summer salad for potlucks, ladies luncheons and picnics. Tricolor spiral pasta and broccoli florets are coated with a mild dressing and bits of bacon.
—Margie Shaw, Americus, Georgia

    1 package (16 ounces) tricolor spiral pasta, cooked, rinsed and drained
    3 cups broccoli florets
  1/3 cup finely chopped onion
  1/2 cup reduced-fat mayonnaise
    2 tablespoons fat-free milk
    1 envelope reduced-fat ranch salad dressing mix
  1/2 teaspoon salt
    6 bacon strips, cooked and crumbled

In a large bowl, combine the pasta, broccoli and onion. In a small bowl, combine mayonnaise, milk, salad dressing mix and salt. Add to pasta mixture; toss to coat evenly. Cover and refrigerate for at least 1 hour. Just before serving, stir in bacon. **Yield:** 12 servings.

Nutritional Analysis: One serving (3/4 cup) equals 213 calories, 6 g fat (1 g saturated fat), 8 mg cholesterol, 568 mg sodium, 33 g carbohydrate, 2 g fiber, 6 g protein.
Diabetic Exchanges: 2 starch, 1 fat.

Favorite Recipe Made Lighter

NOON IS the perfect time for Cindy Harnish and her family to enjoy the flavor of her homemade Spinach Salad Dressing. "This special spinach dressing works on any salad and has just the right sweet-and-sour taste to dress up a lunch salad," says the Wexford, Pennsylvania cook.

"Our triplets are 4 years old," she adds, "and I'm always searching for healthy meals and snacks. Everyone loves the down-home flavor of this family favorite but not all of the oil and sugar. Please help me lighten it up!"

The oil and sugar in Cindy's recipe were what made her tangy dressing so creamy smooth. To keep that consistency, the *Light & Tasty* Test Kitchen turned to one of its favorite light ingredients—applesauce.

Its thickness provided the dressing with body, which allowed our home economists to reduce the oil from 1/3 cup to 2 tablespoons. And because applesauce is naturally sweet, they were able to cut the amount of sugar in half.

Our home economists reduced the vinegar slightly so the dressing wouldn't be too tart. Then a little water was added so the yield would be the same as the original recipe.

Makeover Spinach Salad Dressing is ideal over spinach. It's also a great way to dress up chicken salad or coleslaw. Yet it has less than half the calories and fat of the original dressing and about 40% less carbohydrates.

Spinach Salad Dressing

Low-carb Meatless

2/3 cup sugar
1/3 cup cider vinegar
1/3 cup vegetable oil
1 small onion, finely chopped
4 teaspoons prepared mustard
1 teaspoon salt
1/2 teaspoon coarsely ground pepper
Fresh spinach leaves

Combine the first seven ingredients in a blender or food processor; cover and process until smooth. Serve over fresh spinach. Store leftover dressing in the refrigerator. **Yield:** 1-1/3 cups.

Nutritional Analysis: One serving (2 tablespoons dressing, calculated without spinach) equals 118 calories, 7 g fat (1 g saturated fat), 0 cholesterol, 260 mg sodium, 14 g carbohydrate, trace fiber, trace protein.

Makeover Spinach Salad Dressing

Low-carb Low-fat Meatless

(Pictured below)

1/3 cup sugar
1 small onion, finely chopped
1/4 cup cider vinegar
1/4 cup unsweetened applesauce
2 tablespoons water
2 tablespoons canola oil
4 teaspoons prepared mustard
1 teaspoon salt
1/2 teaspoon coarsely ground pepper
Fresh spinach leaves

Combine the first nine ingredients in a blender or food processor; cover and process until smooth. Serve over fresh spinach. Store leftover dressing in the refrigerator. **Yield:** 1-1/3 cups.

Nutritional Analysis: One serving (2 tablespoons dressing, calculated without spinach) equals 56 calories, 3 g fat (trace saturated fat), 0 cholesterol, 260 mg sodium, 8 g carbohydrate, trace fiber, trace protein.
Diabetic Exchanges: 1/2 starch, 1/2 fat.

Italian Market Salad

Low-carb

(Pictured at right)

I found a recipe in the newspaper that sounded great, but the ingredients were too high in fat for us. So I adapted it and created this salad with good-for-you ingredients like brown rice and turkey pepperoni. The blend of flavors is fantastic.
—Karen Schmidt, Plymouth, Wisconsin

2 cups cooked brown rice, cooled
2 cups (8 ounces) shredded part-skim mozzarella cheese
4 plum tomatoes, seeded and chopped
1/2 medium green pepper, julienned
4 ounces sliced turkey pepperoni, quartered
1/2 cup diced fully cooked turkey ham
4 green onions, sliced
1 can (2-1/4 ounces) sliced ripe olives, drained
1/2 cup reduced-fat Italian salad dressing

In a large bowl, combine the first eight ingredients. Pour dressing over salad; toss to coat. Cover and refrigerate for 2 hours or until chilled. **Yield:** 9 servings.

Nutritional Analysis: One serving (3/4 cup) equals 199 calories, 9 g fat (3 g saturated fat), 36 mg cholesterol, 612 mg sodium, 15 g carbohydrate, 2 g fiber, 13 g protein.
Diabetic Exchanges: 2 lean meat, 1 starch, 1/2 fat.

Ranch-Style Buttermilk Dressing

Low-carb Meatless

(Pictured at right)

This creamy quick-to-fix dressing is pleasantly seasoned with dill and minced parsley...and it whisks together in no time. Store-bought ranch salad dressings just can't compare.
—Shirley Francey, St. Catharines, Ontario

2/3 cup 1% buttermilk
1/3 cup reduced-fat mayonnaise
1/4 cup reduced-fat sour cream
2 tablespoons minced fresh parsley
1 garlic clove, minced
1/2 teaspoon sugar
1/2 teaspoon dill weed
1/4 teaspoon salt
1/4 teaspoon ground mustard
1/8 teaspoon pepper

In a bowl, combine all of the ingredients. Whisk until smooth. Cover and refrigerate until serving. **Yield:** 1 cup.

Nutritional Analysis: One serving (2 tablespoons) equals 54 calories, 4 g fat (1 g saturated fat), 7 mg cholesterol, 179 mg sodium, 3 g carbohydrate, trace fiber, 1 g protein.
Diabetic Exchange: 1 fat.

Roasted Pear Salad

Meatless

Oven-roasted pears take the ho-hum out of this green salad created by our Test Kitchen staff. They tossed together a good-for-you medley of mellow pear slices, crispy greens, nuts and dried cranberries. The creamy dressing carries yet more pear flavor sweetened with just a touch of honey.

2 firm ripe pears, halved and cored
4 teaspoons olive oil, *divided*
2 tablespoons cider vinegar
1 tablespoon water
1 teaspoon honey
1/4 teaspoon salt
1/8 teaspoon white pepper
1 package (10 ounces) mixed baby salad greens
1 cup watercress sprigs
1/4 cup chopped hazelnuts, toasted
1/4 cup dried cranberries

In a bowl, toss pears with 1 teaspoon oil. Arrange on a 15-in. x 10-in. x 1-in. baking pan coated with nonstick cooking spray. Bake at 400° for 10 minutes; turn pears over and bake 5-7 minutes longer or until golden and tender.

When pears are cool enough to handle, remove and discard peel. Thinly slice two pear halves lengthwise and set aside. Place remaining pear halves in a food processor or blender. Add the vinegar, water, honey, salt and pepper; cover and process until smooth. While processing, slowly add remaining oil.

Place salad greens and watercress in a bowl; toss with nuts and cranberries. Arrange pear slices on top; drizzle with dressing. **Yield:** 4 servings.

Nutritional Analysis: One serving equals 174 calories, 9 g fat (1 g saturated fat), 0 cholesterol, 178 mg sodium, 24 g carbohydrate, 5 g fiber, 3 g protein.
Diabetic Exchanges: 2 fat, 1 fruit, 1 vegetable.

🍎 The Benefits of Buttermilk

WITH A NAME like buttermilk, you'd think this dairy product would be loaded with fat. But it's not! Its name simply refers to the milky liquid that is left after butter has been churned from milk or cream.

The thick nutritious milk is lower in fat than whole milk and cream, and high in potassium, calcium and vitamin B-12. Like yogurt and sour cream, it's an acidic ingredient that gives baked goods body and soft texture.

It lends a rich hearty flavor to everything from salad dressing to soup. Buttermilk's tang also complements sweet fruits like peaches and cherries.

Southwestern Macaroni Salad

Meatless

(Pictured below)

*This salad is like having salsa mixed with macaroni.
It's yummy! It serves a lot, which makes it a great
side for any gathering. I sometimes add a little
cayenne pepper for those who like it hot.*
—Nancy Clancy, Standish, Maine

1 package (1 pound) elbow macaroni
1 pound cherry tomatoes, quartered
1 cup frozen corn, thawed
1 medium green pepper, chopped
1 small red onion, chopped
1 can (2-1/4 ounces) sliced ripe olives, drained
1/2 cup lime juice
1/4 cup olive oil
1 tablespoon red wine vinegar
1 tablespoon chili powder
1 tablespoon ground cumin
1 teaspoon sugar
1 teaspoon salt
1 teaspoon garlic powder

Cook pasta according to package directions; drain and rinse
in cold water. In a large bowl, combine the pasta, tomatoes,
corn, green pepper, red onion and olives.

In a jar with a tight-fitting lid, combine the lime juice, oil,
vinegar and seasonings; shake well. Pour over pasta mixture; toss to coat. Cover and refrigerate for 1 hour or until
chilled. **Yield:** about 3 quarts.

Nutritional Analysis: *One serving (3/4 cup) equals 163 calories, 5 g fat (1 g saturated fat), 0 cholesterol, 205 mg sodium, 27
g carbohydrate, 2 g fiber, 4 g protein.*
Diabetic Exchanges: *1-1/2 starch, 1 vegetable, 1/2 fat.*

Pear Gelatin Salad

Low-carb   Low-fat   Low-sodium

*This light and refreshing salad blends fat-free vanilla
yogurt with lime gelatin to showcase convenient
canned pears. I often make a double batch—one for my
family and one to take to a covered-dish supper.*
—Carol Keinard, Elizabethtown, Pennsylvania

1 can (15 ounces) reduced-sugar sliced pears
1 package (.6 ounce) sugar-free lime gelatin
   or 2 packages (.3 ounce *each*) sugar-free
   lime gelatin
2 cups boiling water
1 carton (6 ounces) fat-free reduced-sugar
   vanilla yogurt
1/4 cup cold water

Drain pears, reserving 1/2 cup liquid. In a bowl, dissolve gelatin in boiling water. Place yogurt in a bowl. Gradually whisk
in 1 cup gelatin mixture until blended. Transfer to an 8-in.
square dish coated with nonstick cooking spray. Cover
and refrigerate for 1 hour or until almost set.

Stir cold water and reserved liquid into remaining gelatin mixture (do not refrigerate). Arrange pears on gelatin-yo-
gurt mixture. Carefully spoon remaining gelatin mixture over
pears. Cover and refrigerate for about 2 hours or until firm.
Yield: 6 servings.

Nutritional Analysis: *One piece equals 61 calories, 0 fat (0
saturated fat), 1 mg cholesterol, 90 mg sodium, 11 g carbohydrate,
1 g fiber, 2 g protein.*
Diabetic Exchange: *1 fruit.*

Lemon-Basil Fruit Dressing

Low-fat   Low-sodium   Meatless

*This tempting dressing stirs up in a jiffy. The addition
of basil makes it deliciously different, and honey
balances the tart citrus taste. It enhances the
natural goodness of most any fresh fruit medley.*
—Carol Gano, Ballwin, Missouri

1/2 cup fat-free plain yogurt
1/2 cup reduced-fat sour cream
3 tablespoons orange juice
2 tablespoons minced fresh basil
2 tablespoons honey
1 tablespoon lemon juice
1 tablespoon lime juice
7-1/2 cups assorted fresh fruit

In a bowl, combine the first seven ingredients until blended.
Place fruit in a serving bowl; serve with dressing. **Yield:**
10 servings.

Marinated Vegetable Salad

Low-carb   Low-fat   Meatless

This medley of healthy vegetables is so delicious, no one guesses it's suitable for diabetics. I take it to pitch-in dinners because it can be made in advance. Using a sugar substitute adds a subtle sweetness to the dressing without all the carbohydrates and calories.
—Linda Pruitt, Greenfield, Indiana

3 cups sliced carrots (1/4-inch slices)
1 cup thinly sliced celery
1/2 cup chopped green pepper
1 medium onion, halved and thinly sliced
1 teaspoon celery seed
1/2 cup reduced-fat Italian salad dressing
Sugar substitute equivalent to 1/2 cup sugar
1/4 cup white vinegar
1/4 cup water

Place 1 in. of water in a large saucepan; add carrots. Bring to a boil. Reduce heat; cover and simmer for 6-7 minutes or until carrots are crisp-tender. Drain and rinse in cold water. In a bowl, combine the celery, green pepper, onion, celery seed and carrots.

In a small saucepan, combine the salad dressing, sugar substitute, vinegar and water. Cook and stir until mixture comes to a boil; pour over vegetables. Cover and refrigerate until chilled, stirring several times. Serve with a slotted spoon. **Yield:** 7 servings.

Editor's Note: This recipe was tested with Splenda No Calorie Sweetener. Look for it in the baking aisle of your grocery store.

Nutritional Analysis: One serving (2/3 cup) equals 75 calories, 3 g fat (trace saturated fat), trace cholesterol, 165 mg sodium, 12 g carbohydrate, 3 g fiber, 1 g protein.
Diabetic Exchanges: 2 vegetable, 1/2 fat.

Colorful Bean Salad

Meatless

(Pictured above right)

I can't remember where I found the recipe for this cold bean salad, but it's become one of my favorites. A squeeze of fresh lime juice adds to the flavor.
—Valerie Harmsworth, Orillia, Ontario

1 can (15 ounces) black beans, rinsed and drained
1 can (15 ounces) garbanzo beans *or* chickpeas, rinsed and drained
1 cup fresh *or* frozen corn, thawed
1 medium green pepper, chopped
1 medium sweet red pepper, chopped
1/2 cup chopped red onion
1 jalapeno pepper, seeded and chopped
2 tablespoons canola oil
2 tablespoons red wine vinegar
1 tablespoon balsamic vinegar
1-1/2 teaspoons ground cumin
1-1/2 teaspoons chili powder
1 teaspoon sugar
1/2 teaspoon dried oregano
1 tablespoon lime juice

In a large bowl, combine the black beans, garbanzo beans, corn, green pepper, red pepper, red onion and jalapeno pepper. In a small bowl, whisk together the oil, vinegars, cumin, chili powder, sugar and oregano. Pour over bean mixture; toss to coat. Cover and refrigerate for at least 1 hour. Just before serving, sprinkle with lime juice. **Yield:** 8 servings.

Editor's Note: When cutting or seeding hot peppers, use rubber or plastic gloves to protect your hands. Avoid touching your face.

Nutritional Analysis: One serving (3/4 cup) equals 161 calories, 5 g fat (trace saturated fat), 0 cholesterol, 177 mg sodium, 25 g carbohydrate, 6 g fiber, 6 g protein.
Diabetic Exchanges: 1-1/2 starch, 1 vegetable, 1/2 fat.

🍎 Favorite Fruit Salad

AT FAMILY DINNERS, I am usually asked to bring fruit salad. Typically, I combine pineapple chunks, orange sections, banana slices and miniature marshmallows and dress it all with whipped cream. The last few times, I used fat-free whipped topping mixed with vanilla yogurt. Everyone seems to enjoy it just as much, but it has less calories and fat.
—*Marie Roberts, Lake Charles, Louisiana*

Apple-Raisin Spinach Salad

Low-sodium   Meatless

(Pictured at right)

I first sampled this tart and tangy salad at a parent/teacher potluck in the elementary school where I used to teach. I loved it and had to have the recipe. Since then, I make it frequently. Everybody in my family enjoys it!
—Shirley Saunders, North Attleboro, Massachusetts

1/4 cup white wine vinegar
2 tablespoons canola oil
2 tablespoons chutney
4 teaspoons sugar
1-1/2 teaspoons curry powder
1 teaspoon ground mustard
1/4 teaspoon salt
6 cups packed torn fresh spinach
1-1/2 cups chopped unpeeled green apples
1/2 cup golden raisins
1/4 cup coarsely chopped peanuts
2 tablespoons finely chopped green onion

In a small bowl, whisk together the first seven ingredients. Place spinach in a large salad bowl; top with apples, raisins, peanuts and onion. Drizzle with dressing; toss to coat. Serve immediately. **Yield:** 6 servings.

Nutritional Analysis: One serving (1 cup) equals 160 calories, 8 g fat (1 g saturated fat), 0 cholesterol, 126 mg sodium, 22 g carbohydrate, 3 g fiber, 3 g protein.
Diabetic Exchanges: 1-1/2 fat, 1 fruit, 1 vegetable.

Healthy Potato Salad

Low-fat   Meatless

(Pictured at right)

Here's a heart-healthy version of my longtime favorite potato salad recipe. It's colorful and chock-full of good crunchy ingredients.
—Pat Potter, Calumet City, Illinois

2 pounds small red potatoes, quartered
5 hard-cooked eggs
3/4 cup fat-free mayonnaise
2 tablespoons cider vinegar
1 teaspoon sugar
1 teaspoon ground mustard
1/2 teaspoon salt
1/4 teaspoon pepper
1 large sweet onion, chopped
2 celery ribs, chopped
1/2 cup chopped green onions
1/2 cup julienned sweet red pepper
1/4 cup minced fresh parsley

Place potatoes in a saucepan and cover with water. Bring to a boil. Reduce heat; cover and simmer for 12-14 minutes or until tender. Drain and cool potatoes for 30 minutes. Slice eggs in half (discard yolks or save for another use); slice whites into 1/2-in. pieces.

In a large bowl, combine the mayonnaise, vinegar, sugar, mustard, salt and pepper. Add the potatoes, egg whites, sweet onion, celery, green onions, red pepper and parsley; toss to coat. Cover and refrigerate for 2 hours or until chilled. **Yield:** 10 servings.

Nutritional Analysis: One serving (3/4 cup) equals 110 calories, 1 g fat (trace saturated fat), 2 mg cholesterol, 305 mg sodium, 22 g carbohydrate, 3 g fiber, 4 g protein.
Diabetic Exchanges: 1 starch, 1 vegetable.

Tropical Carrot Salad

Low-sodium   Meatless

Hoping to convince my son to eat his carrots, I came up with this refreshing salad. This colorful spin-off on a traditional carrot and raisin salad tosses dried cranberries, pineapple and mango into the mix, along with a light yogurt and mayonnaise dressing.
—Louise Ross, Santa Rosa, California

1 pound shredded carrots
1/2 cup raisins
1/2 cup dried cranberries
1/2 cup crushed unsweetened pineapple, drained
1/2 cup chopped mango
1/2 cup fat-free plain yogurt
1/4 cup reduced-fat mayonnaise
2 tablespoons orange juice concentrate
1/3 cup chopped salted cashews

In a large bowl, combine the carrots, raisins, cranberries, pineapple and mango. In a small bowl, combine the yogurt, mayonnaise and orange juice concentrate; fold into carrot mixture. Cover and refrigerate for 2 hours. Sprinkle with cashews. **Yield:** 8 servings.

Nutritional Analysis: One serving (3/4 cup) equals 164 calories, 6 g fat (1 g saturated fat), 3 mg cholesterol, 134 mg sodium, 27 g carbohydrate, 3 g fiber, 3 g protein.
Diabetic Exchanges: 1-1/2 fruit, 1 vegetable, 1 fat.

🍎 Tasty Salad Topping

MANY of our favorite vegetable and fruit salad recipes call for sprinkling toasted pecans or almonds on top. On one occasion when I was out of nuts, I used broken pretzel pieces instead.

I crumbled a handful of pretzels on a microwave-safe plate and toasted them in the microwave for 2-3 minutes. (Be sure to watch carefully to prevent burning.)

They added fewer calories and less fat but kept the crunch in the salad. Best of all, the substitution was a hit with my family.
—Joyce Lehman
Davison, Michigan

Southwest Scallop Salad

Low-carb

(Pictured below)

With lots of vegetables and a delicate seafood flavor, this colorful salad is ideal for a summer luncheon. A hint of lime draws out the garden goodness in the tomatoes and avocados. The contrasting textures make each bite enjoyable.
—Marjorie Hennig, Seymour, Indiana

1 pound bay scallops
1/4 cup lime juice
2 tablespoons olive oil
1-1/2 teaspoons sugar
1 teaspoon grated lime peel
1/4 teaspoon salt
1/8 teaspoon pepper
1 green onion, sliced
2 tablespoons minced fresh cilantro
1 teaspoon minced fresh parsley
1 medium ripe avocado, peeled and sliced
1/2 cup julienned roasted sweet red pepper
1 medium tomato, chopped
6 lettuce leaves
1 medium tomato, sliced

In a large saucepan, bring 3 in. of water to a boil. Reduce heat. Add scallops; simmer, uncovered, for 1-2 minutes or until scallops are firm and opaque. Drain immediately and rinse with cold water. Drain again.

In a bowl, whisk the lime juice, oil, sugar, lime peel, salt and pepper. Stir in the green onion, cilantro and parsley. Dip avocado slices in lime juice mixture. Place on a plate; cover and refrigerate. Stir red pepper and scallops into lime juice mixture; cover and refrigerate for 1 hour or until chilled. Just before serving, stir in chopped tomato. Serve on lettuce leaf-lined individual plates with tomato and avocado slices. **Yield:** 4 servings.

Nutritional Analysis: One serving equals 276 calories, 16 g fat (2 g saturated fat), 37 mg cholesterol, 373 mg sodium, 15 g carbohydrate, 4 g fiber, 21 g protein.
Diabetic Exchanges: *3 lean meat, 3 vegetable, 1 fat.*

Blue Cheese Salad Dressing

Low-carb   Meatless

Our family loves blue cheese dressing, but not the fat. I'm happy to share the recipe for this creamy dressing that also makes a great veggie dip. We appreciate this healthier alternative that uses fat-free sour cream, milk and cream cheese.
—Alcy Thorne, Los Molinos, California

2 ounces fat-free cream cheese
1/2 cup fat-free sour cream
1/2 cup reduced-fat mayonnaise
2 to 3 tablespoons fat-free milk
1/2 teaspoon ground mustard
1/8 teaspoon salt
Dash pepper
1/4 cup crumbled blue cheese

In a small mixing bowl, beat cream cheese for 1 minute or until fluffy. Add sour cream; beat until blended. Add the mayonnaise, milk, mustard, salt and pepper; beat until well blended. Stir in blue cheese. Store in the refrigerator. **Yield:** 1-1/4 cups.

Nutritional Analysis: One serving (2 tablespoons) equals 71 calories, 5 g fat (1 g saturated fat), 8 mg cholesterol, 204 mg sodium, 4 g carbohydrate, trace fiber, 2 g protein.
Diabetic Exchange: *1 fat.*

Fruity Rainbow Salad

Low-fat   Low-sodium   Meatless

(Pictured at right)

This is a beautiful salad with all of its colorful fruits. You can use other produce as well, such as melon balls, bananas, apples and such. The sweet and tangy marinade gives the salad a refreshing zip.
—Teri Lindquist, Gurnee, Illinois

1 can (8 ounces) unsweetened pineapple chunks
2 cups sliced fresh strawberries
2 cups green grapes
1 can (15 ounces) mandarin oranges, drained
1 cup fresh blueberries
1 cup sliced nectarines
1/4 cup lemon juice
1/4 cup honey
1/8 teaspoon ground nutmeg

Drain pineapple, reserving 1/4 cup juice. (Discard remaining juice or save for another use.) In a bowl, combine the pineapple, strawberries, grapes, oranges, blueberries and nectarines.

In another bowl, combine the lemon juice, honey, nutmeg and reserved pineapple juice. Pour over fruit; mix gently. Cover and refrigerate for several hours or overnight. **Yield:** 8 servings.

Nutritional Analysis: One serving (3/4 cup) equals 117 calories, 1 g fat (trace saturated fat), 0 cholesterol, 3 mg sodium, 30 g carbohydrate, 3 g fiber, 1 g protein.
Diabetic Exchange: *2 fruit.*

Italian Pasta Salad

Meatless

(Pictured above)

I've served this dish at our children's graduation parties and everyone has asked for the recipe. The chilled pasta salad is perfect for a picnic or potluck. Dressed with a light coating of reduced-fat salad dressing, it's chock-full of cauliflower, carrot and broccoli bits.
—Loretta Conrey, Cedar Rapids, Iowa

8 ounces uncooked spiral pasta
2 cups cauliflowerets
1 cup fresh broccoli florets
1/2 cup chopped carrot
1 tablespoon water
1 can (8 ounces) sliced water chestnuts, drained
1 can (2-1/4 ounces) sliced ripe olives, drained
1/3 cup chopped onion
1 cup reduced-fat creamy Italian salad dressing
1-1/2 teaspoons dill weed
1/4 teaspoon salt

Cook pasta according to package directions; drain. In a microwave-safe dish, combine the cauliflower, broccoli, carrot and water. Cover and microwave on high for 2-3 minutes. Immediately place vegetables in ice water. Drain and pat dry.

In a large bowl, combine the water chestnuts, olives, onion, pasta and vegetables. In another bowl, combine the salad dressing, dill weed and salt. Pour over pasta mixture and toss to coat. Cover and refrigerate until chilled. **Yield:** 10 servings.

Editor's Note: This recipe was tested in a 1,100-watt microwave.

Nutritional Analysis: One serving (3/4 cup) equals 157 calories, 4 g fat (1 g saturated fat), trace cholesterol, 362 mg sodium, 26 g carbohydrate, 2 g fiber, 4 g protein.
Diabetic Exchanges: 1-1/2 starch, 1 vegetable, 1/2 fat.

Honey-Mustard Root Salad

Low-carb   Meatless

When I discovered I didn't have enough carrots for a shredded carrot salad, I improvised by adding parsnips, a leek and red pepper. Since this dish travels well, I took it to a holiday dinner. Now, the first thing I hear when I walk in the door at family gatherings is, "Did you bring the salad?"
—Carolyn Smith, Kalamazoo, Michigan

    1 large leek (white portion only), cut into thin
      strips
    2 teaspoons plus 2 tablespoons olive oil, *divided*
2-1/2 cups shredded parsnips (about 5 medium)
2-1/2 cups shredded carrots (about 5 medium)
    1 medium sweet red pepper, julienned
    2 tablespoons red wine vinegar
    2 teaspoons Dijon mustard
    1 teaspoon honey
  3/4 teaspoon salt

In a large nonstick skillet, saute leek in 2 teaspoons oil for 4 minutes. Add the parsnips, carrots and red pepper; saute 5-7 minutes longer or until vegetables are crisp-tender. Transfer to a large bowl.

In a jar with a tight-fitting lid, combine the vinegar, mustard, honey, salt and remaining oil; shake well. Pour over vegetables and toss to coat. Cover and refrigerate for at least 2 hours before serving. **Yield:** 8 servings.

Nutritional Analysis: *One serving (1/2 cup) equals 101 calories, 5 g fat (1 g saturated fat), 0 cholesterol, 271 mg sodium, 14 g carbohydrate, 4 g fiber, 1 g protein.*
Diabetic Exchanges: *2 vegetable, 1 fat.*

Curried Chicken Tossed Salad

Low-carb

(Pictured at right)

Curry and basil pack plenty of flavor into this lightly dressed salad. With chicken and asparagus, it's a lovely lunch salad.
—Irene Tetreault, South Hadley, Massachusetts

  2 cups water
  2 cups cut fresh asparagus (1-inch pieces)
1/2 cup julienned carrot (2-inch strips)
  4 cups mixed salad greens
  2 cups coarsely chopped spinach
  2 cups cubed cooked chicken breast
  5 tablespoons fat-free mayonnaise
  2 tablespoons olive oil
  2 tablespoons fat-free milk
  1 tablespoon lemon juice
  1 teaspoon thinly sliced green onion
  1 teaspoon honey
3/4 teaspoon dried basil
3/4 teaspoon curry powder
1/4 teaspoon salt
1/8 teaspoon pepper

In a small nonstick skillet, bring water to a boil. Add asparagus; cover and boil for 2 minutes. Add carrots; cover and boil 1-1/2 to 2 minutes longer. Drain and immediately place asparagus and carrots in ice water. Drain and pat dry.

In a large bowl, combine the salad greens, spinach, chicken and blanched vegetables. In a small bowl, whisk together the remaining ingredients. Serve with salad. **Yield:** 4 servings.

Nutritional Analysis: *One serving (2 cups salad with 2 tablespoons dressing) equals 236 calories, 10 g fat (2 g saturated fat), 62 mg cholesterol, 378 mg sodium, 12 g carbohydrate, 4 g fiber, 25 g protein.*
Diabetic Exchanges: *3 lean meat, 1 vegetable, 1/2 starch.*

Cheddar-Apple Turkey Salad

(Pictured at right)

Whenever I take this colorful salad to a potluck, I get compliments. Even my son loves this…and he doesn't care for either cheese or sour cream. The apples add interest and a little crunch…and you can easily substitute cooked chicken for the turkey.
—Luci Knepper, Salem, Ohio

    1 package (3 ounces) ramen noodles
1-1/2 cups cubed red apples
1-1/4 cups cubed cooked turkey breast
  1/2 cup cubed reduced-fat cheddar cheese
  1/2 cup frozen peas, thawed
  1/4 cup thinly sliced green onions
  1/4 cup chopped sweet red pepper
  1/2 cup fat-free poppy seed salad dressing
    2 tablespoons reduced-fat sour cream
  1/4 teaspoon salt

Remove seasoning packet from ramen noodles and discard or save for another use. Prepare noodles according to package directions. Drain and rinse in cold water.

In a bowl, combine the noodles, apples, turkey, cheese, peas, green onions and red pepper. In a small bowl, combine the dressing, sour cream and salt. Stir into noodle mixture. Cover and refrigerate for at least 1 hour. **Yield:** 4 servings.

Nutritional Analysis: *One serving (1-1/4 cups) equals 259 calories, 8 g fat (5 g saturated fat), 24 mg cholesterol, 456 mg sodium, 35 g carbohydrate, 3 g fiber, 11 g protein.*
Diabetic Exchanges: *2 starch, 1 lean meat, 1/2 fruit, 1/2 fat.*

🍎 Doctored Dressing Mix

I DON'T care for bottled fat-free dressings, so I make my own. I start with a packet of ranch salad dressing mix and use fat-free milk and mayonnaise in place of the regular milk and mayonnaise called for on the package. It's so good you won't think it's fat-free.
—Leticia Schrantz
Fort Huachuca, Arizona

Three-Layer Fruit Salad

Low-fat   Low-sodium

I layer bananas, pears and apricots in a loaf pan, then cover them with lime gelatin. Rather than spooning out servings, slice the salad to showcase the pretty layers. Try substituting canned peaches or fruit cocktail for the other canned fruits in the recipe.
—Joyce Siewert, Greendale, Wisconsin

1 can (15 ounces) reduced-sugar pear halves
2 cans (8-1/4 ounces *each*) reduced-sugar apricot halves
2 medium firm bananas, cut into 1/2-inch slices
2 packages (.3 ounces *each*) sugar-free lime gelatin
2 cups boiling water

Drain pears and apricots, reserving 1-1/2 cups syrup. In a 9-in. x 5-in. x 3-in. loaf pan coated with nonstick cooking spray, layer the pears, apricots and bananas. In a large bowl, dissolve gelatin in boiling water. Stir in reserved syrup. Pour gelatin mixture over bananas. Cover and refrigerate until firm. Unmold and slice gelatin. **Yield:** 8 servings.

Nutritional Analysis: One piece equals 76 calories, trace fat (trace saturated fat), 0 cholesterol, 62 mg sodium, 17 g carbohydrate, 2 g fiber, 2 g protein.
Diabetic Exchange: 1 fruit.

Summer Fruit 'n' Pasta Salad

Meatless

(Pictured above)

I'm always making up recipes, and this refreshing salad came about when I wanted something cool yet spicy to eat during hot summers. Serve it as a meatless main course or as a side dish at barbecues.
—Donna Williams, Las Vegas, Nevada

8 ounces uncooked elbow macaroni
3/4 cup fat-free plain yogurt
3/4 cup reduced-fat mayonnaise
4 teaspoons snipped fresh dill
1/4 teaspoon salt
Dash hot pepper sauce
2 medium tart green apples, chopped
2 medium red apples, chopped
1-1/2 cups seedless grapes
2 celery ribs, thinly sliced
1 can (15 ounces) mandarin oranges, drained
2 medium firm bananas, cut into 1/4-inch slices
1/2 cup chopped walnuts

Cook pasta according to package directions. Rinse with cold water and drain. In a bowl, combine the yogurt, mayonnaise, dill, salt and hot pepper sauce. In a large serving bowl, combine the pasta, apples, grapes, celery and mandarin oranges. Gently stir in 1 cup yogurt mixture. Cover and refrigerate salad and remaining yogurt mixture for 2-3 hours. Just before serving, stir in bananas, walnuts and remaining yogurt mixture. **Yield:** 14 servings.

Nutritional Analysis: One serving (1 cup) equals 199 calories, 8 g fat (1 g saturated fat), 5 mg cholesterol, 160 mg sodium, 31 g carbohydrate, 3 g fiber, 4 g protein.
Diabetic Exchanges: 1 starch, 1 fruit, 1 fat.

Tarragon Vinaigrette

Low-carb   Low-fat   Low-sodium

This is a great dressing for perking up any kind of salad. Try mixing it into potato salad... it will tingle your taste buds!
—Tammy Landry, Saucier, Mississippi

2 tablespoons powdered fruit pectin
3 tablespoons boiling water
1/3 cup unsweetened apple juice concentrate
3 tablespoons tarragon vinegar
2 tablespoons Dijon mustard
1 tablespoon olive oil
1 tablespoon minced fresh tarragon
1/4 teaspoon pepper

In a small bowl, dissolve pectin in boiling water; set aside. In a bowl, whisk together the apple juice concentrate, vinegar, mustard, oil, tarragon, pepper and pectin mixture. Cover and refrigerate for at least 1 hour. **Yield:** 6 servings.

Nutritional Analysis: One serving (2 tablespoons) equals 71 calories, 2 g fat (trace saturated fat), 0 cholesterol, 124 mg sodium, 11 g carbohydrate, trace fiber, trace protein.
Diabetic Exchanges: 1/2 fruit, 1/2 fat.

Black-Eyed Pea and Bean Salad

Low-fat   Meatless

I was trying to use up some ingredients I had in our pantry one day and threw this bean salad together.

I served it the next night with chicken, and everyone enjoyed it. Now it's a staple for our weeknight menus.
—Marilyn Gonsman, Blairsville, Georgia

- 1 can (16 ounces) red kidney beans, rinsed and drained
- 1 can (15-1/2 ounces) black-eyed peas, rinsed and drained
- 1 can (15 ounces) black beans, rinsed and drained
- 2 celery ribs, thinly sliced
- 1/2 cup chopped sweet red pepper
- 1/2 cup finely chopped red onion
- 3 tablespoons red wine vinegar
- 3 tablespoons white wine vinegar
- 2 tablespoons olive oil
- 1/2 teaspoon salt

In a large bowl, combine the kidney beans, black-eyed peas, black beans, celery, red pepper and onion. In a small bowl, whisk together the vinegars, oil and salt. Pour over bean mixture; toss to coat. Refrigerate for about 4 hours, stirring occasionally. **Yield:** 8 servings.

Nutritional Analysis: One serving (3/4 cup) equals 169 calories, 3 g fat (trace saturated fat), 0 cholesterol, 414 mg sodium, 26 g carbohydrate, 7 g fiber, 9 g protein.
Diabetic Exchanges: 1-1/2 starch, 1 very lean meat, 1/2 fat.

Grapefruit Shrimp Salad

Low-carb

Perk up seafood salad with a tangy dressing that combines orange juice, red wine vinegar and Dijon mustard. I had tried a similar salad at a restaurant and adapted this version for a fun lunch to take to work. It always gets comments.
—Joanne Beaupre, Manchester, Connecticut

- 1 head Bibb *or* Boston lettuce
- 1 large grapefruit, peeled and sectioned
- 1 medium ripe avocado, peeled and thinly sliced
- 1 pound cooked medium shrimp, peeled and deveined

CITRUS VINAIGRETTE:
- 2 tablespoons orange juice
- 2 tablespoons red wine vinegar
- 1 tablespoon olive oil
- 2 teaspoons honey
- 1-1/4 teaspoons Dijon mustard
- 1/4 teaspoon salt

Place lettuce on four serving plates. Arrange grapefruit, avocado and shrimp over lettuce. In a bowl, whisk together vinaigrette ingredients. Drizzle over each salad. **Yield:** 4 servings.

Nutritional Analysis: One serving equals 266 calories, 12 g fat (2 g saturated fat), 221 mg cholesterol, 445 mg sodium, 14 g carbohydrate, 4 g fiber, 26 g protein.
Diabetic Exchanges: 3 very lean meat, 2 fat, 1 vegetable, 1/2 fruit.

Israeli Pepper Tomato Salad

Low-carb   Meatless

(Pictured below)

This Israeli salad, which is traditionally eaten at breakfast, lends itself to endless variety...you can add foods like olives, beets or potatoes.
—Sandy Long, Lees Summit, Missouri

- 6 medium tomatoes, seeded and chopped
- 1 *each* medium sweet red, yellow and green pepper, chopped
- 1 medium cucumber, seeded and chopped
- 1 medium carrot, chopped
- 3 green onions, thinly sliced
- 1 jalapeno pepper, seeded and chopped
- 2 tablespoons *each* minced fresh cilantro, parsley, dill and mint
- 1/4 cup lemon juice
- 2 tablespoons olive oil
- 3 garlic cloves, minced
- 1/2 teaspoon salt
- 1/4 teaspoon pepper

In a large bowl, combine the tomatoes, sweet peppers, cucumber, carrot, green onions, jalapeno and herbs. In a small bowl, whisk together the remaining ingredients. Pour over the tomato mixture; toss to coat evenly. Cover and refrigerate for at least 1 hour. Serve with a slotted spoon. **Yield:** 9 servings.

Editor's Note: When cutting or seeding hot peppers, use rubber or plastic gloves to protect your hands. Avoid touching your face.

Nutritional Analysis: One serving (1 cup) equals 72 calories, 4 g fat (trace saturated fat), 0 cholesterol, 146 mg sodium, 10 g carbohydrate, 3 g fiber, 2 g protein.
Diabetic Exchanges: 2 vegetable, 1/2 fat.

BLT Bow Tie Pasta Salad

Low-carb Low-sodium

I first had this summery salad at a family reunion. It's one of my husband's favorite dinners. Sometimes, we leave out the chicken and serve it as a side dish instead.
—Jennifer Madsen, Rexburg, Idaho

2-1/2 cups uncooked bow tie pasta
 6 cups torn romaine
1-1/2 cups cubed cooked chicken breast
 1 medium tomato, diced
 4 bacon strips, cooked and crumbled
 1/3 cup reduced-fat mayonnaise
 1/4 cup water
 1 tablespoon barbecue sauce
1-1/2 teaspoons white vinegar
 1/4 teaspoon pepper

Cook pasta according to package directions. Drain and rinse under cold water. In a large serving bowl, combine the pasta, romaine, chicken, tomato and bacon. In a small bowl, whisk together the mayonnaise, water, barbecue sauce, vinegar and pepper. Pour over pasta mixture; toss to coat evenly. Serve immediately. **Yield:** 11 servings.

Nutritional Analysis: One serving (1 cup) equals 134 calories, 5 g fat (1 g saturated fat), 21 mg cholesterol, 125 mg sodium, 14 g carbohydrate, 1 g fiber, 9 g protein.
Diabetic Exchanges: 1 starch, 1 lean meat.

Broccoli Slaw

Low-fat Meatless

I first made this unusual salad for my husband's lunch. It takes just 5 to 10 minutes to put together from start to finish. The crunchy blend of ingredients has a nice zip.
—Betty Kleberger, Florissant, Missouri

 4 cups broccoli coleslaw mix
 1 can (11 ounces) Mexicorn, drained
1/2 cup salsa
 2 tablespoons reduced-fat mayonnaise
 2 teaspoons sugar
1/2 teaspoon salt
1/8 teaspoon coarsely ground pepper
 3 tablespoons cider vinegar

In a bowl, combine the coleslaw mix, corn and salsa. In a small bowl, combine the mayonnaise, sugar, salt and pepper. Gradually whisk in vinegar. Pour over coleslaw mixture; toss to coat evenly. Cover and refrigerate for at least 2 hours. **Yield:** 6 servings.

Editor's Note: Broccoli coleslaw mix may be found in the produce section of most grocery stores.

Nutritional Analysis: One serving (3/4 cup) equals 92 calories, 2 g fat (trace saturated fat), 2 mg cholesterol, 621 mg sodium, 17 g carbohydrate, 4 g fiber, 4 g protein.
Diabetic Exchanges: 1 starch, 1 vegetable.

Three-Step Taco Salad

(Pictured below)

This Southwestern-style salad is layered with crunchy tortilla chips, lettuce, beans, tomatoes, olives, cheese and a zippy meat mixture, then drizzled with a snappy salsa dressing. My family loves it. Yours will, too!
—Phyllis Schmalz, Kansas City, Kansas

 1 pound lean ground beef
3/4 cup water
 1 envelope reduced-sodium taco seasoning
 4 cups baked tortilla chips, broken
 8 cups shredded lettuce, *divided*
 1 can (16 ounces) kidney beans, rinsed and drained
 2 medium tomatoes, seeded and chopped, *divided*
 1 can (2-1/4 ounces) sliced ripe olives, drained
 1 cup (4 ounces) shredded reduced-fat cheddar cheese, *divided*
2/3 cup fat-free sour cream
2/3 cup salsa

In a nonstick skillet, cook beef over medium heat until no longer pink; drain. Add water and taco seasoning; bring to a boil. Reduce heat; simmer, uncovered, for 5 minutes, stirring occasionally.

In a large bowl, layer tortilla chips, 7 cups lettuce, beans, half of tomatoes, olives, half of cheese and meat mixture. Top with remaining tomatoes, cheese and lettuce. In a small bowl, combine sour cream and salsa. Serve with salad. **Yield:** 10 servings.

Nutritional Analysis: One serving (1-1/2 cups salad with 2 tablespoons sour cream mixture) equals 213 calories, 7 g fat (3 g saturated fat), 30 mg cholesterol, 514 mg sodium, 22 g carbohydrate, 4 g fiber, 16 g protein.
Diabetic Exchanges: 2 lean meat, 1 vegetable, 1 starch.

Side Dishes & Condiments

In this chapter, you'll find just the right accompaniment for your meals...from fresh vegetables, pleasing pasta and hearty potatoes to satisfying rice, mouth-watering relishes and perfectly seasoned sauces.

Makeover Sour Cream Potatoes (page 91)

Sesame Green Beans 'n' Water Chestnuts

Low-carb Meatless

Soy sauce and sesame oil make a flavorful base for these good-for-you green beans. Toasted sesame seeds and water chestnuts add texture and crunch to this quick skillet side that goes well with beef or poultry.
—*Dot Christiansen, Bettendorf, Iowa*

1-1/4 pounds fresh green beans (about 5 cups), trimmed
  1 can (8 ounces) sliced water chestnuts, drained
  1 cup sliced fresh mushrooms
  2 garlic cloves, minced
  2 teaspoons canola oil
  2 teaspoons sesame oil
  2 tablespoons water
  4 teaspoons reduced-sodium soy sauce
  2 teaspoons sugar
1/4 teaspoon pepper
1/8 teaspoon salt
  2 teaspoons sesame seeds, toasted

In a nonstick skillet, saute the beans, water chestnuts, mushrooms and garlic in canola and sesame oil for 5-6 minutes or until almost tender. Add the water, soy sauce, sugar, pepper and salt. Reduce heat; cover and simmer for 10-12 minutes or until beans are tender. Sprinkle with sesame seeds. **Yield:** 6 servings.

Nutritional Analysis: *One serving (3/4 cup) equals 87 calories, 4 g fat (trace saturated fat), 0 cholesterol, 189 mg sodium, 12 g carbohydrate, 4 g fiber, 3 g protein.*
Diabetic Exchanges: *2 vegetable, 1/2 fat.*

Vegetables with Brown Rice

Meatless

When garden crops are plentiful, this is a delightful dish to serve. It's convenient for company because the veggies can be precut and refrigerated in plastic bags until cooking time.
—*Patty Kile, Greentown, Pennsylvania*

1/4 cup chopped walnuts
  3 teaspoons canola oil, *divided*
  1 medium sweet red pepper, julienned
  1 cup broccoli florets
  1 medium zucchini, sliced
  1 medium yellow summer squash, sliced
3/4 cup frozen peas
  3 tablespoons water
  1 teaspoon salt
1/8 teaspoon pepper
  2 cups hot cooked brown rice
  3 tablespoons minced fresh parsley

In a large nonstick skillet, saute walnuts in 1 teaspoon oil for 2 minutes or until lightly toasted. Remove walnuts and set aside.
In the same skillet, saute the pepper and broccoli in re-

maining oil for 1 minute. Add the zucchini and yellow squash; saute 1 minute longer. Stir in the peas, water, salt and pepper. Reduce heat; cover and simmer for 5 minutes or until vegetables are tender. Combine rice and parsley; arrange on a serving platter. Top with vegetables and nuts. **Yield:** 8 servings.

Nutritional Analysis: *One serving (3/4 cup) equals 115 calories, 5 g fat (trace saturated fat), 0 cholesterol, 298 mg sodium, 16 g carbohydrate, 3 g fiber, 3 g protein.*
Diabetic Exchanges: *1 vegetable, 1 fat, 1/2 starch.*

Light 'n' Creamy Mashed Potatoes

Low-fat Meatless

(Pictured below)

You'd never know that these mashed potatoes developed in our Test Kitchen are on the lighter side. Garlic and chives season them nicely while sour cream and cream cheese add richness. They're perfect to serve to company.

  6 cups quartered peeled potatoes (about 3 pounds)
  4 ounces fat-free cream cheese, cubed
1/2 cup reduced-fat sour cream
1/2 cup fat-free milk
3/4 teaspoon salt
1/4 teaspoon garlic powder
1/4 teaspoon pepper
  1 tablespoon minced chives
Dash paprika

Place potatoes in a saucepan and cover with water. Bring to a boil. Reduce heat; cover and cook until tender. Drain. In a large mixing bowl, mash the potatoes. Add the cream

cheese, sour cream, milk, salt, garlic powder and pepper; beat until smooth. Stir in chives. Sprinkle with paprika. **Yield:** 8 servings.

Nutritional Analysis: One serving (2/3 cup) equals 140 calories, 2 g fat (1 g saturated fat), 6 mg cholesterol, 322 mg sodium, 26 g carbohydrate, 2 g fiber, 6 g protein.
Diabetic Exchange: 1-1/2 starch.

Seasoned Bread Crumbs

*Low-carb   Low-fat   **Low-sodium***

Our Test Kitchen came up with this better-for-you alternative to high-sodium packaged bread crumbs, using garlic powder and a handful of dried herbs. The crumbs make a savory topping for casseroles and a crispy coating for pork, chicken and fish.

  4 ounces Italian bread, cubed
  1 teaspoon garlic powder
  1 teaspoon dried parsley flakes
  1/2 teaspoon dried oregano
  1/2 teaspoon dried basil
  1/4 teaspoon dried thyme
  1/4 teaspoon dried rosemary, crushed

Place all ingredients in a blender or food processor; cover and process until fine crumbs form. Transfer to a 15-in. x 10-in. x 1-in. baking pan. Bake, uncovered, at 350° for 8-12 minutes or until lightly browned, stirring occasionally. Cool. Store in an airtight container. **Yield:** 1 cup.

Nutritional Analysis: One serving (2 tablespoons) equals 40 calories, 1 g fat (trace saturated fat), 0 cholesterol, 83 mg sodium, 8 g carbohydrate, 1 g fiber, 1 g protein.
Diabetic Exchange: 1/2 starch.

Three-Grain Pilaf

Meatless

(Pictured above right)

This is an old family recipe that everyone still looks forward to. The satisfying combination of brown rice, pearl barley and bulgur makes this tasty side dish special enough for company.
—Mary Knudson, Bermuda Dunes, California

  1 large onion, chopped
  1 garlic clove, minced
  2 tablespoons olive oil
2/3 cup shredded carrot
1/3 cup uncooked brown rice
1/3 cup uncooked medium pearl barley
1/3 cup uncooked bulgur
  2 cups vegetable broth *or* reduced-sodium chicken broth
1/4 cup sherry *or* water
  1 teaspoon minced fresh oregano *or* 1/4 teaspoon dried oregano
  1 teaspoon minced fresh basil *or* 1/4 teaspoon dried basil
1/2 teaspoon salt
1/4 teaspoon pepper

1/3 cup minced fresh parsley
1/3 cup sliced almonds, toasted

In a large nonstick skillet, saute onion and garlic in oil for 2 minutes. Add carrot; saute for 2 minutes or until the vegetables are crisp-tender. Stir in the rice, barley and bulgur; saute for 4 minutes or until grains are lightly browned. Gradually add broth and sherry or water. Bring to a boil. Reduce heat; stir in oregano, basil, salt and pepper. Cover and simmer for 40-45 minutes or until grains are tender and the liquid is absorbed. Stir in parsley and sprinkle with almonds. **Yield:** 5 servings.

Editor's Note: Look for bulgur in the cereal, rice or organic food aisle of your grocery store.

Nutritional Analysis: One serving (3/4 cup) equals 238 calories, 9 g fat (1 g saturated fat), 0 cholesterol, 498 mg sodium, 33 g carbohydrate, 6 g fiber, 7 g protein.
Diabetic Exchanges: 2 starch, 1-1/2 fat.

🍎 A Glossary of Great Grains

LOOKING to bring something new to the table? Consider the bevy of grains commonly available today.

Bulgur. A form of cracked wheat that can be found in the cereal, rice or organic food aisle of most grocery stores, bulgur requires little preparation time. The versatile grain is often used in soups, stews and salads. It also makes a great replacement for some of the meat in meat loaf or burgers.

Rolled Oats. Supermarkets usually carry three types of rolled oats. Old-fashioned oats consist of the entire grain, quick-cooking oats are sliced for a faster cooking time and instant oats are precooked and dried. Be sure to note the type of oats required in the recipe you're following.

Barley. The nutlike flavor of pearl barley makes it a tasty substitution for rice in many dishes. It's also popular in salads and soups. Instant or quick-cooking barley has been flattened and presteamed but offers the same nutrients as pearl barley.

1/2 cup white wine vinegar
1/4 cup water
1 bay leaf
1 whole clove
1/2 to 1 teaspoon pepper
1/2 teaspoon salt
Sugar substitute equivalent to 3 tablespoons sugar
1 can (15 ounces) sliced beets, drained

In a saucepan, bring the vinegar, water, bay leaf, clove, pepper and salt to a boil. Reduce heat; simmer, uncovered, for 5 minutes. Remove from the heat; stir in sugar substitute until dissolved. Pour over beets. Cover and refrigerate for at least 5 hours or overnight. Discard bay leaf and clove. Serve with a slotted spoon. **Yield:** 4 servings.

Editor's Note: This recipe was tested with Splenda No Calorie Sweetener. Look for it in the baking aisle of your grocery store.

Nutritional Analysis: One serving (1/2 cup) equals 37 calories, trace fat (trace saturated fat), 0 cholesterol, 461 mg sodium, 9 g carbohydrate, 2 g fiber, 1 g protein.
Diabetic Exchange: 1 vegetable.

Savory 'n' Saucy Baked Beans

Low-fat **Meatless**

(Pictured above)

Dress up canned baked beans in a jiffy with green pepper, celery and canned tomatoes. A hint of sweetness and a touch of garlic make these beans naturals for summer picnics and patio meals.
—A.G. Strickland, Marietta, Georgia

1/2 cup chopped onion
1/2 cup chopped green pepper
1/2 cup chopped celery
1 can (28 ounces) vegetarian baked beans
1 can (14-1/2 ounces) diced tomatoes, drained
1/2 teaspoon pepper
1/4 teaspoon salt
1/4 teaspoon garlic powder

In a large saucepan coated with nonstick cooking spray, cook the onion, green pepper and celery for 3 minutes or until tender. Stir in the beans, tomatoes, pepper, salt and garlic powder. Bring to a boil. Reduce heat; simmer, uncovered, for 10-15 minutes. **Yield:** 6 servings.

Nutritional Analysis: One serving (3/4 cup) equals 156 calories, trace fat (trace saturated fat), 0 mg cholesterol, 195 mg sodium, 30 g carbohydrate, 8 g fiber, 6 g protein.
Diabetic Exchange: 2 starch.

Diabetic Spiced Beets

Low-carb *Low-fat* **Meatless**

I marinate canned beets in a mixture of vinegar, clove, pepper and bay leaf for a tart side dish that is sure to appeal to even finicky eaters.
—Mae Flint, Ionia, Michigan

Italian Seasoning

Low-carb *Low-fat* **Low-sodium**

Who needs salt when you can give breads, pasta, spaghetti sauce and other dishes an Italian flair with this distinctive dried herb blend from our Test Kitchen?

3 tablespoons *each* dried basil, oregano and parsley flakes
1 tablespoon garlic powder
1 teaspoon dried thyme
1 teaspoon dried rosemary, crushed
1/4 teaspoon pepper
1/4 teaspoon crushed red pepper flakes

Place all the ingredients, in batches if necessary, in a spice grinder or small bowl. Grind or crush with the back of a spoon until mixture becomes a coarse powder. Store in an airtight container for up to 6 months. **Yield:** 7 tablespoons.

Nutritional Analysis: One serving (1/4 teaspoon) equals 1 calorie, trace fat (0 saturated fat), 0 cholesterol, trace sodium, trace carbohydrate, trace fiber, trace protein.
Diabetic Exchanges: Free food.

Confetti Potato Pancakes

Low-fat **Meatless**

My husband's family is Irish, and his mother makes potato pancakes quite often. I like to add other vegetables to give them a more colorful look and heartier texture. Crispy on the outside and soft inside, these receive rave reviews, especially when I serve them to my in-laws!
—Betsy McDaniels, Colfax, Illinois

2 large potatoes (about 1-1/2 pounds), peeled
2 medium zucchini
2 large carrots

1/2 cup finely chopped onion, *divided*
2 eggs, lightly beaten
1/2 cup all-purpose flour
1 to 2 garlic cloves, minced
1/2 teaspoon salt
1/2 teaspoon dried basil
1/4 teaspoon sugar
1 tablespoon canola oil

Coarsely shred the potatoes, zucchini and carrots; drain and pat dry. Place half of the shredded vegetables and 1/4 cup chopped onion in a food processor or blender; cover and process until finely chopped. Transfer to a bowl; add eggs, flour, garlic, salt, basil, sugar and remaining onion and shredded vegetables.

In a large nonstick skillet, heat oil. Drop batter by 1/4 cupfuls into skillet; flatten to form patties. Fry until golden brown; turn and cook the second side. **Yield:** 8 servings.

Nutritional Analysis: One serving (2 pancakes) equals 148 calories, 3 g fat (1 g saturated fat), 53 mg cholesterol, 176 mg sodium, 26 g carbohydrate, 3 g fiber, 5 g protein.
Diabetic Exchanges: 1-1/2 starch, 1 vegetable.

Minty Orzo and Peas

Meatless

(Pictured below)

My grandmother used to serve this side dish along with roast leg of lamb. With its fresh mint taste, it also makes a nice salad served chilled. It's simple but delicious.
—Kristen Dunphy, Haverhill, Massachusetts

1 cup uncooked orzo pasta
1 small onion, finely chopped
1 garlic clove, minced
2 tablespoons butter
2 cups frozen peas
1 teaspoon grated lemon peel
1/4 teaspoon salt

1/8 teaspoon pepper
2 tablespoons finely chopped fresh mint

Prepare orzo according to package directions. Drain and set aside. In a large skillet, saute onion and garlic in butter until tender. Add peas; cook for 2 minutes or until tender. Add the lemon peel, salt, pepper and orzo; heat through. Stir in mint. Serve immediately. **Yield:** 6 servings.

Nutritional Analysis: One serving (2/3 cup) equals 200 calories, 5 g fat (3 g saturated fat), 10 mg cholesterol, 194 mg sodium, 33 g carbohydrate, 3 g fiber, 7 g protein.
Diabetic Exchanges: 2 starch, 1 fat.

Homemade Steak Sauce

Low-carb   Low-fat

This creative condiment features everything from tomato paste and raisins to grapefruit juice, honey, garlic and soy sauce. I think it tastes better than the commercial brands.
—Judy Neil, Royal Oak, Michigan

1/4 cup chopped onion
1 tablespoon olive oil
2 tablespoons honey
1/4 cup reduced-sodium beef broth
1/4 cup Worcestershire sauce
1/4 cup reduced-sodium soy sauce
1/4 cup ruby red grapefruit juice
3 tablespoons tomato paste
2 tablespoons balsamic vinegar
2 tablespoons cider vinegar
2 tablespoons raisins
2 teaspoons garlic powder
1-1/2 teaspoons coarsely crushed pepper
3/4 teaspoon dried thyme
1/2 teaspoon salt

In a nonstick saucepan over medium heat, cook onion in oil until tender. Add honey; cook and stir for 2 minutes. Stir in broth, Worcestershire sauce, soy sauce, grapefruit juice, tomato paste and vinegars until blended. Stir in the raisins, garlic powder, pepper, thyme and salt. Bring to a boil. Reduce heat; simmer, uncovered, for about 20 minutes or until sauce is reduced to about 1-1/4 cups.

Cool to room temperature. Transfer to a blender; cover and process until smooth. Cover and refrigerate. **Yield:** 1-1/4 cups.

Nutritional Analysis: One tablespoon equals 27 calories, 1 g fat (trace saturated fat), trace cholesterol, 222 mg sodium, 5 g carbohydrate, trace fiber, trace protein.
Diabetic Exchange: 1/2 starch.

Macaroni 'n' Cheese Italiano

Meatless

I've always liked macaroni and cheese, but my husband prefers macaroni with tomato sauce. So I added spaghetti sauce and mozzarella to give my mac and cheese an Italian flavor.
—Isabelle Wolters, Scituate, Massachusetts

  2 cups uncooked elbow macaroni
3/4 cup chopped onion
1/4 cup chopped celery
1/4 cup chopped green pepper
  2 teaspoons olive oil
1/2 cup meatless spaghetti sauce
1/2 teaspoon dried basil
1/2 teaspoon dried oregano
  2 tablespoons all-purpose flour
1/2 teaspoon salt
1/4 teaspoon ground nutmeg
1/8 teaspoon cayenne pepper
  2 cups fat-free milk
1-1/4 cups shredded reduced-fat cheddar cheese
1/2 cup shredded part-skim mozzarella cheese
  2 tablespoons grated Parmesan cheese
  2 plum tomatoes, seeded and sliced

Prepare pasta according to package directions until cooked but firm. Meanwhile, in a large nonstick skillet, saute the onion, celery and green pepper in oil until tender. Stir in spaghetti sauce, basil and oregano. Bring to a boil. Reduce heat; simmer, uncovered, for 5 minutes. Drain macaroni; stir into sauce. Transfer to a 2-qt. baking dish coated with nonstick cooking spray; set aside.

In a saucepan, combine the flour, salt, nutmeg and cayenne. Gradually stir in milk until smooth. Bring to a boil over medium heat; cook and stir for 2 minutes or until thickened. Reduce heat; stir in cheddar and mozzarella cheeses until melted. Pour over macaroni mixture. Top with Parmesan cheese and tomatoes. Bake, uncovered, at 350° for 25-30 minutes or until bubbly and golden brown. Let stand for 5 minutes before serving. **Yield:** 6 servings.

Nutritional Analysis: One serving equals 262 calories, 9 g fat (5 g saturated fat), 25 mg cholesterol, 406 mg sodium, 31 g carbohydrate, 2 g fiber, 16 g protein.
Diabetic Exchanges: 2 lean meat, 1-1/2 starch, 1 vegetable, 1/2 fat.

Parmesan Seasoned Breading

Low-carb *Low-fat*

I created this flavorful coating years ago for my family, and it has deliciously stood the test of time. Although my husband and I are alone now, I still rely on this recipe as a quick, crunchy breading for meats. There's always a container in my refrigerator ready to use on pork, fish, chicken and even vegetables.
—Alyce Wyman, Pembina, North Dakota

1 cup (4 ounces) grated Parmesan cheese
1/2 cup cornflake crumbs
1/2 cup Malt-O-Meal hot wheat cereal
  1 tablespoon parsley flakes
  1 teaspoon salt
  1 teaspoon seasoned salt
  1 teaspoon rubbed sage
  1 teaspoon garlic powder
  1 teaspoon onion powder
  1 teaspoon seafood seasoning
  1 teaspoon paprika
1/2 teaspoon ground thyme
1/2 teaspoon pepper

In a bowl, combine all the ingredients; mix well. Store in an airtight container in the refrigerator for up to 6 months. **Yield:** 2 cups.

Editor's Note: Use in place of seasoned bread crumbs called for in recipes for chicken, fish or pork chops.

Nutritional Analysis: One serving (2 tablespoons) equals 54 calories, 2 g fat (1 g saturated fat), 4 mg cholesterol, 398 mg sodium, 7 g carbohydrate, trace fiber, 3 g protein.
Diabetic Exchange: 1/2 starch.

Summer Garden Medley

Meatless

(Pictured below)

This colorful side dish brings back sweet memories of the corn-and-tomato dish my mother often prepared in the summer. Farmers in our area supply us with delicious eggplant...so I sometimes substitute them for the zucchini in veggie recipes like this one.
—Elaine Nelson, Fresno, California

  2 medium zucchini, halved lengthwise and cut into 1/4-inch slices
  1 cup fresh *or* frozen corn
3/4 cup diced green pepper

1 medium leek (white portion only), sliced
1/2 teaspoon seasoned salt
1 tablespoon olive oil
2 medium ripe tomatoes, seeded and diced

In a large nonstick skillet, saute the zucchini, corn, green pepper, leek and seasoned salt in oil until vegetables are tender. Add tomatoes; heat through. **Yield:** 4 servings.

Nutritional Analysis: *One serving (1 cup) equals 113 calories, 4 g fat (1 g saturated fat), 0 mg cholesterol, 202 mg sodium, 19 g carbohydrate, 3 g fiber, 3 g protein.*
Diabetic Exchanges: *2 vegetable, 1/2 starch, 1/2 fat.*

Strawberry Chutney

Low-carb Low-fat **Low-sodium**

I got this recipe at my Weight Watchers meeting during a recipe swap and made some slight alterations. Flavored with orange peel, mustard, raspberry vinegar and raisins, this chutney is great on ham, turkey or pork.
—*Donna Burke, Chatsworth, Illinois*

1/4 cup packed brown sugar
1/4 cup lemon juice
1/4 cup raspberry vinegar
2 tablespoons raisins
2 tablespoons honey
1/4 teaspoon grated orange peel
1/4 teaspoon prepared mustard
2 cups sliced fresh strawberries

In a saucepan, combine the first seven ingredients. Bring to a boil. Reduce heat to medium; cook, uncovered, for 15 minutes or until slightly thickened, stirring occasionally. Stir in strawberries. Reduce heat to low and simmer 10 minutes longer or until thickened, stirring occasionally. Refrigerate overnight. **Yield:** 9 servings.

Nutritional Analysis: *One serving (2 tablespoons) equals 57 calories, trace fat (trace saturated fat), 0 cholesterol, 5 mg sodium, 15 g carbohydrate, 1 g fiber, trace protein.*
Diabetic Exchange: *1 fruit.*

🍎 Baked Fries Are Better

MY FAMILY loves French fries and steak fries, but we bake them to avoid all the fat from deep-frying. For every medium to large potato, we put a tablespoon of olive or canola oil in a resealable plastic bag. We put seasonings in the bag, then add the cut potatoes.

After shaking the potatoes until they are well-coated, we place them on a baking sheet and bake them at 350° until they are brown. They taste delicious—crispy on the outside and moist on the inside.

You can also season the fries according to your taste buds. We love Cajun fries sprinkled with Cajun seasoning and Mexican fries made with taco seasoning. —*Lesa Tyson, Philadelphia, Pennsylvania*

Cheesy Broccoli Casserole

(Pictured above)

My mother-in-law gave me the recipe for this hearty side dish over 30 years ago. It was the only way I could get my husband to eat broccoli—by hiding it in the stuffing!
—*Sheron Hutcheson, Newark, Delaware*

1 package (10 ounces) frozen chopped broccoli, thawed, drained and patted dry
2 cups (8 ounces) shredded reduced-fat cheddar cheese
1 package (6 ounces) reduced-sodium stuffing mix
1 small onion, finely chopped
1 egg, beaten
1/8 teaspoon ground nutmeg
Dash pepper
1 cup fat-free milk
1 cup reduced-sodium chicken broth
2 bacon strips, cooked and crumbled

In a large bowl, combine the broccoli, cheese, stuffing mix, onion, egg, nutmeg and pepper; mix well. Gradually stir in milk and broth.

Transfer to a 2-qt. baking dish coated with nonstick cooking spray. Bake, uncovered, at 325° for 50-55 minutes or until a knife inserted near the center comes out clean. Sprinkle with bacon. **Yield:** 7 servings.

Nutritional Analysis: *One serving (1 cup) equals 246 calories, 10 g fat (6 g saturated fat), 58 mg cholesterol, 389 mg sodium, 25 g carbohydrate, 2 g fiber, 17 g protein.*
Diabetic Exchanges: *2 lean meat, 1-1/2 starch, 1/2 fat.*

Seasoning Blend

Low-carb   Low-fat   Low-sodium

This low-sodium blend can spice up just about anything. Try sprinkling the mild mix of onion powder, garlic powder and thyme on seafood, chicken and steak. For a little more zip, add some cayenne pepper.
—Lesley Tragesser, Charleston, Missouri

> **5 teaspoons onion powder**
> **2-1/2 teaspoons garlic powder**
> **2-1/2 teaspoons ground mustard**
> **2-1/2 teaspoons paprika**
> **3/4 teaspoon thyme leaves, crushed**
> **1/2 teaspoon white pepper**
> **1/4 teaspoon salt**
> **1/4 teaspoon celery seed**

In a small bowl, combine all of the ingredients. Store in an airtight container for up to 6 months. **Yield: about 1/3 cup.**

Nutritional Analysis: One serving (1 teaspoon) equals 8 calories, trace fat (trace saturated fat), 0 cholesterol, 43 mg sodium, 2 g carbohydrate, trace fiber, trace protein.
Diabetic Exchange: Free food.

Dilled Summer Squash

Low-carb   Low-fat   Low-sodium   Meatless

You don't need salt to add a pinch of pizzazz to summer squash. Here is how to turn the garden favorite into a savory side with dill, onion, pepper and butter.
—Shirley Antaya, Arab, Alabama

> **4 cups sliced yellow summer squash**
> **1/4 cup water**
> **2 teaspoons finely chopped onion**
> **2 teaspoons butter**
> **2 teaspoons snipped fresh dill *or* 1/2 teaspoon dill weed**
> **1/8 teaspoon pepper**

In a large saucepan, combine the squash, water and onion. Bring to a boil. Reduce heat. Cover and simmer for 10-15 minutes or until tender; drain. Stir in butter, dill and pepper. **Yield: 4 servings.**

Nutritional Analysis: One serving (3/4 cup) equals 44 calories, 2 g fat (1 g saturated fat), 5 mg cholesterol, 22 mg sodium, 6 g carbohydrate, 2 g fiber, 2 g protein.
Diabetic Exchanges: 1 vegetable, 1/2 fat.

Slow-Roasted Tomatoes

Low-carb   Meatless

Seasoned with oregano and cheese, tomatoes take on a wonderfully intense flavor as they roast in the oven. Serve these warm as a side dish. They are very nice with grilled chicken. This dish is good year-round—even in winter, when tomatoes aren't at their best.
—Martha Chayet, Manchester-by-the-Sea, Massachusetts

> **16 plum tomatoes, halved lengthwise**
> **1/4 cup grated Parmesan cheese**
> **1 tablespoon dried oregano**
> **1 teaspoon sugar**
> **1 teaspoon salt**
> **1/2 teaspoon pepper**
> **2 tablespoons olive oil**

Remove tomato seeds with a spoon. Place tomatoes, cut side up, on baking sheets coated with nonstick cooking spray. Sprinkle with cheese, oregano, sugar, salt and pepper; drizzle with oil. Bake at 250° for 2 hours. **Yield: 8 servings.**

Nutritional Analysis: One serving (4 halves) equals 72 calories, 5 g fat (1 g saturated fat), 2 mg cholesterol, 363 mg sodium, 6 g carbohydrate, 1 g fiber, 2 g protein.
Diabetic Exchanges: 1 vegetable, 1 fat.

Spiced Fruit Bake

Low-fat   Low-sodium   Meatless

(Pictured at right)

Canned fruit makes this easy compote a snap to toss together. Gently spiced with cinnamon and nutmeg, the fruity blend makes a perfect breakfast medley or a comforting dessert.
—Beverly Coyde, Gasport, New York

> **1 can (20 ounces) unsweetened pineapple chunks**
> **1 can (15 ounces) reduced-sugar apricot halves**
> **1 can (14-1/2 ounces) reduced-sugar pear halves**
> **1/4 cup packed brown sugar**
> **1 tablespoon butter, melted**
> **1/4 teaspoon ground cinnamon**
> **1/4 teaspoon ground nutmeg**
> **1/2 cup reduced-fat vanilla yogurt**

Drain fruits, reserving a total of 3/4 cup juice. Place fruit in a 2-qt. baking dish. In a small bowl, combine the brown sugar, butter, cinnamon, nutmeg and reserved juice; pour over fruit. Bake, uncovered, at 350° for 25-30 minutes or until heated through. Serve with a slotted spoon. Top each serving with 1 tablespoon of yogurt. **Yield: 8 servings.**

Nutritional Analysis: One serving (2/3 cup) equals 132 calories, 2 g fat (1 g saturated fat), 5 mg cholesterol, 30 mg sodium, 30 g carbohydrate, 1 g fiber, 1 g protein.
Diabetic Exchange: 2 fruit.

Steamed Winter Vegetables

Low-fat   Meatless

(Pictured above)

Potatoes, parsnips, carrots, brussels sprouts and turnips star in this colorful side dish. A dash of horseradish and dill perk up this vegetable assortment that makes an appealing partner to any winter entree.
—*Marilyn Leedom, Appleton, Wisconsin*

1 pound small red potatoes, cut into 1-inch
   chunks
1/2 pound brussels sprouts, halved
2 medium parsnips, peeled and cut into 1/2-inch
   chunks
1 small turnip, peeled and cut into 1/2-inch
   chunks

2 small carrots, cut into 1/4- to 1/2-inch slices
4-1/2 teaspoons butter
1-1/2 teaspoons snipped fresh dill
1-1/2 teaspoons white vinegar
1-1/2 teaspoons prepared horseradish, drained
1/4 teaspoon salt

Place the vegetables in a steamer basket. Place in a large saucepan over 1 in. of water; bring to a boil. Cover and steam for 10-12 minutes or until crisp-tender. Melt butter in a large nonstick skillet. Stir in the vegetables and toss to coat evenly. In a small bowl, combine the dill, vinegar, horseradish and salt. Pour over the vegetables and toss to coat evenly. Serve immediately. **Yield:** 6 servings.

Nutritional Analysis: One serving (3/4 cup) equals 123 calories, 3 g fat (2 g saturated fat), 8 mg cholesterol, 162 mg sodium, 22 g carbohydrate, 4 g fiber, 3 g protein.
Diabetic Exchanges: 1 starch, 1 vegetable, 1/2 fat.

Stir-Fry Sesame Green Beans

Meatless

(Pictured above)

Looking for a different treatment for garden-fresh green beans? Try this stir-fried side dish from our Test Kitchen. It's nicely seasoned with fresh ginger, sesame oil and sesame seeds.

1 pound fresh green beans, cut into 1-inch pieces
1 tablespoon canola oil
1 cup julienned sweet red pepper
1 cup sliced fresh mushrooms
1/4 cup thinly sliced green onions
2 garlic cloves, minced
3 tablespoons reduced-sodium soy sauce
2 teaspoons minced fresh gingerroot
1/4 cup sliced dried apricots
1 teaspoon sesame oil
2 teaspoons sesame seeds, toasted

In a large nonstick skillet or wok, stir-fry beans over medium-high heat in oil for 2 minutes. Add sweet pepper and mushrooms; stir-fry 2 minutes longer. Add green onions and garlic; stir-fry for 1-2 minutes.

Combine the soy sauce and ginger; stir into skillet. Bring to a boil. Reduce heat; simmer, uncovered, for 2 minutes. Stir in apricots; cook and stir for 1 minute longer. Remove from the heat; stir in sesame oil and sesame seeds. Serve immediately. **Yield:** 4 servings.

Nutritional Analysis: One serving (1 cup) equals 135 calories, 6 g fat (trace saturated fat), 0 cholesterol, 463 mg sodium, 18 g carbohydrate, 5 g fiber, 4 g protein.
Diabetic Exchanges: 2 vegetable, 1 fat, 1/2 fruit.

Great Grain Pilaf

Low-fat   Meatless

If you're bored with boiled rice, try this fun pilaf. It's mild tasting and a great way to include fiber in your diet. Because I like experimenting with different grains, I buy at a bulk food store. Being able to purchase just the amount you need for a recipe is a real advantage.
—Joyce Graves, Sterling Heights, Michigan

1/2 cup chopped green onions
2 garlic cloves, minced
2 teaspoons butter
1 cup uncooked long grain rice
1/2 cup bulgur
1/4 cup quick-cooking barley
3 cups reduced-sodium chicken broth *or* vegetable broth
1/2 teaspoon salt
Dash pepper
1/3 cup minced fresh parsley

In a saucepan, saute onions and garlic in butter until tender. Add the rice, bulgur and barley. Cook and stir for 5 minutes.

Gradually stir in broth, salt and pepper. Bring to a boil. Reduce heat; cover and simmer for 25 minutes or until tender and broth is absorbed. Stir in parsley. **Yield:** 8 servings.

Editor's Note: Look for bulgur in the cereal, rice or organic food aisle of your grocery store.

Nutritional Analysis: One serving (2/3 cup) equals 154 calories, 2 g fat (1 g saturated fat), 4 mg cholesterol, 202 mg sodium, 30 g carbohydrate, 3 g fiber, 5 g protein.
Diabetic Exchange: 2 starch.

Grilled Garlic Cheese Grits

Low-carb   Meatless

Grits are an everyday food here in the South. I came up with this easy recipe one day when I ran out of potatoes. It's a great alternative to a baked potato when served with grilled steak or chicken.
—Holly Bonds, Smyrna, Georgia

4 cups water
1 cup uncooked old-fashioned grits
1 teaspoon salt
1 cup (4 ounces) shredded reduced-fat cheddar cheese
1 to 2 garlic cloves, minced
1 tablespoon olive oil

In a saucepan, bring water to a boil. Slowly add the grits and salt, stirring constantly. Reduce heat; simmer, uncovered, for 40-45 minutes or until thickened, stirring occasionally. Add the cheese and garlic; stir until the cheese is melted. Pour into a 9-in. square baking dish coated with nonstick cooking spray. Cover and refrigerate for 2 to 2-1/2 hours or until firm.

Before starting the grill, coat grill rack with nonstick cooking spray. Cut grits into 3-in. squares; brush both sides with oil. Grill, covered, over medium heat for 4-6 minutes on each side or until lightly browned. **Yield:** 9 servings.

Nutritional Analysis: One piece equals 108 calories, 4 g fat (2 g saturated fat), 7 mg cholesterol, 337 mg sodium, 14 g carbohydrate, trace fiber, 5 g protein.
Diabetic Exchanges: 1 starch, 1/2 fat.

Onion-Basil Grilled Vegetables

Meatless

(Pictured below)

As the caretaker for a private home, I sometimes cook for the young family who lives there. Everyone likes these grilled vegetables.
—Jan Oeffler, Danbury, Wisconsin

3 medium ears fresh corn, cut into 3 pieces
1 pound medium red potatoes, quartered
1 cup fresh baby carrots
1 large green pepper, cut into 1-inch pieces
1 large sweet red pepper, cut into 1-inch pieces
1 envelope onion soup mix
3 tablespoons minced fresh basil *or* 1 tablespoon dried basil
1 tablespoon olive oil
1/4 teaspoon pepper
1 tablespoon butter

In a large bowl, combine the first nine ingredients. Toss to coat. Place on a double thickness of heavy-duty foil (about 28 in. x 18 in.). Dot with butter. Fold foil around the vegetable mixture and seal tightly. Grill, covered, over medium heat for 25-30 minutes or until potatoes are tender, turning once. **Yield:** 6 servings.

Nutritional Analysis: One serving (1-1/2 cups) equals 164 calories, 5 g fat (2 g saturated fat), 5 mg cholesterol, 453 mg sodium, 28 g carbohydrate, 4 g fiber, 4 g protein.
Diabetic Exchanges: 1-1/2 starch, 1 vegetable, 1 fat.

 ## Rooting for Rutabagas

IT MAY look like an oversized turnip, but the rutabaga is a deliciously different root vegetable. Thought to be a cross between a turnip and a wild cabbage, the rutabaga is a relative newcomer to the veggie world. Records of it date back to the 17th century.

Because the rutabaga thrives in cold climates, it became popular in Scandinavia, especially in Sweden. (The name comes from the Swedish "rotabagge", meaning round root.) Europeans still use the nickname "Swedish turnips" or "swedes".

When shopping for rutabagas, select roots that are smooth-skinned, unblemished, heavy, firm and not spongy. Those measuring about 4 inches in diameter, with a deep yellow flesh, have the sweetest flavor.

Lemon Carrots and Rutabaga

Low-carb   Low-sodium   Meatless

Ever since I found this recipe in a newspaper, it's become a side dish staple at my house. It's colorful and tasty and special enough to serve to company.
—Bernice Larsen, Gretna, Nebraska

4 medium carrots, cut into 3-inch julienne strips (about 2 cups)
1 small rutabaga (10 ounces), peeled and cut into 3-inch julienne strips (about 2 cups)
1/2 cup water
2 tablespoons butter
1 tablespoon brown sugar
1 tablespoon lemon juice
1/2 teaspoon grated lemon peel
1/4 teaspoon dill weed

In a saucepan, combine carrots, rutabaga and water. Bring to a boil. Cover and cook over medium heat for 13-15 minutes.

Meanwhile, in a small saucepan, combine remaining ingredients; cook, uncovered, over medium heat for 2-3 minutes or until butter is melted. Drain vegetables; add to butter mixture. Cook 3-4 minutes longer or until vegetables are glazed, stirring occasionally. **Yield:** 5 servings.

Nutritional Analysis: One serving (3/4 cup) equals 93 calories, 5 g fat (3 g saturated fat), 12 mg cholesterol, 77 mg sodium, 13 g carbohydrate, 3 g fiber, 1 g protein.
Diabetic Exchanges: 2 vegetable, 1 fat.

Savory Herb Rice

Low-fat **Meatless**

I got this recipe from the mother of one of my college roommates many years ago and filed it away. I found it one night by accident and made it for dinner. Now it's a staple that I often serve with chicken, beef, pork...or even fish.
—Suzy Mercker, Lawrenceville, Georgia

2 cups water
1 tablespoon butter
1 teaspoon chicken *or* vegetable bouillon granules
1 cup uncooked long grain rice
2 tablespoons reduced-sodium soy sauce
1 teaspoon dried minced onion
1/2 teaspoon onion powder
1/4 teaspoon dried basil
1/4 teaspoon dried marjoram
1/4 teaspoon dried thyme

In a large saucepan, combine the water, butter and bouillon. Bring to a boil. Add remaining ingredients. Reduce heat; cover and simmer for about 15 minutes or until liquid is absorbed and rice is tender. **Yield:** 5 servings.

Nutritional Analysis: One serving (2/3 cup) equals 178 calories, 3 g fat (2 g saturated fat), 6 mg cholesterol, 490 mg sodium, 33 g carbohydrate, 1 g fiber, 4 g protein.
Diabetic Exchanges: 2 starch, 1/2 fat.

Greek Vegetable Bake

Low-fat **Meatless**

My mom got the recipe for this zucchini and green bean casserole from an authentic Greek cook years ago. The ingredients originally included olive oil, but we omitted it...and it tastes even better!
—Angela Berry, Coon Rapids, Minnesota

1 pound fresh green beans, trimmed
1 pound zucchini, cut into 1/4-inch slices
3 small carrots, cut into 1/4-inch slices
1 large potato, peeled, cut into 1/4-inch slices and quartered
1 medium onion, chopped
1 celery rib, thinly sliced
1 can (8 ounces) tomato sauce
2 tablespoons minced fresh parsley
1 teaspoon dried oregano
1/2 teaspoon seasoned salt
1/2 teaspoon garlic salt
1/2 teaspoon lemon-pepper seasoning
1/2 teaspoon pepper

In a 2-qt. baking dish coated with nonstick cooking spray, layer half of beans, zucchini, carrots, potato, onion and celery. Top with half of tomato sauce. Combine the seasonings and sprinkle half over tomato sauce. Repeat layers (dish will be full). Cover and bake at 350° for 70-80 minutes or until vegetables are tender. **Yield:** 6 servings.

Nutritional Analysis: One serving (1 cup) equals 75 calories, trace fat (trace saturated fat), 0 cholesterol, 564 mg sodium, 18 g carbohydrate, 5 g fiber, 4 g protein.
Diabetic Exchanges: 2 vegetable, 1/2 starch.

Light Sweet Potato Casserole

Low-fat **Meatless**

(Pictured below)

You're bound to have sweet potato success when you whip up this casserole recipe from our Test Kitchen. With its rich color, creamy texture and irresistible taste, it is sure to be a popular stop on your holiday buffet table.

3 pounds sweet potatoes, peeled and cut into chunks
1/3 cup fat-free milk
1/4 cup egg substitute
2 tablespoons brown sugar
1/2 teaspoon salt
1/2 teaspoon vanilla extract
1/4 teaspoon ground cinnamon

Place sweet potatoes in a large saucepan or Dutch oven; cover with water. Bring to a boil. Reduce heat; cover and cook for 25-30 minutes or until tender. Drain.

In a large mixing bowl, beat the sweet potatoes, milk, egg substitute, brown sugar, salt and vanilla until smooth. Transfer to a 1-1/2-qt. baking dish coated with nonstick cooking spray. Sprinkle with cinnamon. Bake, uncovered, at 350° for 25-30 minutes or until heated though. **Yield:** 8 servings.

Nutritional Analysis: One serving (2/3 cup) equals 160 calories, trace fat (trace saturated fat), trace cholesterol, 187 mg sodium, 36 g carbohydrate, 2 g fiber, 3 g protein.
Diabetic Exchange: 2 starch.

*way to get my family to eat cooked cabbage...
hidden in Grandma's potatoes!*
—Marie Pagel, Lena, Wisconsin

6 medium potatoes, peeled and cubed
  (about 2-1/2 pounds)
2 cups chopped cabbage
1 large onion, chopped
1 tablespoon butter
1/2 teaspoon salt
1/8 teaspoon pepper

Place potatoes in a large saucepan or Dutch oven; cover with water. Bring to a boil. Cover and cook over medium heat for 8-10 minutes or until potatoes are almost tender. Add cabbage and onion. Cover and simmer for 5-6 minutes or until cabbage is tender. Drain well. Mash with butter, salt and pepper. **Yield:** 7 servings.

Nutritional Analysis: One serving (2/3 cup) equals 148 calories, 2 g fat (1 g saturated fat), 4 mg cholesterol, 195 mg sodium, 31 g carbohydrate, 3 g fiber, 3 g protein.
Diabetic Exchange: 2 starch.

Marinated Green Beans

Low-carb Low-fat **Meatless**

(Pictured above)

For many years, I made this dish with asparagus. At Thanksgiving, green beans were all I had, so I used them instead. Everyone enjoyed it.
—Phy Bresse, Lumberton, North Carolina

2 cups water
1 pound fresh green beans
2 tablespoons reduced-sodium soy sauce
1 tablespoon cider vinegar
1 teaspoon olive oil
1 teaspoon sesame oil
1/4 teaspoon ground ginger
1/4 teaspoon Chinese five-spice powder
Dash pepper
1 tablespoon sesame seeds, toasted

In a large saucepan, bring water to a boil. Add beans; cover and boil for 3-5 minutes or until crisp-tender. Drain and immediately place beans in ice water. Drain and pat dry. Place in a large bowl.

In a small bowl, whisk together the soy sauce, vinegar, olive oil, sesame oil, ginger, five-spice powder and pepper. Pour over beans; toss to coat. Cover and refrigerate for 1 hour or until chilled. Sprinkle with sesame seeds just before serving. **Yield:** 6 servings.

Nutritional Analysis: One serving (3/4 cup) equals 49 calories, 2 g fat (trace saturated fat), 0 cholesterol, 206 mg sodium, 6 g carbohydrate, 3 g fiber, 2 g protein.
Diabetic Exchanges: 1 vegetable, 1/2 fat.

Colcannon Irish Potatoes

Low-fat **Meatless**

My mother came from Ireland as a teen and brought this comforting recipe with her. I find that it's a great

Wild Rice Pilaf

Low-fat **Meatless**

Apricots and wild rice are pleasing companions in this easy pilaf our Test Kitchen staff created. The bits of dried fruit bring sweetness to this side dish that goes great with fish, seafood and poultry.

1/4 cup chopped onion
2 teaspoons canola oil
1 package (6 ounces) long grain and wild rice mix
2-1/3 cups water
1-1/2 cups frozen corn, thawed
1 green onion, thinly sliced
1/2 cup dried apricots, chopped
2 tablespoons minced fresh parsley
2 tablespoons orange juice
2 teaspoons balsamic vinegar
1/2 teaspoon salt
1/8 teaspoon pepper

In a saucepan, saute onion in oil until tender. Add rice mix and water; bring to a boil. Reduce heat; cover and simmer for 25-30 minutes or until liquid is absorbed. Remove from the heat; stir in the remaining ingredients. Cover and let stand for 5 minutes. **Yield:** 8 servings.

Nutritional Analysis: One serving (1/2 cup) equals 139 calories, 2 g fat (trace saturated fat), 0 cholesterol, 383 mg sodium, 29 g carbohydrate, 2 g fiber, 4 g protein.
Diabetic Exchanges: 1-1/2 starch, 1/2 fruit.

Dijon Sauce for Veggies

Low-carb *Low-fat* **Meatless**

(Pictured above)

Here's a deliciously different way to serve good-for-you vegetables to your family. The creamy trimmed-down sauce with its subtle Dijon flavor drapes nicely over cauliflower, carrots or most any vegetable. I like to blanch broccoli florets and toss them with the sauce.
—Jan Allen, Thermopolis, Wyoming

  1/2 cup finely chopped onion
    2 garlic cloves, minced
    1 teaspoon olive oil
2-1/2 cups fat-free milk
    3 tablespoons cornstarch
  1/4 cup vegetable broth
    2 ounces reduced-fat cream cheese, cubed
    2 tablespoons Dijon mustard
  1/4 teaspoon salt
  1/8 teaspoon pepper
Dash ground nutmeg

In a small nonstick saucepan, saute the onion and garlic in oil until tender; stir in milk. Combine cornstarch and broth until smooth; stir into saucepan. Bring to a boil; cook and stir for 1 minute or until thickened.

Remove from the heat. Whisk in cream cheese until melted. Stir in the mustard, salt, pepper and nutmeg. Serve with vegetables. **Yield:** 2-1/2 cups.

Nutritional Analysis: One serving (1/4 cup) equals 58 calories, 2 g fat (1 g saturated fat), 6 mg cholesterol, 212 mg sodium, 7 g carbohydrate, trace fiber, 3 g protein.
Diabetic Exchanges: 1/2 starch, 1/2 fat.

Sweet 'n' Sour Beans

Low-fat

This bean dish is surprisingly low in fat, even with the bacon in it. I adapted it from a higher-calorie version that used ground beef. This is great served as a side dish with grilled meats...or over rice as a main dish.
—Carla Specht, Annawan, Illinois

1/2 cup packed brown sugar
1/4 cup cider vinegar
  1 teaspoon garlic powder
  1 teaspoon ground mustard
  2 large onions, sliced and separated into rings
  1 can (28 ounces) baked beans
  1 can (16 ounces) kidney beans, rinsed and drained
  1 can (15-1/4 ounces) lima beans, rinsed and drained
  4 bacon strips, cooked and crumbled

In a large nonstick skillet, combine the brown sugar, cider vinegar, garlic powder and mustard; bring to a boil. Stir in onions. Reduce heat; simmer, uncovered, for 15-20 minutes or until onions are tender. Add the beans and bacon.

Pour into a 2-qt. baking dish coated with nonstick cooking spray. Cover and bake at 350° for 40-45 minutes or until heated through. **Yield:** 8 servings.

Nutritional Analysis: One serving (2/3 cup) equals 265 calories, 2 g fat (1 g saturated fat), 3 mg cholesterol, 710 mg sodium, 53 g carbohydrate, 10 g fiber, 12 g protein.

Corn Bread Dressing

Meatless

A traditional turkey dinner wouldn't be the same without this old-fashioned dressing. It's jam-packed with a blend of splendid seasonings.
—Drew Weeks, Edisto Island, South Carolina

    1 cup all-purpose flour
    1 cup cornmeal
    2 tablespoons sugar
    1 tablespoon baking powder
  1/2 teaspoon salt
  2/3 cup water
  1/3 cup fat-free milk
  1/4 cup egg substitute
    2 tablespoons canola oil
DRESSING:
   10 slices bread, toasted and cubed
    3 cups chopped celery
1-1/3 cups chopped onion
    1 teaspoon canola oil
    3 teaspoons reduced-sodium chicken *or* vegetable bouillon granules
  1/4 cup boiling water
    1 can (14-1/2 ounces) reduced-sodium chicken broth *or* vegetable broth
  1/2 cup egg substitute

2 teaspoons dried parsley flakes
1-1/2 teaspoons rubbed sage
1 teaspoon *each* poultry seasoning, dried basil
and rosemary, crushed
1/2 teaspoon *each* salt and dried thyme

For corn bread, in a bowl, combine the flour, cornmeal, sugar, baking powder and salt. In a small bowl, combine the water, milk, egg substitute and oil. Stir into flour mixture just until blended. Transfer to an 8-in. square baking dish coated with nonstick cooking spray. Bake at 375° for 15-20 minutes or until a toothpick inserted near the center comes out clean. Cool and crumble into a large bowl.

For stuffing, stir bread cubes into corn bread crumbs. In a nonstick skillet coated with nonstick cooking spray, cook celery and onion in oil for about 6 minutes or until tender. Stir into corn bread mixture. In a small bowl, dissolve bouillon in water. In a large bowl, combine the broth, egg substitute, seasonings and bouillon mixture. Pour over corn bread mixture; toss to coat evenly.

Transfer to a 13-in. x 9-in. x 2-in. baking pan coated with nonstick cooking spray. Cover and bake at 350° for 20 minutes. Uncover; bake 25-30 minutes longer or until lightly browned. **Yield:** 13 servings.

Nutritional Analysis: One serving (3/4 cup) equals 178 calories, 4 g fat (trace saturated fat), trace cholesterol, 628 mg sodium, 31 g carbohydrate, 2 g fiber, 6 g protein.
Diabetic Exchange: 2 starch.

Baked Butternut Squash

Meatless

Take advantage of fabulous fall produce by baking up this scrumptious side dish. Lightly seasoned with cinnamon, nutmeg and brown sugar, the squash offers plenty of harvest-fresh flavor.
—Heidi Vawdrey, Riverton, Utah

1 butternut squash (2 pounds)
2 tablespoons butter, melted
1/4 teaspoon salt
1/8 teaspoon ground cinnamon
1/8 teaspoon ground nutmeg
1/8 teaspoon pepper
6 teaspoons brown sugar, *divided*

Cut squash in half lengthwise; discard seeds. Brush squash halves with butter. Combine the salt, cinnamon, nutmeg and pepper; sprinkle over squash halves. Place 2 teaspoons brown sugar in each half. Sprinkle remaining brown sugar over cut sides of squash.

Place in an 11-in. x 7-in. x 2-in. baking dish coated with nonstick cooking spray. Cover and bake at 350° for 40 minutes. Uncover; bake 15-25 minutes longer until squash is tender. **Yield:** 6 servings.

Nutritional Analysis: One serving (2/3 cup cooked squash) equals 106 calories, 4 g fat (2 g saturated fat), 10 mg cholesterol, 144 mg sodium, 19 g carbohydrate, 4 g fiber, 1 g protein.
Diabetic Exchanges: 1 starch, 1/2 fat.

Vegetable Brown Rice

Meatless

(Pictured below)

Loaded with carrots, onions and peas, this rice makes a terrific side dish, but it can even stand on its own as a light main course. Raisins offer a slight sweetness, and pecans add a little crunch.
—Denith Hull, Bethany, Oklahoma

2 cups water
1 cup uncooked brown rice
1/2 teaspoon dried basil
2 medium carrots, peeled and cut into thin 1-inch strips
1 cup chopped onion
9 green onions, cut into 1-inch strips
1/2 cup raisins
2 tablespoons olive oil
1 package (10 ounces) frozen peas, thawed
1 teaspoon salt
1 cup pecan halves, toasted

In a small saucepan, bring water to a boil. Stir in rice and basil. Reduce heat to medium-low; cover and simmer for 30-35 minutes or until rice is tender and water is absorbed.

In a large nonstick skillet, stir-fry the carrots, onion, green onions and raisins in hot oil for 5-7 minutes or until vegetables are lightly browned. Add the peas and salt. Cook for 1 minute or until vegetables are tender. Stir in pecans and rice; heat through. **Yield:** 9 servings.

Nutritional Analysis: One serving (3/4 cup) equals 242 calories, 11 g fat (1 g saturated fat), 0 cholesterol, 313 mg sodium, 32 g carbohydrate, 5 g fiber, 5 g protein.
Diabetic Exchanges: 2 fat, 1-1/2 starch, 1 vegetable, 1/2 fruit.

Green Beans with Bacon

Low-carb Low-fat

*I give green beans, a favorite everyday vegetable,
a lift with bacon and onion. A dash of
nutmeg adds interest to the simple sauce.
I fix this much-requested side dish often.*
—*Linda Rock, Stratford, Wisconsin*

> 3 cups fresh *or* frozen cut green beans
> 2 bacon strips, diced
> 1/4 cup chopped onion
> 1/4 cup chopped green pepper
> 1-1/2 teaspoons all-purpose flour
> 1/2 cup fat-free milk
> 1/4 teaspoon salt
> Dash white pepper
> Dash ground nutmeg

Place beans in a saucepan and cover with water; bring to
a boil. Cook, uncovered, for 8-10 minutes or until tender.
Meanwhile, in a nonstick skillet, cook bacon over medium
heat until crisp. Remove with a slotted spoon to paper towels. Drain, reserving 1 teaspoon drippings. In the drippings, saute onion and green pepper until tender.

Drain beans; set aside. In a small bowl, combine flour
and milk until smooth; stir into the onion mixture. Add salt,
pepper and nutmeg. Bring to a boil; cook and stir for 2
minutes or until thickened. Add the beans; heat through.
Yield: 4 servings.

*Nutritional Analysis: One serving (3/4 cup) equals 84 calo-
ries, 3 g fat (1 g saturated fat), 4 mg cholesterol, 223 mg sodium,
12 g carbohydrate, 3 g fiber, 4 g protein.*
Diabetic Exchanges: 2 vegetable, 1/2 fat.

the heat. Stir in peas. Cover and let stand for about 5 minutes or until heated through and liquid is absorbed. Stir in
parsley. **Yield:** 6 servings.

*Nutritional Analysis: One serving (3/4 cup) equals 144 calo-
ries, trace fat (trace saturated fat), 0 cholesterol, 294 mg sodium,
30 g carbohydrate, 1 g fiber, 4 g protein.*
Diabetic Exchanges: 1-1/2 starch, 1 vegetable.

Confetti Rice

Low-fat

(Pictured above right)

*I know you'll agree that this is a very good
low-fat recipe. Diced sweet red and green pepper—
along with green peas and fresh parsley—
add bright color to the simple rice dish.*
—*Dorothy Bayes, Sardis, Ohio*

> 1 can (14-1/2 ounces) reduced-sodium chicken
> broth
> 1 cup uncooked long grain rice
> 1/4 cup water
> 1/4 teaspoon salt
> 1/4 teaspoon dried oregano
> 1/8 teaspoon pepper
> 1/2 cup diced sweet red pepper
> 1/2 cup diced green pepper
> 1/2 cup frozen green peas, thawed
> 2 tablespoons minced fresh parsley

In a large saucepan, combine the first six ingredients. Bring
to a boil. Stir in sweet peppers. Reduce heat; cover and simmer for 15-20 minutes or until rice is tender. Remove from

French Herb Seasoning

Low-carb Low-fat Low-sodium

*This versatile seasoning will wake up the flavor in both
meat and vegetables. This zesty mix is so simple to make.
I always have a jar on hand. I especially like it because
it's salt-free, yet it gives food a delicious perk.*
—*Joan Hallford, North Richland Hills, Texas*

> 3 tablespoons *each* dried savory, marjoram and
> thyme
> 1 teaspoon dried basil
> 1 teaspoon dried rosemary, crushed
> 1/2 teaspoon rubbed sage
> 1/2 teaspoon fennel seed, crushed

In a small bowl, combine all ingredients. Store in an airtight container for up to 6 months. **Yield:** 2/3 cup.

*Nutritional Analysis: One serving (1 teaspoon) equals 3 calo-
ries, trace fat (0 saturated fat), 0 cholesterol, trace sodium, 1 g carbohydrate, trace fiber, trace protein.*
Diabetic Exchange: Free food.

Favorite Recipe Made Lighter

POTATOES add comforting appeal to any meal…but recipes for this popular veggie are often laden with fat. That was the case with Sour Cream Potatoes from Dona Dickie of Livermore, California.

To reduce the fat, our home economists swapped the 2 cups of regular sour cream with 1-1/2 cups of the reduced-fat variety and reduced the amount of butter from 1/4 cup to 2 tablespoons. They also cut back on the full-fat cheddar cheese.

The high-sodium celery soup had to go. Our staff replaced it by making a white sauce with fat-free milk and cooking fresh celery and onion with the potatoes. A sprinkling of celery seed further enhanced the flavor. Although a teaspoon of salt was added to the makeover recipe, the overall sodium content was still reduced by 11%.

Makeover Sour Cream Potatoes has a whopping 72% less fat, two-thirds less saturated fat and 44% fewer calories.

Sour Cream Potatoes

Meatless

2-1/2 pounds potatoes, peeled and cubed
3-1/2 cups (14 ounces) shredded cheddar
   cheese, *divided*
   2 cups (16 ounces) sour cream
   1 can (10-3/4 ounces) condensed cream of
   celery soup, undiluted
1/4 cup butter
1/4 cup minced chives, *divided*

Place potatoes in a saucepan; cover with water. Cover and bring to a boil; cook until just tender, about 5 minutes. Drain well. In a bowl, combine 3 cups cheese, sour cream, soup, butter and 3 tablespoons chives. Add potatoes; stir gently until potatoes are coated.

Transfer to a greased 2-1/2-qt. baking dish. Cover and bake at 350° for 35-40 minutes or until heated through. Sprinkle with remaining cheese; bake 2-3 minutes longer or until cheese is melted. Sprinkle with remaining chives. **Yield:** 10 servings.

Nutritional Analysis: One serving (3/4 cup) equals 420 calories, 29 g fat (18 g saturated fat), 78 mg cholesterol, 552 mg sodium, 28 g carbohydrate, 2 g fiber, 14 g protein.

Makeover Sour Cream Potatoes

Meatless

(Pictured at right and on page 75)

2-1/2 pounds potatoes, peeled and cubed
1/2 cup finely chopped celery
1/4 cup finely chopped onion
   2 tablespoons butter
1/4 cup all-purpose flour
   1 teaspoon salt
1/4 teaspoon ground celery seed
1/4 teaspoon pepper
   1 cup fat-free milk
1-1/2 cups reduced-fat sour cream
   1 cup (4 ounces) shredded reduced-fat
   cheddar cheese, *divided*
   2 ounces cubed reduced-fat process cheese
   (Velveeta)
   4 tablespoons minced chives, *divided*

Place potatoes, celery and onion in a large saucepan; cover with water. Cover and bring to a boil; cook until just tender, about 5 minutes. Drain well. Meanwhile, melt butter in a small saucepan. Stir in the flour, salt, ground celery seed and pepper until smooth. Gradually stir in milk. Bring to a boil; cook and stir for 2 minutes or until thickened.

Transfer sauce to a large bowl; stir in the sour cream, 1/2 cup cheddar cheese, process cheese and 3 tablespoons chives. Add potato mixture; stir gently until coated.

Transfer to a 2-1/2-qt. baking dish coated with nonstick cooking spray. Cover and bake at 350° for 35-40 minutes or until heated through. Sprinkle with remaining cheese; cover and let stand for 5 minutes or until cheese is melted. Sprinkle with remaining chives. **Yield:** 10 servings.

Nutritional Analysis: One serving (3/4 cup) equals 237 calories, 8 g fat (6 g saturated fat), 29 mg cholesterol, 492 mg sodium, 31 g carbohydrate, 2 g fiber, 10 g protein.
Diabetic Exchanges: 2 starch, 1 lean meat, 1/2 fat.

Zucchini in Sour Cream Sauce

Low-carb Low-fat

Someone shared this zucchini recipe with me years ago. Light and refreshing, it complements any meat you serve it with. Reduced-fat sour cream helps keep the calorie count down, while dill boosts the flavor. Try the sauce over chicken or grilled fish.
—Sandi Laskowski, Rapid City, South Dakota

```
3 cups cubed unpeeled zucchini
1/4 cup water
2 tablespoons chopped onion
1/2 teaspoon salt
1/2 teaspoon chicken bouillon granules
1/4 teaspoon dill weed
1 tablespoon butter
1 teaspoon sugar
1/2 teaspoon lemon juice
1/4 cup reduced-fat sour cream
1 tablespoon all-purpose flour
```

In a saucepan, combine the zucchini, water, onion, salt, bouillon and dill. Bring to a boil. Reduce heat; cover and simmer for 5 minutes or until zucchini is tender. Remove from heat and stir in the butter, sugar and lemon juice. Combine sour cream and flour until smooth. Gradually add to saucepan. Cook and stir over low heat for 5-7 minutes or until thickened. **Yield:** 6 servings.

Nutritional Analysis: One serving (1/4 cup) equals 50 calories, 3 g fat (2 g saturated fat), 9 mg cholesterol, 320 mg sodium, 5 g carbohydrate, 1 g fiber, 2 g protein.
Diabetic Exchanges: *1 vegetable, 1/2 fat.*

Exceptional Eggplant

EGGPLANT is available all year, but the peak season is from July to October.

The best eggplant is firm, smooth-skinned and heavy for its size…and its flesh springs back when lightly pressed. Avoid eggplant with soft or brown spots.

Eggplant is low in calories, fat-free, sodium-free and cholesterol-free. It is an excellent source of fiber and a fairly good source of potassium and folic acid.

End-of-the-Garden Casserole

Meatless

The conclusion of the growing season is just the beginning of this garden-fresh hot dish. Packed with potatoes, onions, eggplant, tomatoes, zucchini and more, there's a harvest of vitamins and minerals in every forkful. The recipe makes a lot, so you can share the bounty.
—Kathy Crow, Payson, Arizona

```
1 pound medium potatoes, thinly sliced
1 medium zucchini, thinly sliced
1/2 pound medium onions, thinly sliced
1 small eggplant, peeled and sliced
1 pound medium tomatoes, sliced
1-1/2 cups (6 ounces) shredded part-skim mozzarella
   cheese
1/4 cup grated Parmesan cheese
1/2 teaspoon dried basil
1/2 teaspoon salt
1/4 teaspoon pepper
1/4 cup water
```

Layer half of the first 10 ingredients in a 3-qt. baking dish coated with nonstick cooking spray. Repeat layers. Pour water over the top. Cover and bake at 375° for 60-75 minutes or until tender. Uncover; bake 5 minutes longer or until lightly browned. **Yield:** 8 servings.

Nutritional Analysis: One serving (3/4 cup) equals 140 calories, 5 g fat (3 g saturated fat), 15 mg cholesterol, 311 mg sodium, 18 g carbohydrate, 3 g fiber, 9 g protein.
Diabetic Exchanges: *2 vegetable, 1 lean meat, 1/2 starch.*

Almond Vegetable Stir-Fry

Low-carb Meatless

(Pictured below)

While broccoli florets and chunks of red pepper give this dish plenty of color, it's the fresh gingerroot, garlic, soy sauce and sesame oil that round out the flavor.
—Mary Relyea, Canastota, New York

```
1 teaspoon cornstarch
1 teaspoon sugar
3 tablespoons cold water
```

2 tablespoons reduced-sodium soy sauce
1 teaspoon sesame oil
4 cups fresh broccoli florets
2 tablespoons canola oil
1 large sweet red pepper, cut into 1-inch chunks
1 small onion, cut into thin wedges
2 garlic cloves, minced
1 tablespoon minced fresh gingerroot
1/4 cup slivered almonds, toasted

In a small bowl, combine the cornstarch and sugar. Stir in the water, soy sauce and sesame oil until smooth; set aside. In a large nonstick wok or skillet, stir-fry broccoli in hot oil for 3 minutes. Add the pepper, onion, garlic and ginger; stir-fry for 2 minutes. Reduce heat; stir the soy sauce mixture. Stir into vegetables along with nuts. Cook and stir for 2 minutes or until thickened. **Yield:** 5 servings.

Nutritional Analysis: One serving (3/4 cup) equals 143 calories, 10 g fat (1 g saturated fat), 0 cholesterol, 260 mg sodium, 11 g carbohydrate, 3 g fiber, 4 g protein.
Diabetic Exchanges: 2 vegetable, 2 fat.

Mixed Rice and Barley Bake

Low-fat **Meatless**

The mellow flavor of the wholesome grains in this nutritious casserole is enhanced by garlic, onion and thyme. This hearty easy-to-prepare side dish pairs well with meat, fish or poultry. I make it often for my family and for company. Everyone enjoys it.
—Marion Bengson, New Brighton, Minnesota

1/3 cup uncooked wild rice
1/3 cup uncooked long grain brown rice
1/3 cup uncooked pearl barley
1 garlic clove, minced
1 tablespoon butter
1 large sweet onion, chopped
8 ounces fresh mushrooms, sliced
3 cups reduced-sodium beef broth *or* vegetable broth
2 teaspoons dried thyme
3/4 teaspoon salt
1/4 teaspoon pepper
2 tablespoons minced fresh parsley

Rinse wild rice with hot water; drain. Combine the wild rice, brown rice and barley. In a saucepan, saute garlic in butter. Add rice mixture; saute for 2-3 minutes. Add the onion, mushrooms, broth, thyme, salt and pepper. Bring to a boil.

Transfer to a 2-qt. baking dish coated with nonstick cooking spray. Cover and bake at 350° for 70 minutes or until rice and barley are tender. Uncover; bake 5-10 minutes longer or until liquid is absorbed. Stir in parsley. **Yield:** 7 servings.

Nutritional Analysis: One serving (2/3 cup) equals 129 calories, 2 g fat (1 g saturated fat), 4 mg cholesterol, 539 mg sodium, 23 g carbohydrate, 3 g fiber, 5 g protein.
Diabetic Exchange: 1-1/2 starch.

Creamy Skillet Potatoes

Low-fat **Meatless**

(Pictured above)

An envelope of ranch salad dressing mix perks up these saucy potatoes prepared on the stovetop. It's a great side dish with almost any meal.
—Denise Pritchard, Seminole, Oklahoma

7 cups cubed uncooked red potatoes
1/3 cup chopped onion
2 tablespoons all-purpose flour
1 envelope (1 ounce) ranch salad dressing mix
1/2 teaspoon dried parsley flakes
1/4 teaspoon salt
1/4 cup reduced-fat sour cream
2 cups fat-free milk

Place 1 in. of water and potatoes in a large nonstick skillet; bring to a boil. Reduce heat; cover and simmer for 10 minutes or until tender; drain. Coat skillet with nonstick cooking spray; add potatoes and onion. Cook over medium-high heat for 5-7 minutes or until golden brown.

In a saucepan, combine the flour, salad dressing mix, parsley and salt. Stir in the sour cream. Gradually add the milk, stirring until blended. Bring to a boil; cook and stir for 2 minutes or until thickened. Pour over potatoes; toss to coat. **Yield:** 8 servings.

Nutritional Analysis: One serving (3/4 cup) equals 160 calories, 1 g fat (1 g saturated fat), 5 mg cholesterol, 365 mg sodium, 32 g carbohydrate, 2 g fiber, 5 g protein.
Diabetic Exchange: 2 starch.

Baby Carrots 'n' Broccoli

Low-carb Low-sodium Meatless

(Pictured above)

My husband and I eat this quick veggie side dish at least once a week. We enjoy it with just about any main course. It's a light easy way to get extra vegetables into your diet.
—*Ally Fitzgerald, Alpharetta, Georgia*

1-1/2 cups fresh baby carrots
  4 cups fresh broccoli florets
  2 tablespoons olive oil
  1 teaspoon Nature's seasoning blend
  1 teaspoon garlic powder
1/2 teaspoon pepper

In a saucepan, bring 4 cups water to a boil; add carrots. Cover and simmer for 5 minutes; drain and pat dry.

In an ungreased 15-in. x 10-in. x 1-in. baking pan, combine the carrots with remaining ingredients. Bake, uncovered, at 425° for 7-9 minutes or until vegetables are crisp-tender, stirring once. **Yield:** 4 servings.

Editor's Note: This recipe was tested with Morton's Nature's Seasons Seasoning Blend.

Nutritional Analysis: One serving (3/4 cup) equals 98 calories, 7 g fat (1 g saturated fat), 0 cholesterol, 37 mg sodium, 8 g carbohydrate, 3 g fiber, 2 g protein.
Diabetic Exchanges: 1 vegetable, 1 fat.

Fish Seasoning

Low-carb Low-fat Low-sodium

This mild blend gives fish a lift but also adds interest to other meats and vegetables. A neighbor whose husband was on a no-salt diet gave me this recipe over 20 years ago.
—*Kayleen Nichols, Sterling, Virginia*

2 tablespoons dried basil
2 tablespoons dill weed
2 tablespoons onion powder
1 tablespoon garlic powder
1 teaspoon celery seed
1 teaspoon dried oregano
1/4 teaspoon dried grated lemon peel
1/8 teaspoon pepper

In a bowl, combine all ingredients. Store in a cool dry place for up to 6 months. **Yield:** 1/3 cup.

Nutritional Analysis: One serving (1 teaspoon) equals 7 calories, trace fat (trace saturated fat), 0 cholesterol, 2 mg sodium, 2 g carbohydrate, trace fiber, trace protein.
Diabetic Exchange: Free food.

Three-Pepper Corn Pudding

Low-fat Meatless

A trio of peppers livens up this comforting side dish. I've had this recipe for many years. I lightened it up from the original by using reduced-fat sour cream and milk, plus some egg substitute. It tastes just as good...but it's much better for us!
—*Virginia Anthony, Jacksonville, Florida*

1 medium sweet red pepper, chopped
6 green onions, thinly sliced
1 tablespoon olive oil
1 can (4 ounces) chopped green chilies, drained
3 medium jalapeno peppers, seeded and chopped
2 packages (10 ounces *each*) frozen corn, thawed, *divided*
1 can (12 ounces) reduced-fat evaporated milk
1/3 cup reduced-fat sour cream
1/4 cup fat-free milk
3 egg whites
2 eggs
1/4 cup cornstarch
1 teaspoon salt
1 teaspoon ground cumin
3/4 teaspoon ground thyme

In a nonstick skillet, cook red pepper and green onions in oil until tender. Remove from the heat. Stir in the green chilies, jalapeno peppers and one package corn. Transfer to a 13-in. x 9-in. x 2-in. baking dish coated with nonstick cooking spray.

In a blender, combine the remaining ingredients and the remaining corn. Cover and process for 3 minutes or until smooth. Pour over red pepper mixture. Bake, uncovered, at 350° for 45-50 minutes or until a knife inserted near the center comes out clean. **Yield:** 12 servings.

Editor's Note: When cutting or seeding hot peppers, use rubber or plastic gloves to protect your hands. Avoid touching your face.

Nutritional Analysis: One piece equals 119 calories, 3 g fat (1 g saturated fat), 39 mg cholesterol, 298 mg sodium, 18 g carbohydrate, 2 g fiber, 6 g protein.
Diabetic Exchanges: 1 starch, 1/2 fat.

Spanish Rice

Low-fat   Meatless

This rice recipe has been in our family for years. It's handy when you're in a hurry for a side dish to complement any entree, not just Tex-Mex fare.
—Sharon Donat, Kalispell, Montana

1 can (14-1/2 ounces) vegetable broth
1 can (14-1/2 ounces) stewed tomatoes
1 cup uncooked long grain rice
1 teaspoon olive oil
1 teaspoon chili powder
1/4 teaspoon dried oregano
1/4 teaspoon garlic salt

In a large saucepan, combine all ingredients. Bring to a boil. Reduce heat; cover and simmer for 20-25 minutes or until rice is tender and liquid is absorbed. **Yield:** 6 servings.

Nutritional Analysis: One serving (2/3 cup) equals 156 calories, 1 g fat (trace saturated fat), 0 cholesterol, 350 mg sodium, 32 g carbohydrate, 1 g fiber, 4 g protein.
Diabetic Exchange: 2 starch.

Sesame Seed Citrus Noodles

Low-fat   Meatless

(Pictured below)

I make this easy but elegant weeknight recipe often. The noodles have a wonderful citrus tang with a hint of basil and a bit of crunch from the toasted sesame seeds.
—Trisha Kruse, Boise, Idaho

4 cups wide no-yolk noodles
2 tablespoons chopped fresh basil
   or 2 teaspoons dried basil
4-1/2 teaspoons butter, melted

1 tablespoon lemon juice
1/2 teaspoon salt
1/2 teaspoon grated lemon peel
1/2 teaspoon grated orange peel
1-1/2 teaspoons sesame seeds, toasted

Cook noodles according to package directions. Drain, reserving 1/2 cup cooking water. Return noodles to pan. Add the basil, butter, lemon juice, salt and lemon and orange peels. Toss to coat, adding reserved cooking liquid if needed to moisten noodles. Sprinkle with sesame seeds. **Yield:** 6 servings.

Nutritional Analysis: One serving (2/3 cup) equals 136 calories, 3 g fat (2 g saturated fat), 8 mg cholesterol, 241 mg sodium, 21 g carbohydrate, 2 g fiber, 4 g protein.
Diabetic Exchanges: 1-1/2 starch, 1/2 fat.

Maple Barbecue Sauce

Low-carb   Low-fat

Unlike many barbecue sauces, this recipe doesn't use ketchup, which typically contains sugar. The savory sauce, made with sugar-free maple-flavored syrup, gives unbelievable flavor to pork, chicken and spareribs.
—Debbie Purdue, Westland, Michigan

2 cups water
1 can (8 ounces) tomato sauce
1 large onion, chopped
1/4 cup balsamic vinegar
1/4 cup Worcestershire sauce
1 tablespoon chili powder
2 teaspoons paprika
1 teaspoon ground mustard
1 teaspoon black pepper
1/2 teaspoon ground cinnamon
1/4 teaspoon salt
1/8 teaspoon ground cloves
1/2 cup sugar-free maple-flavored syrup

In a large saucepan, combine the first 12 ingredients. Bring to a boil. Reduce heat; simmer, uncovered, for 30 minutes or until the onion is tender. Stir in the syrup; cook until heated through. Store in an airtight container in the refrigerator for up to 3 weeks. Stir before using. **Yield:** 3-1/2 cups.

Nutritional Analysis: One serving (1/4 cup) equals 23 calories, trace fat (trace saturated fat), 0 cholesterol, 185 mg sodium, 6 g carbohydrate, 1 g fiber, 1 g protein.
Diabetic Exchange: 1/2 starch.

Lemony Herbed Rice

Low-fat Meatless

(Pictured above)

I substituted reduced-sodium chicken broth for the rich chicken stock that was originally called for in this recipe. It's a great side dish to serve with grilled fish or chicken for a tasty low-fat meal.
— *Connie Rank-Smith, Sherwood, Wisconsin*

  **3 cups reduced-sodium chicken broth *or*
    vegetable broth**
1-1/3 cups uncooked long grain rice
  **1 can (4-1/2 ounces) chopped green chilies,
    drained**
  3/4 teaspoon salt
  **1 tablespoon *each* minced fresh parsley, cilantro
    and chives**
  1/2 teaspoon grated lemon peel
  1/4 teaspoon pepper

In a large saucepan, combine the broth, rice, chilies and salt; bring to a boil. Reduce heat; cover and simmer for 15-20 minutes or until rice is tender. Remove from the heat; let stand for 5 minutes. Fluff with a fork and stir in the remaining ingredients. **Yield:** 7 servings.

Nutritional Analysis: *One serving (2/3 cup) equals 151 calories, trace fat (trace saturated fat), 0 cholesterol, 578 mg sodium, 32 g carbohydrate, 1 g fiber, 4 g protein.*
Diabetic Exchange: *2 starch.*

Supreme Potato Casserole

Low-fat Meatless

Cottage cheese and sour cream give a delicious creamy coating to the tender cubes of potatoes in this side dish. I usually double the recipe when serving it to guests. They never realize it's light.
— *Joy Allen, Forsyth, Georgia*

  3 medium potatoes (about 1-1/2 pounds)
  1 cup (8 ounces) fat-free cottage cheese
1/2 cup reduced-fat sour cream
  1 tablespoon fat-free milk
  1 teaspoon sugar
1/2 teaspoon salt
1/8 teaspoon garlic powder
  2 tablespoons sliced green onion
1/2 cup shredded reduced-fat cheddar cheese

Place potatoes in a large saucepan; cover with water. Cover and bring to a boil. Reduce heat; cook potatoes until tender. Drain. Peel potatoes and cut into cubes. In a blender or food processor, combine the cottage cheese, sour cream, milk, sugar, salt and garlic powder; cover and process until smooth. In a large bowl, combine potatoes, processed cottage cheese mixture and green onion.

Pour into a 1-qt. baking dish coated with nonstick cooking spray. Bake, uncovered, at 350° for 30 minutes; sprinkle with cheese. Bake 15 minutes longer or until the cheese is melted. **Yield:** 6 servings.

Nutritional Analysis: *One serving (1/2 cup) equals 158 calories, 3 g fat (2 g saturated fat), 15 mg cholesterol, 391 mg sodium, 24 g carbohydrate, 2 g fiber, 12 g protein.*
Diabetic Exchanges: *1-1/2 starch, 1 lean meat.*

Breakfast & Brunch

Breakfast boosts your energy level, which is bound to give you a sunny outlook on the day and help you perform your best. So open your family's eyes to good eating with these day-brightening recipes.

Hearty Oatmeal Pancakes (page 101)

Whole Wheat Waffles

Low-fat **Meatless**

Finding a homemade waffle recipe that's low in calories is difficult. So I modified a recipe I had, substituting fat-free plain yogurt for the oil or margarine.
—*Jessica Beare Edmunds, Kingsland, Georgia*

1/2 cup egg substitute
1-3/4 cups 1% milk
1/2 cup fat-free plain yogurt
1 tablespoon vanilla extract
1 cup all-purpose flour
1 cup whole wheat flour
Sugar substitute equivalent to 1/2 cup sugar
2 tablespoons sugar
4 teaspoons baking powder
1/4 teaspoon salt

In a mixing bowl, beat egg substitute until frothy. Add the milk, yogurt and vanilla; mix well. Combine the flours, sugar substitute, sugar, baking powder and salt; stir into milk mixture just until combined. Bake in a preheated waffle iron according to manufacturer's directions until golden brown. **Yield:** 20 waffles (4-in. x 4-in.).

Editor's Note: This recipe was tested with Splenda No Calorie Sweetener. Look for it in the baking aisle of your grocery store.

Nutritional Analysis: One serving (2 waffles) equals 137 calories, 1 g fat (trace saturated fat), 3 mg cholesterol, 207 mg sodium, 27 g carbohydrate, 2 g fiber, 6 g protein.
Diabetic Exchange: 2 starch.

Creamy Mandarin Cooler

Low-fat

(Pictured at right)

This frothy and flavorful concoction is as fast to fix as it is to refresh. It makes a delicious splash at breakfast or any other time of day. It tastes like an old-fashioned Dreamsicle.
—*Renee Richardson, Pounding Mill, Virginia*

3/4 cup fat-free milk
1/4 cup orange juice
1 can (11 ounces) reduced-sugar mandarin
 oranges, undrained

1 carton (6 ounces) fat-free reduced-sugar
 orange creme yogurt
1 package (1 ounce) sugar-free instant vanilla
 pudding mix
12 to 15 ice cubes

In a blender, combine the milk, orange juice, oranges, yogurt, pudding mix and ice cubes; cover and process for 20 seconds or until smooth. Stir if necessary. Pour into chilled glasses; serve immediately. **Yield:** 5 servings.

Nutritional Analysis: One serving (1 cup) equals 99 calories, trace fat (trace saturated fat), 2 mg cholesterol, 286 mg sodium, 21 g carbohydrate, trace fiber, 3 g protein.
Diabetic Exchanges: 1 fruit, 1/2 fat-free milk.

Early-Riser Oven Omelet

Low-carb

(Pictured at right)

Your gang will look forward to their morning meal when you prepare this omelet. Packed with tomato, broccoli, ham and reduced-fat cheese, it's an easy brunch dish to serve your bunch on Easter Sunday.
—*Wendy Fawcett, Gillam, Manitoba*

10 egg whites
5 eggs
1 cup fat-free milk
1/4 teaspoon seasoned salt
1/4 teaspoon pepper
1-1/2 cups cubed fully cooked lean ham
1 cup chopped fresh broccoli
1 cup (4 ounces) reduced-fat shredded cheddar
 cheese
1 medium tomato, seeded and chopped
3 tablespoons finely chopped onion

In a bowl, beat the egg whites, eggs, milk, seasoned salt and pepper. Pour into a 10-in. ovenproof skillet coated with nonstick cooking spray. Sprinkle with the ham, broccoli, cheese, tomato and onion. Bake, uncovered, at 350° for 30-35 minutes or until eggs are almost set. Broil 4-6 in. from the heat for 1-2 minutes or until the eggs are set and top is lightly browned. **Yield:** 6 servings.

Nutritional Analysis: One slice equals 230 calories, 10 g fat (5 g saturated fat), 210 mg cholesterol, 893 mg sodium, 6 g carbohydrate, 1 g fiber, 27 g protein.
Diabetic Exchanges: 4 lean meat, 1 vegetable.

🍎 An Apple a Day

FOR A MORNING SNACK, I cut up an unpeeled Golden Delicious apple and sprinkle it with a little cinnamon and sugar. Then I microwave it for about 3 minutes. It tastes just like hot apple pie! I have also done the same with nectarines with great results.
—*Laura Maile, Lake Park, Florida*

Nut 'n' Fruit Granola

(Pictured above)

Low-sodium   Meatless

After a friend brought this crunchy fruit-filled treat on a camping trip, I requested the recipe and lightened it up. It's great on its own, but try it over low-fat yogurt or with milk, too.
—Rachel Dandeneau, Dummer, New Hampshire

4 cups old-fashioned oats
1 cup flaked coconut
1/2 cup toasted wheat germ
1/2 cup slivered almonds
1/4 cup unsalted sunflower kernels
1/2 cup honey
1/4 cup orange juice
2 tablespoons canola oil
1-1/2 teaspoons ground cinnamon
1/4 teaspoon salt
1 teaspoon vanilla extract
1 cup dried mixed fruit
1 cup raisins
1/2 cup dried cranberries
Milk, optional

In a large bowl, combine the first five ingredients and set aside. In a small saucepan, combine the honey, orange juice, oil, cinnamon and salt; cook and stir over medium heat for 3 minutes. Remove from the heat; stir in vanilla. Pour over oat mixture; stir to coat.

Transfer to a 15-in. x 10-in. x 1-in. baking pan coated with nonstick cooking spray. Bake at 350° for 25-30 minutes or until golden brown, stirring 3-4 times. Cool on a wire rack. Place oat mixture in a large bowl. Stir in the dried fruit, raisins and cranberries. Store in an airtight container in a cool dry place for up to 2 months. Serve with milk if desired. **Yield:** 9 cups.

Nutritional Analysis: One serving (1/2 cup granola, calculated without milk) equals 237 calories, 8 g fat (2 g saturated fat), 0 cholesterol, 56 mg sodium, 40 g carbohydrate, 4 g fiber, 5 g protein.
Diabetic Exchanges: 1-1/2 starch, 1 fruit, 1 fat.

Blue Cheese Spinach Frittata

Low-carb   Meatless

When my husband and I decided to lose weight, I turned to my cookbook collection and lightened up several recipes. With its fresh spinach salad, this hearty frittata quickly became a favorite.
—Joyce Fairchild, Marina Del Rey, California

1/2 cup chopped onion
4 garlic cloves, minced
1 package (10 ounces) fresh spinach, coarsely chopped
2 cups egg substitute
1-1/2 cups (6 ounces) shredded part-skim mozzarella cheese
1 cup (4 ounces) crumbled blue cheese
2 plum tomatoes, diced
1/4 cup chopped walnuts
SALAD:
2 cups coarsely chopped fresh spinach
2 plum tomatoes, diced
1 teaspoon rice vinegar
1/2 teaspoon olive oil
1/4 teaspoon garlic salt

In a large nonstick skillet coated with nonstick cooking spray, cook onion and garlic over medium heat for 3 minutes or until tender. Remove from the skillet. Add spinach to skillet in batches, cooking for 1 minute or until wilted. Remove from the heat.

In a large bowl, beat the egg substitute until frothy. Stir in the onion mixture, cooked spinach, mozzarella, blue cheese, tomatoes and nuts. Place in a 10-in. ovenproof skillet coated with nonstick cooking spray.

Bake, uncovered, at 400° for 30-35 minutes or until a knife inserted near the center comes out clean. Combine the salad ingredients; serve with frittata. **Yield:** 6 servings.

Nutritional Analysis: One serving (1 piece with 1/3 cup salad) equals 244 calories, 14 g fat (7 g saturated fat), 33 mg cholesterol, 689 mg sodium, 9 g carbohydrate, 3 g fiber, 22 g protein.
Diabetic Exchanges: 3 lean meat, 1 vegetable, 1 fat.

Hearty Oatmeal Pancakes

Meatless

(Pictured below and on page 97)

My husband and I are trying to eat more oatmeal for its health benefits, but we get tired of having a bowlful every day. These moist and fluffy pancakes give us the good grains that we need...and still taste like a treat. We love them with turkey bacon on Sunday morning.
—Kathy Thompson, Glendale, Kentucky

1 cup quick-cooking oats
1/2 cup all-purpose flour
1/2 cup whole wheat flour
1 tablespoon sugar
1 teaspoon baking powder
1/2 teaspoon baking soda
1/4 teaspoon salt
1 egg, lightly beaten
2 cups 1% buttermilk
2 tablespoons canola oil
1 teaspoon vanilla extract
Assorted berries, optional

In a bowl, combine the first seven ingredients. In another bowl, combine the egg, buttermilk, oil and vanilla; mix well. Stir into the dry ingredients just until moistened.

Pour batter by 1/4 cupful onto a hot griddle that has been coated with nonstick cooking spray. Turn when bubbles form on top; cook until the second side is golden brown. Serve with berries if desired. **Yield:** 4 servings.

Nutritional Analysis: One serving (3 pancakes, calculated without berries) equals 328 calories, 11 g fat (2 g saturated fat), 58 mg cholesterol, 509 mg sodium, 45 g carbohydrate, 4 g fiber, 12 g protein.
Diabetic Exchanges: 2-1/2 starch, 1-1/2 fat, 1/2 reduced-fat milk.

A Better Bacon-and-Egg Breakfast

I LIKE to keep a supply of cooked crumbled bacon in the freezer. By sprinkling a little into scrambled eggs, folks feel like they've had "bacon and eggs" for breakfast with only a fraction of the fat and calories.

Before cooking the bacon, I cut the strips into small pieces so they cook faster. *—KK MacCarter Maplewood, Minnesota*

Strawberry Crepe Roll-Ups

Low-fat Meatless

I grew up enjoying these sweet crepes, which my grandmother, aunts and uncles always called "Swedish pancakes". My husband, Chuck, sometimes makes this delicious dietary version for me on weekends.
—Cheryl Erikson, Grass Valley, California

1-1/4 cups fat-free milk
3/4 cup egg substitute
3/4 teaspoon vanilla extract
1 cup all-purpose flour
1 teaspoon sugar
1/4 teaspoon salt
2/3 cup strawberry spreadable fruit
3 cups chopped fresh strawberries
2 teaspoons confectioners' sugar

In a mixing bowl, combine the milk, egg substitute and vanilla. Combine the flour, sugar and salt; add to milk mixture and mix well. Cover and refrigerate for 1 hour.

Coat a 7- or 8-in. nonstick skillet with nonstick cooking spray. Heat skillet over medium heat. Pour about 2 tablespoons batter into the center of skillet. Lift and tilt pan to evenly coat bottom. Cook until top appears dry; turn and cook 15-20 seconds longer. Remove to plate; keep warm. Repeat with remaining batter, coating with additional nonstick cooking spray as needed.

Spread each crepe with about 2 teaspoons spreadable fruit. Top with about 3 tablespoons strawberries. Roll up. Sprinkle with confectioners' sugar. **Yield:** 8 servings.

Nutritional Analysis: One serving (2 filled crepes) equals 137 calories, trace fat (trace saturated fat), 1 mg cholesterol, 145 mg sodium, 28 g carbohydrate, 3 g fiber, 6 g protein.
Diabetic Exchanges: 1 starch, 1 fruit.

Oatmeal Cranberry Breakfast Bake

Meatless

I like to prepare this baked oatmeal on weekend mornings when I have a little extra time. Even guests who typically don't like oatmeal fill their bowls with this hearty version, flavored with dried cranberries, brown sugar and cinnamon.
—Angela Higinbotham, Willits, California

3 cups old-fashioned oats
1 cup dried cranberries
3/4 cup packed brown sugar
2 teaspoons ground cinnamon
1 teaspoon salt
4 egg whites, lightly beaten
3 cups fat-free milk
1/4 cup canola oil
1 tablespoon vanilla extract
Additional milk, optional

In a large bowl, combine the first five ingredients. In another bowl, whisk together the egg whites, milk, oil and vanilla. Stir into the oat mixture just until moistened.

Place in a 13-in. x 9-in. x 2-in. baking dish coated with nonstick cooking spray. Bake at 350° for 50-55 minutes or until oats are tender and liquid is absorbed. Cut into bars. Serve in bowls with milk if desired. **Yield:** 12 servings.

Nutritional Analysis: One serving (1 piece, calculated without additional milk) equals 230 calories, 6 g fat (1 g saturated fat), 1 mg cholesterol, 253 mg sodium, 39 g carbohydrate, 3 g fiber, 7 g protein.
Diabetic Exchanges: 2 starch, 1 fat, 1/2 fruit.

Sausage Breakfast Wraps

(Pictured at right)

I love breakfast burritos, but they're typically high in fat and cholesterol. So I created my own healthier version. Since my wraps freeze beautifully, they make an anytime meal. Let the sausage mix cool for about an hour before assembling and freezing the wraps.
—Ed Rysdyk Jr., Wyoming, Michigan

1 pound turkey Italian sausage links, casings removed
1 medium sweet red pepper, diced
1 small onion, diced
4 cartons (8 ounces *each*) frozen egg substitute, thawed
1 can (4 ounces) chopped green chilies
1 teaspoon chili powder
10 flour tortillas (8 inches), warmed
1-1/4 cups salsa

In a nonstick skillet, cook sausage over medium heat until no longer pink; drain. Transfer to a 13-in. x 9-in. x 2-in. baking dish coated with nonstick cooking spray. Sprinkle with red pepper and onion. Combine the egg substitute, green chilies and chili powder; pour over sausage mixture.

Bake, uncovered, at 350° for 30-35 minutes or until set. Break up sausage mixture with a spoon. Place 2/3 cup down the center of each tortilla; top with salsa. Fold one end over sausage mixture, then fold two sides over. **Yield:** 10 servings.

Nutritional Analysis: One serving (1 breakfast wrap with 2 tablespoons salsa) equals 286 calories, 7 g fat (2 g saturated fat), 24 mg cholesterol, 980 mg sodium, 33 g carbohydrate, 1 g fiber, 21 g protein.
Diabetic Exchanges: 2 starch, 2 lean meat, 1/2 fat.

Crepes with Berries

Low-fat Low-sodium Meatless

(Pictured at right)

Greet the day in a luscious way with homemade crepes served with berries and yogurt. I found this low-fat recipe in a magazine and made it even quicker and lighter. The crepe batter whips up so easily in the blender.
—Leica Merriam, Providence, Utah

2 tablespoons sugar
4 cups blueberries, blackberries *and/or* raspberries
1 cup fat-free milk
1 egg
3 egg whites
1/2 teaspoon almond extract
1/2 teaspoon vanilla extract
2/3 cup all-purpose flour
1/4 cup cornmeal
16 teaspoons reduced-sugar apricot preserves
1 carton (8 ounces) reduced-fat reduced-sugar vanilla yogurt

Sprinkle sugar over berries; gently toss to mix. Cover and refrigerate. In a blender, combine the milk, egg, egg whites and extracts; cover and process until blended. Add the flour and cornmeal; cover and process until blended. Cover and refrigerate for 1 hour.

Coat a 7-in. skillet with nonstick cooking spray. Heat skillet over medium heat. Pour about 2 tablespoons batter into the center of skillet. Lift and tilt pan to evenly coat bottom. Cook until top appears dry; turn and cook 15-20 seconds longer. Remove to a plate; keep warm. Repeat with remaining batter, coating with additional nonstick cooking spray as needed.

Spread each crepe with 1 teaspoon apricot preserves. Fold each crepe into quarters; place two crepes on an individual plate. Top with 2 tablespoons yogurt and 1/2 cup berry mixture. Serve immediately. **Yield:** 8 servings.

Nutritional Analysis: One serving (2 filled crepes with 2 tablespoons yogurt and 1/2 cup berries) equals 156 calories, 1 g fat (trace saturated fat), 28 mg cholesterol, 60 mg sodium, 30 g carbohydrate, 4 g fiber, 6 g protein.
Diabetic Exchanges: 1-1/2 starch, 1/2 fruit.

Puffy Chile Rellenos Casserole

Meatless

(Pictured below)

Here's a wonderfully zesty casserole that's much lower in fat and easier to assemble then traditional chile rellenos. I don't remember where I got the recipe, but I've enjoyed this layered brunch entree for years.
—Marilyn Morey, Mallard, Iowa

- 6 cans (4 ounces *each*) whole green chilies, drained
- 8 flour tortillas (6 inches), cut into 1-inch strips
- 2 cups (8 ounces) shredded part-skim mozzarella cheese
- 2 cups (8 ounces) shredded reduced-fat cheddar cheese
- 3 cups egg substitute
- 3/4 cup fat-free milk
- 1/2 teaspoon garlic powder
- 1/2 teaspoon ground cumin
- 1/2 teaspoon pepper
- 1/4 teaspoon salt
- 1 teaspoon paprika
- 1 cup salsa

Cut along one side of each chili and open to lie flat. Coat a 13-in. x 9-in. x 2-in. baking dish with nonstick cooking spray. Layer half of the chilies, tortilla strips, mozzarella and cheddar cheeses in prepared dish. Repeat layers. In a small bowl, beat the egg substitute, milk, garlic powder, cumin, pepper and salt. Pour over cheese. Sprinkle with paprika.

Bake, uncovered, at 350° for 40-45 minutes or until puffy and a knife inserted 2 in. from the edge of the pan comes out clean. Let stand for 10 minutes before cutting. Serve with salsa. **Yield:** 12 servings.

Editor's Note: When cutting or seeding hot peppers, use rubber or plastic gloves to protect your hands. Avoid touching your face.

Nutritional Analysis: One serving (1 piece with 4 teaspoons salsa) equals 218 calories, 8 g fat (5 g saturated fat), 26 mg cholesterol, 548 mg sodium, 18 g carbohydrate, 1 g fiber, 19 g protein.
Diabetic Exchanges: 2 lean meat, 1 starch, 1 vegetable.

Potato Basil Scramble

Meatless

This potato dish is so popular at our house, we argue over who gets the leftovers. I grow my own herbs, so I usually use fresh basil in this recipe, but dried works just as well. We love this for dinner with fruit salad and English muffins. It also makes a hearty breakfast for the weekend.
—Terri Zobel, Raleigh, North Carolina

- 2 cups cubed potatoes
- 1/2 cup chopped onion
- 1/2 cup chopped green pepper
- 1 tablespoon canola oil
- 2 cups egg substitute
- 2 tablespoons minced fresh basil
- 1/2 teaspoon salt
- 1/8 teaspoon cayenne pepper

Place potatoes in a microwave-safe bowl; add 1 in. of water. Cover and microwave on high for 7 minutes; drain.

In a large nonstick skillet coated with nonstick cooking spray, saute the onion, green pepper and potatoes in oil until tender. Add the egg substitute, basil, salt and pepper. Cook over medium heat until eggs are completely set, stirring occasionally. **Yield:** 4 servings.

Editor's Note: This recipe was tested in a 1,100-watt microwave.

Nutritional Analysis: One serving (1 cup) equals 163 calories, 4 g fat (trace saturated fat), 0 cholesterol, 549 mg sodium, 19 g carbohydrate, 2 g fiber, 14 g protein.
Diabetic Exchanges: 2 lean meat, 1 starch.

Lighten Up Deviled Eggs

Here's a unique way to make healthier deviled eggs—by using up leftover mashed potatoes. I hard-cook the eggs, peel them and cut them in half, then discard the yolks. I stir the seasonings and other ingredients into the mashed potatoes. Then I spoon the potato mixture into the egg white halves. These deviled eggs are lower in fat and cholesterol, and no one will know you used leftovers.
—Sherri Volland, Burlington, Kansas

Skinny Crab Quiche

Low-carb

(Pictured above)

Crabmeat, zucchini, cheddar cheese and green onions flavor this savory crustless quiche. Take it to potlucks, cut into appetizer-size slices. As a diabetic, I know there will be at least one dish there I can eat guilt-free.
—Nancy Romero, Clarkston, Washington

1 can (6 ounces) crabmeat, drained, flaked and cartilage removed
1-1/2 cups (6 ounces) shredded reduced-fat cheddar cheese
1/2 cup shredded zucchini
1/3 cup chopped green onions
1-1/2 cups egg substitute
1 can (12 ounces) fat-free evaporated milk
3/4 teaspoon ground mustard
1/2 teaspoon salt
1/4 teaspoon salt-free lemon-pepper seasoning
Dash paprika

In a bowl, combine the crab, cheese, zucchini and onions. Press onto the bottom and up the sides of a 9-in. deep-dish-pie plate coated with nonstick cooking spray. In another bowl, combine the egg substitute, milk, mustard, salt and lemon-pepper; mix well. Pour into the crust. Sprinkle with paprika.

Bake, uncovered, at 400° for 25-30 minutes or until a knife inserted near the center comes out clean. Let stand for 10 minutes before cutting. **Yield:** 6 servings.

Nutritional Analysis: One slice equals 223 calories, 9 g fat (5 g saturated fat), 50 mg cholesterol, 736 mg sodium, 10 g carbohydrate, trace fiber, 26 g protein.
Diabetic Exchanges: 3 lean meat, 1/2 fat-free milk.

Caramelized Onion Broccoli Quiche

Meatless

(Pictured below)

*This is wonderful for brunch or for supper, paired with
a green salad. The combination of broccoli, sweet
onions and feta cheese is truly delicious.*
—Kim Pettipas, Oromocto, New Brunswick

- 3 cups sliced sweet onions
- 1 teaspoon sugar
- 1/2 teaspoon salt
- 2 teaspoons olive oil
- 2 cups frozen shredded hash brown potatoes, thawed
- 1 tube (11 ounces) refrigerated breadsticks
- 1 package (10 ounces) frozen chopped broccoli, thawed and drained
- 1 cup (4 ounces) crumbled feta cheese
- 2 eggs
- 2 egg whites
- 3/4 cup fat-free milk

In a large nonstick skillet, cook the onions, sugar and salt
in oil over low heat for 40 minutes or until onions are softened and liquid has evaporated. Turn heat to medium-low;
add hash browns. Cook 8-10 minutes longer or until potatoes are golden. Remove from heat and set aside.

To make crust, unroll breadstick dough onto a lightly
floured surface and separate into strips. Pinch several
breadsticks together, end to end, forming a rope. Holding
one end of rope, loosely coil dough to form a circle. Add
remaining breadsticks to coil, one at a time, pinching ends
together. Tuck end under; pinch to seal. Cover and let rest
for 10 minutes. Roll into a 10-1/2-in. to 11-in. circle. Transfer to an ungreased 9-in. pie plate. Spoon onion mixture
into crust. Top with broccoli and cheese.

In a bowl, whisk together eggs, egg whites and milk; pour
over cheese (pie plate will be full). Bake at 350° for 40
minutes. Cover edges with foil. Bake 10-12 minutes longer
or until a knife inserted near the center comes out clean. Let
stand for 10 minutes before cutting. **Yield:** 6 servings.

*Nutritional Analysis: One piece equals 365 calories, 12 g fat
(5 g saturated fat), 94 mg cholesterol, 928 mg sodium, 50 g carbohydrate, 5 g fiber, 14 g protein.*
*Diabetic Exchanges: 2-1/2 starch, 2 vegetable, 1-1/2 fat,
1 lean meat.*

Pennsylvania Dutch Apple Butter

Low-fat   Low-sodium   Meatless

*You can spread this apple butter on thick and still enjoy
a breakfast that's thin on calories. For a smooth texture,
use tender varieties such as McIntosh or Cortland apples.*
—Diane Widmer, Blue Island, Illinois

- 3/4 cup unsweetened apple cider *or* juice
- 1/3 cup sugar
- 1 teaspoon ground cinnamon
- 1/4 teaspoon ground cloves
- 6 medium apples, peeled and quartered (3 pounds)

Place the apple juice, sugar, cinnamon and cloves in a
blender or food processor; cover and process until blended.
Adding 3-4 apple pieces at a time, cover and process until
smooth. Pour into a saucepan. Bring to boil. Reduce heat;
cover and cook over low heat for 1 hour, stirring occasionally. Uncover and cook 1 to 1-1/2 hours longer or until
thickened. Store in airtight containers in the refrigerator.
Yield: 2 cups.

*Nutritional Analysis: One serving (2 tablespoons) equals 66
calories, trace fat (trace saturated fat), 0 mg cholesterol, 1 mg sodium, 17 g carbohydrate, 2 g fiber, trace protein.*
Diabetic Exchange: 1 fruit.

Beefed-Up Main Dishes

Even folks watching their diets can indulge in a meaty entree. The secret is to select lean beef cuts and to trim down the accompanying sauces. No one will guess you cheated these dishes out of fat and calories!

Winter Beef Stew (page 113)

Ginger Beef Stir-Fry

Low-carb

Ginger and red pepper flakes bring a little zip to this beef- and-veggie stovetop supper stirred up by our Test Kitchen staff.

2 teaspoons sugar
1/2 teaspoon *each* **cornstarch and ground ginger**
1/4 teaspoon pepper
1/4 teaspoon crushed red pepper flakes
2 tablespoons sherry *or* **beef broth**
2 tablespoons reduced-sodium soy sauce
1 tablespoon barbecue sauce
1 teaspoon sesame oil
1-1/2 cups julienned carrots
1/2 cup sliced onion
2 teaspoons canola oil
12 ounces boneless beef top round steak, cut into thin strips
2 garlic cloves, minced
1/4 cup sliced green onions
Hot cooked rice, optional

In a bowl, combine the sugar, cornstarch, ginger, pepper and red pepper flakes. Stir in the sherry or broth, soy sauce, barbecue sauce and sesame oil; set aside. In a large non-stick skillet or wok, stir-fry carrots and onion in hot canola oil until crisp-tender; remove and set aside. In the same pan, stir-fry beef and garlic until meat is no longer pink. Stir sauce mixture; stir into pan. Add carrot mixture. Bring to a boil; cook and stir for 2 minutes or until thickened. Garnish with green onions. Serve over rice if desired. **Yield:** 3 servings.

Nutritional Analysis: One serving (1 cup stir-fry mixture, calculated without rice) equals 254 calories, 8 g fat (2 g saturated fat), 64 mg cholesterol, 502 mg sodium, 14 g carbohydrate, 3 g fiber, 27 g protein.
Diabetic Exchanges: 3 lean meat, 1 vegetable, 1/2 starch.

Slow Cooker Beef Au Jus

Low-carb

It's easy to fix this roast, which has lots of onion flavor. Sometimes I also add cubed potatoes and baby carrots to the slow cooker to make a terrific meal plus leftovers.
—Carol Hille, Grand Junction, Colorado

1 boneless beef rump roast (3 pounds)
1 large onion, sliced
3/4 cup reduced-sodium beef broth
1 envelope (1 ounce) au jus gravy mix
2 garlic cloves, halved
1/4 teaspoon pepper

Cut roast in half. In a large nonstick skillet coated with nonstick cooking spray, brown meat on all sides over medium-high heat. Place onion in a 5-qt. slow cooker. Top with meat. Combine the broth, gravy mix, garlic and pepper. Pour over meat. Cover and cook on low for 6-7 hours or until meat and onion are tender.

Remove meat to a cutting board. Let stand for 10 minutes. Thinly slice meat and return to slow cooker. Serve meat with pan juices and onions. **Yield:** 10 servings.

Nutritional Analysis: One serving (3 ounces cooked beef with 1/4 cup pan juices) equals 188 calories, 7 g fat (2 g saturated fat), 82 mg cholesterol, 471 mg sodium, 3 g carbohydrate, trace fiber, 28 g protein.
Diabetic Exchange: 3 lean meat.

Brisket with Gravy

Low-carb

(Pictured below)

Chili sauce, brown sugar and garlic season this robust beef brisket. Topped with tender onions and served with a slightly sweet gravy, the entree tastes special enough for company.
—Pat Patty, Spring, Texas

1 fresh beef brisket (about 4 pounds)
1/2 teaspoon pepper
1 large onion, thinly sliced and separated into rings
1 can (12 ounces) beer *or* **nonalcoholic beer**
1/2 cup chili sauce
3 tablespoons brown sugar
2 garlic cloves, minced
2 tablespoons cornstarch
1/4 cup cold water

Place beef in a roasting pan. Sprinkle with pepper and top with onion. Combine the beer, chili sauce, brown sugar and garlic; stir until sugar is dissolved. Pour over meat. Cover and bake at 325° for 3-1/2 hours. Uncover; bake 15-30 minutes longer or until onions are lightly browned and meat is tender. Remove meat and onions to a serving platter and keep warm.

Pour drippings and loosened browned bits into a saucepan. Skim fat. Combine cornstarch and water until

smooth. Gradually stir into pan drippings. Bring to a boil; cook and stir for 2 minutes or until thickened. Slice meat thinly across the grain. Serve with gravy. **Yield:** 12 servings.

Editor's Note: This is a fresh beef brisket, not corned beef.

Nutritional Analysis: One serving (3 ounces cooked beef with 2 tablespoons gravy) equals 270 calories, 12 g fat (4 g saturated fat), 88 mg cholesterol, 389 mg sodium, 9 g carbohydrate, trace fiber, 28 g protein.
Diabetic Exchanges: 3 lean meat, 1 fat, 1/2 starch.

Beef Chow Mein Skillet

When your family craves an Oriental-style meal, pull out this easy one-dish recipe. It rivals any restaurant version.
—LaVonne Hegland, St. Michael, Minnesota

 1 pound ground beef
 1 large onion, chopped
 4 cups hot water (150° to 160°)
 3 cups chopped celery
 1 package (8 ounces) fresh mushrooms, quartered
1-1/2 cups water
 1 can (8 ounces) sliced water chestnuts, drained
 3 tablespoons reduced-sodium soy sauce
 1 tablespoon brown sugar
 2 teaspoons reduced-sodium beef bouillon granules
 1/4 teaspoon garlic powder
 1/8 teaspoon pepper
 2 tablespoons cornstarch
 3 tablespoons cold water
Hot cooked rice
 1 cup chow mein noodles

In a large nonstick skillet, cook beef and onion over medium heat until meat is no longer pink; drain. Using a slotted spoon, remove beef mixture to several layers of white paper towels. Let stand for 1 minute. Blot top of beef with additional white paper towels. Transfer beef mixture to fine mesh strainer over a 1-1/2-qt. bowl. Pour hot water over beef. Drain for 5 minutes.

Return beef to the skillet. Stir in the celery, mushrooms, water, water chestnuts, soy sauce, brown sugar, bouillon granules, garlic powder and pepper. Bring to a boil. Reduce heat; cover and simmer for 15-20 minutes or until the vegetables are tender.

Combine the cornstarch and cold water until smooth; stir into the beef mixture. Bring to a boil. Reduce heat; cook and stir for 2 minutes or until thickened. Serve over rice if desired. Top with chow mein noodles. **Yield:** 4 servings.

Nutritional Analysis: One serving (1-1/2 cups beef mixture and 1/4 cup chow mein noodles, calculated without rice) equals 296 calories, 9 g fat (1 g saturated fat), 50 mg cholesterol, 1,017 mg sodium, 31 g carbohydrate, 5 g fiber, 25 g protein.
Diabetic Exchanges: 3 lean meat, 2 vegetable, 1-1/2 starch.

Mexican Spaghetti Sauce

Low-fat

(Pictured above)

Green chilies, black beans, chili powder and corn give this spaghetti a satisfying Southwestern zip.
—Sandi Leonard, Peculiar, Missouri

 1 pound ground beef
3/4 cup chopped onion
 4 cups hot water (150° to 160°)
 1 jar (26 ounces) meatless spaghetti sauce
 1 can (15 ounces) black beans, rinsed and drained
 1 can (14-1/2 ounces) diced tomatoes
 1 cup frozen yellow and white corn, thawed
 1 cup salsa
 1 can (4 ounces) chopped green chilies
 1 tablespoon chili powder
 1/4 teaspoon salt
 1/4 teaspoon pepper
Hot cooked spaghetti

In a large nonstick skillet, cook beef and onion over medium heat until meat is no longer pink; drain. Using a slotted spoon, remove beef mixture to several layers of white paper towels. Let stand for 1 minute. Blot top of beef with additional white paper towels. Transfer beef mixture to fine mesh strainer over a 1-1/2-qt. bowl. Pour hot water over beef. Drain for 5 minutes.

In a large saucepan, combine spaghetti sauce, beans, tomatoes, corn, salsa, chilies, chili powder, salt and pepper. Stir in beef mixture. Bring to a boil. Reduce heat; simmer, uncovered, for 10-15 minutes. Serve over spaghetti. **Yield:** 10 servings.

Nutritional Analysis: One serving (3/4 cup sauce, calculated without spaghetti) equals 163 calories, 3 g fat (trace saturated fat), 20 mg cholesterol, 583 mg sodium, 22 g carbohydrate, 5 g fiber, 12 g protein.
Diabetic Exchanges: 3 vegetable, 1 lean meat, 1/2 starch.

🍎 Hamburger History

WHO would have guessed that hamburgers could be controversial? But that's the case when it comes to discerning the origin of this all-American favorite. At least four "inventions" are credited with being the first hamburger:

Frank and Charles Menches, from Stark County, Ohio, ran a traveling concession stand in the early 1880s. When they ran out of sausage patties at a fair in Hamburg, New York, the brothers ground up beef, added seasonings and served it on buns.

Charles Nagreen, a vendor at a local fair in 1885 in Seymour, Wisconsin, flattened homemade meatballs and put them between two slices of bread to make them portable.

In 1890, Louis Lassen, owner of a turn-of-the-century luncheonette in New Haven, Connecticut, ground up beef and made a sandwich using two slices of bread.

Fletch Davis, who owned a lunch counter in Athens, Texas, sold his ground beef patty sandwiches on toast at the St. Louis World's Fair in 1904.

Zippy Burgers

Our Test Kitchen concocted this easy recipe, enhancing lean ground beef with onion powder, chili powder and red pepper flakes.

    1/4 cup beer *or* beef broth
    2 tablespoons Worcestershire sauce
    2 teaspoons chili powder
    1 teaspoon onion powder
    1/2 teaspoon crushed red pepper flakes
    1/4 teaspoon salt
    1/4 teaspoon pepper
    1 pound lean ground beef
    4 hamburger buns, split

In a bowl, combine the first seven ingredients. Crumble beef over mixture and mix well. Shape into four patties.

If grilling the hamburgers, coat grill rack with nonstick cooking spray before starting the grill. Grill hamburgers, covered, over medium heat or broil 4 in. from the heat for 6-8 minutes on each side or until a meat thermometer reads 160°. Serve on buns. **Yield:** 4 servings.

Nutritional Analysis: One hamburger equals 314 calories, 12 g fat (4 g saturated fat), 70 mg cholesterol, 557 mg sodium, 25 g carbohydrate, 2 g fiber, 25 g protein.
Diabetic Exchanges: 3 lean meat, 1-1/2 starch.

Mexican-Style Goulash

This is among the tastiest and speediest recipes in my collection...and it's my husband's favorite one-pot dish.
—Maurane Ramsey, Fort Wayne, Indiana

    1 pound lean ground beef
    1 cup chopped onion

    1 can (14-1/2 ounces) diced tomatoes, undrained
    1 can (8 ounces) tomato sauce
    1 cup fresh *or* frozen corn
    1/2 cup water
  1-1/4 teaspoons chili powder
    1 teaspoon dried oregano
    1/2 teaspoon salt
    2/3 cup uncooked elbow macaroni
    2/3 cup shredded reduced-fat cheddar cheese

In a large nonstick skillet, cook beef and onion over medium heat until meat is no longer pink; drain. Stir in the tomatoes, tomato sauce, corn, water, chili powder, oregano and salt. Bring to a boil. Add macaroni. Reduce heat; cover and simmer for 20-25 minutes or until macaroni is tender. Sprinkle with cheese; cover and cook 2-3 minutes longer or until cheese is melted. **Yield:** 5 servings.

Nutritional Analysis: One serving (1 cup) equals 303 calories, 10 g fat (5 g saturated fat), 55 mg cholesterol, 743 mg sodium, 28 g carbohydrate, 4 g fiber, 26 g protein.
Diabetic Exchanges: 3 lean meat, 2 vegetable, 1 starch.

Stir-Fried Beef on Lettuce

Low-carb

(Pictured at right)

Being from the Philippines, I'm partial to stir-fries. My husband especially likes this refreshing combination of steak and crisp shredded lettuce.
—Niñez McConnell, Mill Creek, Washington

    1/3 cup reduced-sodium soy sauce
    1/3 cup white wine *or* chicken broth
    1 pound boneless beef sirloin steak, cut into 1/8-inch strips
    1 teaspoon cornstarch
    1/2 pound fresh mushrooms, sliced
    2 cups fresh snow peas
    4 teaspoons canola oil, *divided*
    4 cups shredded lettuce

In a small bowl, combine the soy sauce and wine or broth. Reserve 1/4 cup. Place beef in a resealable plastic bag. Add remaining soy sauce mixture; seal and mix. Refrigerate for 15 minutes. Place cornstarch in a small bowl. Stir in reserved soy sauce mixture until smooth; set aside.

In a nonstick skillet, stir-fry mushrooms and snow peas in 2 teaspoons hot oil for 3-4 minutes or until snow peas are crisp-tender. Remove and keep warm. Drain and discard marinade from beef. In same skillet, stir-fry beef in remaining oil for 2 minutes. Stir cornstarch mixture; add to skillet. Bring to a boil; cook and stir for 1-2 minutes or until slightly thickened. Place lettuce on four serving plates. Top with beef mixture and snow pea mixture. **Yield:** 4 servings.

Nutritional Analysis: One serving (1 cup stir-fry mixture with 1 cup lettuce) equals 246 calories, 10 g fat (2 g saturated fat), 64 mg cholesterol, 856 mg sodium, 8 g carbohydrate, 3 g fiber, 26 g protein.
Diabetic Exchanges: 3 lean meat, 1 vegetable, 1 fat.

Shredded Beef Sandwiches

(Pictured above)

Cola is the secret ingredient in this delicious slow-cooked beef. Coated with a well-seasoned sauce, the tender meat gets its zip from chili powder and cayenne pepper.
—Marie Basinger, Connellsville, Pennsylvania

3/4 cup cola
1/4 cup Worcestershire sauce
2 garlic cloves, minced
1 tablespoon white vinegar
1 teaspoon reduced-sodium beef bouillon granules
1/2 teaspoon chili powder
1/2 teaspoon ground mustard
1/4 teaspoon cayenne pepper
1 boneless beef rump roast (2 pounds)
2 teaspoons canola oil
2 medium onions, chopped
1/2 cup ketchup
8 kaiser rolls

In a 4-cup measuring cup, combine the cola, Worcestershire sauce, garlic, vinegar, bouillon and seasonings; set aside. Cut roast in half. In a nonstick skillet, brown meat in oil on all sides. Place onions in a 3-qt. slow cooker. Top with meat. Pour half of cola mixture over meat. Cover and cook on low for 8-10 hours or until meat is tender. Cover and refrigerate remaining cola mixture.

Remove meat from cooking liquid and cool. Strain cooking liquid, reserving onions and discarding the liquid. When meat is cool enough to handle, shred with two forks. Return meat and onions to the slow cooker. In a small saucepan, combine ketchup and reserved cola mixture; heat through. Pour over meat mixture and heat through. Serve on rolls. **Yield:** 8 servings.

Nutritional Analysis: One serving (1/2 cup meat mixture with roll) equals 354 calories, 10 g fat (2 g saturated fat), 59 mg cholesterol, 714 mg sodium, 40 g carbohydrate, 2 g fiber, 26 g protein.
Diabetic Exchanges: 3 lean meat, 2-1/2 starch.

Chuck Wagon Beans

You won't have to ring the dinner bell twice when these hearty Western-style beans are on the menu. Rinsing the browned ground beef makes the entree leaner on calories but not on taste. Since I began fixing lighter meals for my husband, I've learned lots of tricks to lower the fat in foods.
—Connie Staal, Greenbrier, Arkansas

2 pounds ground beef
1/2 cup chopped celery
1/2 cup chopped green pepper
1/2 cup chopped onion
8 cups hot water (150° to 160°)
2 cans (15 ounces *each*) pork and beans
1 can (10-3/4 ounces) reduced-fat reduced-sodium condensed tomato soup, undiluted
1/4 cup water
2 tablespoons cider vinegar
1 tablespoon brown sugar
1 teaspoon ground mustard

In a nonstick skillet, cook the beef, celery, green pepper and onion over medium heat until meat is no longer pink; drain. Using a slotted spoon, place beef mixture on several sheets of white paper towels; drain. Let stand for 1 minute. Blot top of beef mixture with additional white paper towels. Transfer half of beef mixture to a fine mesh strainer over a 1-1/2-qt. bowl. Pour half of hot water over beef. Drain for 5 minutes. Repeat with remaining beef mixture and hot water.

In a bowl, combine the pork and beans, tomato soup, water, vinegar, brown sugar, mustard and beef mixture. Transfer to a shallow 2-1/2-qt. baking dish coated with nonstick cooking spray. Bake, uncovered, at 375° for 40-50 minutes or until heated through and mixture reaches desired thickness. **Yield:** 8 servings.

Nutritional Analysis: One serving (1 cup) equals 272 calories, 7 g fat (1 g saturated fat), 54 mg cholesterol, 495 mg sodium, 29 g carbohydrate, 6 g fiber, 24 g protein.
Diabetic Exchanges: 3 lean meat, 1-1/2 starch.

Grilled Citrus Steak

Low-carb

(Pictured below)

We invite someone for dinner almost every weekend, and this recipe has never failed us. It can be prepared in just a few minutes. I like to serve it with vegetables and a salad.
—Joan Whyte-Elliott, Fenelon Falls, Ontario

2/3 cup reduced-sugar orange marmalade
1/3 cup reduced-sodium soy sauce
1/3 cup lemon juice
1 tablespoon canola oil
2 pounds boneless beef top round steak
(2 inches thick)

In a bowl, combine the orange marmalade, soy sauce, lemon juice and oil; mix well. Pour 1 cup marinade into a large resealable plastic bag. Score the surface of the steak with shallow diagonal cuts, making diamond shapes. Add the steak to the marinade. Seal bag and turn to coat; refrigerate for 6-8 hours, turning occasionally. Cover and refrigerate remaining marinade.

Coat grill rack with nonstick cooking spray before starting the grill for indirect heat. Drain and discard marinade from beef. Grill beef, covered, over direct medium-hot heat for 6-8 minutes or until browned, turning once. Place beef over indirect heat and continue grilling for 25-30 minutes or until beef reaches desired doneness (for rare, a meat thermometer should read 140°; medium, 160°; well-done, 170°), basting occasionally with reserved marinade. **Yield:** 6 servings.

Nutritional Analysis: One serving (4 ounces cooked beef) equals 243 calories, 7 g fat (2 g saturated fat), 96 mg cholesterol, 337 mg sodium, 6 g carbohydrate, trace fiber, 37 g protein.
Diabetic Exchanges: 4 lean meat, 1/2 fruit.

Grilling Is Good for You!

GRILLING lends unique flavor to meat, fish, vegetables and fruits without adding fat.

Lean meat in particular stays lean because fat drips away as it cooks. By trimming any visible fat from the meat before cooking, you can reduce the total fat per serving by almost 50%.

Rubs—blends of dried herbs and spices worked into the surface of meat or seafood—are a great way to add low-fat flavor.

Most marinades call for a fair amount of oil; however, only 1 to 2 tablespoons are necessary to help enhance the flavor of the meat. When using 1 to 2 tablespoons of oil, coat the cool grill top with nonstick cooking spray to prevent sticking.

Winter Beef Stew

(Pictured on page 107)

This warming main dish is a favorite after a day of play around our home. It's no fuss, too—I can put it in the oven and practically forget about it.
—Ruth Ann Harker, Jerome, Idaho

1-1/2 pounds boneless chuck roast, cut
into 1-1/4-inch pieces
1 cup chopped onion
2 garlic cloves, minced
2 teaspoons canola oil
1-1/2 pounds small red potatoes, cut into chunks
3 medium carrots, cut into 1-inch pieces
2 medium onions, quartered
1/2 pound fresh mushrooms, halved
1 can (14-1/2 ounces) reduced-sodium beef broth
1 cup unsweetened apple juice
1/4 cup tomato paste
1/2 cup minced fresh parsley
2 bay leaves
1/2 teaspoon salt
1/2 teaspoon dried thyme
1/2 teaspoon pepper
1 bacon strip, cooked and crumbled

In a Dutch oven, cook the meat, chopped onion and garlic in oil over medium-high heat until meat is browned on all sides; drain. Add the potatoes, carrots, quartered onions and mushrooms. In a bowl, combine the broth, apple juice, tomato paste, parsley, bay leaves, salt, thyme and pepper. Pour over meat.

Cover and bake at 325° for 2 hours. Stir. Bake, uncovered, for 30-45 minutes longer or until stew reaches desired thickness. Discard bay leaves; sprinkle with bacon. **Yield:** 6 servings.

Nutritional Analysis: One serving (1-1/2 cups) equals 364 calories, 9 g fat (3 g saturated fat), 79 mg cholesterol, 544 mg sodium, 39 g carbohydrate, 6 g fiber, 32 g protein.
Diabetic Exchanges: 3 lean meat, 3 vegetable, 1-1/2 starch.

Stir-fry carrots in remaining oil for 2 minutes. Add the green pepper, celery and mushrooms; stir-fry for 3 minutes. Add the water chestnuts and onions; stir-fry for 2 minutes or until vegetables are crisp-tender. Stir cornstarch mixture and add to the pan. Bring to a boil; cook and stir for 2 minutes. Add spinach and beef; cook and stir until spinach is wilted and beef is heated through. Serve over rice if desired. **Yield:** 4 servings.

Nutritional Analysis: One serving (1-1/4 cups stir-fry, calculated without rice) equals 280 calories, 13 g fat (3 g saturated fat), 63 mg cholesterol, 597 mg sodium, 16 g carbohydrate, 6 g fiber, 25 g protein.
Diabetic Exchanges: 3 lean meat, 2 vegetable, 1/2 starch, 1/2 fat.

Spinach Beef Stir-Fry

(Pictured above)

With tender strips of steak and fresh colorful vegetables, this mouth-watering stir-fry sizzles with flavor! My versatile entree can also be made with chicken breasts instead of beef. If you like zucchini or squash, toss some in. A bag of frozen mixed vegetables can also be used.
—LaVerne Heath, Fountain, North Carolina

1/4 cup reduced-sodium soy sauce
1 boneless beef sirloin steak (1 pound), cut into thin strips
2 teaspoons cornstarch
1/2 teaspoon beef bouillon granules
1/2 teaspoon Chinese five-spice powder
1/2 cup water
2 tablespoons canola oil, *divided*
1 cup sliced fresh carrots
1 medium green pepper, julienned
1 cup sliced celery
1 cup sliced fresh mushrooms
1 can (8 ounces) sliced water chestnuts, drained
1/2 cup sliced green onions
6 cups torn fresh spinach
Hot cooked rice, optional

Place soy sauce in a large resealable plastic bag; add steak. Seal bag and turn to coat; refrigerate for up to 2 hours. Drain and discard soy sauce.

In a bowl, combine the cornstarch, bouillon, five-spice powder and water until smooth; set aside. In a large non-stick skillet or wok, stir-fry the beef in batches in 1 tablespoon hot oil until beef is no longer pink. Remove from skillet and set aside.

Sweet 'n' Tangy Pot Roast

Low-carb

I fixed this roast the first time I cooked for my husband-to-be more than 20 years ago. For dessert, I made chocolate pudding spooned over marshmallows. He thought he'd died and gone to heaven!
—Carol Mulligan, Honeoye Falls, New York

1 boneless beef chuck roast (3 pounds)
1/2 teaspoon salt
1/2 teaspoon pepper
1 cup water
1 cup ketchup
1/4 cup red wine *or* beef broth
1 envelope brown gravy mix
2 teaspoons Dijon mustard
1 teaspoon Worcestershire sauce
1/8 teaspoon garlic powder
3 tablespoons cornstarch
1/4 cup cold water

Cut meat in half and place in a 5-qt. slow cooker. Sprinkle with salt and pepper. In a bowl, combine the water, ketchup, wine or broth, gravy mix, mustard, Worcestershire sauce and garlic powder; pour over meat. Cover and cook on low for 9-10 hours or until meat is tender.

Combine cornstarch and cold water until smooth. Stir into slow cooker. Cover and cook on high for 30 minutes or until gravy is thickened. Remove meat from slow cooker. Slice and serve with gravy. **Yield:** 8 servings.

Nutritional Analysis: One serving (3 ounces cooked beef with 1/2 cup gravy) equals 249 calories, 8 g fat (3 g saturated fat), 89 mg cholesterol, 748 mg sodium, 13 g carbohydrate, 1 g fiber, 30 g protein.
Diabetic Exchanges: 3 lean meat, 1 starch.

Favorite Recipe Made Lighter

Our home economists tastefully trimmed down Lasagna with Two Sauces from Suzanne Dole of Claremont, New Hampshire.

Lasagna with Two Sauces

1-1/2 pounds *each* ground beef and ground pork
1 cup finely chopped onion
4 garlic cloves, minced
1 teaspoon dried oregano
2 tablespoons olive oil
1 cup dry red wine *or* beef broth
4 cans (15 ounces *each*) tomato sauce
1/2 teaspoon salt
1/4 teaspoon pepper
Dash paprika
15 uncooked lasagna noodles
CREAM CHEESE SAUCE:
1/2 cup butter
1 cup all-purpose flour
4 cups milk
1 package (8 ounces) cream cheese, softened
1/4 teaspoon *each* salt and ground nutmeg
1/8 teaspoon pepper
1-1/2 cups (6 ounces) grated Parmesan cheese

In a large skillet, cook meat, onion, garlic and oregano in oil until meat is no longer pink; drain. Stir in the wine or broth. Simmer, uncovered, until wine is almost completely reduced. Add tomato sauce and seasonings. Bring to a boil. Reduce heat; simmer, uncovered, for 3 hours, stirring occasionally.

Cook lasagna noodles according to package directions; drain. In a large saucepan, melt butter. Stir in flour; cook and stir until lightly browned, about 6-8 minutes. Gradually stir in milk until smooth. Add cream cheese and seasonings. Cook and stir over low heat until smooth and thickened.

In a greased 13-in. x 9-in. x 3-in. lasagna dish, spread 1 cup meat sauce. Layer with 5 noodles, a third each cream cheese and meat sauces and 1/2 cup Parmesan cheese. Repeat layers. Top with remaining noodles, cream cheese sauce, meat sauce and Parmesan cheese. (Pan will be full.) Cover and bake at 350° for 45 minutes. Uncover; bake for 15 minutes. Let stand for 20 minutes before cutting. **Yield:** 15 servings.

Nutritional Analysis: One piece equals 517 calories, 32 g fat (15 g saturated fat), 107 mg cholesterol, 1,069 mg sodium, 30 g carbohydrate, 2 g fiber, 27 g protein.

Makeover Lasagna With Two Sauces

(Pictured at right)

1 pound lean ground beef
1/2 pound lean ground pork
1 cup finely chopped onion
4 garlic cloves, minced
1 cup dry red wine *or* beef broth
4 cans (15 ounces *each*) tomato sauce
2 teaspoons sugar
1 teaspoon dried oregano
1/4 teaspoon pepper
Dash paprika
2/3 cup bulgur
2 cups boiling water
12 uncooked lasagna noodles
CREAM CHEESE SAUCE:
1/4 cup butter
1 cup all-purpose flour
4 cups fat-free milk
1 package (8 ounces) reduced-fat cream cheese, cubed
1/4 teaspoon *each* salt and ground nutmeg
1/8 teaspoon pepper
1 cup (4 ounces) shredded Parmesan cheese

In a large nonstick skillet, cook meat, onion and garlic until meat is no longer pink; drain. Stir in the wine or broth. Simmer, uncovered, until wine is almost completely reduced. Add tomato sauce and seasonings. Bring to a boil. Reduce heat; simmer, uncovered, for 3 hours, stirring occasionally.

Place bulgur in a bowl; add boiling water and let stand for 1 hour. Drain; set aside. Cook lasagna noodles according to package directions; drain. In a saucepan, heat butter over medium heat until golden brown, about 4 minutes. Remove from the heat. In a bowl, whisk flour and milk until smooth; stir into butter. Bring to a boil; cook and stir for 2 minutes. Reduce heat to low; add cream cheese and seasonings. Cook and stir until smooth. Stir bulgur into meat sauce.

In a 13-in. x 9-in. x 3-in. lasagna dish coated with nonstick cooking spray, spread 1 cup meat sauce. Layer with 4 noodles, a third each cream cheese and meat sauces and a 1/3 cup Parmesan cheese. Repeat layers. Top with remaining noodles, sauces and Parmesan cheese. (Pan will be full.) Cover and bake at 350° or 45 minutes. Uncover; bake for 15 minutes. Let stand for 20 minutes before cutting. **Yield:** 15 servings.

Nutritional Analysis: One piece equals 334 calories, 13 g fat (7 g saturated fat), 50 mg cholesterol, 926 mg sodium, 33 g carbohydrate, 3 g fiber, 20 g protein.

Diabetic Exchanges: 2 starch, 2 lean meat, 1 vegetable, 1 fat.

Hearty Beef Vegetable Stew

(Pictured below)

I received this wonderful recipe from a co-worker. It's awesome! It is a hit with everyone, including our two young children. And it's good for you, too.
—*Angela Nelson, Ruther Glen, Virginia*

1 can (28 ounces) crushed tomatoes, undrained
3 tablespoons quick-cooking tapioca
2 tablespoons dried basil
1 tablespoon sugar
1/2 teaspoon salt
1/8 teaspoon pepper
1-1/2 pounds red potatoes, cut into 1-inch cubes
3 medium carrots, cut into 1-inch slices
1 medium onion, chopped
1/2 cup chopped celery
1-1/2 pounds lean chuck roast, cut into 1-inch cubes
2 teaspoons canola oil

In a bowl, combine the tomatoes, tapioca, basil, sugar, salt and pepper; let stand for 15 minutes. Place the potatoes, carrots, onion and celery in a 5-qt. slow cooker.

In a large nonstick skillet, brown meat in oil over medium heat. Drain and transfer meat to slow cooker. Pour tomato mixture over the top. Cover and cook on high for 5-6 hours or until meat and vegetables are tender. **Yield:** 6 servings.

Nutritional Analysis: *One serving (1-1/3 cups) equals 380 calories, 8 g fat (3 g saturated fat), 78 mg cholesterol, 458 mg sodium, 46 g carbohydrate, 7 g fiber, 31 g protein.*
Diabetic Exchanges: *3 lean meat, 2 starch, 2 vegetable.*

Pepper Steak Stir-Fry

Low-carb

I make my own picante sauce for this beefy dish, but you can also use a store-bought brand. My husband doesn't care for Oriental food but he likes this great dish with its Mexican flair.
—*Judy Brown, Rockdale, Texas*

1 tablespoon cornstarch
1/2 cup water
1/2 cup picante sauce
2 tablespoons reduced-sodium soy sauce
2 teaspoons minced fresh gingerroot
1 pound boneless beef sirloin steak, cut into 1-inch strips
3 teaspoons canola oil, *divided*
1 medium green pepper, julienned
1 cup sliced fresh mushrooms
6 green onions, cut into 1/4-inch pieces
1 garlic clove, minced
Hot cooked rice, optional

In a bowl, combine the cornstarch and water until smooth. Stir in the picante sauce, soy sauce and ginger; set aside.

In a large nonstick skillet or wok, stir-fry meat for 1-2 minutes in 2 teaspoons hot oil. Remove meat with a slotted spoon and keep warm. Add the pepper, mushrooms, onions, garlic and remaining oil to the skillet. Stir-fry for 3 minutes. Stir picante mixture and add to skillet along with meat. Bring to a boil; cook and stir for 1-2 minutes or until thickened and vegetables are crisp-tender. Serve over rice if desired. **Yield:** 4 servings.

Nutritional Analysis: *One serving (1 cup stir-fry mixture, calculated without rice) equals 218 calories, 9 g fat (2 g saturated fat), 63 mg cholesterol, 614 mg sodium, 9 g carbohydrate, 1 g fiber, 23 g protein.*
Diabetic Exchanges: *3 lean meat, 1 vegetable.*

Onion Beef Stroganoff

This lightened-up Stroganoff is sure to become a family favorite. The tender strips of beef, sliced mushrooms and onion are coated in a pleasing sauce made with fat-free yogurt and served over noodles.
—*Beth Bries, Farley, Iowa*

1 tablespoon cornstarch
1 envelope onion mushroom soup mix
1/4 teaspoon salt
1/4 teaspoon pepper
1 cup fat-free evaporated milk
1 pound boneless beef sirloin steak, cut into
  thin strips
2 teaspoons canola oil
1/2 medium onion, sliced and separated into rings
1 garlic clove, minced
1-1/2 cups sliced fresh mushrooms
1 cup (8 ounces) fat-free plain yogurt
Hot cooked noodles
1 tablespoon minced fresh parsley

In a saucepan, combine the first four ingredients. Gradually stir in the milk until blended. Bring to a boil; cook and stir 2 minutes or until thickened. Remove from the heat; keep warm.

In a nonstick skillet, brown beef in oil. Add onion and garlic; cook and stir for 2 minutes. Add mushrooms; cook 1 minute longer or until mushrooms are tender. Reduce heat to low; stir in yogurt and reserved sauce. Cook and stir for 3-5 minutes on low until heated through. Serve over noodles; sprinkle with parsley. **Yield:** 4 servings.

Nutritional Analysis: One serving (3/4 cup beef mixture, calculated without noodles) equals 303 calories, 9 g fat (2 g saturated fat), 75 mg cholesterol, 755 mg sodium, 21 g carbohydrate, 1 g fiber, 34 g protein.
Diabetic Exchanges: 3 lean meat, 1 fat-free milk, 1/2 starch.

🍎 Sirloin Tips

WHEN BUYING sirloin, choose steaks that are firm to the touch and check the "sell by" date on the package.

Store sirloin in its original packaging in the refrigerator for 2 to 3 days, or freeze for up to 2 weeks.

For a quick marinade, blend light soy sauce with a little sugar and ginger. Marinate the steak overnight, then grill or broil.

Stir-fry frozen vegetables with thin slices of sirloin, soy sauce, cornstarch and beef broth and serve over rice for a quick-fix dinner.

Sirloin Veggie Kabobs

(Pictured above right)

*Planning your next cookout menu will be
no work at all when you have this
classic kabob recipe to call on. Feel free to use
cauliflower or any of your other favorite vegetables.*
—Trisha Ward, Atlanta, Georgia

2/3 cup chili sauce
1/2 cup dry red wine *or* beef broth
1/2 cup balsamic vinegar
2 tablespoons canola oil
4-1/2 teaspoons Worcestershire sauce
4-1/2 teaspoons dried minced onion
1 garlic clove, minced
1/2 teaspoon ground mustard
1/4 teaspoon salt
1 pound boneless beef sirloin steak, cut
  into 3/4-inch cubes
16 fresh baby portobello *or* large white
  mushrooms, halved
2 medium red onions, cut into wedges
1 medium sweet red pepper, cut into 3/4-inch
  pieces
1 medium sweet yellow pepper, cut into 3/4-inch
  pieces

In a bowl, combine the first nine ingredients; mix well. Pour half into a large resealable plastic bag. Add beef; seal bag and turn to coat. Pour remaining marinade in another large resealable plastic bag; add vegetables. Seal bag and turn to coat. Refrigerate beef and vegetables for up to 4 hours.

If grilling the kabobs, coat grill rack with nonstick cooking spray before starting the grill. Drain and discard marinade from beef. Drain vegetables, reserving marinade for basting. On eight metal or soaked wooden skewers, alternately thread beef and vegetables.

Grill, covered, over medium heat or broil 4-6 in. from the heat for 3-4 minutes on each side or until beef reaches desired doneness, turning three times. Baste frequently with reserved marinade. **Yield:** 4 servings.

Nutritional Analysis: Two kabobs equals 268 calories, 10 g fat (2 g saturated fat), 63 mg cholesterol, 480 mg sodium, 20 g carbohydrate, 2 g fiber, 24 g protein.
Diabetic Exchanges: 3 lean meat, 2 vegetable, 1/2 starch.

Asparagus Beef Stir-Fry

Low-carb

Chinese food is a big hit with my family, so this stir-fry is popular at our house...especially when I put a little extra bite in it with the red pepper flakes. To make sure the steak is tender, cut it into thin strips across the grain.
—*Debby Petersen, Niagara, Wisconsin*

2 tablespoons reduced-sodium soy sauce, *divided*
2 tablespoons dry white wine *or* beef broth, *divided*
1/2 pound boneless beef sirloin steak, cut into thin strips
1 tablespoon cornstarch
1/2 cup water
4 teaspoons canola oil, *divided*
1 small onion, thinly sliced
1 pound asparagus, sliced into 1-inch pieces
2 celery ribs, thinly sliced
1 garlic clove, minced
1/8 to 1/4 teaspoon crushed red pepper flakes
Hot cooked rice, optional

In a large resealable plastic bag, combine 1 tablespoon soy sauce and 1 tablespoon wine or broth; add beef. Seal bag and turn to coat; refrigerate for 30 minutes. In a small bowl, combine the cornstarch, water and remaining soy sauce and wine or broth until smooth; set aside.

In a large nonstick skillet or wok, stir-fry beef in 2 teaspoons oil for 3-4 minutes or until beef is no longer pink. Remove with a slotted spoon and keep warm. Stir-fry onion in remaining oil for 1 minute. Add asparagus; stir-fry for 2 minutes. Add celery, garlic and red pepper flakes; stir-fry 4-6 minutes longer or until vegetables are crisp-tender.

Stir cornstarch mixture and add to the skillet. Bring to a boil; cook and stir for 2 minutes or until thickened. Add beef; heat through. Serve over rice if desired. **Yield:** 3 servings.

Nutritional Analysis: One serving (1-1/3 cups beef mixture, calculated without rice) equals 211 calories, 10 g fat (2 g saturated fat), 42 mg cholesterol, 461 mg sodium, 11 g carbohydrate, 3 g fiber, 18 g protein.
Diabetic Exchanges: 2 lean meat, 2 vegetable, 1 fat.

Steak with Three Peppers

(Pictured at right and on the cover)

Fresh ginger and garlic season this mouth-watering mixture of beef strips, sweet peppers, romaine lettuce and crunchy water chestnuts. My husband loves stir-fry. I like it, too, because it's quick, easy and cleanup is a breeze since everything cooks in one pan.
—*Katherine Prier, Conway, Missouri*

4 teaspoons cornstarch, *divided*
1/2 teaspoon sugar
3 tablespoons reduced-sodium soy sauce, *divided*
1 tablespoon sherry *or* reduced-sodium beef broth
3 tablespoons additional reduced-sodium beef broth
3 teaspoons sesame oil, *divided*
3/4 teaspoon hot pepper sauce
1 pound boneless beef sirloin steak, cut into 1/2-inch strips
4 teaspoons canola oil, *divided*
1 *each* medium sweet red, yellow and orange peppers, cut into 1/4-inch slices
1 medium onion, cut into thin wedges
3 garlic cloves, minced
1 tablespoon minced fresh gingerroot
6 romaine lettuce leaves, cut into 1/2-inch strips
1 can (8 ounces) sliced water chestnuts, drained
Hot cooked rice, optional

In a bowl, combine 2 teaspoons cornstarch and sugar. Stir in 2 tablespoons soy sauce, sherry or broth, additional broth, 1 teaspoon sesame oil and hot pepper sauce until smooth; set aside.

In another bowl, combine the remaining cornstarch, soy sauce and sesame oil until smooth. Add beef and stir gently to coat. Cover and refrigerate for 1 hour.

In a large nonstick skillet or wok, stir-fry beef in 1 teaspoon hot canola oil for 3 minutes or until no longer pink. Remove and keep warm.

In the same skillet, stir-fry the peppers, onion, garlic and ginger in remaining canola oil for 3 minutes or until vegetables are crisp-tender. Stir reserved soy sauce mixture until smooth. Bring to a boil; cook and stir for 1-2 minutes or until thickened. Stir in the lettuce, water chestnuts and reserved beef. Cook and stir for 1 minute or until heated through. Serve over rice if desired. **Yield:** 4 servings.

Nutritional Analysis: One serving (1-1/4 cups stir-fry mixture, calculated without rice) equals 306 calories, 14 g fat (3 g saturated fat), 67 mg cholesterol, 489 mg sodium, 18 g carbohydrate, 5 g fiber, 27 g protein.
Diabetic Exchanges: 3 lean meat, 2 vegetable, 1 fat, 1/2 starch.

Rice Makes It Nice

INSTEAD of using the pound of ground beef called for when making taco meat, sloppy joes or soups, I cook a half pound of ground beef.

After draining the meat, I add 1-1/2 cups of cooked brown rice to make up for the missing meat. This is a good way to stretch ground beef and make healthier dishes. It also is a great way to use up leftover rice.
—*Krista Frank*
Rhododendron, Oregon

Braised Beef and Mushrooms

Low-carb Low-sodium

Knowing folks on restricted diets need to please their taste buds, too, our home economists came up with this flavorful treatment for beef. Bits of vegetables in a hearty wine-flavored sauce make the meat moist and delicious. Even without salt, it's a mouth-watering choice for dinner!

1-1/2 pounds boneless beef chuck roast, cut
    into 3/4-inch cubes
1 tablespoon olive oil
1 cup finely chopped turnip
1/2 cup finely chopped onion
3 cups sliced fresh mushrooms
6 garlic cloves, minced
1-3/4 cups red wine *or* reduced-sodium beef broth
1-1/4 cups water
1/4 cup tomato paste
2 envelopes very low-sodium beef bouillon
    granules
2 teaspoons prepared horseradish
1-1/2 teaspoons dried tarragon
1/4 teaspoon pepper
4 teaspoons cornstarch
2 tablespoons cold water
Hot cooked noodles, optional

In a large nonstick saucepan, brown meat in oil; drain. Remove meat from pan; set aside. In same pan, cook turnip and onion for 3 minutes or until lightly browned. Stir in mushrooms and garlic; cook and stir for 3-4 minutes or until turnips are tender.

In a small bowl, combine the wine or broth, water, tomato paste, bouillon granules, horseradish, tarragon and pepper until smooth. Gradually stir into skillet. Return meat to pan. Bring to a boil. Reduce heat; cover and simmer for about 1-1/4 hours or until meat is tender. Uncover; simmer 15 minutes longer.

In a small bowl, combine cornstarch and cold water until smooth. Gradually stir into pan. Bring to a boil; cook and stir for 2 minutes or until thickened. Serve over noodles if desired. **Yield:** 4 servings.

Nutritional Analysis: One serving (1 cup beef mixture, calculated without noodles) equals 298 calories, 11 g fat (3 g saturated fat), 90 mg cholesterol, 134 mg sodium, 14 g carbohydrate, 2 g fiber, 33 g protein.
Diabetic Exchanges: 4 lean meat, 2 vegetable, 1/2 fat.

Texas Ranch-Style Stew

Ground beef, beans and pasta thicken this hearty stew that's perfect for brisk autumn days. The zippy sauce, made with canned vegetable juice, gives the chunky mixture a western flair.
—Mrs. J.W. West, Alvord, Texas

1 cup small shell pasta
1 pound lean ground beef
1 medium onion, chopped

1 medium green pepper, chopped
2 garlic cloves, minced
3 cans (5-1/2 ounces *each*) reduced-sodium
    V8 juice
1 can (15 ounces) ranch-style beans *or* baked
    beans, undrained
1 can (14-1/2 ounces) southwestern diced
    tomatoes, undrained
1/2 cup frozen corn, thawed
1 tablespoon chili powder
1/2 teaspoon salt
1/4 teaspoon pepper

Cook the pasta according to package directions. Meanwhile, in a large nonstick skillet, cook the beef, onion, green pepper and garlic over medium heat until meat is no longer pink; drain. Stir in the remaining ingredients. Bring to a boil. Reduce heat; simmer, uncovered, for 10 minutes, stirring occasionally. Drain the pasta. Stir into the stew. **Yield:** 6 servings.

Nutritional Analysis: One serving (1-1/3 cups) equals 307 calories, 7 g fat (3 g saturated fat), 37 mg cholesterol, 886 mg sodium, 37 g carbohydrate, 7 g fiber, 22 g protein.
Diabetic Exchanges: 3 lean meat, 2 vegetable, 1-1/2 starch.

Hearty Backyard Burgers

(Pictured below)

I like to toast rye rolls or whole wheat hamburger buns on the grill for a few minutes while the burgers finish cooking. Then I top the burgers with ketchup and pickle planks right before serving.
—Paula LeFevre, Garden, Michigan

1/2 cup finely chopped onion
1/4 cup beer *or* nonalcoholic beer
1 tablespoon Worcestershire sauce
2 garlic cloves, minced
1 teaspoon salt
1/4 teaspoon pepper
1-1/2 pounds lean ground beef
6 rye rolls *or* whole wheat hamburger buns, split
6 lettuce leaves
12 tomato slices

In a bowl, combine the first six ingredients. Crumble beef over mixture and mix well. Shape into six patties. Coat grill rack with nonstick cooking spray before starting the grill. Cover and grill over medium-high heat for 4-5 minutes on each side or until no longer pink and a meat thermometer reads 160°. Serve on rolls with lettuce and tomato slices. **Yield:** 6 servings.

Nutritional Analysis: *One burger equals 307 calories, 12 g fat (4 g saturated fat), 70 mg cholesterol, 686 mg sodium, 25 g carbohydrate, 4 g fiber, 25 g protein.*
Diabetic Exchanges: *3 lean meat, 1-1/2 starch.*

Braised Southwest Beef Roast

Low-carb

Seasoned with Southwestern zest, this lean beef roast is fork-tender and gets a little kick from salsa. My husband, Phillip, and our two young daughters raise our own cattle and hogs on a farm. This is one of our favorite ways to eat beef. Enjoy!
—*Cathy Sestak, Freeburg, Missouri*

1-1/2 teaspoons chili powder
1 teaspoon ground cumin
1/2 teaspoon garlic powder
1/2 teaspoon dried oregano
1 beef eye of round roast (2 pounds)
1 tablespoon canola oil
1 cup reduced-sodium beef broth
1-1/4 cups salsa
1/4 cup water
1 bay leaf

In a small bowl, combine the chili powder, cumin, garlic power and oregano; rub over roast. In a Dutch oven, brown meat in oil. Remove from the pan.

Gradually add broth, stirring to loosen any browned bits from pan. Stir in salsa, water and bay leaf; return meat to pan. Bring to a boil. Reduce heat; cover and simmer for 2-1/4 to 2-1/2 hours or until meat is fork-tender.

Set meat aside and keep warm. Bring pan juices to a boil. Cook, uncovered, for 10-15 minutes or until sauce is reduced to about 1-1/3 cups; skim fat. Discard bay leaf. Serve sauce with meat. **Yield:** 5 servings.

Nutritional Analysis: *One serving (4 ounces cooked beef with 1/4 cup sauce) equals 249 calories, 9 g fat (2 g saturated fat), 80 mg cholesterol, 696 mg sodium, 8 g carbohydrate, 1 g fiber, 34 g protein.*
Diabetic Exchanges: *4 lean meat, 1 vegetable.*

Teriyaki Flank Steak

Low-carb

(Pictured above)

Teriyaki sauce, Chinese five-spice powder, ginger and sesame oil combine in this overnight marinade that gives plenty of Oriental flair to grilled flank steak.
—*Nancy Fairless, Clifton, New Jersey*

1-1/2 pounds beef flank steak
3/4 cup reduced-sodium teriyaki sauce
2 tablespoons sesame oil
1-1/2 teaspoons ground ginger *or* 2 tablespoons minced fresh gingerroot
5 garlic cloves, minced
1/2 teaspoon Chinese five-spice powder
1/4 teaspoon pepper
2 green onions, thinly sliced

Score the surface of the steak with shallow diagonal cuts, making diamond shapes. In a bowl, combine the teriyaki sauce, oil, ginger, garlic, five-spice powder and pepper; mix well. Pour 2/3 cup marinade into a large resealable plastic bag; add the steak and green onions. Seal bag and turn to coat; refrigerate for at least 8 hours or overnight. Cover and refrigerate remaining marinade.

If grilling the steak, coat grill rack with nonstick cooking spray before starting the grill. Drain and discard marinade from meat. Grill steak, covered, over medium-hot heat or broil 4-6 in. from the heat for 5-6 minutes on each side or until meat reaches desired doneness (for rare, a meat thermometer should read 140°; medium, 160°; well-done, 170°), brushing occasionally with reserved marinade. **Yield:** 6 servings.

Nutritional Analysis: *One serving (3 ounces cooked steak) equals 207 calories, 10 g fat (4 g saturated fat), 54 mg cholesterol, 388 mg sodium, 4 g carbohydrate, trace fiber, 23 g protein.*
Diabetic Exchanges: *3 lean meat, 1/2 fat.*

Autumn Pot Roast

(Pictured above)

*Good old-fashioned pot roast has a
new mouth-watering flavor prepared this way.
This colorful dish makes an appealing holiday meal.
The cranberries mixed with horseradish give the
beef terrific taste. You can add any
vegetables you like to make it more unique.*
—*Deby Kominski, Honesdale, Pennsylvania*

  1 **boneless beef rump roast (about 3 pounds),**
    tied
1/4 **teaspoon salt**
1/4 **teaspoon pepper**
  2 **teaspoons canola oil**
3/4 **cup fresh *or* frozen cranberries**
1/2 **cup water**
1/4 **cup sugar**
  1 **cup reduced-sodium beef broth**
1/3 **cup prepared horseradish, drained**
  1 **cinnamon stick (3 inches)**
  3 **whole cloves**
 16 **pearl onions**
  2 **medium sweet potatoes (about 1-1/2 pounds),**
    peeled and cut into 3/4-inch cubes
 16 **baby carrots**
  4 **teaspoons cornstarch**
  2 **tablespoons cold water**

Sprinkle meat with salt and pepper. In a Dutch oven, brown meat in oil. Drain and remove from the heat. In a large saucepan, combine the cranberries, water and sugar. Cook and stir over medium heat until cranberries pop and liquid is slightly thickened, about 8 minutes. Remove from the heat.

Add the broth and horseradish; pour over meat. Place cinnamon stick and cloves in a double thickness of cheesecloth; bring up corners of cloth and tie with kitchen string to form a bag. Add to Dutch oven.

Cover and bake at 325° for 2 hours. Meanwhile, in a large saucepan, bring 6 cups water to a boil. Add pearl onions; boil for 3 minutes. Drain and rinse in cold water; peel and set aside. Add sweet potatoes to Dutch oven. Cover and cook 15 minutes longer. Add carrots and onions; cover and cook 30-40 minutes more or until vegetables and meat are tender. Remove meat and vegetables; keep warm. Discard spice bag.

Cool pan juices for 10 minutes; transfer to a blender. Cover and process until smooth; return to pan. Combine the cornstarch and cold water until smooth. Gradually whisk into the pan juices. Bring to a boil; cook and stir for 1-2 minutes or until thickened. Serve with the meat and vegetables. **Yield:** 8 servings.

Nutritional Analysis: One serving (3 ounces cooked beef with 3/4 cup vegetables and 3 tablespoons gravy) equals 328 calories, 9 g fat (3 g saturated fat), 83 mg cholesterol, 235 mg sodium, 31 g carbohydrate, 4 g fiber, 29 g protein.

Diabetic Exchanges: 3 lean meat, 1-1/2 starch, 1 vegetable.

Chicken & Turkey Entrees

You don't have to eat like a bird—or forego flavor—in order to trim down on fat and calories. A simple solution is to choose chicken and turkey. Your family will flock to the table for these enticing entrees.

Garlic Onion Turkey Burgers (page 128)

Lemon Turkey Stir-Fry

The recipe for this tender turkey stir-fry has a hint of lemon, which accents the flavor.
—Audrey Thibodeau, Mesa, Arizona

2 teaspoons cornstarch
2 teaspoons Worcestershire sauce
1 teaspoon reduced-sodium soy sauce
2 teaspoons lemon peel
1 teaspoon chicken bouillon granules
1 teaspoon honey
2/3 cup boiling water
1 pound turkey breast, cubed
2 tablespoons canola oil, *divided*
1/2 cup *each* sliced green onions and celery
1/2 cup chopped red pepper
1 can (8 ounces) water chestnuts, drained
1 package (6 ounces) frozen snow peas, thawed
2 tablespoons lemon juice
1/4 teaspoon coarsely ground pepper
Hot cooked rice, optional

In a small bowl, combine the first four ingredients until smooth. Dissolve bouillon and honey in boiling water; stir into the cornstarch mixture. Set aside.

In a large nonstick skillet or wok, stir-fry the turkey in 1 tablespoon hot oil until no longer pink; remove and keep warm. In the same skillet, stir-fry the green onions, celery and red pepper in remaining oil until crisp-tender; return turkey to pan. Stir bouillon mixture and add to the pan. Bring to a boil; cook and stir for 2 minutes or until thickened. Add the water chestnuts and pea pods; heat through. Stir in the lemon juice and pepper. Serve over rice if desired. **Yield:** 4 servings.

Nutritional Analysis: *One serving (1 cup stir-fry mixture, calculated without rice) equals 264 calories, 8 g fat (1 g saturated fat), 70 mg cholesterol, 444 mg sodium, 17 g carbohydrate, 4 g fiber, 30 g protein.*
Diabetic Exchanges: *3 lean meat, 2 vegetable, 1/2 starch.*

Fettuccine Primavera

(Pictured above right)

A mild lemon sauce seasoned with thyme lightly coats this attractive medley of tender chicken, pasta, asparagus, red pepper and peas.
—Marietta Howell, Okmulgee, Oklahoma

8 ounces uncooked fettuccine
1 cup julienned sweet red pepper
1 tablespoon canola oil
1/2 pound boneless skinless chicken breasts, cut into 1/4-inch strips
6 green onions, sliced
1/2 pound fresh asparagus, trimmed and cut into 1-inch pieces
3/4 cup chicken broth
1-1/2 teaspoons lemon juice
1/2 teaspoon salt

1/2 teaspoon dried thyme
1/2 teaspoon grated lemon peel
2/3 cup frozen peas, thawed
2 teaspoons cornstarch
1 tablespoon water
2 tablespoons reduced-fat sour cream
1/4 cup shredded Parmesan cheese

Cook pasta according to package directions. Meanwhile, in a 12-in. nonstick skillet, saute red pepper in oil for 3 minutes until crisp-tender. Stir in the chicken, onions, asparagus, broth, lemon juice, salt, thyme and lemon peel. Cook for 1 minute or until asparagus is crisp-tender. Stir in peas; saute for 1 minute or until heated through.

Combine cornstarch and water until smooth; stir into chicken mixture. Bring to a boil; cook and stir for 1-2 minutes or until thickened and chicken is no longer pink. Remove from the heat; stir in sour cream.

Pour the chicken mixture into a large bowl. Drain pasta and add to chicken mixture. Sprinkle with Parmesan cheese and toss to coat. **Yield:** 6 servings.

Nutritional Analysis: *One serving (1-1/3 cups) equals 274 calories, 6 g fat (2 g saturated fat), 27 mg cholesterol, 431 mg sodium, 38 g carbohydrate, 4 g fiber, 18 g protein.*
Diabetic Exchanges: *2 starch, 1 vegetable, 1 very lean meat, 1 fat.*

Tarragon Poached Chicken

Low-carb Low-fat

A delectable sauce starring Dijon mustard and white wine tops off the poached chicken in this delightful meal-in-one dinner. People who taste this unique dish can't believe I found it in a collection of lighter recipes. Carrots and onions are cooked with the chicken and round out the meal nicely.
—*Herbert Bray, Johnstown, Pennsylvania*

1-1/2 cups reduced-sodium chicken broth
  1/2 cup dry white wine *or* additional reduced-sodium chicken broth
    2 medium celery ribs, thinly sliced
    2 medium carrots, thinly sliced
    1 medium onion, thinly sliced
    2 teaspoons dried tarragon
  1/2 teaspoon salt
  1/8 teaspoon pepper
    4 boneless skinless chicken breast halves
      (4 ounces *each*)
    2 tablespoons cornstarch
    2 tablespoons water
    1 teaspoon Dijon mustard
  1/8 teaspoon browning sauce, optional
    1 tablespoon chopped fresh parsley
Hot cooked rice, optional

In a large nonstick skillet, combine the first eight ingredients. Bring to a boil. Reduce heat; simmer, uncovered, for 10 minutes. Add chicken; cover and simmer 15-20 minutes longer or until chicken juices run clear. With a slotted spoon, remove chicken and vegetables to a serving dish.

Combine cornstarch, water, mustard and browning sauce if desired until smooth; whisk into poaching liquid. Bring to a boil; cook and stir for 2 minutes or until thickened. Spoon over chicken and vegetables; sprinkle with parsley. Serve over hot cooked rice if desired. **Yield:** 4 servings.

Nutritional Analysis: One serving (1 chicken breast half with vegetables and 1/4 cup sauce, calculated without rice) equals 206 calories, 2 g fat (trace saturated fat), 66 mg cholesterol, 673 mg sodium, 13 g carbohydrate, 2 g fiber, 29 g protein.
Diabetic Exchanges: 3 lean meat, 2 vegetable.

Braised Turkey Thighs

Low-carb

(Pictured at right)

Folks who enjoy dark meat will appreciate this treatment for turkey thighs. An oven bag keeps them nice and moist during baking. Little bits of vegetables add taste and texture to the flavorful gravy.
—*Loretta Paulus, Venice, Florida*

    1 cup *each* finely chopped onion, celery and
      carrots
  1/3 cup ketchup
1-1/4 teaspoons salt
  1/2 teaspoon paprika
  1/8 teaspoon pepper
    4 pounds turkey thighs
    2 tablespoons all-purpose flour, *divided*
    1 oven bag (20-inch x 14-inch)
  1/2 cup reduced-sodium chicken broth
  1/3 cup dry white wine *or* additional reduced-sodium chicken broth
    1 teaspoon dried oregano
    2 bay leaves
  1/4 cup cold water

In a bowl, combine the onion, celery, carrots, ketchup, salt, paprika and pepper. Pat onto turkey thighs. Place 1 tablespoon flour in oven bag; shake to coat. Transfer turkey thighs to oven bag. Place in a 13-in. x 9-in. x 2-in. baking dish. Combine the broth, wine or additional broth, oregano and bay leaves. Pour into bag; seal. Cut 2 slits into the top of the bag. Bake at 350° for 1-1/2 hours or until a meat thermometer reads 180° and turkey juices run clear.

Remove turkey to a serving platter; keep warm. Pour pan juices into a small saucepan; skim fat and discard bay leaves. Bring to a boil. Reduce heat; simmer, uncovered, for 5 minutes or until mixture is reduced to 1-3/4 cups.

Place remaining flour in a bowl. Stir in cold water until smooth. Stir into saucepan. Bring to a boil; cook and stir for 2 minutes or until thickened. Remove skin and bones from turkey; cut turkey into slices. Serve gravy with turkey. **Yield:** 8 servings.

Nutritional Analysis: One serving (4 ounces cooked turkey with 1/4 cup gravy) equals 255 calories, 9 g fat (3 g saturated fat), 91 mg cholesterol, 629 mg sodium, 8 g carbohydrate, 1 g fiber, 33 g protein.
Diabetic Exchanges: 4 lean meat, 1 vegetable.

spoons of water or flour if needed). When cycle is completed, turn dough onto a lightly floured surface. Divide dough in half. Cover and let stand for 10 minutes.

Roll into two 14-in. circles. Transfer to two 14-in. pizza pans coated with nonstick cooking spray. Spread oil over each crust. Top with pizza sauce, oregano, mozzarella cheese, pepperoni, Parmesan cheese, onion and green pepper. Bake at 450° for 15-20 minutes or until crust is golden brown. **Yield:** 2 pizzas (6 slices each).

Nutritional Analysis: One slice equals 343 calories, 11 g fat (5 g saturated fat), 29 mg cholesterol, 611 mg sodium, 43 g carbohydrate, 4 g fiber, 19 g protein.
Diabetic Exchanges: 2-1/2 starch, 2 lean meat, 1 vegetable, 1/2 fat.

Whole Wheat Pepperoni Pizzas

(Pictured above)

People say that the crispy whole wheat crust of this pizza recipe is the best they've tasted. Plus, it's so easy to prepare in the bread machine...and it makes enough for two pizzas.
—Beth Zaring, Wellston, Ohio

1-2/3 cups water
   2 tablespoons olive oil
   2 tablespoons sugar
   2 tablespoons nonfat dry milk powder
   1 teaspoon salt
   1 teaspoon lemon juice
2-1/2 cups bread flour
   2 cups whole wheat flour
   2 teaspoons active dry yeast
TOPPINGS:
   4 teaspoons olive oil
   1 can (15 ounces) pizza sauce
   2 teaspoons dried oregano
   4 cups (16 ounces) part-skim mozzarella cheese
   2 ounces turkey pepperoni, diced
  1/4 cup grated Parmesan cheese
  2/3 cup chopped onion
  2/3 cup chopped green pepper

In bread machine pan, place the first nine ingredients in order suggested by manufacturer. Select dough setting (check dough after 5 minutes of mixing; add 1 to 2 table-

Creamy Curried Turkey

A subtle hint of curry and a snappy crunch from apple and celery make this a fun variation on the classic creamed turkey. This is so popular at our house, I've occasionally cooked a turkey just to have leftovers to make it. Spooned over biscuits, it's a nice light lunch, supper or potluck dish.
—Maureen Dufraimont, Guelph, Ontario

   2 cups fat-free milk
   1 tablespoon lemon juice
   1 tablespoon reduced-fat sour cream
   1 tablespoon reduced-fat mayonnaise
   1 teaspoon salt
  1/2 teaspoon curry powder
  1/8 teaspoon pepper
   1 cup sliced fresh mushrooms
   1 medium apple, peeled and chopped
   1 celery rib, chopped
  1/4 cup chopped green pepper
   2 tablespoons butter
  1/4 cup all-purpose flour
   3 cups cubed cooked turkey breast
  1/2 cup frozen peas
   5 toasted reduced-fat biscuits, split

In a small bowl, combine the first seven ingredients; set aside. In a large nonstick skillet, saute the mushrooms, apple, celery and green pepper in butter until tender. Stir in flour until blended; gradually add milk mixture. Bring to a boil; cook and stir for 1-2 minutes or until thickened. Add turkey and peas; heat through. Serve over biscuits. **Yield:** 5 servings.

Nutritional Analysis: One serving (1 cup turkey mixture with 1 biscuit) equals 416 calories, 8 g fat (4 g saturated fat), 88 mg cholesterol, 1,220 mg sodium, 50 g carbohydrate, 2 g fiber, 36 g protein.
Diabetic Exchanges: 3 starch, 3 very lean meat, 1 fat, 1/2 fat-free milk.

Quick Turkey Casserole

I whip up this fast-to-fix main dish in the microwave. Everyone loves this creamy casserole, and it's a great way to use up leftover rice and turkey.
—Ann Hanel, San Jacinto, California

2 cups sliced onions
1/2 teaspoon sugar
2 teaspoons butter
2 teaspoons canola oil
3 ounces reduced-fat cream cheese
1 can (10-3/4 ounces) condensed reduced-fat
   reduced-sodium cream of mushroom soup,
   undiluted
2 cups cooked long grain rice
1-1/2 cups cubed cooked turkey
2 tablespoons minced fresh parsley
1/4 teaspoon salt
1/8 teaspoon pepper
1/4 cup fine cornflake crumbs
1/8 teaspoon paprika

In a nonstick skillet, cook onions and sugar in butter and oil over low heat for 15-20 minutes or until onions are golden brown, stirring frequently.

Meanwhile, place cream cheese in a shallow microwave-safe bowl; cover and microwave on high for 20-30 seconds or until softened. Add soup; stir until blended. Add the rice, turkey, parsley, salt and pepper. Cover and microwave on high for 3-4 minutes or until heated through. Toss onions with cornflake crumbs; arrange over turkey mixture. Sprinkle with paprika. Microwave, uncovered, on high for 1-2 minutes or until topping is heated through. **Yield:** 4 servings.

Editor's Note: This recipe was tested in a 1,100-watt microwave.

Nutritional Analysis: One serving (3/4 cup) equals 375 calories, 13 g fat (5 g saturated fat), 63 mg cholesterol, 625 mg sodium, 42 g carbohydrate, 2 g fiber, 22 g protein.
Diabetic Exchanges: *3 lean meat, 2-1/2 starch, 1 vegetable.*

Taco Noodle Dish

(Pictured at right)

I got creative while we were housebound during a snowstorm one winter and used ingredients I had on hand to come up with this hearty casserole. Later, I modified it so it has less fat and fewer calories.
—Judy Munger, Warren, Minnesota

2 cups uncooked yolk-free wide noodles
2 pounds lean ground turkey
1 can (8 ounces) tomato sauce
1/2 cup water
1 can (4 ounces) chopped green chilies
1 envelope reduced-sodium taco seasoning
1 teaspoon onion powder
1 teaspoon chili powder
1/2 teaspoon garlic powder
1 cup (4 ounces) shredded reduced-fat cheddar
   cheese
2 cups shredded lettuce
1 cup diced fresh tomatoes
1/3 cup sliced ripe olives, drained
1/2 cup taco sauce
1/2 cup fat-free sour cream

Cook noodles according to package directions. Meanwhile, in a large nonstick skillet, cook the turkey over medium heat until no longer pink; drain. Stir in the tomato sauce, water,

green chilies, taco seasoning, onion powder, chili powder and garlic powder. Bring to a boil. Reduce heat; simmer, uncovered, for 5 minutes. Drain noodles; place in an 11-in. x 7-in. x 2-in. baking dish coated with nonstick cooking spray. Spread the turkey mixture over the top. Sprinkle with cheese. Bake, uncovered, at 350° for 10-15 minutes or until cheese is melted. Let stand for 10 minutes.

Top with the lettuce, tomatoes, olives and taco sauce. Dollop each serving with 1 tablespoon of sour cream. **Yield:** 8 servings.

Nutritional Analysis: One serving equals 312 calories, 13 g fat (5 g saturated fat), 100 mg cholesterol, 788 mg sodium, 18 g carbohydrate, 2 g fiber, 27 g protein.
Diabetic Exchanges: *3 lean meat, 1 starch, 1 vegetable, 1 fat.*

🍎 Choice Chicken Tips

KEEP the following in mind when buying, storing and cooking chicken:

- Check the "sell by" date on the label to be sure the chicken is fresh. The color of a chicken's skin has no bearing on its quality, but it should be opaque. Avoid frozen chicken that has ice crystals or freezer burns.

- Keep safety in mind when handling uncooked chicken. To prevent contamination to other foods, use hot soapy water to wash your hands as well as any knives, cutting boards or countertops that may have come in contact with the uncooked chicken.

- Never serve undercooked chicken. Chicken is thoroughly cooked when its juices run clear. Golden brown skin does not necessarily mean that a chicken is fully cooked.

Almond Turkey Stir-Fry

Need a wholesome meal that's full of fresh flavor and quick to fix? Try this delicious dish!
—*Lori Johnson, Four Corners, Wyoming*

1 tablespoon cornstarch
1 cup reduced-sodium chicken broth
1/4 cup water
2 tablespoons reduced-sodium soy sauce
1 teaspoon sugar
1/4 teaspoon salt
1/4 teaspoon pepper
1 pound turkey breast tenderloin, cubed
4 teaspoons canola oil, *divided*
1 cup chopped celery
1/2 cup shredded carrot
1/2 cup chopped onion
1/2 cup sliced fresh mushrooms
1/2 cup sliced green onions
1 garlic clove, minced
1 can (8 ounces) sliced water chestnuts, drained
1/2 cup slivered almonds, toasted
Hot cooked rice, optional

In a small bowl, combine the first seven ingredients until smooth; set aside. In a nonstick skillet, stir-fry turkey in 2 teaspoons hot oil until no longer pink. Remove and keep warm. In the same skillet, stir-fry the celery, carrot, onion, mushrooms, green onions and garlic in remaining oil until crisp-tender, about 5-6 minutes.

Add water chestnuts and turkey; heat through. Stir broth mixture and add to the pan. Bring to a boil; cook and stir for 1-2 minutes or until thickened. Sprinkle with almonds. Serve over hot cooked rice if desired. **Yield:** 4 servings.

Nutritional Analysis: One serving (1 cup stir-fry mixture, calculated without rice) equals 303 calories, 12 g fat (1 g saturated fat), 70 mg cholesterol, 697 mg sodium, 16 g carbohydrate, 4 g fiber, 33 g protein.
Diabetic Exchanges: 4 lean meat, 1 vegetable, 1/2 starch.

Garlic-Onion Turkey Burgers

(Pictured on page 123)

Even if you're not on a restricted diet, you'll enjoy these tasty burgers. The ground turkey and beef patties are moist, hearty and seasoned to please. I came up with this recipe as a more nutritious alternative to store-bought hamburger patties.
—*Lisa Stavropoulos, Stouffville, Ontario*

3 small onions, quartered
1 small carrot, cut into chunks
3 garlic cloves, peeled
1/2 cup dry bread crumbs
1/3 cup fat-free milk
1 egg, beaten
1 teaspoon salt
1/2 teaspoon dried basil
1/2 teaspoon dried thyme
1 teaspoon Worcestershire sauce
2 pounds lean ground turkey
1 pound lean ground beef
12 hamburger buns, split

In a food processor, combine the onions, carrot and garlic; cover and process until finely chopped. Transfer mixture to a large bowl. Add the bread crumbs, milk, egg, salt, basil, thyme and Worcestershire sauce. Crumble turkey and beef over mixture; mix well. Shape into 12 patties.

Coat grill rack with nonstick cooking spray before starting the grill. Grill, covered, over medium-hot heat for 5-7 minutes on each side or until a meat thermometer reads 165° and juices run clear. Serve on buns. **Yield:** 12 servings.

Nutritional Analysis: One hamburger equals 327 calories, 12 g fat (4 g saturated fat), 96 mg cholesterol, 589 mg sodium, 27 g carbohydrate, 2 g fiber, 26 g protein.
Diabetic Exchanges: 3 lean meat, 2 starch.

Vegetable Chicken Stir-Fry

Low-carb

(Pictured at right)

This light and lively stir-fry provides the perfect mix of good taste and nutrition.
—*Michelle Haviland, Healdsburg, California*

1 tablespoon cornstarch
1 cup reduced-sodium chicken broth
1/4 cup reduced-sodium soy sauce
1 pound boneless skinless chicken breasts, cut into strips
3 garlic cloves, minced
Dash ground ginger
2 tablespoons olive oil, *divided*
2 cups fresh broccoli florets
1 cup each sliced carrots and cauliflowerets
1 cup fresh *or* frozen snow peas
1 teaspoon sesame seeds, toasted

In a bowl, combine cornstarch, broth and soy sauce until smooth; set aside. In a large nonstick skillet or wok, stir-fry the chicken, garlic and ginger in hot oil for 4-5 minutes or until chicken is no longer pink. Remove and keep warm.

In skillet, stir-fry broccoli, carrots and cauliflower in the remaining oil for 4 minutes or until crisp-tender. Add snow peas; stir-fry for 2 minutes. Stir broth mixture; add to pan. Bring to a boil; cook and stir for 1 minute or until thickened. Add chicken; heat through. Top with sesame seeds. **Yield:** 4 servings.

Nutritional Analysis: One serving (1-1/2 cups) equals 256 calories, 9 g fat (1 g saturated fat), 66 mg cholesterol, 862 mg sodium, 13 g carbohydrate, 2 g fiber, 31 g protein.
Diabetic Exchanges: 3 lean meat, 2 vegetable, 1 fat.

Chicken on a Stick

Low-carb Low-sodium

Chicken is my family's favorite meat, whether it's roasted, barbecued or whatever. I make these skewered chicken strips often, especially during the summer months. They're popular at our annual family picnic, too.
—Susan Post, Baltimore, Ontario

    2 tablespoons canola oil
    2 tablespoons lemon juice
    2 tablespoons reduced-sodium soy sauce
    4 garlic cloves, minced
    2 teaspoons honey
    1 teaspoon ground cumin
    1 teaspoon ground coriander
  1/2 teaspoon ground ginger
  3/4 pound boneless skinless chicken breasts, cut
      into thin strips

In a bowl, combine the oil, lemon juice, soy sauce, garlic, honey and seasonings; mix well. Pour 1/4 cup marinade into a large resealable plastic bag; add the chicken. Seal bag and turn to coat; refrigerate for at least 3-4 hours. Cover and refrigerate remaining marinade.

Coat grill rack with nonstick cooking spray before starting the grill. Drain and discard marinade from chicken. On metal or soaked wooden skewers, thread chicken. Grill, uncovered, over medium-hot heat for 3-4 minutes on each side or until chicken juices run clear, basting frequently with reserved marinade and turning once. **Yield:** 6 servings.

Nutritional Analysis: One serving equals 97 calories, 4 g fat (1 g saturated fat), 31 mg cholesterol, 70 mg sodium, 2 g carbohydrate, trace fiber, 12 g protein.
Diabetic Exchange: *2 lean meat.*

Turkey Skillet Supper

This quick and filling one-dish meal won't taste like "diet" fare to your family. Chili powder livens up this satisfying mixture of ground turkey, macaroni and canned tomatoes.
—Connie Thomas, Jensen, Utah

    1 pound lean ground turkey
    1 medium onion, chopped
    1 can (28 ounces) crushed tomatoes
    2 cups uncooked elbow macaroni
    1 medium green pepper, chopped
    1 can (8 ounces) tomato sauce
  1/2 cup water
    2 tablespoons chili powder
    6 tablespoons reduced-fat sour cream

In a nonstick skillet, cook turkey and onion over medium heat until meat is no longer pink; drain. Add the tomatoes, macaroni, green pepper, tomato sauce, water and chili powder. Bring to a boil. Reduce heat; cover and simmer for 20 minutes or until macaroni is tender. Garnish servings with sour cream. **Yield:** 6 servings.

Nutritional Analysis: One serving (1-1/4 cups turkey mixture with 1 tablespoon sour cream) equals 341 calories, 8 g fat (2 g saturated fat), 60 mg cholesterol, 515 mg sodium, 48 g carbohydrate, 6 g fiber, 23 g protein.
Diabetic Exchanges: *3 vegetable, 2 starch, 2 lean meat.*

Lemon Honey Turkey

Low-fat Low-sodium

(Pictured below)

Folks will be smacking their lips when they taste these tender slices of turkey draped in a sweet and tangy sauce. I love cooking with lemon and honey and experimenting with herbs. This dish is so easy to make.
—Judith Harris, Brainerd, Minnesota

  1/3 cup honey
  1/4 cup lemon juice
    2 teaspoons dried rosemary, crushed
  1/4 teaspoon crushed red pepper flakes
    2 turkey breast tenderloins (12 ounces *each*)
    1 teaspoon cornstarch
    1 teaspoon water
  1/8 teaspoon browning sauce, optional

In a small bowl, combine the first four ingredients. Place tenderloins in an 11-in. x 7-in. x 2-in. baking dish coated with nonstick cooking spray. Brush with half the sauce. Bake, uncovered, at 350° for 40-45 minutes or until a meat thermometer reads 170°, basting occasionally with remaining sauce. Remove turkey to a plate and keep warm.

Transfer drippings to a small saucepan. Combine cornstarch and water until smooth; stir into drippings. Bring to

a boil; cook and stir for 1-2 minutes or until thickened. Stir in browning sauce if desired. Serve sauce over turkey. **Yield:** 6 servings.

Nutritional Analysis: One serving (3 ounces cooked turkey with 4 teaspoons sauce) equals 196 calories, 1 g fat (trace saturated fat), 82 mg cholesterol, 53 mg sodium, 17 g carbohydrate, trace fiber, 30 g protein.
Diabetic Exchanges: 3 very lean meat, 1 starch.

Green Vegetables with Brown Rice

Here's a great way to use up leftover chicken and rice!
The vibrant medley of veggies and crunchy almonds gets
plenty of flavor from soy sauce, garlic and gingerroot.
—Kristen Feola, Springfield, Missouri

1/2 cup broccoli florets
1 tablespoon olive oil
1/2 medium green pepper, cut into 1-inch pieces
1 small onion, cut into 1-inch pieces
2 garlic cloves, minced
1/2 teaspoon minced fresh gingerroot
1/4 teaspoon pepper
2 cups cubed cooked chicken breast
1-1/2 cups cooked brown rice
4 green onions, sliced
1/4 cup fresh *or* frozen peas
1/4 cup pineapple juice
1/4 cup reduced-sodium soy sauce
2 tablespoons slivered almonds, toasted

In a large nonstick skillet or wok, stir-fry broccoli in oil for 3 minutes. Add the green pepper and onion; stir-fry for 5-6 minutes. Add the garlic, ginger and pepper; stir-fry 1 minute longer. Add the chicken, rice, green onions, peas, pineapple juice and soy sauce; bring to a boil. Cook and stir until vegetables are crisp-tender. Just before serving, sprinkle with almonds. **Yield:** 4 servings.

Nutritional Analysis: One serving (1 cup) equals 295 calories, 8 g fat (1 g saturated fat), 60 mg cholesterol, 674 mg sodium, 27 g carbohydrate, 4 g fiber, 27 g protein.
Diabetic Exchanges: 3 lean meat, 1-1/2 starch, 1 vegetable.

🍎 Simple Salt-Free Chicken Stock

INSTEAD of buying salt-free chicken stock, I make it myself. I put three pounds of chicken, several black peppercorns, a celery rib and carrot in my slow cooker. I quarter an onion and press a few cloves into each piece and add that to the pot. Then I pour in a cup of dry vermouth and a bay leaf. I cook this on low for 7-8 hours.

I end up with nicely-flavored poached chicken and a cup of stock. And I don't miss the salt.
—Marijane Rea, Milwaukie, Oregon

Grilled Turkey Kabobs

(Pictured above)

I tried these kabobs at a friend's barbecue and asked
for the recipe. Marinating them overnight really gives
the flavor a chance to soak in. They make a tangy
light meal served with fruited rice pilaf.
—Marilyn Rodriguez, Fairbanks, Alaska

1/3 cup chili sauce
2 tablespoons lemon juice
1 tablespoon sugar
2 bay leaves
1 pound turkey breast tenderloins, cut
  into 1-1/2 cubes
2 medium zucchini, cut into 1/2-inch slices
2 small green peppers, cut into 1-1/2 squares
2 small onions, quartered
8 medium fresh mushrooms
8 cherry tomatoes
1 tablespoon canola oil

In a bowl, combine the chili sauce, lemon juice, sugar and bay leaves; mix well. Pour 1/4 cup marinade into a large resealable plastic bag; add the turkey. Seal bag and turn to coat; refrigerate for at least 2 hours or overnight. Cover and refrigerate remaining marinade.

Coat grill rack with nonstick cooking spray before starting the grill. Drain and discard marinade. Discard bay leaves from reserved marinade. On eight metal or soaked wooden skewers, alternately thread turkey and vegetables. Brush lightly with oil. Grill, uncovered, over medium-hot heat for 3-4 minutes on each side or until juices run clear, basting frequently with reserved marinade and turning three times. **Yield:** 4 servings.

Nutritional Analysis: One serving (2 kabobs) equals 254 calories, 5 g fat (1 g saturated fat), 82 mg cholesterol, 695 mg sodium, 21 g carbohydrate, 3 g fiber, 33 g protein.
Diabetic Exchanges: 3 lean meat, 2 vegetable, 1/2 starch.

Chutney-Glazed Chicken

Low-carb

(Pictured below)

Basting bone-in chicken breasts with chutney while grilling results in a mouth-watering moist entree. They make a really delicious meal when served with a tossed salad and dinner rolls. Garnishing with chives is a nice touch.
—*Angie Ridgway, Fairfield, Nebraska*

1/2 cup mango chutney
2 tablespoons sherry *or* apple juice
2 tablespoons Dijon mustard
1 teaspoon curry powder
6 bone-in chicken breast halves (about 8 ounces *each*), skin removed

Coat grill rack with nonstick cooking spray before starting the grill for indirect heat. In a small bowl, combine the chutney, sherry or apple juice, mustard and curry powder. Grill chicken meaty side down over indirect medium heat for 15 minutes. Turn; grill 15-20 minutes longer or until a meat thermometer reads 170°, basting occasionally with chutney mixture. **Yield:** 6 servings.

Nutritional Analysis: One serving (1 chicken breast half) equals 243 calories, 5 g fat (1 g saturated fat), 102 mg cholesterol, 220 mg sodium, 10 g carbohydrate, 1 g fiber, 38 g protein. **Diabetic Exchanges:** 4 lean meat, 1/2 starch.

Cobb Salad Wraps

(Pictured above)

A homemade dressing lightens up these refreshing tortilla wraps. The avocado, bacon, blue cheese and tomato deliver the flavors I enjoy most while keeping me on my healthy eating plan.
—*Lynne Van Wagenen, Salt Lake City, Utah*

1/2 pound boneless skinless chicken breasts, cooked and shredded
1/2 cup chopped avocado
4 bacon strips, cooked and crumbled
1 celery rib, thinly sliced
1 green onion, sliced
2 tablespoons chopped ripe olives
2 tablespoons crumbled blue cheese
2 tablespoons lemon juice
1 tablespoon honey
1-1/2 teaspoons Dijon mustard
1 garlic clove, minced
1/4 teaspoon dill weed
1/4 teaspoon salt
1/8 teaspoon pepper
1 tablespoon olive oil
4 romaine leaves, torn
4 whole wheat flour tortillas (8 inches), warmed
1 medium tomato, chopped

In a small bowl, combine the chicken, avocado, bacon, celery, onion, olives and cheese. In another small bowl, combine the lemon juice, honey, mustard, garlic, dill weed, salt and pepper. Whisk in the oil. Pour over the chicken mixture; toss to coat. Place romaine on each tortilla; top with 2/3 cup chicken mixture, then with tomatoes. Roll up tortilla. **Yield:** 4 servings.

Turkey with Cranberry-Grape Sauce

Our son-in-law brought home wild turkey, which inspired this delectable main dish. The sauce stirs up quickly...and you can grill the turkey in just minutes.
—Marguerite Shaeffer, Sewell, New Jersey

1 teaspoon cornstarch
1/2 cup orange juice
1/4 cup dried cranberries
4-1/2 teaspoons honey
1 tablespoon lemon juice
2 turkey tenderloins (12 ounces *each*), halved widthwise
2 teaspoons olive oil
1 teaspoon coarsely ground pepper
1/2 teaspoon salt
1-1/2 cups green grapes, halved

In a saucepan, combine the first five ingredients until smooth. Bring to a boil; cook and stir for 1-2 minutes or until thickened. Cover and refrigerate.

If grilling, coat grill rack with nonstick cooking spray before starting the grill. Flatten turkey to 3/4-in. thickness. Combine oil, pepper and salt; rub over both sides of turkey. Grill turkey, covered, over direct medium heat or broil 4-6 in. from the heat for 5-7 minutes on each side or until a meat thermometer reads 170°. Just before serving, stir grapes into sauce. Serve turkey with cranberry-grape sauce. **Yield:** 4 servings.

Nutritional Analysis: One serving (5 ounces cooked turkey with 1/3 cup sauce) equals 328 calories, 4 g fat (1 g saturated fat), 123 mg cholesterol, 372 mg sodium, 27 g carbohydrate, 1 g fiber, 45 g protein.
Diabetic Exchanges: 5 very lean meat, 2 fruit, 1/2 fat.

Chinese Chicken Spaghetti

(Pictured at right)

It's hard to believe that something that comes together this easily could be tasty and lower in fat. This dish is pretty zippy, but if you like your stir-fries extra spicy, increase the red pepper flakes a bit.
—Jenna Noel, Glendale, Arizona

8 ounces uncooked spaghetti
1 tablespoon cornstarch
4 tablespoons reduced-sodium soy sauce, *divided*
2 tablespoons sesame oil, *divided*
1 pound boneless skinless chicken breasts, cut into 2-inch pieces
2 tablespoons white vinegar

1 tablespoon sugar
1 tablespoon canola oil
2 cups fresh snow peas
2 cups shredded carrots
3 green onions, chopped
3/8 teaspoon ground ginger *or* 1-1/2 teaspoons minced fresh gingerroot
1/2 teaspoon crushed red pepper flakes

Cook pasta according to package directions. In a small bowl, whisk cornstarch and 1 tablespoon soy sauce until smooth; stir in 1 tablespoon sesame oil. Transfer to a large resealable plastic bag. Add chicken; seal bag and turn to coat. Let stand for 10 minutes. In a small bowl, combine the vinegar, sugar, remaining soy sauce and sesame oil; set aside.

In a large nonstick skillet or wok, stir-fry chicken in canola oil until juices run clear. Remove to a platter and keep warm. In the same skillet, stir-fry peas and carrots for 5 minutes. Add the green onions, ginger and pepper flakes. Cook and stir until vegetables are crisp-tender. Return chicken to pan. Add soy sauce mixture; mix well. Drain pasta; add to skillet. Toss until combined. **Yield:** 6 servings.

Nutritional Analysis: One serving (1 cup) equals 329 calories, 9 g fat (1 g saturated fat), 44 mg cholesterol, 465 mg sodium, 37 g carbohydrate, 3 g fiber, 24 g protein.
Diabetic Exchanges: 3 lean meat, 2 starch, 1 vegetable.

Basil Chicken Sandwiches

(Pictured above)

*My mother-in-law has food allergies, my
father-in-law has some very specific food preferences
and my parents appreciate light meals. So I created
this chicken sandwich with fresh basil.*
—*Kerry Durgin Krebs, New Market, Maryland*

1/2 teaspoon pepper
1/4 teaspoon salt
Dash paprika
  1 pound boneless skinless chicken breasts, cut
    into 1/2-inch slices
  6 tablespoons olive oil vinaigrette salad
    dressing, *divided*
  6 Italian *or* French sandwich rolls (5 inches), split
18 basil leaves
  1 jar (7 ounces) roasted sweet red peppers in
    water, drained
1/4 cup shredded Romano cheese

In a bowl, combine the pepper, salt and paprika; sprinkle
over chicken slices. In a nonstick skillet over medium-high
heat, cook chicken in 2 tablespoons salad dressing for 4-5
minutes on each side or until chicken juices run clear. Brush
remaining salad dressing on rolls. Place basil leaves on
rolls; top with chicken and red peppers. Sprinkle with Romano cheese. **Yield:** 6 servings.

*Nutritional Analysis: One sandwich equals 309 calories, 7 g
fat (2 g saturated fat), 48 mg cholesterol, 698 mg sodium, 36 g carbohydrate, 1 g fiber, 24 g protein.*
Diabetic Exchanges: *2 lean meat, 2 starch, 1 vegetable.*

Brown Rice 'n' Apple Stuffed Turkey

*Mouth-watering flavors of autumn permeate
this lovely stuffing concocted by our
Test Kitchen home economists.*

  1 can (14-1/2 ounces) reduced-sodium chicken
    broth
1/2 cup unsweetened apple juice, *divided*
1/2 teaspoon salt, *divided*
  1 cup uncooked long grain brown rice
1/3 cup raisins
1/2 cup chopped celery
1/2 cup chopped onion
  1 tablespoon butter
  1 cup chopped tart apple
  1 teaspoon poultry seasoning
1/4 teaspoon pepper
  1 turkey (10 to 12 pounds)

In a saucepan, combine the broth, 1/3 cup apple juice and
1/4 teaspoon salt. Bring to a boil. Stir in the rice and
raisins. Return to a boil. Reduce heat; cover and simmer for
40-50 minutes or until rice is tender.

Meanwhile, in a nonstick skillet, cook celery and onion
in butter for 2 minutes. Add apple; cook and stir for 3 minutes or until vegetables are tender. Combine the rice mixture, apple mixture, poultry seasoning, pepper and remaining apple juice and salt.

Just before baking, loosely stuff turkey. Skewer turkey
openings; tie drumsticks together. Place breast side up on
a rack in a roasting pan. Bake, uncovered, at 325° for 2-
3/4 to 3 hours or until a meat thermometer reads 180° for
the turkey and 165° for the stuffing. (Cover loosely with foil
if turkey browns too quickly.)

Cover turkey and let stand for 20 minutes. Remove stuffing and carve turkey, discarding skin. If desired, thicken pan
drippings for gravy. **Yield:** 6 servings with leftovers.

Editor's Note: Stuffing may be prepared as directed and
baked separately in a 1-1/2-qt. baking dish coated with nonstick cooking spray. Cover and bake at 325° for 25 minutes. Uncover; bake 10-15 minutes longer or until heated
through.

*Nutritional Analysis: One serving (3 ounces cooked turkey
with 3/4 cup stuffing, calculated without gravy) equals 286 calories, 8 g fat (3 g saturated fat), 51 mg cholesterol, 443 mg sodium, 37 g carbohydrate, 3 g fiber, 17 g protein.*
Diabetic Exchanges: *2-1/2 starch, 1 lean meat.*

🍎 Winging It with Leftovers

AFTER you finish a feast featuring roasted turkey,
give thanks for leftovers—the salvation of busy
cooks during hectic weeks.

The National Turkey Federation suggests play-
ing it safe with leftovers. Within 2 hours after roasting the bird, remove the stuffing, carve any additional meat off the bones and store in the refrigerator or freezer.

Wrap turkey meat and stuffing separately, refrigerate and use within 3 days. Or freeze, wrapping separately in heavy-duty foil or freezer wrap or placing
in freezer containers or bags. For best flavor, use
stuffing within 1 month and turkey within 2 months.

Favorite Recipe Made Lighter

TO SATISFY hearty appetites, Yvonne Shannon of Cobourg, Ontario prepares Creamy Italian Sausage Pasta. "My husband and I love any kind of pasta," she explains.

"This recipe is lovely, but I know it's high in fat and calories," she admits. "Can you help me lighten it so I don't feel guilty when I eat it?"

Our Test Kitchen found several ways to reduce the whopping 54 grams of fat found in each serving. First, they replaced the pork-based Italian sausage with turkey Italian sausage, which trimmed the fat by more than 11 grams a serving.

There was no need to use oil and butter to cook the sausage, so eliminating them removed 4 grams of fat per serving.

But the biggest reduction in fat came from revising the thick sauce. Instead of heavy cream, a combination of fat-free half-and-half, whole milk and a little flour was used—resulting in a reduction of 28 grams of fat per serving!

The slimmed-down version of Yvonne's savory supper has just half the calories, 20% of the fat, 15% of the saturated fat and about 40% of the cholesterol. Yet the full-flavored result is one her family—and yours—can enjoy without the guilt.

Creamy Italian Sausage Pasta

    8 ounces uncooked spiral pasta
  3/4 pound bulk Italian sausage
4-1/2 teaspoons olive oil
1-1/2 teaspoons butter
  3/4 cup chopped sweet red pepper
  1/2 cup chopped onion
  1/2 cup dry white wine *or* chicken broth
    2 cups heavy whipping cream
  1/2 cup grated Romano cheese
  1/2 teaspoon salt
  1/4 teaspoon pepper
    1 tablespoon chopped fresh parsley

Cook pasta according to package directions. In a large skillet, cook sausage in oil and butter over medium heat for 5 minutes. Add red pepper and onion; cook and stir until vegetables are tender and sausage is no longer pink. Add wine or broth; cook for 2 minutes. Add the cream, cheese, salt and pepper. Bring to a boil. Reduce heat; cook over low heat for 8-10 minutes, stirring occasionally.

Drain pasta. In a large bowl, combine sausage mixture and pasta. Before serving, sprinkle with parsley. **Yield:** 6 servings.

Nutritional Analysis: One serving (1 cup) equals 697 calories, 54 g fat (27 g saturated fat), 163 mg cholesterol, 754 mg sodium, 34 g carbohydrate, 2 g fiber, 18 g protein.

Makeover Creamy Italian Sausage Pasta

(Pictured below)

    8 ounces uncooked spiral pasta
  3/4 pound turkey Italian sausage links, casings removed
  3/4 cup chopped sweet red pepper
  1/2 cup chopped onion
    1 tablespoon all-purpose flour
    1 cup fat-free half-and-half
    1 cup milk
  1/2 cup dry white wine *or* chicken broth
  1/2 cup grated Romano cheese
  1/4 teaspoon salt
  1/4 teaspoon pepper
  1/8 teaspoon paprika
    1 tablespoon minced fresh parsley

Cook pasta according to package directions. In a large nonstick skillet, cook the sausage, red pepper and onion over medium heat until sausage is no longer pink and vegetables are tender; drain and return to the pan. In a small bowl, combine the flour, half-and-half, milk, wine or chicken broth, cheese, salt, pepper and paprika until blended. Add to the sausage mixture. Bring to a boil; cook and stir for 1 minute or until thickened. Remove from the heat.

Drain pasta. In a large bowl, combine sausage mixture and pasta. Before serving, sprinkle with parsley. **Yield:** 6 servings.

Nutritional Analysis: One serving (1 cup) equals 343 calories, 11 g fat (4 g saturated fat), 61 mg cholesterol, 600 mg sodium, 38 g carbohydrate, 2 g fiber, 21 g protein.

Diabetic Exchanges: 2 starch, 2 lean meat, 1 fat, 1/2 reduced-fat milk.

Apple-Swiss Turkey Sandwiches

Honey mustard adds a sweet tang to this hearty concoction. Apple slices, Swiss cheese, cucumber and turkey are layered between slices of nutritious multigrain bread. These delicious sandwiches pack well to take to the office or on the trail.
—Gloria Updyke, Front Royal, Virginia

3 tablespoons honey mustard
8 slices multigrain bread, toasted
2 medium unpeeled apples, cored and thinly sliced
8 slices reduced-fat Swiss cheese
1/2 cup thinly sliced cucumber
8 ounces thinly sliced cooked turkey breast

Lightly spread mustard on each slice of toast; set aside. Place apples on a microwave-safe plate and microwave, uncovered, on high for 1 to 1-1/2 minutes or until slightly softened. Arrange half of the apple slices and cheese on 4 slices of toast. Top with cucumber and turkey. Add remaining apple and cheese slices. Top with remaining toast, mustard side down. **Yield:** 4 servings.

Nutritional Analysis: One sandwich equals 323 calories, 6 g fat (3 g saturated fat), 56 mg cholesterol, 406 mg sodium, 41 g carbohydrate, 6 g fiber, 27 g protein.
Diabetic Exchanges: 3 lean meat, 2 starch, 1/2 fruit.

Baked Chicken and Mushrooms

Low-carb

I made up this dish years ago, and it still remains a family favorite. It's a fast and healthy weeknight meal, but the fresh mushrooms and sherry make it special enough for a weekend dinner party.
—Lise Prestine, South Bend, Indiana

6 boneless skinless chicken breast halves
(4 ounces *each*)
1/4 teaspoon paprika
1/2 pound fresh mushrooms, sliced
1 tablespoon butter
1/2 cup sherry *or* chicken broth
3 green onions, chopped
1 garlic clove, minced
1/2 teaspoon salt
1/8 teaspoon pepper
3/4 cup shredded part-skim mozzarella cheese

Arrange chicken in a 13-in. x 9-in. x 2-in. baking dish coated with nonstick cooking spray. Sprinkle with paprika. Bake, uncovered, at 350° for 15 minutes.

Meanwhile, in a large nonstick skillet, saute mushrooms in butter for 5 minutes. Add the sherry or broth, green onions, garlic, salt and pepper. Bring to a boil. Pour over chicken. Bake 10-15 minutes longer or until chicken juices run clear. Top with cheese. Bake for 3-5 minutes or until cheese is melted. **Yield:** 6 servings.

Nutritional Analysis: One serving (1 chicken breast half) equals 198 calories, 6 g fat (3 g saturated fat), 79 mg cholesterol, 361 mg sodium, 3 g carbohydrate, 1 g fiber, 31 g protein.
Diabetic Exchange: 4 lean meat.

Grilled Chicken with Peaches

(Pictured below)

My grandmother gave me this recipe, which I lightened up. My children loved it when they were little, and now my grandchildren ask for it when they come over. The peaches are delicious hot off the grill.
—Linda McCluskey, Cullman, Alabama

1 cup 100% peach spreadable fruit
2 tablespoons olive oil
4 teaspoons reduced-sodium soy sauce
1 tablespoon ground mustard
1 garlic clove, minced
1/2 teaspoon salt
1/4 teaspoon pepper
1/4 teaspoon cayenne pepper
8 bone-in skinless chicken breast halves
(8 ounces *each*)
8 medium ripe peaches, halved and pitted

Coat grill rack with nonstick cooking spray before starting grill for indirect heat. In a small bowl, combine the first eight ingredients; set aside. Grill chicken, covered, over indirect medium heat for 10 minutes on each side. Brush chicken with glaze. Grill 10-15 minutes longer or until juices run clear, turning every 5 minutes and brushing with glaze. Transfer to a serving platter and keep warm.

Grill peach halves cut side down over indirect heat for 2 minutes. Turn; brush with glaze and grill for 3-4 minutes

longer or until tender. Serve grilled peaches with chicken.
Yield: 8 servings.

Nutritional Analysis: One serving (1 chicken breast half with 2 peach halves) equals 348 calories, 8 g fat (2 g saturated fat), 97 mg cholesterol, 333 mg sodium, 31 g carbohydrate, 2 g fiber, 37 g protein.
Diabetic Exchanges: 4 lean meat, 2 fruit.

Hawaiian Stir-Fry

*With its appealing tropical twist,
this recipe is sure to win raves.*
—Georgiana Weathers, Orlando, Florida

  1 can (8 ounces) unsweetened pineapple chunks
  2 tablespoons brown sugar
  1 tablespoon cornstarch
1/3 cup water
  2 tablespoons reduced-sodium soy sauce
  1 carrot, cut into 2-inch julienne strips
  2 tablespoons canola oil, *divided*
  2 celery ribs, thinly sliced
  1 medium sweet red pepper, julienned
  1 medium sweet yellow pepper, julienned
  1 medium onion, cut into thin wedges
  2 cups frozen sugar snap peas, thawed
  1 pound boneless skinless chicken breasts, cut
     into 2-1/2-inch strips
Hot cooked rice, optional

Drain pineapple, reserving juice. In a small bowl, combine brown sugar and cornstarch. Stir in the water, soy sauce and reserved pineapple juice until smooth; set aside. In a large nonstick skillet or wok, stir-fry carrot in 1 tablespoon hot oil for 1 minute. Stir in the celery, sweet peppers and onion; stir-fry for 3 minutes. Add sugar snap peas; stir-fry about 1 minute longer or until vegetables are crisp-tender. Remove vegetables and keep warm.

In the same skillet, stir-fry chicken in remaining oil for 3-4 minutes or until no longer pink. Stir soy sauce mixture; gradually stir into skillet. Bring to a boil; cook and stir for 1-2 minutes or until thickened. Stir in vegetable mixture and pineapple chunks; heat through. Serve over rice if desired.
Yield: 4 servings.

Nutritional Analysis: One serving (1-1/2 cups stir-fry mixture, calculated without rice) equals 314 calories, 9 g fat (1 g saturated fat), 66 mg cholesterol, 413 mg sodium, 29 g carbohydrate, 5 g fiber, 29 g protein.
Diabetic Exchanges: 3 lean meat, 3 vegetable, 1 fruit.

Open-Faced Chicken Sandwiches

(Pictured above)

Caramelized onions, mushrooms and two types of cheese make these my favorite sandwiches. I invented them for a last-minute picnic by combining items I had on hand. They've been a hit ever since.
—Lynda Clark, Spokane, Washington

  1 loaf (8 ounces and 8 inches long) French bread
  1 pound fresh mushrooms, sliced
  1 large sweet onion, sliced
  1 cup fat-free mayonnaise
1/2 cup crumbled blue cheese
1/4 teaspoon pepper
  1 pound boneless skinless chicken breasts,
     grilled and sliced
  1 cup (4 ounces) shredded part-skim mozzarella
     cheese

Cut bread into eight 1-in. slices and toast slices. Meanwhile, in a large nonstick skillet coated with nonstick cooking spray, saute mushrooms and onion for 15-20 minutes or until onion is tender and golden brown; set aside.

In a small bowl, combine the mayonnaise, blue cheese and pepper; mix well. Spread blue cheese mixture over each bread slice. Top with chicken, mushroom mixture and mozzarella cheese. Place on a broiler pan. Broil 4-6 in. from the heat for 3-4 minutes or until cheese is melted. **Yield:** 8 servings.

Nutritional Analysis: One open-faced sandwich equals 276 calories, 8 g fat (4 g saturated fat), 66 mg cholesterol, 618 mg sodium, 23 g carbohydrate, 3 g fiber, 27 g protein.
Diabetic Exchanges: 3 lean meat, 1 starch, 1 vegetable.

Cajun Chicken Sandwiches

(Pictured below)

*This is my favorite sandwich. The seasoning
mixture is enough to give a mild flavor to several
chicken breasts or a spicy taste to just a few.*
—Amber Peterson, Oakes, North Dakota

  **6 boneless skinless chicken breast halves
    (4 ounces *each*)**
  1 tablespoon olive oil
1/2 teaspoon celery salt
1/2 teaspoon garlic salt
1/2 teaspoon lemon-pepper seasoning
1/4 teaspoon cayenne pepper
1/4 teaspoon paprika
1/4 teaspoon pepper
  6 kaiser rolls, split and toasted
 12 slices tomato
  6 lettuce leaves

Flatten chicken to 1/2-in. thickness. Brush both sides with
oil. Combine the seasonings; rub over both sides of chick-
en. Arrange in a 13-in. x 9-in. x 2-in. baking dish. Cover
and refrigerate for at least 2 hours or overnight.

Coat grill rack with nonstick cooking spray before starting the grill. Grill, covered, over medium heat for 3-5 minutes on each side or until chicken juices run clear. Serve on
rolls with tomato and lettuce. **Yield:** 6 servings.

*Nutritional Analysis: One sandwich equals 323 calories, 6 g
fat (1 g saturated fat), 66 mg cholesterol, 701 mg sodium, 33 g carbohydrate, 2 g fiber, 32 g protein.*
Diabetic Exchanges: 3 lean meat, 2 starch.

Italian Sausage 'n' Peppers Supper

(Pictured above)

*I created this sausage and pepper dish after I enjoyed
something similar at an Italian restaurant. My
young son loves it even though it is a little spicy.*
—Teresa Puszkar, Harrowsmith, Ontario

  2 cups uncooked penne pasta
  1 pound turkey Italian sausage links
**1/2 cup *each* julienned sweet red, yellow and green
    pepper**
  **1 tablespoon minced fresh basil *or* 1 teaspoon
    dried basil**
  3 garlic cloves, minced
1/4 teaspoon dried oregano
1/4 teaspoon dried thyme
1/4 teaspoon caraway seeds
  1 tablespoon olive oil
  **2 cans (14-1/2 ounces *each*) diced tomatoes,
    drained**

Cook pasta according to package directions. In a large nonstick skillet, brown sausage over medium heat; drain. Cut
sausage into 1/4-in. slices. In the same skillet, saute the
peppers, basil, garlic, oregano, thyme, caraway seeds and
sliced sausage in oil until peppers are crisp-tender. Stir in
tomatoes. Cook and stir until heated through. Drain pasta;
add to skillet and mix well. **Yield:** 5 servings.

*Nutritional Analysis: One serving (1-1/2 cups) equals 327
calories, 12 g fat (3 g saturated fat), 49 mg cholesterol, 845 mg
sodium, 33 g carbohydrate, 3 g fiber, 21 g protein.*
*Diabetic Exchanges: 2 vegetable, 2 lean meat, 1-1/2 starch,
1 fat.*

🍎 Savory Un-Stuffed Chicken

I LIKE to make what I call "stuffed" chicken legs. I remove the skin from the legs and instead of coating them in melted butter, I use chicken broth. (If you're using the no-salt-added broth, spice it up with some garlic or curry.) Then I roll the legs in crushed stuffing mix before baking. The result is not as rich as using butter, but it's still very tasty.

—Pat Fischer, Stratford, Connecticut

Marinated Turkey Tenderloins

Low-carb

These moist grilled tenderloins marinate overnight in a savory teriyaki and soy sauce mixture. I had used this recipe for years on pork tenderloin and decided to give turkey a try.
—Linda Gregg, Spartanburg, South Carolina

- 1/4 cup canola oil
- 1/4 cup reduced-sodium soy sauce
- 1/4 cup reduced-sodium teriyaki sauce
- 2 tablespoons red wine vinegar
- 1 tablespoon lime juice
- 1 tablespoon Dijon mustard
- 2 garlic cloves, minced
- 2 teaspoons coarsely ground pepper
- 1-1/2 teaspoons dried parsley flakes
- 1-1/2 teaspoons dried basil
- 1/2 teaspoon onion powder
- 2 pounds turkey tenderloins

In a 2-cup measuring cup, combine the first 11 ingredients. Pour 2/3 cup into a large resealable plastic bag; add turkey. Seal bag and turn to coat; refrigerate for 8 hours or overnight. Cover and refrigerate remaining marinade.

Before starting the grill, coat grill rack with nonstick cooking spray. Drain and discard marinade from turkey. Grill, covered, over medium heat for 7-9 minutes; baste with reserved marinade. Turn and grill 7-9 minutes longer or until juices run clear. **Yield:** 8 servings.

Nutritional Analysis: *One serving (3 ounces cooked turkey) equals 165 calories, 5 g fat (1 g saturated fat), 77 mg cholesterol, 314 mg sodium, 2 g carbohydrate, trace fiber, 28 g protein.*
Diabetic Exchange: *3 lean meat.*

Bombay Chicken

Low-carb

(Pictured above)

This grilled dinner always turns out moist and tender. The marinade has a Middle Eastern flair, giving the dish a zesty flavor. It makes a beautiful presentation as well.
—June Thomas, Chesterton, Indiana

- 1-1/2 cups (12 ounces) fat-free plain yogurt
- 1/4 cup lemon juice
- 2 tablespoons chili powder
- 2 tablespoons paprika
- 2 tablespoons olive oil
- 1-1/2 teaspoons salt
- 1/2 to 1 teaspoon cayenne pepper
- 1/2 teaspoon garlic powder
- 1/4 teaspoon ground ginger
- 1/4 teaspoon ground cardamom
- 1/8 teaspoon ground cinnamon
- 4 to 5 pounds bone-in chicken thighs and legs, skin removed

In a large resealable plastic bag, combine the first 11 ingredients. Add the chicken; seal bag and turn to coat. Refrigerate overnight.

Coat grill rack with nonstick cooking spray before starting grill. Drain and discard marinade. Grill chicken, covered, over direct medium-hot heat for 15 minutes. Turn; grill for 10-15 minutes longer or until juices run clear. **Yield:** 8 servings.

Nutritional Analysis: *One serving (4 ounces cooked dark meat) equals 255 calories, 13 g fat (3 g saturated fat), 106 mg cholesterol, 344 mg sodium, 3 g carbohydrate, 1 g fiber, 31 g protein.*
Diabetic Exchange: *4 lean meat.*

Chicken Chop Suey

This is my favorite stir-fry dish. It's so versatile because you can change the meat or veggies to suit your taste... or according to what's in the refrigerator.
—Arleen Gibson, Simcoe, Ontario

3 tablespoons reduced-sodium soy sauce
1 tablespoon dark brown sugar
1 pound boneless skinless chicken breasts, thinly sliced
3 medium onions, sliced
2 garlic cloves, minced
2 tablespoons canola oil
6 celery ribs with leaves, cut into 1/2-inch pieces
1/2 pound small fresh mushrooms
1 large green pepper, cut into 1-inch pieces
4-1/2 teaspoons cornstarch
1 cup water
2 cups canned bean sprouts
1/4 teaspoon salt
1/4 teaspoon pepper
Hot cooked rice, optional

In a large resealable plastic bag, combine soy sauce and brown sugar; add the chicken. Seal bag and turn to coat; refrigerate for 20-30 minutes.

In a large nonstick skillet or wok, stir-fry onions and garlic in oil until tender. Remove with a slotted spoon to a bowl. Add celery, mushrooms and green pepper to skillet; stir-fry 3-4 minutes or until crisp-tender. Remove with a slotted spoon to bowl. Add chicken and marinade to skillet; stir-fry for 5-7 minutes or until chicken is no longer pink. Return vegetables to skillet.

Combine cornstarch and water until smooth; stir into chicken mixture. Bring to a boil; cook and stir for 2 minutes or until thickened. Add the bean sprouts, salt and pepper; cook and stir for 2 minutes or until heated through. Serve over rice if desired. **Yield:** 6 servings.

Nutritional Analysis: One serving (1-1/2 cups chop suey, calculated without rice) equals 308 calories, 9 g fat (1 g saturated fat), 66 mg cholesterol, 822 mg sodium, 26 g carbohydrate, 5 g fiber, 32 g protein.
Diabetic Exchanges: 4 vegetable, 3 lean meat, 1/2 starch.

Creamy Chicken and Thyme

Low-carb

Thyme gives this simple chicken dish its unique flavor. I lightened up the original recipe by using reduced-fat sour cream. My husband loves this, as do friends from my Weight Watchers group.
—Harriet Johnson, Champlin, Minnesota

4 boneless skinless chicken breast halves (4 ounces *each*)
1 can (14-1/2 ounces) reduced-sodium chicken broth, *divided*
1 tablespoon all-purpose flour
1/2 cup reduced-fat sour cream
1/2 teaspoon dried parsley flakes
1/4 teaspoon salt
1/4 teaspoon dill weed
1/4 teaspoon dried thyme
1/8 teaspoon onion salt
1/8 teaspoon pepper
Hot cooked yolk-free noodles, optional

Place chicken breasts in a large nonstick skillet. Add 1/2 cup of broth. Bring to boil. Reduce heat; cover and simmer for 10-12 minutes or until juices run clear, turning once. Remove chicken from pan; keep warm. Add remaining broth to skillet and bring to a boil; reduce heat to low.

In a small bowl, combine the flour and sour cream. Whisk into pan. Stir in the parsley, salt, dill weed, thyme, onion salt and pepper. Simmer, uncovered, for 5 minutes or until slightly thickened. Place chicken breasts over hot cooked noodles if desired. Drizzle with sauce. **Yield:** 4 servings.

Nutritional Analysis: One serving (1 chicken breast half with 1/4 cup sauce, calculated without noodles) equals 179 calories, 4 g fat (2 g saturated fat), 76 mg cholesterol, 569 mg sodium, 4 g carbohydrate, trace fiber, 30 g protein.
Diabetic Exchange: 3 lean meat.

Walnut Chicken Stir-Fry

Low-carb

(Pictured at right)

During the holidays, I fix meals that are simple, light and nutritious. This is one of our favorites.
—Sharon Fleming, Bogota, Colombia

2 tablespoons cornstarch, *divided*
4 teaspoons canola oil, *divided*
1 tablespoon reduced-sodium soy sauce
2 teaspoons chicken bouillon granules
1 teaspoon ground ginger
1 teaspoon chili powder
3/4 pound boneless skinless chicken breasts, cut into 1-inch cubes
4 cups fresh broccoli florets
1 large onion, cut into 8 wedges
1 medium sweet red pepper, julienned
1 cup water
1/4 cup walnut halves
Hot cooked rice, optional

In a large resealable plastic bag, combine 1 tablespoon cornstarch, 1 teaspoon oil, soy sauce, bouillon granules, ginger and chili powder; add chicken. Seal bag and turn to coat; refrigerate for 15 minutes to 1 hour.

In a large nonstick skillet or wok, stir-fry chicken and marinade in remaining oil until chicken is no longer pink. Remove chicken with a slotted spoon and keep warm. In the same skillet, stir-fry broccoli for 8 minutes. Add onion and red pepper; stir-fry 6-8 minutes longer or until vegetables are crisp-tender.

Return chicken to the skillet. Combine remaining cornstarch and water until smooth. Add to the skillet. Bring to a boil; cook and stir for 2 minutes or until thickened. Sprinkle with nuts. Serve over rice if desired. **Yield:** 4 servings.

Nutritional Analysis: One serving (1-1/2 cups chicken mixture, calculated without rice) equals 253 calories, 11 g fat (1 g saturated fat), 50 mg cholesterol, 811 mg sodium, 15 g carbohydrate, 4 g fiber, 24 g protein.
Diabetic Exchanges: 3 lean meat, 3 vegetable, 1/2 fat.

Marinated Barbecued Chicken

Low-carb *Low-fat*

Every time I make this tender chicken, people ask for the recipe. A friend of mine shared the recipe, which she got from her sister-in-law who's from the Philippines.
—Deborah DiLaura English, Casper, Wyoming

```
2/3 cup sugar
2/3 cup reduced-sodium soy sauce
1/2 cup lemon-lime soda
1/2 cup lemon juice
  2 tablespoons garlic powder
  1 teaspoon pepper
1/2 teaspoon salt
  8 bone-in skinless chicken breast halves
    (7 ounces each)
  2 tablespoons barbecue sauce
```

In a bowl, combine the first seven ingredients. Pour 1-1/2 cups marinade into a large resealable plastic bag; add the chicken. Seal bag and turn to coat; refrigerate overnight. Cover and refrigerate remaining marinade.

Coat grill rack with nonstick cooking spray before starting the grill. Drain and discard marinade from chicken. Add barbecue sauce to reserved marinade. Grill chicken, covered, over indirect medium heat for 35-50 minutes or until a meat thermometer reads 170°, turning and basting occasionally with marinade. Before serving, brush with remaining marinade. **Yield:** 8 servings.

Nutritional Analysis: *One serving (1 chicken breast half) equals 205 calories, 3 g fat (1 g saturated fat), 79 mg cholesterol, 590 mg sodium, 12 g carbohydrate, trace fiber, 30 g protein.*
Diabetic Exchanges: *4 lean meat, 1/2 starch.*

Tangy Turkey Tostadas

(Pictured above right)

My husband and I have busy schedules, so I often turn to this nutritious variation on fast-food tacos. They're so tasty and easy to make. I serve them with a tossed green salad and Spanish rice.
—Julie Lee, Memphis, Tennessee

```
1-1/4 pounds lean ground turkey
  1/2 cup chopped onion
    1 cup chopped green pepper
    2 garlic cloves, minced
  3/4 cup sliced fresh mushrooms
    1 can (16 ounces) kidney beans, rinsed and
      drained
    1 cup salsa
    1 can (4 ounces) chopped green chilies
    1 tablespoon chili powder
    1 teaspoon ground cumin
  1/2 teaspoon salt
    4 drops hot pepper sauce
1-1/2 cups (6 ounces) reduced-fat Mexican cheese
      blend
  1/2 cup frozen corn, thawed
   16 corn tostadas (5 inches)
    2 cups shredded lettuce
    1 cup chopped tomatoes
  1/4 cup minced fresh cilantro
```

In a large nonstick skillet, cook turkey over medium heat until no longer pink; drain. Add the onion, green pepper and garlic. Cook and stir for 3 minutes or until onion is tender. Stir in the mushrooms; cook 1 minute longer. Stir in the beans, salsa, chilies, chili powder, cumin, salt and hot pepper sauce. Cook for 5 minutes or until heated through. Stir in cheese and corn; heat through. Spread about 1/3 cup filling on each tostada shell. Sprinkle with lettuce, tomatoes and cilantro. **Yield:** 8 servings.

Nutritional Analysis: *Two tostadas equals 371 calories, 16 g fat (5 g saturated fat), 56 mg cholesterol, 595 mg sodium, 36 g carbohydrate, 7 g fiber, 26 g protein.*
Diabetic Exchanges: *3 lean meat, 2 starch, 1 vegetable, 1 fat.*

Spinach Turkey Noodle Bake

This creamy, comforting casserole is a terrific way to use up leftover turkey. I usually freeze diced cooked turkey in 2-cup portions and have them ready to use when someone requests this popular dish.
—Ramona Fish, Columbus, Indiana

```
2-1/2 cups uncooked yolk-free noodles
    2 cups diced cooked turkey breast
    1 can (10-3/4 ounces) reduced-fat reduced-
      sodium cream of chicken soup, undiluted
  1/4 teaspoon garlic salt
  1/8 teaspoon dried rosemary, crushed
Dash pepper
    1 package (10 ounces) frozen chopped spinach,
      thawed and squeezed dry
    1 cup (8 ounces) fat-free cottage cheese
```

3/4 cup shredded part-skim mozzarella cheese, *divided*
1/8 teaspoon paprika

Cook noodles according to package directions; drain. Meanwhile, in a bowl, combine the turkey, soup, garlic salt, rosemary and pepper. In another bowl, combine the spinach, cottage cheese and 1/2 cup mozzarella cheese.

In a 2-qt. baking dish coated with nonstick cooking spray, layer half of the noodles, turkey mixture and cottage cheese mixture. Repeat layers. Cover and bake at 350° for 35 minutes. Uncover; sprinkle with remaining mozzarella cheese. Bake 10-15 minutes longer or until edges are lightly browned; sprinkle with paprika. Let stand for 5 minutes before serving. **Yield:** 6 servings.

Nutritional Analysis: One serving (1 cup) equals 242 calories, 4 g fat (2 g saturated fat), 53 mg cholesterol, 568 mg sodium, 21 g carbohydrate, 3 g fiber, 26 g protein.
Diabetic Exchanges: 3 very lean meat, 1-1/2 starch, 1/2 fat.

Chicken Cutlets with Mushroom Sauce

Low-carb   Low-fat

For a quick hearty entree, make these no-fuss poultry cutlets that brown on the stovetop in no time.
—Judy Grebetz, Racine, Wisconsin

4 boneless skinless chicken breast halves **(4 ounces** *each***)**
1/4 teaspoon salt
1/2 teaspoon pepper, *divided*
2 teaspoons butter
2 tablespoons chopped green onion
2 garlic cloves, minced
2 cups sliced fresh mushrooms
1/2 cup reduced-sodium chicken broth
1-1/2 teaspoons minced fresh tarragon *or* **1/2 teaspoon dried tarragon**
2 teaspoons cornstarch
1/4 cup red wine *or* **additional reduced-sodium chicken broth**
2 to 3 drops browning sauce, optional

Pound chicken to 1/4-in. thickness. Sprinkle both sides with salt and 1/4 teaspoon pepper. In a large nonstick skillet, cook chicken for 4-5 minutes on each side or until juices run clear.

Meanwhile, in a saucepan, melt the butter over medium-low heat. Add the green onion and garlic; saute for 2 minutes. Add the mushrooms and cook until softened, about 2 minutes. Stir in the chicken broth, tarragon and remaining pepper. Cook over medium heat until mushrooms are tender.

In a small bowl, combine the cornstarch and wine or additional broth until smooth. Stir into the mushroom mixture. Bring to a boil; cook and stir for 2 minutes or until thickened. Stir in browning sauce if desired. Serve sauce over chicken. **Yield:** 4 servings.

Nutritional Analysis: One serving (1 chicken breast half with 1/3 cup sauce) equals 169 calories, 3 g fat (2 g saturated fat), 71 mg cholesterol, 321 mg sodium, 3 g carbohydrate, 1 g fiber, 28 g protein.
Diabetic Exchanges: 3 lean meat, 1 vegetable.

Chicken Artichoke Skillet

Low-carb

(Pictured below)

This quick-to-fix chicken entree featuring artichokes and olives has a real Greek flair. Seasoned with lemon juice and oregano, the stovetop chicken turns out moist and tender. I like to vary the olives—Greek, green, black or a mixture.
—Carol Latimore, Arvada, Colorado

4 boneless skinless chicken breast halves **(4 ounces** *each***)**
1/4 teaspoon salt
1/4 teaspoon pepper
2 teaspoons olive oil
2/3 cup reduced-sodium chicken broth
1 can (14 ounces) water-packed artichoke hearts, rinsed, drained and quartered
1/4 cup halved stuffed olives
1/4 cup halved pitted Greek olives
2 tablespoons fresh minced oregano *or* **2 teaspoons dried oregano**
1 tablespoon lemon juice

Sprinkle chicken with salt and pepper. In a large nonstick skillet, cook chicken in oil over medium-high heat for 3 minutes on each side. Combine the broth, artichoke hearts, olives, oregano and lemon juice; add to skillet. Bring to a boil. Reduce heat; cover and simmer for 4-6 minutes or until chicken juices run clear. **Yield:** 4 servings.

Nutritional Analysis: One serving equals 207 calories, 6 g fat (1 g saturated fat), 66 mg cholesterol, 1,057 mg sodium, 8 g carbohydrate, 3 g fiber, 29 g protein.
Diabetic Exchanges: 3 lean meat, 1 vegetable.

Turkey Salad Wraps

(Pictured above)

Your family will be happy to take the "wrap" when it's loaded with luscious turkey salad dressed with a light mix of yogurt, mayonnaise, garlic and curry. This is excellent for lunch boxes, and the tortilla is a fun replacement for bread. To add a bit of color, choose red or green tortillas.
—Janet Knickerbocker, Palmyra, Missouri

2 cups cubed cooked turkey breast
1 medium sweet onion, chopped
3/4 cup chopped celery
1/2 cup fat-free plain yogurt
1/4 cup reduced-fat mayonnaise
1/2 teaspoon garlic salt
1/2 teaspoon curry powder
2 medium tomatoes, thinly sliced
1 cup torn leaf lettuce
4 spinach flour tortillas (8 inches), warmed if desired

In a large bowl, combine the turkey, onion and celery. In another bowl, whisk together the yogurt, mayonnaise, garlic salt and curry. Pour over turkey mixture; toss to coat. Layer tomatoes and lettuce on tortillas. Top with turkey mixture; roll up and secure with toothpicks. **Yield:** 4 servings.

Nutritional Analysis: One wrap equals 305 calories, 9 g fat (2 g saturated fat), 66 mg cholesterol, 358 mg sodium, 28 g carbohydrate, 4 g fiber, 29 g protein.
Diabetic Exchanges: 3 lean meat, 2 vegetable, 1 starch.

Chicken with Roasted Red Pepper Sauce

Low-carb

I created this recipe as a way to introduce different vegetables to my family. My 3-year-old son said it was the best chicken he'd ever tasted.
—Kelly Cobb, Mason, Ohio

3 medium sweet red peppers, cut in half lengthwise and seeded
1 large whole garlic bulb
1 teaspoon plus 1 tablespoon olive oil, *divided*
4 boneless skinless chicken breast halves (4 ounces *each*)
1/2 teaspoon salt, *divided*
1/4 teaspoon pepper, *divided*
1/2 cup sliced leek (white portion only)
1/2 cup reduced-sodium chicken broth
Hot cooked pasta, optional
1/4 cup shredded Parmesan cheese

Broil peppers 4 in. from the heat until skins blister, about 15 minutes. Immediately place peppers in a bowl; cover and let stand for 15-20 minutes. Peel off and discard charred skin. Coarsely chop peppers; transfer to a food processor.

Remove papery outer skin from garlic (do not peel or separate cloves); cut top off of garlic bulb. Brush with 1 teaspoon oil. Wrap bulb in heavy-duty foil. Bake at 425° for 30-35 minutes or until softened. Cool for 10-15 minutes. Squeeze softened garlic into the food processor with peppers; cover and process until almost smooth. Set aside.

Sprinkle both sides of chicken with 1/4 teaspoon salt and 1/8 teaspoon pepper. In a large nonstick skillet, cook chicken in remaining oil over medium heat for 3-4 minutes on each side or until lightly browned. Remove and keep warm.

In the same skillet, cook leek for 2 minutes or until leek is lightly browned. Add broth, stirring to loosen any browned bits from pan. Add red pepper mixture, chicken and remaining salt and pepper. Bring to a boil. Reduce heat; cover and simmer for 3 minutes until the chicken juices run clear. Uncover; cook until sauce is slightly thickened. Serve chicken and red pepper sauce over pasta if desired. Sprinkle with Parmesan cheese. **Yield:** 4 servings.

Nutritional Analysis: One serving (1 chicken breast half with 1/3 cup sauce and 1 tablespoon Parmesan cheese, calculated without pasta) equals 239 calories, 8 g fat (2 g saturated fat), 69 mg cholesterol, 537 mg sodium, 12 g carbohydrate, 3 g fiber, 30 g protein.
Diabetic Exchanges: 3 lean meat, 2 vegetable.

Hot Swiss Chicken Sandwiches

(Pictured below)

I've been making these open-faced sandwiches for years, and people always ask for the recipe. I sometimes put the filling on slices of sourdough or into pitas. No matter how you serve it, folks gobble it up!
—Edith Tabor, Vancouver, Washington

    1/4 cup reduced-fat mayonnaise
    1/4 teaspoon salt
    1/4 teaspoon lemon juice
1-1/2 cups cooked diced chicken breast
    2/3 cup chopped celery
    1/2 cup shredded reduced-fat Swiss cheese
      4 teaspoons butter, softened
      6 slices Italian bread (about 3/4 inch thick)
      6 tomato slices
    3/4 cup shredded lettuce

In a bowl, combine the mayonnaise, salt and lemon juice. Stir in the chicken, celery and cheese. Spread butter on each slice of bread; top each with 1/3 cup of the chicken mixture.

   Place sandwiches on a 15-in. x 10-in. x 1-in. baking pan; broil 4-6 in. from the heat for 3-4 minutes or until heated through. Top sandwiches with tomato and lettuce. Serve immediately. **Yield:** 6 servings.

   Nutritional Analysis: *One sandwich equals 218 calories, 9 g fat (3 g saturated fat), 44 mg cholesterol, 438 mg sodium, 17 g carbohydrate, 1 g fiber, 17 g protein.*
   Diabetic Exchanges: *2 lean meat, 1 starch, 1/2 fat.*

Southwest Turkey Stew

Low-fat

(Pictured above)

I prefer main dishes that enable me to stay on my diet but still eat what the rest of the family eats. This stew is a hit with my husband and our young children.
—Stephanie Wilson, Helix, Oregon

1-1/2 pounds turkey tenderloins, cubed
      2 teaspoons canola oil
      1 can (15 ounces) turkey chili with beans, undrained
      1 can (14-1/2 ounces) diced tomatoes, undrained
      1 medium sweet red pepper, cut into 3/4-inch pieces
      1 medium green pepper, cut into 3/4-inch pieces
    3/4 cup chopped onion
    3/4 cup salsa
      3 garlic cloves, minced
1-1/2 teaspoons chili powder
    1/2 teaspoon salt
    1/2 teaspoon ground cumin
      1 tablespoon minced fresh cilantro, optional

In a nonstick skillet, brown turkey in oil; transfer to a 3-qt. slow cooker. Stir in the chili, tomatoes, peppers, onion, salsa, garlic, chili powder, salt and cumin. Cover and cook on low for 5-6 hours or until turkey juices run clear. Garnish with cilantro if desired. **Yield:** 6 servings.

   Nutritional Analysis: *One serving (1-1/4 cups) equals 252 calories, 3 g fat (1 g saturated fat), 80 mg cholesterol, 1,006 mg sodium, 19 g carbohydrate, 5 g fiber, 35 g protein.*
   Diabetic Exchanges: *5 very lean meat, 2 vegetable, 1/2 starch.*

Chicken and Mandarin Oranges

Low-carb

I created this recipe after my husband and I moved to Wisconsin from sunny Florida. The citrus flavor certainly brings back lots of warm memories of our former home. Because it calls for canned mandarin oranges, I can bring a bit of the Sunshine State to my table throughout the year!
—Mary Rogers, Greendale, Wisconsin

  1/2 teaspoon salt
  1/2 teaspoon ground ginger
  1/4 teaspoon pepper
    4 boneless skinless chicken breast halves
      (4 ounces *each*)
    1 tablespoon canola oil
    1 can (11 ounces) mandarin oranges
    1 small onion, chopped
  1/8 teaspoon crushed red pepper flakes
Hot cooked rice
    2 teaspoons cornstarch
    2 tablespoons water
  1/4 cup minced fresh cilantro

In a small bowl, combine the salt, ginger and pepper. Sprinkle over both sides of chicken. In a nonstick skillet, saute chicken in oil for 2 minutes on each side or until browned. Remove chicken to plate and keep warm.

Reduce heat to medium-low. Drain oranges, reserving juice. Stir juice, onion and red pepper flakes into skillet. Cook and stir for about 3 minutes or until onion is tender. Bring to a boil. Return chicken to skillet. Reduce heat; cover and cook for about 10 minutes or until chicken juices run clear. Place chicken over rice; keep warm.

Combine cornstarch and water until smooth. Gradually stir into skillet. Bring to a boil; cook and stir for about 2 minutes or until mixture is thickened. Add mandarin oranges; heat through. Pour sauce over chicken. Sprinkle with cilantro. **Yield:** 4 servings.

Nutritional Analysis: *One serving (1 chicken breast half with sauce, calculated without rice) equals 202 calories, 5 g fat (1 g saturated fat), 66 mg cholesterol, 370 mg sodium, 11 g carbohydrate, 2 g fiber, 27 g protein.*
Diabetic Exchanges: *3 lean meat, 1 fruit.*

Spinach Turkey Roll

Low-carb

(Pictured above)

My husband doesn't care much for garlic, so I use elephant garlic, which is milder. He never mentions the garlic being too strong in this recipe, so we're both satisfied with the results.
—Delia Kennedy, Deer Park, Washington

    1 cup meatless spaghetti sauce, *divided*
    2 eggs, lightly beaten
    1 cup soft whole wheat bread crumbs
  1/4 cup finely chopped onion
    2 garlic cloves, minced
    1 teaspoon dried basil
    1 teaspoon dried oregano
    1 teaspoon ground mustard
    1 pound lean ground turkey
    1 package (10 ounces) frozen chopped spinach,
      thawed and squeezed dry
  1/2 cup shredded part-skim mozzarella cheese

In a bowl, combine 1/4 cup spaghetti sauce, eggs, bread crumbs, onion, garlic, basil, oregano and mustard. Crumble turkey over mixture and mix well.

On a sheet of waxed paper, pat turkey mixture into a 12-in. x 8-in. rectangle. Sprinkle with spinach and cheese. Roll up jelly-roll style, starting with a short side and peeling waxed paper away while rolling. Seal seam and ends. Place seam side down in a 15-in. x 10-in. x 1-in. baking pan coated with nonstick cooking spray.

Bake, uncovered, at 350° for 50-60 minutes or until a meat thermometer reads 165°. Let stand for 5 minutes before slicing. Heat remaining spaghetti sauce; serve over turkey. **Yield:** 6 servings.

Nutritional Analysis: *One serving equals 230 calories, 11 g fat (4 g saturated fat), 137 mg cholesterol, 395 mg sodium, 12 g carbohydrate, 3 g fiber, 20 g protein.*
Diabetic Exchanges: *3 lean meat, 2 vegetable.*

Favorite Recipe Made Lighter

WHEN cooking for family or company, Paula Hairford of Plaucheville, Louisiana relies on Chicken Enchiladas to please different palates. But she asked our Test Kitchen staff to lighten up the recipe.

Chicken Enchiladas

  1 pound boneless skinless chicken breasts
1/2 cup water
  5 teaspoons minced garlic, *divided*
  1 cup finely chopped onion
  3 tablespoons butter
  2 cans (4 ounces *each*) chopped green chilies
  1 tablespoon chili powder
1-1/2 teaspoons salt
1/2 teaspoon *each* ground cumin and dried oregano
1/4 teaspoon pepper
1/2 cup all-purpose flour
  1 cup chicken broth
  1 cup heavy whipping cream
  2 cups (8 ounces) shredded Monterey Jack cheese, *divided*
1/3 cup vegetable oil
 12 corn tortillas (6 inches)
  1 cup thinly sliced green onions, *divided*

In a saucepan, bring the chicken, water and 2 teaspoons garlic to a boil. Reduce heat; cover and simmer for 15-20 minutes or until chicken is no longer pink. Remove chicken; reserve liquid. Cut chicken into thin strips. Set aside.

In a skillet, saute onion in butter until tender. Add remaining garlic and saute for 1 minute. Add chilies and seasonings; saute 1 minute. Stir in flour until blended. Gradually stir in chicken broth, cream and reserved liquid. Bring to a boil over medium heat; cook and stir 2 minutes or until thickened. Remove from the heat. Stir in 1 cup cheese until melted. Combine 1 cup of the cheese sauce and chicken; set aside.

In a large skillet, heat oil. Dip tortillas, one at a time, in hot oil just until limp, about 5 seconds on each side. Place on paper towels to drain. Spoon about 1/4 cup chicken mixture down the center of each tortilla; sprinkle with 1 tablespoon green onion. Roll up and place seam side down in a greased 13-in. x 9-in. x 2-in. baking dish. Pour remaining sauce evenly over tortillas. Cover and bake at 400° for 20-25 minutes or until heated through and bubbly. Sprinkle with remaining cheese; bake 3-4 minutes longer or until cheese is melted. Garnish with remaining green onions. **Yield:** 6 servings.

Nutritional Analysis: Two enchiladas equals 706 calories, 48 g fat (22 g saturated fat), 149 mg cholesterol, 1,289 mg sodium, 40 g carbohydrate, 5 g fiber, 32 g protein.

Makeover Chicken Enchiladas

  1 pound boneless skinless chicken breasts
1/2 cup water
  5 teaspoons minced garlic, *divided*
  1 cup finely chopped onion
  4 teaspoons canola oil
  2 cans (4 ounces *each*) chopped green chilies
  4 teaspoons chili powder
1-1/4 teaspoons salt
  1 teaspoon *each* ground cumin and dried oregano
1/4 teaspoon pepper
1/2 cup all-purpose flour
1-1/2 cups reduced-sodium chicken broth, *divided*
  1 cup fat-free milk
  2 cups (8 ounces) shredded reduced-fat Mexican cheese blend, *divided*
 12 corn tortillas (6 inches)
  1 cup thinly sliced green onions, *divided*

In a saucepan, bring the chicken, water and 2 teaspoons garlic to a boil. Reduce heat; cover and simmer for 15-20 minutes or until chicken is no longer pink. Remove chicken; reserve liquid. Cut chicken into thin strips. Set aside.

In a nonstick skillet, saute onion in oil until tender. Add remaining garlic and saute for 1 minute. Add chilies and seasonings; saute 1 minute. Stir in flour until blended. Gradually stir in 1 cup chicken broth, milk and reserved liquid. Bring to a boil over medium heat; cook and stir 2 minutes or until thickened. Remove from the heat. Stir in 1 cup cheese until melted. Combine 1 cup of cheese sauce and chicken; set aside.

In a large nonstick skillet, heat remaining chicken broth. Dip tortillas, one at a time, in hot broth just until limp, about 4 seconds on each side. Spoon about 1/4 cup chicken mixture down the center of each tortilla; sprinkle with 1 tablespoon green onion. Roll up and place seam side down in a 13-in. x 9-in. x 2-in. baking dish coated with nonstick cooking spray. Pour remaining sauce evenly over tortillas. Cover and bake at 400° for 20-25 minutes or until heated through and bubbly. Sprinkle with remaining cheese; cover and let stand for 5 minutes. Garnish with remaining green onions. **Yield:** 6 servings.

Nutritional Analysis: Two enchiladas equals 418 calories, 15 g fat (5 g saturated fat), 72 mg cholesterol, 1,197 mg sodium, 41 g carbohydrate, 6 g fiber, 35 g protein.
Diabetic Exchanges: 4 lean meat, 2 starch, 2 vegetable.

Turkey Fajitas

I prepare these quick and easy fajitas about once a week, and my family never gets tired of them. I like to serve them with salsa and light sour cream on the side.
—*Bonnie Basinger, Lees Summit, Missouri*

  1 **pound boneless turkey tenderloins, cut into thin strips**
  1 **tablespoon canola oil**
  1 *each* **medium green, sweet red and yellow peppers, cut into 1/4-inch strips**
  1 **medium onion, thinly sliced and separated into rings**
  1 **garlic clove, minced**
1/2 **teaspoon salt**
1/2 **teaspoon ground cumin**
1/2 **teaspoon pepper**
1/4 **teaspoon cayenne pepper**
1/2 **cup minced fresh cilantro**
1/4 **cup lime juice**
  8 **flour tortillas (6 inches), warmed**

In a large nonstick skillet, saute turkey in oil for 2 minutes. Add the peppers, onion, garlic, salt, cumin, pepper and cayenne. Cook and stir for 5 minutes or until turkey is no longer pink and peppers are crisp-tender. Stir in cilantro and lime juice; cook 1 minute longer. Serve in tortillas. **Yield:** 4 servings.

   Nutritional Analysis: Two fajitas equals 369 calories, 7 g fat (trace saturated fat), 45 mg cholesterol, 448 mg sodium, 42 g carbohydrate, 4 g fiber, 37 g protein.
   Diabetic Exchanges: 3 lean meat, 2 vegetable, 2 starch.

Crispy Oven-Baked Chicken

(Pictured above)

This is a delicious way to fix chicken that has all the flavor without all the calories. The cornflake coating is dressed up with a pleasant mixture of herbs and seasonings.
—*Alice Nulle, Woodstock, Illinois*

1-1/4 **cups crushed cornflakes**
  1 **teaspoon onion powder**
  1 **teaspoon poultry seasoning**
  1 **teaspoon paprika**
1/2 **teaspoon salt**
1/2 **teaspoon garlic powder**
1/2 **teaspoon dried marjoram**
1/2 **teaspoon dried thyme**
1/2 **teaspoon pepper**
1/4 **cup lemon juice**
1/4 **cup reduced-fat French salad dressing**
  6 **bone-in chicken breasts (8 ounces *each*), skin removed**

In a shallow bowl, combine the first nine ingredients. In another shallow bowl, combine the lemon juice and salad dressing. Dip chicken in lemon juice mixture, then coat with cornflake mixture. Arrange chicken on a rack in a foil-lined 15-in. x 10-in. x 1-in. baking pan. Bake, uncovered, at 400° for 40-50 minutes or until juices run clear. **Yield:** 6 servings.

   Nutritional Analysis: One chicken breast equals 288 calories, 5 g fat (1 g saturated fat), 102 mg cholesterol, 506 mg sodium, 19 g carbohydrate, trace fiber, 39 g protein.
   Diabetic Exchanges: 4 lean meat, 1 starch.

🍎 Try Other Tortillas

- To lighten up Mexican dishes, substitute corn tortillas when flour tortillas are called for in recipes. Yellow or white corn tortillas have less fat and fewer calories than flour tortillas.
   —*L. Patricia Campbell, San Antonio, Texas*
- Many recipes recommend frying corn tortillas in hot fat so they will not break when folded or rolled for enchiladas or other Mexican specialties. I found a healthier way to accomplish this. I spray the tortillas with butter-flavored nonstick spray, then fry in a hot dry skillet for about 30 seconds on each side.

   They don't end up greasy, and can be folded and rolled without breaking. To make your own taco shells, fry them a bit longer and fold while hot.   —*Bruce Watson, Canon City, Colorado*

Pork & Lamb Favorites

Lean cuts of pork and lamb
are ideal for people who are
eating a little lighter. Plus, with
a quick cooking time, versatile pork
and lamb are mealtime mainstays.

Marmalade Raisin Glazed Ham (page 152)

Maple Pork Slices

Low-carb

I combine fresh garlic, herbs and sugar-free maple syrup to turn pork tenderloin into a distinctive entree. The touch of sweetness makes this meat dish a big hit with my family.
—*Lori Comstock, Chesterfield, Virginia*

1 pork tenderloin (1 pound), cut into 1-inch slices
1 garlic clove, minced
1 teaspoon dried marjoram
1 teaspoon dried thyme
1/4 teaspoon salt
1/4 teaspoon onion powder
1 tablespoon butter
2 tablespoons sugar-free maple syrup

Flatten meat to 1/2-in. thickness. In a resealable plastic bag, combine the garlic, marjoram, thyme, salt and onion powder. Add meat, a slice at a time; shake to coat evenly.

In a nonstick skillet, cook meat in butter over medium heat for 2-3 minutes on each side or until meat is no longer pink. Drain and discard pan juices. Add syrup to meat in skillet. Cook over medium-high heat, turning several times, for about 3 minutes or until syrup is absorbed. Serve immediately. **Yield:** 4 servings.

Nutritional Analysis: One serving (3 ounces cooked pork) equals 171 calories, 7 g fat (3 g saturated fat), 75 mg cholesterol, 226 mg sodium, 2 g carbohydrate, trace fiber, 24 g protein.
Diabetic Exchange: *3 lean meat.*

Cider Pork Roast

Apple cider, dried cherries and fresh rosemary put the pizzazz in this pleasing pork roast. It's even more flavorful when drizzled with the sweet pan juices.
—*Terry Danner, Rochelle, Illinois*

1 boneless pork loin roast (2 pounds)
3/4 teaspoon salt
1/4 teaspoon pepper
2 cups apple cider *or* unsweetened apple juice, *divided*
3 sprigs fresh rosemary
1/2 cup dried cherries
5 teaspoons cornstarch

Sprinkle pork with salt and pepper. In a nonstick skillet coated with nonstick cooking spray, brown pork for about 4 minutes on each side. Pour 1 cup apple cider in a 3-qt. slow cooker. Place two sprigs rosemary in slow cooker; top with meat and remaining rosemary. Place cherries around roast. Cover and cook on low for 5-6 hours or until a meat thermometer reads 160°.

Remove meat; keep warm. Strain cooking liquid; reserve liquid and transfer to a small saucepan. Stir in 3/4 cup cider; bring to a boil. Combine cornstarch and remaining cider until smooth. Gradually whisk into cider mixture. Bring to a boil; cook and stir for 1-2 minutes or until thickened. Serve with meat. **Yield:** 6 servings.

Nutritional Analysis: One serving (4 ounces cooked pork with 1/4 cup gravy) equals 298 calories, 9 g fat (3 g saturated fat), 89 mg cholesterol, 368 mg sodium, 20 g carbohydrate, 1 g fiber, 32 g protein.
Diabetic Exchanges: *4 lean meat, 1-1/2 fruit.*

Oven Cassoulet

(Pictured below)

This tasty casserole can be put together quickly and is so warm and satisfying on a wintry night. We enjoy it with a lettuce salad or cooked vegetables.
—*Diane Molberg, Emerald Park, Saskatchewan*

1/2 pound reduced-fat fully cooked kielbasa *or* Polish sausage, cut into 1/2-inch cubes
1 cup chopped onion
2 medium carrots, thinly sliced
2 celery ribs, chopped
1 garlic clove, minced
1 can (14-1/2 ounces) diced tomatoes, drained
3/4 cup reduced-sodium chicken broth
1 bay leaf
1/2 teaspoon dried thyme
1/4 teaspoon pepper
1/8 teaspoon ground cloves
2 cans (15-1/2 ounces *each*) great northern beans, rinsed and drained
1-1/2 cups soft bread crumbs
2 tablespoons butter, melted
2 tablespoons minced fresh parsley

In a nonstick saucepan coated with nonstick cooking spray, cook and stir the sausage, onion, carrots, celery and garlic for 4-5 minutes or until onion is tender. Stir in the tomatoes, broth, bay leaf, thyme, pepper and cloves. Bring to a boil. Reduce heat; simmer, uncovered, for about 15 minutes

or until carrots are tender and liquid is slightly thickened. Discard bay leaf. Stir in beans.

Transfer to a 2-qt. baking dish coated with nonstick cooking spray. Combine the bread crumbs, butter and parsley. Sprinkle over sausage mixture. Bake, uncovered, at 350° for 30-35 minutes or until edges are bubbly and top is golden brown. **Yield:** 6 servings.

Nutritional Analysis: One serving (1-1/4 cups) equals 270 calories, 6 g fat (3 g saturated fat), 23 mg cholesterol, 809 mg sodium, 40 g carbohydrate, 10 g fiber, 14 g protein.
Diabetic Exchanges: 2 lean meat, 2 vegetable, 1-1/2 starch.

Slow-Cooker Pork And Apple Curry

Low-carb

Here's a gentle curry dish that's sure to please American palates. For fun, try varying the garnish... add a few chopped peanuts or a little chutney.
—Nancy Reck, Mill Valley, California

    2 pounds boneless pork loin roast, cut
      into 1-inch cubes
    1 medium tart apple, peeled and chopped
    1 small onion, chopped
  1/2 cup orange juice
    1 tablespoon curry powder
    1 teaspoon chicken bouillon granules
    1 garlic clove, minced
  1/2 teaspoon salt
  1/2 teaspoon ground ginger
  1/4 teaspoon ground cinnamon
    2 tablespoons cornstarch
    2 tablespoons cold water
Hot cooked rice, optional
  1/4 cup raisins
  1/4 cup flaked coconut, toasted

In a 3-qt. slow cooker, combine the first 10 ingredients. Cover and cook on low for 5-6 hours or until meat is tender. Increase heat to high.

In a small bowl, combine cornstarch and water until smooth; stir into slow cooker. Cover and cook for 30 minutes or until thickened, stirring once. Serve over rice if desired. Sprinkle with raisins and coconut. **Yield:** 8 servings.

Nutritional Analysis: One serving (2/3 cup with 1-1/2 teaspoons each raisins and coconut, calculated without rice) equals 235 calories, 9 g fat (4 g saturated fat), 68 mg cholesterol, 341 mg sodium, 13 g carbohydrate, 1 g fiber, 25 g protein.
Diabetic Exchanges: 3 lean meat, 1 fruit.

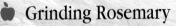

Grinding Rosemary

I PUT dry rosemary in a clean coffee grinder and grind it into a powder. Then I sprinkle the rosemary powder on chicken or turkey. The house smells so good while it cooks, and everyone enjoys the meal.
—*Charley Gomes, Tucson, Arizona*

Rosemary Roasted Pork Tenderloin

Low-carb

(Pictured above)

This is one of my favorite herb recipes and really showcases the rosemary. The tender pork also picks up a slightly sweet taste from apple juice concentrate. This recipe has a short list of ingredients but tastes like you fussed.
—Carolyn Scheider, Austin, Texas

  1/2 cup apple juice concentrate
  1/4 cup Dijon mustard
  1/4 cup fresh rosemary sprigs, chopped
    8 garlic cloves, minced
  3/4 teaspoon coarsely ground pepper
    3 pork tenderloins (1 pound *each*)

In a bowl, combine the first five ingredients; mix well. Set aside 1/3 cup; cover and refrigerate. In a large resealable plastic bag, combine the pork and remaining marinade. Seal bag and turn to coat; refrigerate overnight.

Drain and discard marinade from meat. Place meat in a roasting pan coated with nonstick cooking spray. Pour the reserved marinade on top. Bake, uncovered, at 350° for 40-45 minutes or until a meat thermometer reads 160°. Let stand for 10 minutes before slicing. **Yield:** 9 servings.

Nutritional Analysis: One serving (4 ounces cooked pork) equals 223 calories, 7 g fat (2 g saturated fat), 90 mg cholesterol, 320 mg sodium, 7 g carbohydrate, trace fiber, 33 g protein.
Diabetic Exchange: 4 lean meat.

Lime-Glazed Pork Chops

Low-sodium

(Pictured above)

A wonderful sweet-sour citrus glaze makes these tender chops tangy and tasty. Quick and easy to prepare, the grilled chops are perfect for picnics and barbecues.
—Jacqui Correa, Landing, New Jersey

　1/3 cup orange marmalade
　　1 jalapeno pepper, seeded and finely chopped
　　2 tablespoons lime juice
　　1 teaspoon grated fresh gingerroot
　　4 bone-in pork loin chops (8 ounces *each*)
　　4 teaspoons minced fresh cilantro
Lime wedges

In a small saucepan, combine the first four ingredients. Cook and stir over medium heat for 5 minutes or until marmalade is melted. Set aside.

Coat grill rack with nonstick cooking spray before starting the grill. Grill chops, covered, over medium heat for 6-7 minutes on each side or until juices run clear, brushing with the glaze during the last 5 minutes of grilling. Sprinkle with cilantro and serve with lime wedges. **Yield:** 4 servings.

Editor's Note: When cutting or seeding hot peppers, use rubber or plastic gloves to protect your hands. Avoid touching your face.

Nutritional Analysis: One pork chop equals 286 calories, 8 g fat (3 g saturated fat), 86 mg cholesterol, 85 mg sodium, 18 g carbohydrate, trace fiber, 34 g protein.
Diabetic Exchanges: 4 lean meat, 1 fruit.

Marmalade Raisin Glazed Ham

Low-carb

(Pictured on page 149)

I always get requests for this entree on special occasions. A spiced marmalade glaze and plump golden raisins add sweetness to every slice.
—Barbara Nowakowski, Mesa, Arizona

　1/2 boneless fully cooked lean ham (4 pounds)
　　1 cup water
　2/3 cup orange juice, *divided*
　1/2 cup orange marmalade spreadable fruit
　1/4 cup golden raisins
　1/4 cup raisins
　1/8 teaspoon ground allspice
　1/8 teaspoon ground cinnamon
　　2 tablespoons cornstarch

Line a shallow roasting pan with foil. Place ham on a rack in prepared pan. Bake, uncovered, at 325° for 45 minutes.

Meanwhile, combine the water, 1/2 cup orange juice, marmalade, raisins and spices in a saucepan. Bring to a boil. Reduce heat; simmer, uncovered, for 20 minutes or until raisins are softened and mixture is reduced to 1-3/4 cups.

Combine cornstarch and remaining orange juice until smooth. Gradually stir into glaze. Bring to a boil; cook and stir for 1-2 minutes or until thickened. Brush ham with glaze. Bake 1 to 1-1/2 hours longer or until a meat thermometer reads 140°, brushing occasionally with glaze. **Yield:** 16 servings.

Nutritional Analysis: One serving (3 ounces cooked ham) equals 163 calories, 4 g fat (1 g saturated fat), 58 mg cholesterol, 1,177 mg sodium, 11 g carbohydrate, trace fiber, 21 g protein.
Diabetic Exchanges: 3 lean meat, 1/2 fruit.

Creole Sausage and Vegetables

If you're a fan of okra, you'll get a kick out of this zippy smoked sausage and vegetable mix. When served over rice, this dish makes a hearty meal with generous portions.
—Jill Holland, Florence, Alabama

　　1 pound reduced-fat fully cooked sausage, cut
　　　into 1/2-inch slices
　　1 large onion, chopped
　1/2 cup chopped green pepper
　1/2 cup chopped sweet red pepper
　　2 garlic cloves, minced

2 teaspoons canola oil
4 cups chopped fresh tomatoes
1 tablespoon Worcestershire sauce
1/2 teaspoon sugar
1/2 teaspoon lemon juice
1/4 teaspoon salt
1/4 teaspoon crushed red pepper flakes
1/4 teaspoon pepper
1/4 teaspoon seafood seasoning
4 cups frozen cut okra
Hot cooked rice, optional

In a large skillet, cook the sausage, onion, sweet peppers and garlic in oil over medium heat until vegetables are tender. Stir in the tomatoes, Worcestershire sauce, sugar, lemon juice and seasonings. Bring to boil. Reduce heat; simmer, uncovered, for 15 minutes.

Add okra; return to a boil. Reduce heat; simmer, uncovered, for 7 minutes or just until okra is tender. Serve with rice if desired. **Yield:** 5 servings.

Nutritional Analysis: One serving (1-1/2 cups sausage mixture, calculated without rice) equals 227 calories, 5 g fat (1 g saturated fat), 32 mg cholesterol, 952 mg sodium, 31 g carbohydrate, 7 g fiber, 16 g protein.
Diabetic Exchanges: 4 vegetable, 2 lean meat, 1/2 starch.

Pork Chops with Nectarine Salsa

(Pictured below)

This special pork dish has a zesty flair and is a snap to prepare. A sweet fruity salsa balances perfectly with

the spicy rub that coats the pan-fried chops. Serve this entree with a simple green salad for a mouth-watering meal.
—Bonnie Bufford, Nicholson, Pennsylvania

2 teaspoons chili powder
1 teaspoon ground coriander
1/2 teaspoon ground cumin
1/2 teaspoon paprika
1/4 teaspoon salt
1/4 teaspoon pepper
4 boneless pork loin chops (4 ounces *each* and 1/2 inch thick)
1 teaspoon olive oil
1/4 cup salsa
2 tablespoons apricot spreadable fruit
2 cups sliced peeled nectarines *or* peaches
2 tablespoons minced fresh cilantro
1 tablespoon minced fresh oregano *or* 1 teaspoon dried oregano

In a small bowl, combine the first six ingredients. Rub over both sides of pork chops. In a large nonstick skillet coated with nonstick cooking spray, cook pork chops in oil over medium-high heat for 5-6 minutes on each side or until juices run clear. Remove to a serving platter and keep warm.

In the same skillet, combine salsa and spreadable fruit. Bring to a boil. Reduce heat; cook and stir over medium heat for 1 minute. Stir in nectarines, cilantro and oregano; cook 2-3 minutes longer or until heated through. Serve with pork. **Yield:** 4 servings.

Nutritional Analysis: One serving (1 pork chop with 1/2 cup salsa) equals 236 calories, 8 g fat (3 g saturated fat), 67 mg cholesterol, 320 mg sodium, 16 g carbohydrate, 2 g fiber, 24 g protein.
Diabetic Exchanges: 3 lean meat, 1 fruit.

Keen on Nectarines

THE DIFFERENCE between a nectarine and a peach is skin-deep. Due to one unlike gene, their skin texture varies—making peaches dull and fuzzy and nectarines shiny and smooth.

Both stone fruits probably originated in China over 2,000 years ago. It is said that a Chinese emperor so loved nectarines, he described them as the "nectar of the gods". That sweet-sounding name suits the tasty nature of over 100 varieties today.

Available early spring through September, nectarines reach their peak in July and August. The pick of the crop has a fresh peachy fragrance, deep golden skin (often with blushes of red) and gives slightly to the touch. Underripe nectarines should be left at room temperature for a couple of days and then refrigerated and eaten within a week.

Grilled Rubbed Pork

Low-carb Low-sodium

(Pictured below)

I like to perk up pork tenderloin with an easy rub that's both sweet and spicy. We make this dish all summer long, and I get loads of requests for the recipe because the meat is so moist and flavorful. The leftovers make great sandwiches, too.
—Susan Tuma, Faribault, Minnesota

2 pork tenderloins (1 pound *each***)**
3 tablespoons brown sugar
2 teaspoons garlic powder
2 teaspoons chili powder
1/2 teaspoon dried oregano
1/2 teaspoon pepper

Place pork in a 13-in. x 9-in. x 2-in. dish. Combine the brown sugar, garlic powder, chili powder, oregano and pepper; rub over pork. Cover and refrigerate for up to 3 hours.

Coat grill rack with nonstick cooking spray before starting the grill. Grill pork, covered, over indirect medium heat for 18-20 minutes or until a meat thermometer reads 160°; turning occasionally. Let stand for 5 minutes before slicing. **Yield:** 6 servings.

Nutritional Analysis: One serving (4 ounces cooked pork) equals 220 calories, 6 g fat (2 g saturated fat), 91 mg cholesterol, 76 mg sodium, 8 g carbohydrate, trace fiber, 33 g protein.
Diabetic Exchanges: 4 lean meat, 1/2 starch.

Pork Chops with Pizza Sauce

Low-carb

This recipe was passed down to me from Mom, who got it from her mother. Oregano and basil in the tomato sauce and in the coating on these tender moist chops give this entree its Italian flavor.
—Joanna Iovino, Commack, New York

2 to 4 teaspoons dried oregano, *divided*
2 to 4 teaspoons dried basil, *divided*
1/2 teaspoon salt, *divided*
1/2 teaspoon pepper, *divided*
4 bone-in center loin pork chops (7 ounces *each***)**
1 tablespoon olive oil
3 medium onions, thinly sliced
4 garlic cloves, minced
2 cans (8 ounces *each***) tomato sauce**
1/2 cup water
2 cups hot cooked noodles

In a small bowl, combine 1-1/2 to 3 teaspoons oregano, 1-1/2 to 3 teaspoons basil, 1/4 teaspoon salt and 1/4 teaspoon pepper. Sprinkle over both sides of chops. In a large nonstick skillet, brown pork on both sides in oil over medium heat; remove from skillet.

In the same skillet, saute onions and garlic until tender. Add the tomato sauce, water and the remaining oregano, basil, salt and pepper. Bring to a boil. Return pork to the skillet. Reduce heat; cover and simmer for 15-20 minutes or until a meat thermometer reads 160°. Serve with hot noodles. **Yield:** 4 servings.

Nutritional Analysis: One serving (1 pork chop and 3/4 cup sauce with 1/2 cup noodles) equals 302 calories, 12 g fat (4 g saturated fat), 86 mg cholesterol, 882 mg sodium, 14 g carbohydrate, 3 g fiber, 33 g protein.
Diabetic Exchanges: 4 lean meat, 3 vegetable.

Apple Braised Pork

Low-carb

Apples add fruity flavor to the gravy that's served with this tender herb-rubbed pork roast. Try serving it with baked apple slices, boiled potatoes or French bread.
—Diane Hixon, Niceville, Florida

1 teaspoon dried thyme
1 teaspoon rubbed sage

1 teaspoon pepper
1 boneless rolled pork loin roast (3 pounds)
1 tablespoon canola oil
1 cup chopped onion
3 garlic cloves, minced
1 large apple, peeled, cored and chopped
1/2 cup frozen unsweetened apple juice
   concentrate, thawed
1/2 teaspoon salt

Combine the thyme, sage and pepper; rub over pork. In a Dutch oven, brown meat on all sides in oil; remove and keep warm. In the same pan, saute onion and garlic until tender. Add the apple, apple juice concentrate and salt; bring to a boil. Return meat to the pan. Cover and bake at 325° for 55-75 minutes or until a meat thermometer reads 160°, basting occasionally with juices. Remove to a serving platter and keep warm.

Pour cooking liquid into a measuring cup; skim off fat. Cool cooking liquid slightly; place in a blender or food processor. Cover and process until smooth. Serve with the roast. **Yield:** 12 servings.

Nutritional Analysis: One serving (3 ounces cooked pork with 2 tablespoons gravy) equals 219 calories, 9 g fat (3 g saturated fat), 68 mg cholesterol, 144 mg sodium, 8 g carbohydrate, 1 g fiber, 25 g protein.
Diabetic Exchanges: 3 lean meat, 1/2 fruit.

Roast Pork Paprikash

Low-carb

(Pictured at right)

My Ukrainian great-grandmother made something similar to this roast when I was young. I don't have her recipe, so I adapted one from a Russian cookbook to suit my family's tastes. It's well worth the effort. The velvety gravy is absolutely delicious!
—Michelle Nichol, Bedford, Nova Scotia

7 garlic cloves, *divided*
1 boneless whole pork loin roast (3 pounds)
1 teaspoon salt, *divided*
1/4 teaspoon pepper
2 tablespoons Dijon mustard
2 large tomatoes, peeled, seeded and quartered
3 medium onions, coarsely chopped
2 celery ribs, chopped
1 medium green pepper, chopped
1 can (14-1/2 ounces) beef broth
2 teaspoons paprika, *divided*
1/2 pound fresh mushrooms, sliced
2 tablespoons butter
2 teaspoons all-purpose flour
1 tablespoon lemon juice
1/2 teaspoon dried thyme

Cut six garlic cloves into slices. With a knife, cut slits in roast; insert garlic slices. Rub meat with 3/4 teaspoon salt and pepper. In a large nonstick skillet coated with nonstick cooking spray, brown meat on all sides. Remove pork from pan. With a spatula, spread mustard over roast.

In a roasting pan, place the tomatoes, onions, celery and green pepper. Add broth. Place roast on vegetables. Sprinkle roast and vegetables with 1/2 teaspoon paprika. Bake, uncovered, at 350° for 65-75 minutes or until a meat thermometer reads 160°. Remove meat to a serving platter and keep warm.

For gravy, strain vegetables, reserving cooking liquid. Set vegetables aside. Skim fat from liquid. In a food processor or blender, puree vegetables and 1/2 cup cooking liquid until smooth. Combine 1 cup pureed vegetables and remaining cooking liquid. Add enough water to measure 2-1/2 cups; set aside.

In a saucepan, cook mushrooms and remaining garlic in butter until tender. Stir in flour until blended; cook and stir for 1-2 minutes. Add lemon juice, thyme, remaining salt and paprika and reserved pureed vegetable mixture. Bring to a boil; cook and stir for 2 minutes or until thickened. Serve with roast. **Yield:** 12 servings.

Nutritional Analysis: One serving (3 ounces cooked pork with 1/4 cup gravy) equals 221 calories, 9 g fat (4 g saturated fat), 72 mg cholesterol, 446 mg sodium, 8 g carbohydrate, 2 g fiber, 28 g protein.
Diabetic Exchanges: 3 lean meat, 1 vegetable.

Pork and Fruit Kabobs

Low-sodium

*The original version of this recipe called for beef.
But I use pork for a change of pace. A delightful
honey-sweetened marinade brings out the
best in this healthy selection of vegetables
and lean tenderloin cubes.*
—*Karen Salyer, Campobello, South Carolina*

```
  3/4 cup apricot nectar
    6 tablespoons dry white wine or lemon juice
    3 tablespoons honey
    3 tablespoons lime juice
    2 garlic cloves, minced
1-1/2 teaspoons dried thyme
    1 pork tenderloin (1 pound), cut into 1-inch cubes
    2 medium sweet potatoes (about 1 pound),
      peeled and cubed
    2 medium zucchini, cut into 1/2-inch slices
   16 dried apricots, halved
```

In a bowl, combine the first six ingredients; mix well. Pour
1/2 cup marinade into a large resealable plastic bag; add
the pork. Seal bag and turn to coat; refrigerate for at least
8 hours or overnight.

Meanwhile, place sweet potatoes in a saucepan; cover
with water. Cover and bring to a boil. Cook until tender,
about 8-10 minutes; drain well. Pour remaining marinade into another resealable plastic bag. Add potatoes and zucchini. Seal bag and turn to coat; refrigerate for at least 8
hours or overnight.

Coat grill rack with nonstick cooking spray before starting the grill. Drain pork and discard marinade. Drain vegetables, reserving marinade for basting. On eight metal or
soaked wood skewers, alternately thread pork, potatoes,
zucchini and apricots.

Grill, uncovered, over medium heat for 3 minutes on
each side. Baste with reserved marinade. Grill 4-5 minutes
longer or until meat juices run clear, turning and basting frequently with reserved marinade. **Yield:** 4 servings.

*Nutritional Analysis: Two kabobs equals 354 calories, 5 g fat
(2 g saturated fat), 67 mg cholesterol, 69 mg sodium, 50 g carbohydrate, 5 g fiber, 28 g protein.*
Diabetic Exchanges: 3 lean meat, 2 starch, 1 fruit.

Cajun Pork Roast

Low-carb

*My husband likes his food spicy, so this pork
roast is a favorite. It can be baked in the oven or on
the grill. I like to serve it with roasted new potatoes
seasoned with garlic and rosemary.*
—*Christine Wall, Bartlett, Illinois*

```
2 pounds boneless pork loin roast
2 teaspoons olive oil
3 tablespoons paprika
2 tablespoons dried oregano
2 tablespoons dried thyme
1 tablespoon garlic powder
```

```
1/2 teaspoon each salt, crushed red pepper flakes,
    ground cumin and white pepper
1/4 teaspoon ground nutmeg
```

Rub pork roast with oil. Combine remaining ingredients and
rub over roast. Cover and refrigerate for 1-3 hours.

Bake, uncovered, at 325° for 1-1/4 to 1-1/2 hours or until a meat thermometer reads 160°. Transfer to a serving
platter. Let stand for 10-15 minutes before slicing. **Yield:** 8
servings.

*Nutritional Analysis: One serving (3 ounces cooked pork)
equals 197 calories, 9 g fat (3 g saturated fat), 67 mg cholesterol,
205 mg sodium, 3 g carbohydrate, 2 g fiber, 24 g protein.*
Diabetic Exchange: 3 lean meat.

Oriental Pork Cabbage Stir-Fry

(Pictured at right)

*Pork paired with crisp cabbage and carrots makes
a stirring combination in this tasty main dish. It's a
quick-fix dish when unexpected company arrives.
I got the recipe from a friend when I was in college.*
—*Jane Goldsmith, Bloomfield, Indiana*

```
  6 cups cabbage chunks (1-inch pieces)
  3 teaspoons canola oil, divided
  4 medium carrots, julienned
  1 pork tenderloin (about 1 pound), cut
    into 3/4-inch cubes
  2 tablespoons minced fresh gingerroot
  1 cup reduced-sodium chicken broth, divided
1/4 cup reduced-sodium soy sauce
  4 teaspoons cornstarch
Hot cooked rice, optional
```

In a large nonstick skillet or wok, stir-fry cabbage in 1 teaspoon hot oil for 1-2 minutes. Add carrots; stir-fry 3-4 minutes longer or until carrots are crisp-tender. Remove and
keep warm.

Stir-fry the pork in remaining oil for 2 minutes. Add ginger and stir-fry for 2 minutes or until pork is lightly browned.
Stir in 3/4 cup broth and soy sauce. Bring to a boil. Reduce heat; cover and simmer for 3 minutes or until meat
juices run clear.

Combine cornstarch and remaining broth until smooth.
Gradually stir into pan. Return cabbage and carrots to skillet. Bring to a boil; cook and stir for 2-3 minutes or until thickened. Serve over rice if desired. **Yield:** 4 servings.

*Nutritional Analysis: One serving (2 cups stir-fry, calculated
without rice) equals 252 calories, 8 g fat (2 g saturated fat), 63
mg cholesterol, 855 mg sodium, 19 g carbohydrate, 5 g fiber, 27
g protein.*
Diabetic Exchanges: 3 lean meat, 3 vegetable.

Curried Lamb Stew

This is without a doubt the yummiest stew I've ever tasted. My mom often made it for special occasions when I was growing up. It's been popular with our family for the past 40 years. You can make it ahead and reheat before serving.
—Lorna Irving, Holberg, British Columbia

2 pounds lean lamb stew meat, cut into 3/4-inch cubes
4 teaspoons olive oil
1 medium onion, chopped
2 garlic cloves, minced
1 tablespoon curry powder
1 teaspoon salt
1/4 teaspoon pepper
1/8 teaspoon *each* ground coriander, cumin and cinnamon
1/8 teaspoon cayenne pepper
1/4 cup all-purpose flour
1-1/4 cups water
1 cup unsweetened pineapple juice
1 medium tart apple, peeled, cored and chopped
1/4 cup tomato sauce
1/2 cup reduced-fat sour cream
Hot cooked rice *or* noodles, optional

In a Dutch oven, brown meat in oil in batches. Cook onion and garlic in drippings until onion is softened. Add the curry, salt, pepper, coriander, cumin, cinnamon and cayenne; cook and stir for 2 minutes. Sprinkle with flour; cook and stir for 2-3 minutes. Stir in the water, pineapple juice, apple and tomato sauce.

Return meat to Dutch oven. Bring to a boil. Reduce heat; cover and simmer for about 60 minutes or until meat is tender. Remove from the heat. Stir in sour cream. Serve over hot cooked rice or noodles if desired. **Yield:** 6 servings.

Nutritional Analysis: One serving (1 cup stew, calculated without rice or noodles) equals 310 calories, 12 g fat (4 g saturated fat), 95 mg cholesterol, 533 mg sodium, 18 g carbohydrate, 2 g fiber, 31 g protein.
Diabetic Exchanges: 4 lean meat, 1/2 fruit, 1/2 starch.

Pasta Pork Medley

(Pictured at right)

After having peanut sauce in an Asian restaurant, I fell in love with the flavor and began experimenting. I came up with my own lower-fat version. We eat this pasta dish often.
—Lynne Van Wagenen, Salt Lake City, Utah

3 tablespoons reduced-sodium soy sauce
4 teaspoons rice vinegar
1 garlic clove, minced
1 teaspoon minced fresh gingerroot
1/2 teaspoon Chinese five-spice powder
2 pork tenderloins (3/4 pound *each*)
5 quarts water

1 package (7 ounces) uncooked spaghetti
1 pound fresh snow peas
PEANUT SAUCE:
3/4 cup reduced-sodium chicken broth
1/3 cup reduced-fat peanut butter
2 tablespoons rice vinegar
2 teaspoons sesame oil
2 teaspoons minced fresh gingerroot
2 garlic cloves, minced
1-1/2 teaspoons reduced-sodium soy sauce
1/4 to 1/2 teaspoon crushed red pepper flakes
1 pint grape *or* cherry tomatoes
1/4 cup sliced green onions

In a small bowl, combine the first five ingredients. Place pork in a large resealable plastic bag; add the marinade. Seal bag and turn to coat; refrigerate overnight.

Drain and discard marinade. Place pork on a rack coated with nonstick cooking spray in a shallow roasting pan. Bake, uncovered, at 425° for 30-35 minutes or until a meat thermometer reads 160°. Cover with foil; let stand for 10 minutes before cutting into thin slices.

Place 5 qts. water in a soup kettle; bring to a boil. Add pasta; cook, uncovered, in boiling water for 10 minutes. Add snow peas; cook 1-2 minutes longer or until pasta and peas are tender; drain.

In a large nonstick skillet, whisk the broth, peanut butter, vinegar, oil, ginger, garlic, soy sauce and pepper flakes until blended. Bring to a boil. Reduce heat; simmer for 2-3 minutes. Add the pasta mixture and tomatoes; heat through. Arrange sliced pork over pasta mixture. Sprinkle with onions. Serve immediately. **Yield:** 6 servings.

Nutritional Analysis: One serving (1-1/3 cups) equals 420 calories, 11 g fat (3 g saturated fat), 67 mg cholesterol, 421 mg sodium, 40 g carbohydrate, 5 g fiber, 35 g protein.
Diabetic Exchanges: 4 lean meat, 2 starch, 2 vegetable.

Chinese Pork Chops

Low-carb

Brewed tea, soy sauce and salt-free seasoning blend lend an Oriental flavor to these tender boneless pork chops. The recipe makes plenty of gravy for drizzling over the tasty chops.
—Rose Grace, Fall River, Massachusetts

  6 lean boneless pork loin chops (4 ounces *each*)
1/2 teaspoon salt-free seasoning blend
1/4 teaspoon pepper
  2 tablespoons reduced-fat stick margarine
  2 cups brewed tea
  2 cups sliced celery
  1 large onion, halved and sliced
1/4 cup reduced-sodium soy sauce
  2 teaspoons cornstarch
  1 tablespoon water

Season both sides of pork chops with seasoning blend and pepper. In a large nonstick skillet, brown meat in margarine on each side over medium-high heat. Add the tea, celery, onion and soy sauce; bring to a boil. Reduce heat; cover and simmer for 30-40 minutes or until meat and vegetables are tender.

Remove meat to serving dish. Strain cooking liquid, reserving vegetables. Place vegetables in serving dish with meat. Combine cornstarch and water in a small saucepan until smooth. Stir in 1 cup cooking liquid. Bring to a boil; cook and stir for 2 minutes or until thickened. Serve over pork chops. **Yield:** 6 servings.

Editor's Note: This recipe was tested with Parkay Light stick margarine.

Nutritional Analysis: One serving (1 pork chop with vegetables and 2 tablespoons gravy) equals 218 calories, 10 g fat (3 g saturated fat), 63 mg cholesterol, 518 mg sodium, 6 g carbohydrate, 1 g fiber, 26 g protein.
Diabetic Exchanges: 3 lean meat, 1 vegetable.

Barbecued Smoked Sausage And Lima Beans

(Pictured above right)

There's a slightly sweet flavor to this filling blend of sausage, lima beans and tomatoes. The last time I made this dish, I used homemade sausage from a local store and it was delicious!
—Myrna Wingate, Irons, Michigan

  1 cup chopped sweet onion
  1 cup chopped green pepper
  4 garlic cloves, minced
  2 teaspoons olive oil
  1 package (16 ounces) reduced-fat fully cooked smoked Polish sausage, cut into 3/4-inch slices
  2 cans (14-1/2 ounces *each*) diced tomatoes, undrained
1/2 cup packed brown sugar
1/4 cup cider vinegar
1-1/2 teaspoons ground mustard
  1 teaspoon chili powder
1/2 teaspoon ground ginger
1/4 teaspoon salt
1/4 teaspoon pepper
  2 packages (10 ounces *each*) frozen baby lima beans
Hot cooked rice

In a large nonstick skillet, saute the onion, green pepper and garlic in oil for 1 minute. Add sausage; cook and stir 4-5 minutes longer or until sausage is lightly browned. Stir in the tomatoes, brown sugar, vinegar, mustard, chili powder, ginger, salt and pepper. Bring to a boil. Stir in lima beans. Return to a boil. Reduce heat; cover and simmer for 10 minutes or until heated through. Serve over rice. **Yield:** 6 servings.

Nutritional Analysis: One serving (1-1/3 cups sausage mixture, calculated without rice) equals 367 calories, 9 g fat (4 g saturated fat), 41 mg cholesterol, 1,003 mg sodium, 53 g carbohydrate, 6 g fiber, 21 g protein.

Pork Tenderloin with Red Pepper Sauce

Low-carb

Tofu gives the rich sauce served with this tender stuffed pork a thick creamy consistency without all the fat. The colorful spinach and red pepper stuffing adds tasty appeal to this special entree.
—*Jenni Dise, Phoenix, Arizona*

  2 pork tenderloins (1 pound *each*)
1/2 cup finely chopped sweet red pepper
1/2 cup finely chopped red onion
  3 garlic cloves, minced
  1 tablespoon olive oil
  1 cup finely chopped fresh spinach
1/8 teaspoon salt
1/8 teaspoon pepper
  1 package (12.3 ounces) firm silken tofu, drained (about 1-1/2 cups)
  1 cup roasted red peppers, finely chopped
  2 tablespoons minced fresh parsley
  2 tablespoons grated Romano cheese

Cut a lengthwise slit down the center of each tenderloin to within 1/2 in. of bottom. Open tenderloins so they lie flat; cover with plastic wrap. Flatten to 1/2-in. thickness. Remove plastic; set tenderloins aside.

In a nonstick skillet, saute sweet red pepper, onion and garlic in oil until tender; add spinach and cook 2 minutes longer. Spread over tenderloins; sprinkle with salt and pepper. Roll up; tie several times with kitchen string and secure ends with toothpicks.

Bake, uncovered, at 400° for 45-60 minutes or until meat thermometer reads 160°. Transfer to a warm serving platter. Let stand for 5-10 minutes before slicing.

Meanwhile, combine the tofu, roasted red peppers, parsley and cheese in a food processor or blender; cover and process until smooth. Transfer to a saucepan; heat through (do not boil). Serve with tenderloin. **Yield:** 6 servings.

Nutritional Analysis: *One serving (6 ounces cooked stuffed pork tenderloin with 1/3 cup sauce) equals 276 calories, 10 g fat (3 g saturated fat), 86 mg cholesterol, 439 mg sodium, 8 g carbohydrate, 1 g fiber, 36 g protein.*
Diabetic Exchanges: *5 lean meat, 1 vegetable.*

Texas-Flavored Pork Chops

Low-carb

(Pictured above)

I like my food spicy, and my husband likes his mild. This pleasantly spiced dish makes us both happy—and our son enjoys it, too. It's easy to make, and I always have all the ingredients on hand.
—*Andrea Keith, Kentwood, Michigan*

3/4 cup seasoned bread crumbs
  3 tablespoons chili powder
1/2 teaspoon seasoned salt
  1 egg
1/4 cup fat-free milk
  6 bone-in pork rib chops (about 7 ounces *each*, 3/4 inch thick)

In a shallow bowl, combine the bread crumbs, chili powder and seasoned salt. In another shallow bowl, combine the egg and milk. Dip chops in egg mixture, then coat with crumbs.

Transfer to a 15-in. x 10-in. x 1-in. baking pan coated with nonstick cooking spray. Bake at 350° for 20-25 minutes or until a meat thermometer reads 160°. **Yield:** 6 servings.

Nutritional Analysis: *One pork chop equals 299 calories, 12 g fat (4 g saturated fat), 120 mg cholesterol, 448 mg sodium, 12 g carbohydrate, 1 g fiber, 34 g protein.*
Diabetic Exchanges: *4 lean meat, 1 starch.*

🍎 Tofu Tips

HERE ARE some tasty ways to incorporate tofu into your meals:

- Mash soft tofu and cook it like scrambled eggs. Add your favorite seasonings.
- Replace the oil or sour cream in salad dressing recipes with pureed tofu.
- Use silken soft tofu instead of mayonnaise or sour cream in dips and spreads.
- Layer tofu in lasagna instead of ricotta cheese.
- Cube precooked flavored tofu and serve with dip as an appetizer.

Fish & Seafood Fare

Fabulous fish dinners and sensational seafood entrees can add appetizing variety to any cook's healthy menu planning. You'll quickly get hooked on these from-the-sea favorites swimming in fantastic flavor!

Grilled Tuna with Pineapple Salsa (page 170)

Onion Peppered Roughy

Low-carb

(Pictured above)

My family is Polish and it's custom to serve a "meatless" meal on Christmas Eve. So I tried this fish a few years ago. My family loved it. It's easy to make and very elegant, too.
—Elizabeth Harrer, Lockport, New York

6 orange roughy or whitefish fillets (6 ounces each)
2 tablespoons butter, melted, divided
1/4 teaspoon salt
1/4 teaspoon pepper
1/2 cup each julienned sweet red, yellow and green pepper
1/2 cup thinly sliced onion
3/4 cup reduced-fat sour cream
Paprika, optional

Pat fish fillets dry with paper towels; place in a 15-in. x 10-in. x 1-in. baking pan coated with nonstick cooking spray. Drizzle fish with 1 tablespoon butter; sprinkle with salt and pepper. Bake, uncovered, at 350° for 10 minutes or until fish flakes easily with a fork.

Meanwhile, in a skillet, saute sweet peppers and onion in remaining butter until almost tender. Dollop fish with sour cream; top with vegetable mixture. Bake 2-3 minutes longer or until heated through. Sprinkle with paprika if desired. **Yield:** 6 servings.

Nutritional Analysis: One serving equals 206 calories, 8 g fat (4 g saturated fat), 54 mg cholesterol, 363 mg sodium, 6 g carbohydrate, 1 g fiber, 28 g protein.
Diabetic Exchanges: 4 very lean meat, 1 vegetable, 1 fat.

Veggie-Topped Fillets

Low-carb

These easy-to-prepare sole fillets are baked in a mild tomato-flavored sauce.
—Joan Shirley, Trego, Montana

4 sole or walleye fillets (6 ounces each)
3/4 teaspoon salt, divided
1/8 teaspoon pepper
1-1/2 cups V8 juice
1/2 cup chopped celery
1/2 cup chopped onion
1/4 cup chopped green pepper
1 tablespoon lemon juice
1 teaspoon sugar
1 tablespoon butter
Hot cooked rice, optional

Place fillets in a 13-in. x 9-in. x 2-in. baking dish coated with nonstick cooking spray; sprinkle with 1/2 teaspoon salt and pepper. In a saucepan, combine the V8 juice, celery, onion, green pepper, lemon juice, sugar and remaining salt; bring to a boil. Cook over medium-low heat for 5-6 minutes or until vegetables are tender. Pour over fish; dot with butter.

Bake, uncovered, at 350° for 10-15 minutes or until fish flakes easily with a fork. Serve with rice if desired. **Yield:** 4 servings.

Nutritional Analysis: One serving (1 fillet with 1/2 cup sauce, calculated without rice) equals 199 calories, 5 g fat (2 g saturated fat), 88 mg cholesterol, 779 mg sodium, 8 g carbohydrate, 1 g fiber, 29 g protein.
Diabetic Exchanges: 4 very lean meat, 1 vegetable, 1/2 fat.

Lemon-Soy Roughy

Low-carb   Low-fat

(Pictured below)

I enjoy fish very much, and I especially like it fried. But my doctor has said it's a no-no! So this is a

very tasty way to prepare fish without adding lots of extra fat and calories.
—Anne Powers, Munford, Alabama

1/4 cup lemon juice
1/4 cup reduced-sodium soy sauce
1 tablespoon sugar
1/2 teaspoon ground ginger
4 fresh *or* frozen orange roughy fillets (6 ounces each), thawed
1/2 teaspoon salt-free lemon-pepper seasoning

In a large resealable plastic bag, combine the lemon juice, soy sauce, sugar and ginger; add fish. Seal bag and turn to coat; refrigerate for 30 minutes.

Drain and discard marinade. Arrange fish in a 15-in. x 10-in. x 1-in. baking pan coated with nonstick cooking spray; sprinkle with lemon-pepper. Bake, uncovered, at 350° for 12-15 minutes or until fish flakes easily with a fork. **Yield:** 4 servings.

Nutritional Analysis: One fillet equals 124 calories, 1 g fat (trace saturated fat), 34 mg cholesterol, 258 mg sodium, 1 g carbohydrate, trace fiber, 25 g protein.
Diabetic Exchange: 4 very lean meat.

Scallop Stir-Fry

This saucy seafood stir-fry from our Test Kitchen features scallops, curry, ginger and a colorful medley of vegetables.

12 ounces fresh *or* frozen sea scallops, thawed
1 tablespoon cornstarch
1 teaspoon sugar
1/4 teaspoon salt
1 cup water
2 teaspoons reduced-sodium soy sauce
2 medium carrots, thinly sliced
3 celery ribs, thinly sliced
3 teaspoons canola oil, *divided*
4 ounces fresh mushrooms, quartered
4 green onions, cut into 1-inch pieces
4 garlic cloves, minced
1 teaspoon curry powder
1/2 teaspoon ground ginger *or* 2 teaspoons minced fresh gingerroot
Hot cooked rice, optional

If scallops are large, cut in half and set aside. In a bowl, combine the cornstarch, sugar and salt. Stir in water and soy sauce until smooth; set aside. In a nonstick skillet, saute carrots and celery in 1-1/2 teaspoons hot oil for 4 minutes. Add mushrooms and green onions; stir-fry for 2-3 minutes or until crisp-tender. Add the garlic, curry powder and ginger; stir-fry for 1 minute. Remove vegetable mixture and set aside.

In the same skillet, stir-fry scallops in remaining oil for 2-3 minutes or until scallops turn opaque. Stir sauce; add to the pan. Bring to a boil; cook and stir for 1-2 minutes or until thickened. Return vegetables to pan; heat through. Serve over hot cooked rice if desired. **Yield:** 3 servings.

Nutritional Analysis: One serving (1 cup stir-fry mixture, calculated without rice) equals 213 calories, 6 g fat (trace saturated fat), 37 mg cholesterol, 581 mg sodium, 18 g carbohydrate, 3 g fiber, 22 g protein.
Diabetic Exchanges: 3 lean meat, 2 vegetable, 1/2 starch.

Broccoli Shrimp Pasta Toss

(Pictured below)

After a long day of shopping, an hour's drive home and another hour putting everything away, I needed to fix something for supper in a hurry. I came up with this tasty dish, and my husband and kids ate every bite.
—Natalie vanViegen, Port Alberni, British Columbia

2 cups uncooked bow tie pasta
1/4 cup chopped onion
3 garlic cloves, minced
1 tablespoon butter
1 tablespoon olive oil
2 cups fresh broccoli florets
1/4 teaspoon salt
8 ounces uncooked medium shrimp, peeled and deveined
1/4 cup grated Parmesan cheese

Cook pasta according to package directions. In a large nonstick skillet, saute onion and garlic in butter and oil until tender. Add broccoli and salt; cook and stir over medium-high heat for 8 minutes. Add shrimp; cook and stir 2-3 minutes longer or until shrimp turn pink and broccoli is tender. Drain pasta; transfer to a serving bowl. Add the broccoli mixture; toss gently. Sprinkle with Parmesan cheese. **Yield:** 4 servings.

Nutritional Analysis: One serving (1-1/4 cups) equals 196 calories, 9 g fat (3 g saturated fat), 79 mg cholesterol, 358 mg sodium, 17 g carbohydrate, 2 g fiber, 13 g protein.
Diabetic Exchanges: 1 starch, 1 lean meat, 1 fat, 1 vegetable.

A Little Lemon Goes a Long Way

I LIKE to keep fresh lemon juice on hand because it's such an easy way to add refreshing flavor to many recipes. After juicing the lemons, I freeze the juice in ice cube trays. Then I simply defrost them and use in fish and seafood recipes, iced or hot teas, and many other dishes. *—Judy Manuel South Bend, Indiana*

Salmon with Ginger Pineapple Salsa

Low-carb

(Pictured at right)

Here in Oregon, fresh fish is a staple in my life. I eat salmon at least twice a week and usually grill it, but it's just as delicious baked with this zesty ginger pineapple salsa.
—Kathleen Kelley, Days Creek, Oregon

1 can (20 ounces) unsweetened pineapple tidbits
1 cup chopped seeded ripe tomatoes
3 green onions, sliced
1 jalapeno pepper, seeded and chopped
2 tablespoons cider vinegar
2 garlic cloves, minced
1-1/2 teaspoons sesame oil
1 teaspoon honey
1/2 teaspoon ground ginger *or* 1-1/2 teaspoons minced fresh gingerroot
1/4 teaspoon crushed red pepper flakes
3/4 teaspoon salt, *divided*
6 salmon fillets (6 ounces *each*)
3/4 teaspoon ground cumin
1/4 teaspoon pepper

Drain pineapple, reserving 1/4 cup juice. In a bowl, combine the tomatoes, green onions, jalapeno, vinegar, garlic, sesame oil, honey, ginger, red pepper flakes, 1/4 teaspoon salt, pineapple and reserved juice; mix well. Cover and refrigerate until serving.

Pat the salmon dry with paper towels. Sprinkle with the cumin, pepper and remaining salt. Place skin side down in a 13-in. x 9-in. x 2-in. baking dish coated with nonstick cooking spray. Bake, uncovered, at 350° for 10-15 minutes or until fish flakes easily with a fork. Serve with salsa. **Yield:** 6 servings.

Editor's Note: When cutting or seeding hot peppers, use plastic gloves to protect your hands. Avoid touching your face.

Nutritional Analysis: *One serving (1 fillet with 1/2 cup salsa) equals 374 calories, 20 g fat (4 g saturated fat), 100 mg cholesterol, 405 mg sodium, 14 g carbohydrate, 1 g fiber, 34 g protein.*
Diabetic Exchanges: *5 lean meat, 1 fruit, 1 fat.*

Seafood Triangles

Low-carb

(Pictured at right)

One chilly Easter, my creative clan was looking for an appetizer that would break family traditions and warm hearts... and we came up with these spicy bites filled with shrimp and crabmeat.
—Tarsia Nichols, Spirit Lake, Idaho

3 tablespoons chopped green onions
3 tablespoons butter, *divided*
1/2 pound uncooked shrimp, peeled, deveined and quartered
1/4 cup dry white wine *or* chicken broth
4 teaspoons cornstarch
1/3 cup 2% milk
1/2 cup grated Parmesan cheese
1 can (6 ounces) crabmeat, drained, flaked and cartilage removed
1 teaspoon sugar
1 teaspoon lemon juice
1/4 teaspoon cayenne pepper
1/8 teaspoon white pepper, optional
22 sheets phyllo dough (14 inches x 9 inches)
1 egg white

In a large nonstick skillet, saute green onions in 1 tablespoon butter until tender. Add shrimp and wine or broth; cook and stir over medium-high heat for 2 minutes or until shrimp turn pink; drain, reserving liquid. Combine cornstarch and milk until smooth.

In the same skillet, combine milk mixture and reserved liquid. Bring to a boil; cook and stir for 2 minutes or until thickened. Reduce heat to low. Stir in the cheese, crab, sugar, lemon juice, cayenne, white pepper if desired and shrimp. Remove from the heat and allow to cool.

On a dry surface, carefully remove two sheets of phyllo dough and place on top of each other (keeping remaining dough covered with plastic wrap to prevent drying). Melt remaining butter. Cut sheets widthwise into six strips about 2 in. wide. Lightly brush the tops with butter. Place a rounded teaspoon filling near lower right corner of strip. Fold left corner of dough over filling, forming a triangle. Fold triangle up, then fold over, forming another triangle. Continue folding like a flag for the length of the strip.

Place triangles on ungreased baking sheets. Brush tops with egg white. Bake at 400° for 7-10 minutes or until golden brown. **Yield:** 5-1/2 dozen.

Nutritional Analysis: *One serving (4 triangles) equals 110 calories, 4 g fat (2 g saturated fat), 37 mg cholesterol, 218 mg sodium, 10 g carbohydrate, trace fiber, 7 g protein.*
Diabetic Exchanges: *1 very lean meat, 1 fat, 1/2 starch.*

Breaded Flounder Fillets

Low-carb *Low-fat*

(Pictured below)

I use flounder in this recipe, but any fish fillets can be prepared with this tasty coating. It's quick and easy when time is short.
—Michelle Smith, Sykesville, Maryland

1/4 cup all-purpose flour
1/4 cup cornmeal
1 teaspoon salt
1/2 teaspoon paprika
1/2 teaspoon pepper
2 egg whites
1/4 cup fat-free milk
4 flounder fillets (6 ounces *each*)
1 tablespoon grated Parmesan cheese

In a shallow bowl, combine the flour, cornmeal, salt, paprika and pepper. In another shallow bowl, beat egg whites and milk. Coat fish with cornmeal mixture, then dip into egg white mixture. Coat fish again in cornmeal mixture.

In a 15-in. x 10-in. x 1-in. baking pan coated with nonstick cooking spray, arrange fish in a single layer. Sprinkle with Parmesan cheese. Bake, uncovered, at 425° for 8-10 minutes or until fish flakes easily with a fork. **Yield:** 4 servings.

Nutritional Analysis: One fillet equals 236 calories, 3 g fat (1 g saturated fat), 83 mg cholesterol, 789 mg sodium, 14 g carbohydrate, 1 g fiber, 37 g protein.
Diabetic Exchanges: *5 very lean meat, 1 starch.*

Seafood Stir-Fry

This delightfully different stir-fry features tuna steaks, broccoli and pasta. The sauce offers a delicate balance of flavors, ranging from zesty red pepper flakes to Parmesan cheese.
—Robin Chamberlin, La Costa, California

6 ounces uncooked linguine, broken in half
1 tablespoon cornstarch
3/4 cup dry white wine *or* reduced-sodium chicken broth
1/2 cup additional reduced-sodium chicken broth
1 teaspoon dried thyme
1/2 teaspoon salt
1/8 to 1/4 teaspoon crushed red pepper flakes
2 cups broccoli florets
4 teaspoons canola oil
1 large sweet yellow, red *or* green pepper, julienned
2 garlic cloves, minced
2 tuna *or* swordfish steaks (8 ounces *each*), cut into 1-inch cubes
1/4 cup shredded Parmesan cheese

Cook pasta according to package directions. In a bowl, combine the cornstarch, wine or chicken broth, additional chicken broth, thyme, salt and pepper flakes until smooth; set aside.

In a large nonstick skillet, stir-fry broccoli in hot oil for 4 minutes. Add sweet pepper and garlic; stir-fry for 4 minutes. Stir cornstarch mixture and add to pan along with tuna; stir-fry 3-4 minutes or until fish flakes easily with a fork and sauce is thickened. Drain pasta; add to stir-fry and toss to coat. Sprinkle with cheese. **Yield:** 4 servings.

Nutritional Analysis: One serving (1-1/2 cups) equals 399 calories, 9 g fat (2 g saturated fat), 57 mg cholesterol, 521 mg sodium, 39 g carbohydrate, 3 g fiber, 35 g protein.
Diabetic Exchanges: *4 lean meat, 2 starch, 1 vegetable.*

Pasta with White Clam Sauce

Garlic and oregano enhance the seafood flavor of this delicious main dish. An Italian friend of my mom's passed on the recipe to her, and I began preparing it when I was 14. For convenience, it can be made in advance…and leftovers are just as good.
—Kelli Soike, Tallahassee, Florida

12 ounces uncooked linguine
2 garlic cloves, minced
1 can (2 ounces) anchovies, undrained
1 tablespoon olive oil
1 bottle (8 ounces) clam juice
1 can (6-1/2 ounces) minced clams, undrained
1/3 cup water
2 tablespoons dried oregano
1 tablespoon minced fresh parsley

1/4 teaspoon salt
1/2 teaspoon pepper
  5 tablespoons shredded Parmesan cheese

Cook pasta according to package directions. In a saucepan, saute garlic and anchovies in oil for 3 minutes, breaking up anchovies. Stir in the clam juice, clams, water, oregano, parsley, salt and pepper. Bring to a boil. Reduce heat; simmer, uncovered, for 15 minutes or until sauce is reduced by half. Drain pasta; toss with clam sauce. Sprinkle with Parmesan. **Yield:** 5 servings.

Nutritional Analysis: One serving (1 cup) equals 379 calories, 13 g fat (2 g saturated fat), 19 mg cholesterol, 874 mg sodium, 50 g carbohydrate, 4 g fiber, 16 g protein.
  Diabetic Exchanges: 3 starch, 2 fat, 1 lean meat.

🍎 Lighter Fried Fish

I RECENTLY experimented with a lighter and zestier version of fried fish. I lightly brushed tilapia fillets with fat-free Italian salad dressing, then coated them with bread crumbs.

I pan-fried the fillets in a small amount of olive oil and I Can't Believe It's Not Butter spray. This eliminated the need for eggs, plus gave the fish zippy flavor without requiring additional seasonings.
  —*Marti Brisky, Valley View, Ohio*

Italian Orange Roughy

Low-carb Low-fat

(Pictured above)

This dish is delicious, foolproof and very low in fat. I prepare it on weeknights when I need a quick supper, but I've also used it for company meals. The Italian tomatoes and lemon-pepper seasoning give the mild fillets a little zest.
  —*Michelle Haerr, Cedarville, Ohio*

4 orange roughy fillets (6 ounces *each*)
1/4 teaspoon lemon-pepper seasoning
1/4 teaspoon salt
1/4 cup finely chopped onion
1/4 cup finely chopped celery
  1 can (14-1/2 ounces) Italian diced tomatoes, undrained

Arrange the fish fillets in an ungreased 13-in. x 9-in. x 2-in. baking dish. Sprinkle with lemon-pepper and salt. Cover with the onion and celery. Top with the tomatoes. Bake at 350° for 30-40 minutes or until fish flakes easily with a fork. **Yield:** 4 servings.

Nutritional Analysis: One serving equals 145 calories, 1 g fat (trace saturated fat), 34 mg cholesterol, 620 mg sodium, 7 g carbohydrate, 2 g fiber, 26 g protein.
  Diabetic Exchanges: 4 very lean meat, 1 vegetable.

Flounder with Shrimp Sauce

Low-carb

I wrap flounder around succulent shrimp in this elegant from-the-sea favorite. Its delicate fish flavor melds perfectly with the mild mustard sauce.
—Carolyn Glassmoyer, Shillington, Pennsylvania

- **4 flounder fillets (6 ounces *each*)**
- **2 teaspoons lemon juice**
- **1/2 teaspoon salt, *divided***
- **1/8 teaspoon pepper**
- **1/4 pound uncooked medium shrimp, peeled and deveined**
- **4 teaspoons butter**
- **4 teaspoons all-purpose flour**
- **1 cup 2% milk**
- **4 teaspoons Dijon mustard**
- **1/8 teaspoon white pepper**

Sprinkle each flounder fillet with lemon juice, 1/4 teaspoon salt and pepper. Roll each fillet around a shrimp and secure with a toothpick. Chop remaining shrimp; set aside. Arrange rolled fillets seam side down in an 11-in. x 7-in. x 2-in. baking dish coated with nonstick cooking spray. Cover and bake at 425° for 20-25 minutes or until fish flakes easily with a fork and shrimp turn pink.

Meanwhile, in a saucepan, melt butter over medium heat. Stir in flour; gradually add the milk, mustard, white pepper and remaining salt until blended. Add remaining shrimp. Bring to a boil; cook and stir for 1-2 minutes or until thickened and shrimp turn pink. Serve sauce over fish. **Yield:** 4 servings.

Nutritional Analysis: *One serving (one stuffed fillet with 1/4 cup sauce) equals 253 calories, 8 g fat (4 g saturated fat), 130 mg cholesterol, 666 mg sodium, 6 g carbohydrate, trace fiber, 38 g protein.*
Diabetic Exchanges: *5 very lean meat, 1 fat, 1/2 starch.*

Citrus Fish Tacos

(Pictured at right)

Fun fish tacos bring a deliciously different twist to a Southwest standby! Combine halibut or cod with a fruity salsa and zesty seasoning, then tuck the fish inside wholesome corn tortillas.
—Maria Baldwin, Mesa, Arizona

- **1-1/2 cups finely diced fresh pineapple**
- **1 can (11 ounces) mandarin oranges, drained and cut in half**
- **1 envelope reduced-sodium taco seasoning, *divided***
- **3 tablespoons orange juice concentrate, *divided***
- **3 tablespoons lime juice, *divided***
- **1 jalapeno pepper, seeded and finely chopped**
- **1-1/2 pounds halibut *or* cod, cut into 3/4-inch cubes**
- **8 corn tortillas (6 inches), warmed**
- **3 cups shredded lettuce**

In a bowl, combine the pineapple, oranges, 1 tablespoon taco seasoning, 1 tablespoon orange juice concentrate, 1 tablespoon lime juice and jalapeno pepper. Cover and refrigerate.

Place fish in an ungreased shallow 2-qt. baking dish. In a small bowl, combine the remaining orange juice concentrate, lime juice and taco seasoning. Add to fish; toss gently to coat. Cover and bake at 375° for 12-16 minutes or until fish flakes easily with a fork.

Place a spoonful of fish on each tortilla. Top each with lettuce and pineapple salsa; fold over. **Yield:** 4 servings.

Editor's Note: When cutting or seeding hot peppers, use rubber or plastic gloves to protect your hands. Avoid touching your face. To warm the tortillas, coat a nonstick skillet with nonstick cooking spray. Heat over medium-low heat. Warm each tortilla in skillet for 10-15 seconds on each side. Repeat, coating with nonstick cooking spray as needed.

Nutritional Analysis: *One serving (2 tacos) equals 411 calories, 6 g fat (1 g saturated fat), 54 mg cholesterol, 670 mg sodium, 52 g carbohydrate, 5 g fiber, 40 g protein.*
Diabetic Exchanges: *5 very lean meat, 2 starch, 1-1/2 fruit.*

Cajun-Style Catfish

Low-carb Low-sodium

(Pictured at right)

These nicely spiced fillets are sure to win you a boatload of compliments! I got the original recipe from a chef in the culinary arts department of a college where I used to work.
—Dolores Barnas, Blasdell, New York

- **4-1/2 teaspoons paprika**
- **1 teaspoon onion powder**
- **1 teaspoon dried oregano**
- **1 teaspoon pepper**
- **1/2 teaspoon white pepper**
- **1/2 teaspoon dried thyme**
- **1/4 teaspoon cayenne pepper**
- **4 catfish fillets (6 ounces *each*)**
- **Refrigerated butter-flavored spray**

In a shallow bowl, combine the first seven ingredients. Spritz both sides of fish with butter-flavored spray. Dip one side of each fillet in spice mixture; place spice side down in a large skillet coated with butter-flavored spray. Cook over medium-high heat for 8-10 minutes or until fish flakes easily with a fork, turning once. **Yield:** 4 servings.

Editor's Note: This recipe was tested with I Can't Believe It's Not Butter Spray.

Nutritional Analysis: *One fillet equals 236 calories, 13 g fat (3 g saturated fat), 80 mg cholesterol, 91 mg sodium, 1 g carbohydrate, 1 g fiber, 27 g protein.*
Diabetic Exchange: *4 lean meat, 1/2 fat.*

Grilled Tuna with Pineapple Salsa

Low-carb

(Pictured above and on page 161)

*While spending some time in Honolulu,
I came upon this tropical treatment for tuna.
Now as a personal chef, I still prepare the
pineapple salsa as a tangy-sweet garnish for
everything from grilled fish to pork and poultry.*
—*Beveylon Concha, Chesapeake, Virginia*

1/2 medium fresh pineapple, peeled and cut
    into 1/2-inch slices
1 small onion, diced
2 jalapeno peppers, seeded and diced
2 tablespoons minced fresh cilantro
2 tablespoons lime juice
4 tuna steaks (6 ounces *each*)
1 tablespoon olive oil
1/4 teaspoon salt
1/4 teaspoon pepper

Grill pineapple slices, uncovered, over medium heat for
5-7 minutes on each side. Remove and chill pineapple for
30 minutes. Dice chilled pineapple. In a bowl, combine the
pineapple, onion, jalapeno peppers, cilantro and lime
juice. Refrigerate for 1 hour or until chilled.

Brush tuna with oil. Sprinkle with salt and pepper. Grill,
covered, over medium heat for 5 minutes on each side or until the fish flakes easily with a fork. Serve with salsa. **Yield:**
4 servings.

Editor's Note: When cutting or seeding hot peppers, use
rubber or plastic gloves to protect your hands. Avoid
touching your face.

Nutritional Analysis: *One serving (1 tuna steak with 1/2 cup
salsa) equals 252 calories, 5 g fat (1 g saturated fat), 77 mg cholesterol, 212 mg sodium, 10 g carbohydrate, 1 g fiber, 40 g protein.*
Diabetic Exchanges: *5 very lean meat, 1 fruit, 1/2 fat.*

Dilled Tuna Sandwiches

Low-carb

*Fishing for a better-tasting tuna sandwich? Put
pizzazz in your tuna salad by adding dill weed,
carrot and onion. My family loves tuna salad
sandwiches, and this recipe is their favorite.*
—*Sue Gronholz, Beaver Dam, Wisconsin*

1/4 cup fat-free mayonnaise
1/4 cup reduced-fat sour cream
3/4 teaspoon dill weed
1/2 teaspoon sugar
1/8 teaspoon pepper
2 cans (6 ounces *each*) light water-packed tuna,
    drained and flaked
1/4 cup shredded carrot
1-1/2 teaspoons finely chopped onion
3 English muffins, split and toasted
6 lettuce leaves
6 slices reduced-fat process American cheese
    product

In a bowl, combine the mayonnaise, sour cream, dill weed,
sugar and pepper until smooth. Stir in the tuna, carrot and
onion. Top each English muffin half with a lettuce leaf,
cheese and 1/2 cup tuna mixture. **Yield:** 6 servings.

Nutritional Analysis: *One open-faced sandwich equals 182
calories, 5 g fat (3 g saturated fat), 31 mg cholesterol, 636 mg sodium, 13 g carbohydrate, 2 g fiber, 22 g protein.*
Diabetic Exchanges: *3 very lean meat, 1 starch.*

Honey-Mustard Grilled Trout

Low-carb

*This easy-to-prepare dish is a favorite with family. We
like the honey-mustard sauce so much, I make a double
batch and keep some in the fridge to use as dressing.*
—*Charlene Cronin, Kenner, Louisiana*

1/4 cup reduced-fat mayonnaise
1 tablespoon cider vinegar
1 tablespoon prepared mustard
1 tablespoon honey
1/8 teaspoon cayenne pepper
4 large onions, cut into 1/2-inch slices
6 trout fillets (6 ounces *each*)

Coat grill rack with nonstick cooking spray before starting
the grill. In a bowl, combine the first five ingredients. Place
onions cut side down on grill rack with sides touching.
Arrange fillets on onion slices. Cover and grill over medium-

● Read Up on Gingerroot

Fresh gingerroot is available in the produce section of most major grocery stores. Select gingerroot with a smooth skin. If wrinkled or cracked, the root is dry and past its prime.

When stored in a heavy-duty bag, unpeeled gingerroot can be frozen up to 1 year. When needed, simply peel and grate the ginger into your recipe.

—*Judy Manuel, South Bend, Indiana*

hot heat for 5 minutes. Baste with mustard mixture. Cook 5-6 minutes longer or until fish flakes easily with a fork, basting frequently. Discard onion slices. **Yield:** 6 servings.

Nutritional Analysis: One trout fillet equals 295 calories, 15 g fat (2 g saturated fat), 100 mg cholesterol, 201 mg sodium, 4 g carbohydrate, trace fiber, 35 g protein.
Diabetic Exchange: 5 lean meat.

Salsa Catfish

Give your fish a Southwestern "kick" with this change-of-pace preparation. My sister doesn't like seafood, so I figured I'd disguise it with a mix of interesting tastes and textures. Everyone was surprised by the slightly crunchy tortilla chip coating.
—*Teresa Hubbard, Russellville, Alabama*

  1 cup finely crushed baked tortilla chips
1/2 to 1 teaspoon chili powder
  3 tablespoons lemon juice
  1 tablespoon canola oil
  4 catfish fillets (4 ounces *each***)**
  1 cup salsa, warmed

In a shallow bowl, combine tortilla chip crumbs and chili powder. In another bowl, combine lemon juice and oil. Dip fish in lemon mixture, then coat with crumb mixture.

Place in a 13-in. x 9-in. x 2-in. baking dish coated with nonstick cooking spray. Sprinkle with any remaining crumbs. Bake at 450° for 8-10 minutes or until fish easily flakes with a fork. Serve with salsa. **Yield:** 4 servings.

Nutritional Analysis: One serving (1 fillet with 1/4 cup salsa) equals 317 calories, 13 g fat (2 g saturated fat), 53 mg cholesterol, 547 mg sodium, 30 g carbohydrate, 3 g fiber, 21 g protein.
Diabetic Exchanges: 3 lean meat, 1-1/2 starch, 1 vegetable, 1/2 fat.

Easy Fish Fillets

For folks who want to cook fish in a flash, this recipe is quite a catch. These fillets always turn out moist and flaky.
—*Theresa Stewart, New Oxford, Pennsylvania*

3/4 cup seasoned bread crumbs
1/3 cup reduced-fat Italian salad dressing
  4 catfish fillets (5 ounces *each***), patted dry**

Place bread crumbs in a shallow bowl. Place dressing in another shallow bowl. Dip fish in dressing, then coat with

crumbs. Place fish on a rack in a 15-in. x 10-in. x 1-in. baking pan. Bake, uncovered, at 450° for 15-20 minutes or until the fish flakes easily with a fork. **Yield:** 4 servings.

Nutritional Analysis: One fillet equals 300 calories, 14 g fat (3 g saturated fat), 67 mg cholesterol, 512 mg sodium, 16 g carbohydrate, 1 g fiber, 25 g protein.
Diabetic Exchanges: 4 lean meat, 1 starch.

Glazed Salmon Fillet

Low-carb

(Pictured below)

I love to cook and usually try a new recipe at least once a week. This salmon has wonderful flavor. I've served it to company several times, and they always love it.
—*Sherry West, New River, Arizona*

1/4 cup reduced-sodium soy sauce
  2 tablespoons brown sugar
1/4 teaspoon crushed red pepper flakes
1/4 teaspoon ground ginger
1/8 teaspoon sesame oil
  1 salmon fillet (1-1/2 pounds)

In a bowl, combine the first five ingredients. If grilling the salmon, coat grill rack with nonstick cooking spray before starting the grill. Grill salmon, covered, over medium heat or broil 4-6 in. from the heat for 5-6 minutes on each side or until salmon flakes easily with a fork, basting frequently with glaze. **Yield:** 6 servings.

Nutritional Analysis: One serving (4 ounces cooked salmon) equals 233 calories, 12 g fat (3 g saturated fat), 67 mg cholesterol, 472 mg sodium, 5 g carbohydrate, trace fiber, 23 g protein.
Diabetic Exchanges: 3 lean meat, 1/2 fat, 1/2 starch.

Maritime Grilled Fish

Low-carb Low-fat

Sweet honey and zippy red pepper flakes accent the herb-enhanced marinade I use for grilled fish. It's also good on chicken.
—*Julie Craghead, Peoria, Illinois*

1/4 cup dry white wine *or* chicken broth
1/4 cup reduced-sodium soy sauce
  3 tablespoons honey
  1 tablespoon olive oil
  3 to 4 garlic cloves, minced
1/4 teaspoon crushed red pepper flakes
1/8 teaspoon pepper
1/8 teaspoon *each* dried basil, thyme and rosemary, crushed
1/8 teaspoon dill weed
  4 orange roughy fillets (6 ounces *each*)

In a large resealable plastic bag, combine the wine, soy sauce, honey, oil, garlic and seasonings; add the fish. Seal bag and turn to coat; refrigerate for up to 1 hour.

If grilling the fish, coat grill rack with nonstick cooking spray before starting the grill. Drain and discard marinade. Grill fish, covered, over medium heat or broil 4-6 in. from heat for 5-6 minutes on each side or until fish flakes easily with a fork. **Yield:** 4 servings.

Nutritional Analysis: *One fillet equals 136 calories, 2 g fat (trace saturated fat), 34 mg cholesterol, 259 mg sodium, 2 g carbohydrate, trace fiber, 25 g protein.*
Diabetic Exchange: *4 very lean meat.*

Baked Salmon with Herbs

Low-carb

(Pictured at right)

The fish dishes I rely on are all family approved. They especially love this salmon…and I like that it's so good for us!. I grow my own herbs and love using them in recipes like this one.
—*Melissa Merrill, Hatteras, North Carolina*

2-1/2 cups soft bread crumbs (about 5 slices)
  4 garlic cloves, minced
  2 tablespoons grated Parmesan cheese
  2 teaspoons dried parsley flakes
  1 teaspoon dried thyme
  1 teaspoon dried rosemary, crushed
1/2 teaspoon salt
1/4 teaspoon pepper
  2 tablespoons butter, melted
  1 salmon fillet (3 pounds)

Line a 15-in. x 10-in. x 1-in. baking pan with foil; coat foil with nonstick cooking spray. Set aside. In a bowl, combine the bread crumbs, garlic, Parmesan cheese, parsley, thyme, rosemary, salt and pepper. Add butter; toss to coat evenly.

Place salmon on prepared pan. Spray with nonstick cooking spray and pat with bread crumb mixture. Bake, uncovered, at 350° for 35-40 minutes or until fish flakes easily with a fork. **Yield:** 8 servings.

Nutritional Analysis: *One serving equals 313 calories, 14 g fat (4 g saturated fat), 102 mg cholesterol, 343 mg sodium, 8 g carbohydrate, 1 g fiber, 36 g protein.*
Diabetic Exchanges: *5 lean meat, 1/2 starch.*

Tilapia with Cucumber Relish

Low-carb

(Pictured at right)

This is a recipe that lures even landlubbers to my fish suppers. I spotted this easy entree on a recipe card in my local fish market. Although my husband isn't big on fish, he enjoys this mild-tasting tilapia. The relish adds garden-fresh flavor and pretty color to the lightly browned fillets.
—*Mary VanHollebeke, Wyandotte, Michigan*

2/3 cup chopped seeded cucumber
1/2 cup chopped radishes
  1 tablespoon tarragon vinegar
  1 teaspoon olive oil
1/2 teaspoon salt, *divided*
1/4 teaspoon pepper, *divided*
1/8 teaspoon sugar
1/8 teaspoon paprika
  4 tilapia fillets (6 ounces *each*)
  1 tablespoon butter

In a small bowl, combine cucumber and radishes. In another small bowl, whisk the vinegar, oil, 1/4 teaspoon salt, 1/8 teaspoon pepper and sugar. Pour over cucumber mixture; toss to coat evenly. Combine paprika and remaining salt and pepper; sprinkle over fillets.

In a large nonstick skillet coated with nonstick cooking spray, melt butter. Add fish; cook for 3-4 minutes on each side or until fish flakes easily with a fork. Serve with cucumber relish. **Yield:** 4 servings.

Nutritional Analysis: *One serving (1 fish fillet with 3 tablespoons relish) equals 181 calories, 6 g fat (3 g saturated fat), 90 mg cholesterol, 388 mg sodium, 1 g carbohydrate, trace fiber, 32 g protein.*
Diabetic Exchanges: *4 very lean meat, 1 fat.*

Taco Fish

Low-carb

Since I live on a lake and have a husband who's an avid angler, fish tops my list of mealtime ingredients. Here, I use delicate fillets as the base for a tempting bake with a mild taco flavor. Kids and adults alike will go for the crunchy tortilla chip topping sprinkled with reduced-fat cheddar cheese.
—Evelyn Eyermann, Cuba, Missouri

4 orange roughy *or* bass fillets (6 ounces *each*)
1/2 teaspoon salt
1/4 teaspoon chili powder
1/2 cup taco sauce
1/3 cup crushed tortilla chips
1/3 cup shredded reduced-fat cheddar cheese

Place fish in a 13-in. x 9-in. x 2-in. baking dish coated with nonstick cooking spray; sprinkle with salt and chili powder. Cover and bake at 350° for 20 minutes. Pour taco sauce over fish. Bake, uncovered, for 5-8 minutes longer or until heated through. Immediately sprinkle with tortilla chips and cheese. **Yield:** 4 servings.

Nutritional Analysis: One fillet equals 199 calories, 5 g fat (2 g saturated fat), 41 mg cholesterol, 684 mg sodium, 9 g carbohydrate, trace fiber, 28 g protein.
Diabetic Exchanges: 4 very lean meat, 1/2 starch, 1/2 fat.

Salmon Casserole

Canned salmon is the key ingredient in this old-fashioned casserole. Bread crumbs give it a soft texture...and mayonnaise, mustard and cheese add comforting flavor.
—Agnes Moon, Ionia, Michigan

1 can (7-1/2 ounces) salmon, drained, bones and skin removed
4 cups soft bread crumbs
1/2 cup chopped celery
1/2 cup chopped green pepper
1/4 cup chopped onion
1 tablespoon minced fresh parsley
3/4 cup fat-free milk
1 tablespoon reduced-fat mayonnaise
1 teaspoon ground mustard
1/4 teaspoon pepper
1 tablespoon grated Parmesan cheese
1/4 teaspoon paprika

In a bowl, combine the salmon, bread crumbs, celery, green pepper, onion and parsley. In another bowl, combine the milk, mayonnaise, ground mustard and pepper. Pour over salmon mixture; toss to coat evenly.

Transfer to a 1-qt. baking dish coated with nonstick cooking spray. Sprinkle with Parmesan cheese and paprika. Bake, uncovered, at 350° for 30-35 minutes or until top is golden brown and casserole is heated through. **Yield:** 4 servings.

Nutritional Analysis: One serving (3/4 cup) equals 242 calories, 7 g fat (1 g saturated fat), 33 mg cholesterol, 361 mg sodium, 28 g carbohydrate, 2 g fiber, 17 g protein.
Diabetic Exchanges: 2 lean meat, 1-1/2 starch, 1 vegetable.

Thai Shrimp Stir-Fry

Low-carb

(Pictured at right)

Peanut butter gives this tasty blend of red peppers, snow peas and shrimp its Thai flavor, while ginger and red pepper flakes spice it up. I like to serve the colorful main dish over pasta.
—Jeanne Fisher, Simi Valley, California

2 medium sweet red peppers, cut into thin slices
1 teaspoon canola oil
1 cup fresh snow peas
1/2 cup thinly sliced green onions
1 garlic clove, minced
1/2 cup reduced-sodium chicken broth
2 tablespoons reduced-fat peanut butter
4-1/2 teaspoons reduced-sodium soy sauce
1 tablespoon rice vinegar
1 teaspoon sesame oil
1 teaspoon minced fresh gingerroot
1/2 teaspoon crushed red pepper flakes
1 pound uncooked medium shrimp, peeled and deveined
Hot cooked fettuccine

In a large nonstick skillet or wok, stir-fry red peppers in hot canola oil for 1 minute. Add the snow peas, green onions and garlic; stir-fry 2-3 minutes longer or until vegetables are crisp-tender. Remove and keep warm.

In the same skillet, combine the broth, peanut butter, soy sauce, vinegar, sesame oil, ginger and pepper flakes. Cook and stir until peanut butter is melted and mixture comes to a boil. Stir in shrimp. Cook and stir for 2 minutes or until shrimp turn pink. Return red pepper mixture to skillet; heat through. Serve over fettuccine. **Yield:** 4 servings.

Nutritional Analysis: One serving (1 cup stir-fry mixture, calculated without pasta) equals 206 calories, 8 g fat (1 g saturated fat), 168 mg cholesterol, 565 mg sodium, 12 g carbohydrate, 3 g fiber, 22 g protein.
Diabetic Exchanges: 3 very lean meat, 1 vegetable, 1 fat, 1/2 starch.

Poached Salmon with Tarragon Sauce

Low-carb

(Pictured above)

When I don't want to heat up the kitchen, I reach for the recipe for this poached salmon. Fixing the sauce first allows the herb seasonings to meld and enhance the mild-tasting steaks. Use two slotted spatulas to remove the poached fish from the pan. Poached fish is delicate and tends to break apart easily.
—Laura Perry, Phoenixville, Pennsylvania

1/3 cup plain yogurt
1/4 cup fat-free mayonnaise
  2 tablespoons thinly sliced green onion
  2 tablespoons minced fresh parsley
  1 teaspoon chopped fresh tarragon *or* 1/2
    teaspoon dried tarragon
1/4 teaspoon salt

1/4 teaspoon white pepper, *divided*
  1 cup reduced-sodium chicken broth
1/2 cup water
1/4 cup lemon juice
  1 bay leaf
  4 salmon steaks (5 ounces *each*)

In a bowl, combine the yogurt, mayonnaise, onion, parsley, tarragon, salt and 1/8 teaspoon pepper. Cover and refrigerate.

In a large nonstick skillet, combine the broth, water, lemon juice, bay leaf and remaining pepper. Bring to a boil. Reduce heat; add the salmon. Cover and poach for 8-10 minutes or until fish is firm and flakes easily with a fork. Remove from poaching liquid. Serve with tarragon sauce. **Yield:** 4 servings.

Nutritional Analysis: One serving (1 salmon steak with 2 tablespoons sauce) equals 261 calories, 12 g fat (3 g saturated fat), 77 mg cholesterol, 500 mg sodium, 5 g carbohydrate, 1 g fiber, 32 g protein.
Diabetic Exchanges: 4 lean meat, 1/2 starch.

Meatless Main Dishes

You won't find any meat in these main dishes …but you won't miss it, either. This hearty vegetarian fare is so delightfully satisfying, even your most ardent meat-and-potatoes lovers will give it rave reviews.

Chili-Stuffed Potatoes (page 184)

Basil Parmesan Pasta Sauce

Low-carb Meatless

As a busy home health nurse, I'm committed to preparing meals that are quick and nutritious. I came up with this rich and creamy sauce that is lower in fat than traditional white sauce. Dinner guests never believe it is made with fat-free milk.
—Susan Houser, Anchorage, Alaska

1 garlic clove, minced
1/4 cup olive oil
1/4 cup all-purpose flour
1-1/2 teaspoons salt
1/4 teaspoon pepper
4 cups fat-free milk
1/4 cup grated Parmesan cheese
2 tablespoons chopped fresh basil
Hot cooked spaghetti *or* linguine

In a nonstick skillet, saute garlic in oil until tender. Stir in flour, salt and pepper until blended (mixture will be thick). Gradually add milk, stirring constantly. Bring to a boil; cook and stir for 2 minutes or until thickened. Remove from the heat; gradually stir in Parmesan cheese and basil until cheese is melted. Serve over pasta. **Yield:** 8 servings.

Nutritional Analysis: One serving (1/2 cup sauce, calculated without pasta) equals 132 calories, 8 g fat (1 g saturated fat), 4 mg cholesterol, 554 mg sodium, 10 g carbohydrate, trace fiber, 6 g protein.
Diabetic Exchanges: 1-1/2 fat, 1 fat-free milk.

Black Bean Fajitas

Meatless

For lunch one day, I dreamed up these fajitas using leftover black beans I had in the refrigerator and a tomato and peppers from my visit to the local farmers market. It made a fast and satisfying light meal.
—Linda Rock, Stratford, Wisconsin

1/2 cup *each* julienned sweet yellow and red pepper
1 can (15 ounces) black beans, rinsed and drained
4 flour tortillas (6 inches), warmed
1 medium tomato, seeded and chopped
1/2 cup salsa
1/2 cup reduced-fat shredded cheddar cheese
1/4 cup fat-free sour cream

Place yellow and red pepper in a microwave-safe bowl. Cover and microwave on high for 2 minutes or until crisp-tender. Add beans; cover and cook 1 minute longer or until heated through. Spoon 1/2 cupful down the center of each tortilla; top with the tomato, salsa, cheese and sour cream. Fold in half. **Yield:** 4 servings.

Nutritional Analysis: One serving (1 fajita) equals 253 calories, 6 g fat (2 g saturated fat), 11 mg cholesterol, 739 mg sodium, 36 g carbohydrate, 5 g fiber, 13 g protein.
Diabetic Exchanges: 2 starch, 1 lean meat, 1 vegetable.

Spinach Vegetable Lasagna

Meatless

(Pictured below)

This mildly seasoned lasagna is chock-full of fresh spinach, mushrooms, carrots and onions. It even pleases nonvegetarians whenever I serve it.
—Vicki Boman, Ponca City, Oklahoma

3 tablespoons butter
1/2 cup all-purpose flour
2-3/4 cups fat-free milk, *divided*
1-1/2 cups plus 2 tablespoons grated Parmesan cheese, *divided*
3 tablespoons Dijon mustard
1/2 teaspoon salt, *divided*
1/4 teaspoon hot pepper sauce
1/2 pound sliced fresh mushrooms
2 medium onions, chopped
2 cups chopped carrots
4 garlic cloves, minced
1 tablespoon olive oil
1 pound fresh spinach, chopped
9 lasagna noodles, cooked, rinsed and drained

In a saucepan, melt butter. Stir in flour until smooth. Add 2-1/2 cups milk. Bring to a boil; cook and stir for 1-2 minutes or until thickened. Remove from the heat. Stir in 1-1/2 cups Parmesan cheese, mustard, 1/4 teaspoon salt and hot pepper sauce; set aside.

In a large nonstick skillet, saute the mushrooms, onions, carrots and garlic in oil until tender. Stir in spinach and remaining salt. Cook and stir for 2 minutes or until spinach is wilted; drain. Remove from the heat; stir in 1-1/2 cups cheese sauce. Combine the remaining cheese sauce and milk. Spread half of the cheese sauce in a 13-in. x 9-in. x 2-in. baking dish coated with nonstick cooking spray. Top with three noodles and half the vegetable mixture; repeat

noodle and vegetable mixture layers. Top with remaining noodles and cheese sauce. Sprinkle with remaining cheese. Bake, uncovered, at 375° for 25-30 minutes or until heated through. Let stand for 10 minutes before cutting. **Yield:** 12 servings.

Nutritional Analysis: One piece equals 222 calories, 8 g fat (4 g saturated fat), 17 mg cholesterol, 496 mg sodium, 27 g carbohydrate, 3 g fiber, 12 g protein.
Diabetic Exchanges: 1 lean meat, 1 starch, 1 vegetable, 1 fat, 1/2 fat-free milk.

Vegetable Lo Mein

Meatless

Crisp-tender veggies and soy sauce are combined with linguine noodles in this colorful main dish. I got this recipe from a radio program several years ago.
—Sara Tatham, Plymouth, New Hampshire

   6 ounces uncooked linguine
   1 teaspoon cornstarch
   1 teaspoon vegetable bouillon granules
1/2 cup water
1/4 cup reduced-sodium soy sauce
1/2 pound fresh mushrooms, quartered
   2 tablespoons canola oil, *divided*
1/2 pound fresh snow peas
   8 green onions, sliced
   4 celery ribs with leaves, sliced
   1 large sweet red pepper, thinly sliced
   1 can (14 ounces) bean sprouts, rinsed and drained

Cook pasta according to package directions; drain and set aside. In a small bowl, combine the cornstarch and bouillon granules; stir in the water and soy sauce and set aside.

In a nonstick skillet, stir-fry mushrooms in 1 tablespoon oil 3 minutes or until tender; remove and keep warm. In same pan, heat remaining oil. Add remaining vegetables; stir-fry 5 minutes or until crisp-tender. Stir soy sauce mixture; add to pan. Bring to a boil; cook and stir for 2 minutes or until thickened. Add pasta and mushrooms. Heat through. **Yield:** 4 servings.

Nutritional Analysis: One serving (1-1/2 cups) equals 327 calories, 8 g fat (1 g saturated fat), trace cholesterol, 1,081 mg sodium, 50 g carbohydrate, 7 g fiber, 12 g protein.
Diabetic Exchanges: 3 vegetable, 2 starch, 1-1/2 fat.

Garlic Broccoli Pasta

Meatless

(Pictured above)

This recipe takes under a half hour to fix and makes a great weeknight entree or side dish. It's one of my 4-year-old's favorites. He calls the broccoli and pasta combination "noodles and trees".
—Michele Thompson, Santa Clarita, California

   6 ounces uncooked rigatoni *or* large tube pasta
   2 cups fresh broccoli florets
   3 garlic cloves, minced
4-1/2 teaspoons olive oil
1/4 cup shredded Parmesan cheese
1/2 teaspoon salt
1/8 teaspoon white pepper

Cook pasta according to package directions. Meanwhile, place broccoli in a steamer basket. Place in a saucepan over 1 in. of water; bring to a boil. Cover and steam for 4-5 minutes or until crisp-tender.

In a saucepan, saute garlic in oil until tender. Drain pasta; add to saucepan and toss to coat. Add the broccoli, Parmesan cheese, salt and pepper; toss to combine. **Yield:** 4 servings.

Nutritional Analysis: One serving (1 cup) equals 231 calories, 8 g fat (2 g saturated fat), 4 mg cholesterol, 464 mg sodium, 34 g carbohydrate, 3 g fiber, 9 g protein.
Diabetic Exchanges: 2 starch, 1 vegetable, 1 fat.

Black Bean Medley

Meatless

This sassy Southwestern-style entree stars a blend of corn, black beans, sweet peppers and zesty stewed tomatoes that's spooned over brown rice. I like to serve it for lunch. It's also tasty made with salsa instead of the tomatoes.
—*Sandra Shafer, Mountain View, California*

    1 cup uncooked brown rice
    1 cup chopped onion
  1/2 cup chopped sweet red pepper
  1/2 cup chopped green pepper
    2 garlic cloves, minced
    1 tablespoon olive oil
1-1/2 cups frozen corn
    1 can (15 ounces) black beans, rinsed and
      drained
    1 can (14-1/2 ounces) Mexican stewed tomatoes
    2 tablespoons red wine vinegar
  1/4 teaspoon salt
  1/4 teaspoon pepper

Cook rice according to package directions. Meanwhile, in a nonstick skillet, saute the onion, sweet peppers and garlic in oil until tender. Add the corn. Reduce heat to medium; cook and stir for 5 minutes or until corn is tender. Add the black beans, tomatoes, vinegar, salt and pepper. Cook and stir for 5 minutes or until heated through. Serve over the brown rice. **Yield:** 5 servings.

Nutritional Analysis: One serving (1 cup bean mixture with 2/3 cup rice) equals 328 calories, 5 g fat (1 g saturated fat), 0 cholesterol, 536 mg sodium, 62 g carbohydrate, 10 g fiber, 11 g protein.

🍎 Black Bean Basics

DON'T know beans about black beans? If you're a fan of Mexican or Caribbean cooking, you've probably enjoyed this versatile bean in burritos, dips, soups or stews.

Native to southern Mexico and Central America, black beans are thought to be more than 7,000 years old. Also called turtle beans, they have a soft texture and mild, earthy flavor. And like other beans, they're a good source of fiber and protein.

Season cooked black beans with balsamic vinegar, sour cream or salsa. Serve on the side along with rice and grilled meat.

Linguine with Marinated Tomato and Basil

Meatless

Tired of pasta weighted down by sauce? Opt for this nutritious toss-up of marinated tomatoes, linguine and cheese. This recipe comes from my husband's

Baked Ziti Casserole

Meatless

(Pictured above)

With its rich Italian flavor and generous combination of cheeses, it's hard to believe this pasta entree is light. It's sure to become a favorite with your family, too!
—*Paula Zsiray, Logan, Utah*

  1 package (16 ounces) ziti *or* small tube pasta
  1 egg, lightly beaten
  1 carton (15 ounces) part-skim ricotta cheese
1/2 cup grated Parmesan cheese, *divided*
  1 jar (28 ounces) meatless spaghetti sauce
  2 cups (8 ounces) shredded part-skim mozzarella
    cheese

Cook pasta according to package directions. Drain pasta; set aside. In a bowl, combine the egg, ricotta and 1/4 cup Parmesan cheese. Spread 1 cup spaghetti sauce in a 13-in. x 9-in. x 2-in. baking dish coated with nonstick cooking spray. Top with a third of the pasta, half of the ricotta mixture, 2/3 cup mozzarella cheese, 1 tablespoon Parmesan cheese and 1 cup sauce.

Repeat layers of pasta, ricotta mixture and mozzarella cheese. Sprinkle with 2 tablespoons Parmesan cheese. Top with remaining pasta, sauce, mozzarella cheese and Parmesan cheese. Cover and bake at 375° for 45-50 minutes or until heated through. **Yield:** 12 servings.

Nutritional Analysis: One serving equals 284 calories, 8 g fat (5 g saturated fat), 43 mg cholesterol, 508 mg sodium, 36 g carbohydrate, 2 g fiber, 17 g protein.
Diabetic Exchanges: 2 starch, 2 lean meat, 1 vegetable.

sister, Allison, and is in our family cookbook. It is one of our favorite summer meals. The leftovers make a great cold pasta salad.
—Linda Nichols, Atlantic, Iowa

    6 plum tomatoes, diced
  3/4 cup shredded part-skim mozzarella
  3/4 cup chopped fresh basil
    3 garlic cloves, minced
    3 tablespoons olive oil
    1 teaspoon salt
  1/2 teaspoon pepper
    1 package (16 ounces) linguine
  1/4 cup shredded Parmesan cheese

In a large bowl, combine the first seven ingredients; toss to coat. Let stand at room temperature for 1 hour. Meanwhile, prepare linguine according to package directions; drain. Add to the tomato mixture; toss to coat. Sprinkle with Parmesan cheese. Serve warm. **Yield:** 8 servings.

Nutritional Analysis: One serving (1 cup) equals 321 calories, 9 g fat (2 g saturated fat), 9 mg cholesterol, 403 mg sodium, 48 g carbohydrate, 4 g fiber, 12 g protein.
Diabetic Exchanges: 3 starch, 1-1/2 fat, 1 vegetable.

Bell Peppers and Pasta

Meatless

(Pictured below)

This meatless entree is always a hit. In fact, I double it whenever I know I'm going to feed some big eaters, and it still disappears.
—Sharon Csubta, Wadsworth, Ohio

2-1/4 cups uncooked penne *or* medium tube pasta
  3/4 cup chopped onion
    1 tablespoon olive oil
    3 garlic cloves, minced
    1 cup chopped sweet red pepper
    1 cup chopped green pepper
  1/4 cup sliced ripe olives
    1 teaspoon dried oregano
  1/4 teaspoon salt
  1/8 teaspoon cayenne pepper
  1/4 cup water
  1/2 cup crumbled feta cheese

Cook pasta according to package directions. In a nonstick skillet, saute onion in oil for 1-1/2 minutes. Add garlic; cook 30 seconds longer. Add the sweet peppers; cook and stir for 2-3 minutes or until vegetables are tender. Stir in the olives, oregano, salt and cayenne. Add water; cook and stir until mixture comes to a boil. Drain pasta and stir into skillet. Remove from the heat. Stir in cheese. Serve immediately. **Yield:** 4 servings.

Nutritional Analysis: One serving (1-1/4 cups) equals 274 calories, 9 g fat (4 g saturated fat), 17 mg cholesterol, 434 mg sodium, 40 g carbohydrate, 4 g fiber, 9 g protein.
Diabetic Exchanges: 2 starch, 2 vegetable, 1-1/2 fat.

Vegetarian Nut Loaf

Meatless

When I made this moist and tasty loaf for my vegetarian friends one Thanksgiving, they all took the recipe home with them.
—Sherry Barber, Whittier, California

    2 large onions, finely chopped
    1 cup chopped fresh mushrooms
  1/4 cup finely chopped green pepper
    2 tablespoons butter
    3 cups grated carrots
1-1/2 cups finely chopped celery
    5 eggs, beaten
  1/2 cup chopped walnuts
  1/4 cup unsalted sunflower kernels
  1/2 teaspoon salt
  1/2 teaspoon dried basil
  1/2 teaspoon dried oregano
  1/4 teaspoon pepper
    3 cups soft whole wheat bread crumbs (about 6 slices)

In a nonstick skillet, saute onions, mushrooms and green pepper in butter until tender. In a bowl, combine the mushroom mixture, carrots, celery, eggs, walnuts, sunflower kernels, salt, basil, oregano and pepper. Stir in bread crumbs.

Coat a 9-in. x 5-in. x 3-in. loaf pan with nonstick cooking spray, then line with waxed paper. Transfer vegetable mixture to prepared pan. Bake at 350° for 1 hour or until a meat thermometer reads 160°. Let stand for 10 minutes before slicing. **Yield:** 8 servings.

Nutritional Analysis: One slice equals 223 calories, 13 g fat (3 g saturated fat), 140 mg cholesterol, 321 mg sodium, 19 g carbohydrate, 4 g fiber, 9 g protein.
Diabetic Exchanges: 2 vegetables, 1-1/2 fat, 1 lean meat, 1/2 starch.

Millet-Stuffed Red Peppers

Meatless

(Pictured below)

Tired of tuna-filled tomatoes and stuffed green peppers? Try this vibrant alternative. The out-of-the-ordinary filling is made with millet.
—Kitty Jones, Chicago, Illinois

1/2 cup uncooked millet, rinsed and drained
1-1/2 cups vegetable broth
4 medium sweet red peppers
3/4 cup frozen corn, thawed
1 medium onion, finely chopped
1/3 cup finely chopped celery
1/4 cup chopped walnuts
1 green onion, finely chopped
1 tablespoon chopped fresh mint *or* 1 teaspoon dried mint flakes
2 teaspoons shredded lemon peel
1-1/2 teaspoons fresh chopped oregano *or* 1/2 teaspoon dried oregano
1 garlic clove, minced
1/2 teaspoon salt
1/4 teaspoon pepper
2 tablespoons olive oil

In a saucepan, simmer millet in broth until tender and broth is absorbed, about 30-35 minutes. Transfer to a large bowl and cool. Meanwhile, cut tops off sweet peppers and remove seeds. In a large kettle, cook peppers in boiling water for 3-5 minutes. Drain and rinse in cold water; set aside.

With a fork, fluff cooled millet. Add next 11 ingredients; blend well. Spoon into sweet peppers. Drizzle with oil. Place in a baking dish coated with nonstick cooking spray. Cov-

er; bake at 350° for 55-60 minutes or until tender. **Yield:** 4 servings.

Editor's Note: Look for millet in the grains or natural food aisle of your grocery store. 1-1/2 cups cooked couscous may be substituted for the millet and vegetable broth.

Nutritional Analysis: One stuffed pepper equals 281 calories, 13 g fat (1 g saturated fat), 0 cholesterol, 684 mg sodium, 37 g carbohydrate, 6 g fiber, 8 g protein.
Diabetic Exchanges: 2 starch, 2 fat, 1 vegetable.

Make It Millet

NOT FAMILIAR with this age-old cereal grain? Millet was one of the first grains used by man in ancient China, India, Egypt and Africa…and it's still a staple in Asia and Africa.

With a chewy texture and slightly nutty taste, millet is cooked like rice and often teamed up with sauces, vegetables or beans. It can also be added to soups and casseroles, served as cereal or ground into flour.

Because it is gluten-free, millet cannot be used in leavened bread unless it's combined with wheat, but it's ideal for flatbread recipes.

Stuffed Vegetarian Shells

Meatless

When my aunt first told me about these shells, they sounded like a lot of work—but the recipe whips up in no time. Sometimes I add a little cooked bacon to the ricotta filling.
—Amelia Hopkin, Salt Lake City, Utah

24 uncooked jumbo pasta shells
1 carton (15 ounces) part-skim ricotta cheese
1 package (10 ounces) frozen chopped broccoli, thawed and drained
1 cup (4 ounces) shredded part-skim mozzarella cheese
2 egg whites
1 tablespoon minced fresh basil *or* 1 teaspoon dried basil
1/2 teaspoon garlic salt
1/4 teaspoon pepper
1 jar (26 ounces) meatless spaghetti sauce
2 tablespoons shredded Parmesan cheese

Cook pasta according to package directions. In a bowl, combine the ricotta, broccoli, mozzarella, egg whites and seasonings; mix well. Drain pasta.

Spread half of the spaghetti sauce into a 13-in. x 9-in. x 2-in. baking dish coated with nonstick cooking spray. Stuff pasta shells with ricotta mixture; arrange over spaghetti sauce. Pour remaining sauce over pasta shells. Cover and bake at 375° for 25 minutes. Uncover; sprinkle with Parmesan cheese. Bake 5 minutes longer or until heated through. **Yield:** 8 servings.

Nutritional Analysis: One serving (3 stuffed shells) equals 296 calories, 9 g fat (5 g saturated fat), 29 mg cholesterol, 640 mg sodium, 37 g carbohydrate, 4 g fiber, 17 g protein.
Diabetic Exchanges: 3 vegetable, 2 lean meat, 1-1/2 starch.

Greek Spaghetti

Meatless

Out of all our recipes for pasta, this simple meatless main dish is our favorite. We can hardly wait for summer to arrive so we can use our garden-fresh tomatoes and minced basil in this recipe. The entree's Mediterranean flair comes from feta cheese, oregano, olive oil and lemon.
—*Christa and Holly Hageman, Telford, Pennsylvania*

6 ounces uncooked thin spaghetti
1 teaspoon dried oregano
1 garlic clove, minced
2 teaspoons olive oil
3 cups chopped seeded plum tomatoes
1/2 cup sliced green onions
1/4 cup minced fresh parsley, *divided*
2 tablespoons minced fresh basil
2 tablespoons lemon juice
1 cup (4 ounces) crumbled feta cheese, *divided*
1/2 teaspoon salt
1/8 teaspoon pepper

Cook pasta according to package directions. In a nonstick skillet, saute oregano and garlic in oil for 1 minute or until garlic is tender. Add the tomatoes, green onions, 2 tablespoons parsley, basil and lemon juice; cook and stir for 2 minutes or until heated through. Remove from the heat.

Drain spaghetti and add to tomato mixture. Add 3/4 cup feta cheese, salt and pepper; toss to combine. Transfer to serving plates. Sprinkle with remaining feta and parsley. Serve immediately. **Yield:** 4 servings.

Nutritional Analysis: One serving (1-1/2 cups) equals 311 calories, 10 g fat (5 g saturated fat), 25 mg cholesterol, 628 mg sodium, 50 g carbohydrate, 5 g fiber, 12 g protein.
Diabetic Exchanges: 3 starch, 1 vegetable, 1 lean meat, 1 fat.

Stir-Fried Veggies with Pasta

Meatless

(Pictured above right)

We never feel like we're missing out on meat when this super supper is on the table. Not only is it a quick dinner to whip up on warm summer nights, but it is one of the meals that my husband requests most.
—*Tracy Holaday, Muncie, Indiana*

2 cups uncooked spiral pasta
2 medium carrots, julienned
1 medium leek, julienned
2 small zucchini, julienned
1 *each* medium sweet red, yellow and green pepper, cut into thin strips
1 cup fresh green beans, cut into 1-inch pieces
1 tablespoon olive oil
1 tablespoon sesame oil
2 tablespoons rice vinegar
2 tablespoons honey
1/2 teaspoon salt
1/4 teaspoon chili powder
1/4 teaspoon ground ginger

Cook pasta according to package directions. In a large nonstick skillet or wok, stir-fry the carrots, leek, zucchini, peppers and green beans in hot olive oil for 3-4 minutes or until vegetables are crisp-tender.

Drain pasta. Add pasta and sesame oil to skillet; stir-fry 2 minutes longer. In a bowl, combine the vinegar, honey, salt, chili powder and ginger. Add to the vegetable mixture; toss to coat. Serve immediately. **Yield:** 6 servings.

Nutritional Analysis: One serving (1-1/2 cups) equals 210 calories, 5 g fat (1 g saturated fat), 0 cholesterol, 218 mg sodium, 37 g carbohydrate, 4 g fiber, 5 g protein.
Diabetic Exchanges: 2 vegetable, 1-1/2 starch, 1 fat.

Vegetarian Spinach Curry

Meatless

Having lost weight with Weight Watchers, I'm always on the lookout for tasty low-calorie meals. I found this recipe in a newspaper a few years ago. It's great because it's low in fat, high in fiber, plus it's easy to make.
—*Diane Toomey, Methuen, Massachusetts*

1 cup chopped onion
2 garlic cloves, minced
1 tablespoon curry powder
1 tablespoon canola oil
1 can (8 ounces) tomato sauce
1 package (10 ounces) frozen chopped spinach, thawed and squeezed dry
1 can (16 ounces) garbanzo beans *or* chickpeas, rinsed and drained, *divided*
1 cup reduced-sodium chicken broth *or* vegetable broth
1/4 teaspoon salt
1/4 teaspoon pepper
Hot cooked couscous, optional

In a nonstick skillet, cook the onion, garlic and curry powder in oil for 3-4 minutes or until onion is tender. Stir in the tomato sauce, spinach and 1 cup garbanzo beans. In a blender, combine the broth and remaining garbanzo beans; cover and blend until smooth, about 2 minutes. Stir into skillet. Sprinkle with salt and pepper. Cook and stir until mixture is heated through. Serve over couscous if desired. **Yield:** 4 servings.

Nutritional Analysis: One serving (1 cup curry, calculated without couscous) equals 193 calories, 6 g fat (trace saturated fat), 0 cholesterol, 764 mg sodium, 28 g carbohydrate, 8 g fiber, 9 g protein.
Diabetic Exchanges: 2 vegetable, 1 starch, 1 lean meat, 1/2 fat.

Chili-Stuffed Potatoes

Meatless

(Pictured on page 177)

Microwave baked potatoes and convenient canned vegetarian chili make this hearty dish a snap to take to the table! It's colorful, too, topped with goodies like fresh tomatoes, reduced-fat sour cream and shredded cheese. These potatoes are great for cookouts or picnic meals.
—*Laura Perry, Exton, Pennsylvania*

4 large baking potatoes (about 2 pounds)
1 can (15 ounces) vegetarian chili
1/2 cup shredded reduced-fat Mexican cheese blend
1 cup chopped seeded fresh tomatoes
1/4 cup reduced-fat sour cream
1/4 cup minced fresh cilantro

Scrub and pierce the potatoes; place on a microwave-safe plate. Microwave, uncovered, on high for 12-14 minutes or until tender, turning once. Meanwhile, in a saucepan, heat chili. With a sharp knife, cut an "X" in each potato; fluff with a fork. Spoon chili over each potato; sprinkle with the cheese. Top with the tomatoes, sour cream and cilantro. **Yield:** 4 servings.

Editor's Note: This recipe was tested in a 1,100-watt microwave.

Nutritional Analysis: One serving (1 stuffed potato with toppings) equals 354 calories, 4 g fat (3 g saturated fat), 10 mg cholesterol, 466 mg sodium, 66 g carbohydrate, 9 g fiber, 15 g protein.

Pesto Vegetable Pizza

Meatless

(Pictured below)

My family loves pizza, but we rarely have it delivered since I created this fresh and flavorful version. Always a winner in my house, it is a fast and delicious meal that even my young son looks forward to.
—*Kate Selner, Lino Lakes, Minnesota*

1 prebaked thin crust Italian bread shell (10 ounces)
2 garlic cloves, halved
1/2 cup pesto sauce
3/4 cup packed fresh spinach, chopped
2 large portobello mushrooms, thinly sliced
1 medium sweet yellow pepper, julienned
2 plum tomatoes, seeded and sliced
1/3 cup packed fresh basil, chopped

**1 cup (4 ounces) shredded reduced-fat
mozzarella cheese
1/4 cup grated Parmesan cheese
1/2 teaspoon dried oregano**

Place crust on an ungreased 12-in. pizza pan. Rub cut side of garlic cloves over crust; discard garlic. Spread crust with pesto. Top with the spinach, mushrooms, yellow pepper, tomatoes and basil. Sprinkle with cheeses and oregano. Bake at 450° for 10-15 minutes or until cheese is melted. **Yield:** 6 servings.

Nutritional Analysis: One slice equals 298 calories, 14 g fat (4 g saturated fat), 15 mg cholesterol, 656 mg sodium, 30 g carbohydrate, 3 g fiber, 13 g protein.
Diabetic Exchanges: 2 fat, 1-1/2 starch, 1 lean meat.

Zucchini 'n' Potato Pie

Meatless

My sister-in-law served this savory pie when we visited her in Illinois, and my husband, who is not fond of zucchini, actually had seconds. With its hash brown crust and quiche-like filling, it's really tasty!
—Kailene Stewart, Oceanside, California

**3 cups frozen shredded hash brown potatoes,
thawed
1 egg
1/4 cup finely chopped onion
1/4 cup grated Parmesan cheese
1/4 teaspoon salt**
FILLING:
**2-1/2 cups thinly sliced zucchini
1 garlic clove, minced
1 tablespoon olive oil
4 egg whites
2 eggs
3/4 cup shredded reduced-fat Swiss cheese
1/2 cup fat-free milk
1/2 teaspoon dried oregano
1/4 teaspoon salt
1/4 teaspoon pepper**

In a large bowl, combine the hash browns, egg, onion, Parmesan and salt. Press onto the bottom and up the sides of a 9-in. pie plate. Bake at 400° for 20 minutes.

In a large nonstick skillet, saute zucchini and garlic in oil until crisp-tender. Cool for 5 minutes. Spoon into potato crust. Combine the remaining ingredients. Pour over zucchini mixture. Reduce oven temperature to 350°; bake zucchini pie for 25-30 minutes or until a knife inserted near the center comes out clean. Let stand for 5-10 minutes before cutting. **Yield:** 6 servings.

Nutritional Analysis: One piece equals 212 calories, 14 g fat (6 g saturated fat), 119 mg cholesterol, 398 mg sodium, 18 g carbohydrate, 2 g fiber, 14 g protein.
Diabetic Exchanges: 2 lean meat, 1 starch, 1/2 fat.

Spicy Beans 'n' Rice

Low-fat Meatless

(Pictured above)

Savory Cajun flavor zips up this quick skillet dish that's loaded with beans, tomatoes, rice and seasonings. It's delicious served with corn bread muffins.
—Ranae Jones, Fort Rucker, Alabama

**1/2 cup coarsely chopped green pepper
1/2 cup coarsely chopped onion
2 garlic cloves, minced
1 tablespoon canola oil
1 can (14-1/2 ounces) stewed tomatoes, cut up
1 can (8 ounces) tomato sauce
1/2 teaspoon Italian seasoning
1/4 teaspoon cayenne pepper
1/8 teaspoon fennel seed, crushed
1 can (16 ounces) kidney beans, rinsed and
drained
1 can (15-1/4 ounces) butter beans, rinsed and
drained
2-1/2 cups cooked rice**

In a nonstick skillet, saute the green pepper, onion and garlic in oil until tender. Stir in the stewed tomatoes, tomato sauce, Italian seasoning, cayenne and fennel seed. Bring to a boil. Reduce heat; cover and simmer for 10 minutes. Stir in the beans. Cover and simmer 5-10 minutes longer or until beans are heated through. Serve with rice. **Yield:** 5 servings.

Nutritional Analysis: One serving (1 cup bean mixture with 1/2 cup rice) equals 298 calories, 3 g fat (trace saturated fat), 0 cholesterol, 888 mg sodium, 59 g carbohydrate, 10 g fiber, 14 g protein.

White Beans with Rigatoni

Meatless

*My husband and I are fans of canned beans...
especially when they're combined with pasta.
This quick-to-fix recipe makes a wonderful after-work
meal served with whole wheat rolls and
a salad with light vinaigrette dressing.*
—Carol Gaus, Itasca, Illinois

    8 ounces rigatoni *or* large tube pasta
1/2 cup chopped onion
    1 garlic clove, minced
    1 tablespoon olive oil
    1 package (8 ounces) sliced fresh mushrooms
    1 can (15 ounces) white kidney *or* cannellini
       beans, rinsed and drained
    1 can (14-1/2 ounces) diced tomatoes, undrained
    2 tablespoons minced fresh sage
1/2 teaspoon salt
1/4 teaspoon pepper
    2 cups chopped kale
1/4 cup shredded Parmesan cheese

Cook pasta according to package directions. In a large saucepan, saute onion and garlic in oil until tender. Stir in the mushrooms; cook about 5 minutes longer or until mushrooms are almost tender.

Stir in the beans, tomatoes, sage, salt and pepper. Bring to a boil. Reduce heat; simmer, uncovered, for 5 minutes. Stir in the kale. Return to a boil. Cover and cook for 3-4 minutes or until kale is wilted and tender. Drain pasta; add to bean mixture and heat through. Sprinkle with Parmesan cheese. **Yield:** 5 servings.

Nutritional Analysis: One serving (1-1/2 cups) equals 319 calories, 6 g fat (1 g saturated fat), 3 mg cholesterol, 537 mg sodium, 55 g carbohydrate, 8 g fiber, 14 g protein.

Spinach Manicotti

Meatless

(Pictured above)

*Stuffed with ricotta cheese and spinach, this
Italian-style entree is flavorful and filling. I particularly
like this meatless dish because I don't have
to cook the pasta before assembling.*
—Mary Steiner, West Bend, Wisconsin

    1 carton (15 ounces) fat-free ricotta cheese
    2 cups (8 ounces) shredded part-skim mozzarella
       cheese, *divided*
    1 package (10 ounces) frozen chopped spinach,
       thawed and squeezed dry
1/2 cup reduced-fat sour cream
1/4 cup dry bread crumbs
    1 tablespoon Italian seasoning
    1 teaspoon garlic powder
    1 teaspoon onion powder
    2 cups tomato juice
    1 cup chunky salsa
    1 can (15 ounces) crushed tomatoes
   14 uncooked manicotti shells

In a large bowl, combine the ricotta, 1-1/2 cups mozzarella cheese, spinach, sour cream, bread crumbs, Italian seasoning, garlic powder and onion powder. Combine the tomato juice, salsa and crushed tomatoes; spread 1 cup sauce in an ungreased 13-in. x 9-in. x 2-in. baking dish. Stuff uncooked manicotti with spinach mixture; arrange over sauce. Pour remaining sauce over manicotti.

Cover and bake at 350° for 55 minutes. Uncover; sprinkle with remaining mozzarella cheese. Bake 15 minutes longer or until noodles are tender. **Yield:** 7 servings.

Nutritional Analysis: One serving (2 stuffed manicotti) equals 341 calories, 8 g fat (5 g saturated fat), 34 mg cholesterol, 883 mg sodium, 45 g carbohydrate, 4 g fiber, 21 g protein.
Diabetic Exchanges: 2 starch, 2 lean meat, 2 vegetable.

Smart Substitutions for Meat

WHETHER you want to serve your gang more meatless meals or simply reduce some of the meat in family favorites, consider the following ideas for savvy stand-ins:

- **Cut Back with Casseroles.** Replace some of the meat called for in your best hot dish with a combination of finely chopped carrots, celery and nuts. Or substitute a portion of the meat with grains such as cooked rice, couscous, barley or bulgur.
- **Believe in Beans.** Legumes are protein-rich substitutes for the meat and poultry found in many dishes—particularly soups and stews. Feel free to experiment and get creative with beans that you're not familiar with.
- **Make Pasta a Preference.** Skip the ground beef usually added to spaghetti sauce, and stir in sliced mushrooms or chopped peppers instead. And you won't miss the meat in your lasagna if you replace it with sauteed vegetables such as sliced zucchini or eggplant.

From the Bread Basket

Is your family getting enough grains?
It's easy to ingrain the goodness of wheat,
oats, rye and more into your meal plans
when you present an incredible assortment
of breads, rolls and muffins.

Maple Walnut Banana Bread (page 192)

Apple Nut Coffee Cake

Low-sodium   Meatless

When I was growing up, my mother used to make this during apple season. The original recipe called for butter and an egg, but I replaced them with applesauce and an egg substitute.
—Debbie Tilley, Riverview, Florida

    1 cup sugar
1/2 cup unsweetened applesauce
1/4 cup egg substitute
    1 cup all-purpose flour
    1 teaspoon ground cinnamon
1/2 teaspoon baking powder
1/2 teaspoon baking soda
1/4 teaspoon salt
    1 cup sliced peeled tart apple (about 1 medium)
1/2 cup coarsely chopped pecans
TOPPING:
1/4 cup packed brown sugar
1/4 cup chopped pecans
    1 tablespoon butter, melted
1/4 teaspoon ground cinnamon

In a mixing bowl, combine the sugar, applesauce and egg substitute; mix well. Combine the flour, cinnamon, baking powder, baking soda and salt; add to the applesauce mixture. Stir in apple and pecans.

Spread in an 8-in. square baking dish coated with nonstick cooking spray. In a bowl, combine the brown sugar, pecans, butter and cinnamon; sprinkle over apple mixture. Bake at 350° for 30-35 minutes or until a toothpick inserted near the center comes out clean. Cool on a wire rack. **Yield:** 12 servings.

Nutritional Analysis: *One piece equals 192 calories, 6 g fat (1 g saturated fat), 3 mg cholesterol, 134 mg sodium, 33 g carbohydrate, 1 g fiber, 2 g protein.*
Diabetic Exchanges: *2 starch, 1 fat.*

Cardamom Braid

Low-sodium   Meatless

(Pictured at right)

This version of Finnish "pulla" has always been an important part of our family celebrations. The recipe is special because it can be made in a bread machine.

Cooks who do not deal well with yeast dough will find that this adaptation is just what they've been looking for.
—Doris Lystila, Townsend, Massachusetts

    1 cup warm fat-free milk (70° to 80°)
1/4 cup butter, softened
    2 eggs, lightly beaten
3-3/4 cups bread flour
1/2 cup sugar
    1 to 2 teaspoons ground cardamom
1/2 teaspoon salt
2-1/2 teaspoons active dry yeast
TOPPING:
    1 egg
    2 tablespoons water
    2 teaspoons sugar
1/4 cup sliced almonds

In bread machine pan, place the first eight ingredients in order suggested by manufacturer. Select dough setting (check dough after 5 minutes of mixing; add 1 to 2 tablespoons of water or flour if needed).

When cycle is completed, turn dough onto a lightly floured surface; divide into thirds. Shape each into a 20-in. rope. Place ropes on a parchment-lined baking sheet; braid. Pinch ends to seal and tuck under. Cover and let rise in a warm place until doubled, about 30 minutes.

In a small bowl, beat egg and water; brush over dough. Sprinkle with sugar and almonds. Bake at 350° for 30-35 minutes or until golden brown. Remove from pan to a wire rack to cool. **Yield:** 1 loaf (20 slices).

Editor's Note: If your bread machine has a time-delay feature, we recommend you do not use it for this recipe.

Nutritional Analysis: *One slice equals 141 calories, 4 g fat (2 g saturated fat), 38 mg cholesterol, 99 mg sodium, 23 g carbohydrate, 1 g fiber, 5 g protein.*
Diabetic Exchanges: *1-1/2 starch, 1 fat.*

Roasted Garlic Bread

Low-carb *Low-fat* *Low-sodium* *Meatless*

I came up with this bread recipe one very stormy morning when we lived on the beach in the Florida Panhandle. While lightning blinked over the Gulf and rain tap-tap-tapped on our balcony, the wonderful aroma of this bread baking gave me such a cozy feeling.
—*Barb Alexander, Princeton, New Jersey*

2 medium whole garlic bulbs
2 teaspoons olive oil
1 package (1/4 ounce) active dry yeast
1 cup warm water (110° to 115°)
1 tablespoon sugar
1 teaspoon salt
2-1/2 to 3 cups all-purpose flour
  2 tablespoons minced fresh sage *or* 2 teaspoons
    rubbed sage
  2 teaspoons minced fresh marjoram *or* 3/4
    teaspoon dried marjoram
  1 teaspoon minced fresh rosemary *or* 1/2
    teaspoon dried rosemary, crushed
  2 tablespoons grated Parmesan cheese
  1 tablespoon butter, melted

Remove papery outer skin from garlic (do not peel or separate cloves). Cut top off of garlic bulbs. Brush with oil. Wrap each bulb in heavy-duty foil. Bake at 425° for 30-35 minutes or until softened. Cool for 10-15 minutes. Squeeze softened garlic into a bowl and set aside.

In a large mixing bowl, dissolve yeast in warm water. Add the sugar, salt and 1 cup flour. Beat until smooth. Stir in enough remaining flour to form a soft dough.

Turn onto a lightly floured surface; knead until smooth and elastic, about 6-8 minutes. Place in a bowl coated with nonstick cooking spray, turning once to coat top. Cover and let rise in a warm place until doubled, about 45 minutes. Meanwhile, add the sage, marjoram and rosemary to the reserved roasted garlic; set aside.

Punch dough down. Turn onto a lightly floured surface; divide in half. Roll each portion into a 10-in. x 8-in. rectangle. Spread garlic mixture to within 1/2 in. of edges. Sprinkle with Parmesan cheese. Roll up jelly-roll style, starting with a long side; pinch seam and ends to seal. Coat a baking sheet with nonstick cooking spray. Place loaves seam side down on pan; tuck ends under. With a sharp knife, make several slashes across the top of each loaf. Cover and let rise until doubled, about 30 minutes.

Bake at 375° for 20-25 minutes or until golden brown. Remove to wire racks; brush with butter. **Yield:** 2 loaves (10 slices each).

Nutritional Analysis: *One slice equals 84 calories, 1 g fat (1 g saturated fat), 2 mg cholesterol, 136 mg sodium, 15 g carbohydrate, 1 g fiber, 2 g protein.*
Diabetic Exchange: *1 starch.*

Dill Bread

Low-fat *Meatless*

(Pictured above)

This golden-brown loaf is moist and flavorful. Dill weed gives each wedge an herbed zest, making it a nice complement to most any meal. What's more, this easy yeast bread requires no kneading!
—*Corky Huffsmith, Salem, Oregon*

1 package (1/4 ounce) active dry yeast
1/4 cup warm water (110° to 115°)
1 cup small-curd 2% cottage cheese
1/4 cup snipped fresh dill *or* 4 teaspoons dill weed
1 tablespoon butter, melted
1-1/2 teaspoons salt
  1 teaspoon sugar
  1 teaspoon dill seed
  1 egg, beaten
2-1/4 to 2-3/4 cups all-purpose flour

In a mixing bowl, dissolve yeast in warm water. Heat cottage cheese to 110°-115°; add to yeast mixture. Add the fresh dill, butter, salt, sugar, dill seed, egg and 1 cup flour; beat well. Stir in enough remaining flour to form a soft dough. Do not knead. Cover and let rise in a warm place until doubled, about 1 hour.

Punch dough down. Turn onto a lightly floured surface; shape into a 6-in. circle. Transfer to a 9-in. round baking pan coated with nonstick cooking spray. Cover and let rise until doubled, about 45 minutes.

Bake at 350° for 35-40 minutes or until bread sounds hollow when tapped. Remove from pan to a wire rack to cool. Cut into wedges before serving. **Yield:** 12 servings.

Nutritional Analysis: *One piece equals 118 calories, 2 g fat (1 g saturated fat), 22 mg cholesterol, 385 mg sodium, 19 g carbohydrate, 1 g fiber, 6 g protein.*
Diabetic Exchanges: *1 starch, 1/2 fat.*

Cinnamon Apple Muffins

Low-fat   Meatless

*These muffins smell delicious coming out of the oven.
But we usually burn our fingers getting them out
of the pan, we're so eager to eat them! Reduced-fat
milk, buttermilk and ricotta cheese keep the fat
count down in these moist and tender muffins,
while apple bits add sweetness to every bite.*
— *Amy Hunter, Renton, Washington*

  2-1/3 cups all-purpose flour
    1 cup plus 2 tablespoons sugar, *divided*
    3 teaspoons ground cinnamon, *divided*
    2 teaspoons baking powder
    1 teaspoon baking soda
  1/2 teaspoon salt
    1 egg
    2 egg whites
    1 cup 1% buttermilk
  1/3 cup 2% milk
  1/3 cup reduced-fat ricotta cheese
    3 tablespoons canola oil
    2 teaspoons vanilla extract
  1-1/2 cups finely chopped peeled tart apples

In a bowl, combine the flour, 1 cup sugar, 2 teaspoons cinnamon, baking powder, baking soda and salt. In another bowl, beat the egg, egg whites, buttermilk, milk, ricotta cheese, oil and vanilla. Stir into dry ingredients just until moistened. Fold in apples.

Coat muffin cups with nonstick cooking spray or use paper-liners; fill three-fourths full. Combine remaining sugar and cinnamon; sprinkle over batter. Bake at 400° for 18-20 minutes or until a toothpick comes out clean. Cool for 5 minutes before removing from pans to wire racks. **Yield:** 1-1/2 dozen.

Nutritional Analysis: One muffin equals 155 calories, 3 g fat (1 g saturated fat), 14 mg cholesterol, 193 mg sodium, 28 g carbohydrate, 1 g fiber, 4 g protein.
Diabetic Exchanges: 1 starch, 1/2 fruit, 1/2 fat.

Green Onion Biscuits

Low-carb   Low-fat   Low-sodium   Meatless

(Pictured above)

*The savory flavor of green onions comes through
in our Test Kitchen's easy drop biscuits,
which are best right out of the oven.
They have a crusty exterior and soft interior.*

    2 cups all-purpose flour
    1 teaspoon baking powder
  1/2 teaspoon salt
  1/4 teaspoon baking soda
  1/4 teaspoon onion powder
    1 cup 1% buttermilk
  1/2 cup finely chopped green onions
    3 tablespoons canola oil
Refrigerated butter-flavored spray

In a large bowl, combine the first five ingredients. Combine the buttermilk, onions and oil. Stir into dry ingredients just until moistened.

Drop by heaping tablespoonfuls 2 in. apart onto baking sheets coated with nonstick cooking spray. Spritz tops with butter-flavored spray. Bake at 400° for 14-18 minutes or until golden brown. Serve warm. **Yield:** 16 biscuits.

Editor's Note: This recipe was tested with I Can't Believe It's Not Butter spray.

Nutritional Analysis: One biscuit equals 85 calories, 3 g fat (trace saturated fat), 1 mg cholesterol, 124 mg sodium, 12 g carbohydrate, 1 g fiber, 2 g protein.
Diabetic Exchange: 1 starch.

🍎 Sweet Substitutions

SUGAR adds sweetness, tenderness and color to baked goods. But if you're watching your sugar intake, you do have other options. Keep these general guidelines in mind:

- You may be able to reduce the sugar by a third in some recipes for baked goods without significantly changing the taste and texture. Do a little experimenting and see if your family can tell the difference.

- To enhance flavor, use sweet spices like cinnamon, cardamom, allspice, nutmeg and mace. Also consider extracts, such as vanilla and almond, to add more flavor.

Favorite Recipe Made Lighter

IN Michelle Eder's home, a slice of Streusel Coffee Cake makes for a sweet morning snack with hot coffee.

"I love this cake from my Aunt Suzie—especially the nice moist texture and the sweet surprise of the brown sugar-nut mixture inside. It's decadent with a cup of joe," says Michelle from her Grand Rapids, Michigan home.

"However, with all its rich ingredients, it packs on the pounds! I've tried to change it to no avail. I'm hoping you can help."

Our home economists were eager to try. Their goal was to reduce the cake's fat, cholesterol and sugar while keeping its wonderful texture and cinnamon-spiced nut layer.

Our Test Kitchen makeover cut the calorie count by nearly 30%, the total fat by more than 40%, and the saturated fat and cholesterol by about 55%. But the trimmed-down treat has all the moistness and cinnamon crunch flavor of the original.

Streusel Coffee Cake

Meatless

- 1 cup chopped walnuts
- 1/2 cup packed brown sugar
- 2 tablespoons butter, melted
- 1/2 teaspoon ground cinnamon

COFFEE CAKE:
- 1 cup butter, softened
- 1-3/4 cups sugar
- 4 eggs, *separated*
- 1 teaspoon vanilla extract
- 3 cups all-purpose flour
- 2 teaspoons baking powder
- 1/2 teaspoon baking soda
- 1/4 teaspoon salt
- 1 cup (8 ounces) sour cream
- 2 teaspoons confectioners' sugar

In a small bowl, combine the nuts, brown sugar, butter and cinnamon; set aside. In a large mixing bowl, cream butter and sugar. Beat in egg yolks, one at a time, beating well after each addition. Beat in vanilla. Combine the dry ingredients; add to creamed ingredients alternately with sour cream. In another mixing bowl, beat egg whites on high speed until stiff peaks form. Fold into batter.

Pour half of the batter into a greased and floured 10-in. fluted tube pan; sprinkle with nut mixture. Pour in remaining batter. Bake at 350° for 45-55 minutes or until a toothpick inserted near the center comes out clean. Cool for 10 minutes before removing from pan to a wire rack to cool completely. Sprinkle with confectioners' sugar. **Yield:** 14 servings.

Nutritional Analysis: One slice equals 461 calories, 24 g fat (12 g saturated fat), 112 mg cholesterol, 335 mg sodium, 54 g carbohydrate, 1 g fiber, 7 g protein.

Makeover Streusel Coffee Cake

Meatless

(Pictured below)

- 2/3 cup chopped walnuts
- 1/3 cup packed brown sugar
- 1 tablespoon butter, melted
- 1/2 teaspoon ground cinnamon

COFFEE CAKE:
- 1/4 cup butter, softened
- 1-1/4 cups sugar
- 2 egg yolks
- 1/4 cup canola oil
- 1/4 cup unsweetened applesauce
- 1 teaspoon vanilla extract
- 3 cups cake flour
- 2 teaspoons baking powder
- 1 teaspoon baking soda
- 1/4 teaspoon salt
- 1-1/2 cups reduced-fat sour cream
- 4 egg whites
- 2 teaspoons confectioners' sugar

In a small bowl, combine the nuts, brown sugar, butter and cinnamon; set aside. In a large mixing bowl, beat the butter and sugar until light and crumbly. Beat in the egg yolks, oil, applesauce and vanilla. Combine the dry ingredients; add to sugar mixture alternately with sour cream. In another mixing bowl, beat egg whites on high speed until stiff peaks form. Fold into batter.

Pour half of the batter into a 10-in. fluted tube pan coated with nonstick cooking spray and floured; sprinkle with nut mixture. Pour in remaining batter. Bake at 350° for 45-55 minutes or until a toothpick inserted near the center comes out clean. Cool for 10 minutes before removing from pan to a wire rack to cool completely. Sprinkle with confectioners' sugar. **Yield:** 14 servings.

Nutritional Analysis: One slice equals 328 calories, 14 g fat (5 g saturated fat), 50 mg cholesterol, 288 mg sodium, 48 g carbohydrate, 1 g fiber, 5 g protein.
Diabetic Exchanges: 3 starch, 2 fat.

Swedish Rye Loaves

(Pictured below)

Low-fat   Meatless

Old-fashioned oats, brown sugar and molasses make these down-home loaves the best-tasting rye bread I've ever had. In fact, guests often ask me for the recipe. Slices are wonderful for sandwiches.
—*Iola Egle, Bella Vista, Arkansas*

1/4 cup old-fashioned oats
1/3 cup packed brown sugar
1/4 cup molasses
  5 tablespoons butter, *divided*
  2 teaspoons salt
  2 cups boiling water
  3 cups bread flour
  2 packages (1/4 ounce *each*) active dry yeast
  3 cups rye flour
  1 teaspoon caraway seeds

In a bowl, combine the oats, brown sugar, molasses, 4 tablespoons butter and salt; stir in boiling water. Let stand until mixture cools to 120°-130°, stirring occasionally. In a large mixing bowl, combine 2 cups bread flour and yeast. Add the molasses mixture just until moistened. Stir in rye flour and enough of the remaining bread flour to form a medium stiff dough. Turn onto a floured surface; knead about 6-8 minutes. Place in a bowl coated with nonstick cooking spray, turning once to coat the top. Cover and let rise in a warm place until doubled, about 1 hour.

Punch down dough; cover and let rise in a warm place until doubled, about 30 minutes. Punch down dough. Turn onto a lightly floured surface; divide into three portions. Shape into loaves. Place on baking sheets coated with non-stick cooking spray. Cover and let rise until doubled, about 30 minutes.

Bake at 375° for 25-30 minutes or until golden brown.

Cool on wire racks. Melt remaining butter; brush over loaves and sprinkle with caraway seeds. Cool. **Yield:** 3 loaves (12 slices each).

Nutritional Analysis: *One slice equals 102 calories, 2 g fat (1 g saturated fat), 4 mg cholesterol, 149 mg sodium, 19 g carbohydrate, 2 g fiber, 2 g protein.*
Diabetic Exchange: *1 starch.*

Maple Walnut Banana Bread

Meatless

(Pictured on page 187)

Loaded with banana flavor and a hint of maple, this old-fashioned walnut-topped loaf is easy to prepare and tastes wonderful warm from the oven.
—*Amy Hawk, Seabrook, New Jersey*

1-3/4 cups all-purpose flour
  1/3 cup sugar
  1/3 cup packed brown sugar
  2 teaspoons baking powder
  1/2 teaspoon baking soda
  1/4 teaspoon salt
  2 eggs
  1 cup mashed ripe bananas (2 to 3 medium)
  3 tablespoons butter, melted
  2 tablespoons fat-free milk
  1/4 teaspoon maple flavoring
  1/4 cup chopped walnuts

In a bowl, combine the first six ingredients. Combine the eggs, bananas, butter, milk and flavoring; mix well. Stir into dry ingredients just until moistened. Spoon into an 8-in. x 4-in. x 2-in. loaf pan coated with nonstick cooking spray. Sprinkle with walnuts.

Bake at 350° for 50-55 minutes or until a toothpick inserted near the center comes out clean. Cool for 10 minutes before removing from pan to a wire rack. **Yield:** 1 loaf (12 slices).

Nutritional Analysis: *One slice equals 197 calories, 6 g fat (2 g saturated fat), 43 mg cholesterol, 184 mg sodium, 34 g carbohydrate, 1 g fiber, 4 g protein.*
Diabetic Exchanges: *1-1/2 starch, 1 fat, 1/2 fruit.*

Crunchy Apple Muffins

Meatless

I enjoy baking muffins, especially when they feature healthy ingredients like these do. The crunchy topping and juicy apple bits add just the right sweetness to these jumbo muffins.
—*Elaine Anderson, Aliquippa, Pennsylvania*

  1 cup all-purpose flour
1/2 cup whole wheat flour
1/2 cup sugar
  2 teaspoons baking powder
1/2 teaspoon ground cinnamon
1/4 teaspoon salt
  1 egg

1/2 cup fat-free milk
  2 tablespoons butter, melted
  1 cup chopped peeled tart apples
TOPPING:
  1/4 cup reduced-fat granola cereal
  2 tablespoons chopped walnuts
  1 tablespoon brown sugar
  1/2 teaspoon ground cinnamon
  2 teaspoons fat-free milk

In a large bowl, combine flours, sugar, baking powder, cinnamon and salt. In another bowl, beat egg, milk and butter. Stir into dry ingredients just until moistened. Fold in apples. Coat jumbo muffin cups with nonstick cooking spray; fill half full.

For topping, combine the cereal, walnuts, brown sugar, cinnamon and milk. Sprinkle over muffins. Bake at 375° for 20-25 minutes or until a toothpick comes out clean. Cool for 5 minutes before removing from pan to a wire rack. Serve warm. **Yield:** 6 muffins.

Nutritional Analysis: One muffin equals 282 calories, 7 g fat (3 g saturated fat), 46 mg cholesterol, 248 mg sodium, 50 g carbohydrate, 3 g fiber, 6 g protein.

Raspberry Lemon Loaf

Meatless

(Pictured above)

This easy-to-prepare quick bread is flavored with tangy lemon peel and fresh raspberries.

It's refreshing as a snack, at breakfast…or any time of day. If your family loves this as much as mine does, one loaf won't last long around your house!
—Carol Dodds, Aurora, Ontario

1-3/4 cups all-purpose flour
  1/2 cup sugar
    1 teaspoon baking powder
  1/2 teaspoon baking soda
  1/2 teaspoon salt
    1 egg
    2 egg whites
    1 cup reduced-fat lemon yogurt
  1/4 cup canola oil
    2 teaspoons grated lemon peel
    1 cup fresh raspberries

In a large bowl, combine the dry ingredients. In another bowl, whisk together the egg, egg whites, yogurt, oil and lemon peel. Add to the dry ingredients just until moistened. Fold in the raspberries.

Transfer to an 8-in. x 4-in. x 3-in. loaf pan coated with nonstick cooking spray. Bake at 350° for 60-65 minutes or until a toothpick inserted near the center comes out clean. Cool for 10 minutes before removing from pan to a wire rack to cool completely. **Yield:** 1 loaf (12 slices).

Nutritional Analysis: One slice equals 176 calories, 6 g fat (1 g saturated fat), 50 mg cholesterol, 218 mg sodium, 26 g carbohydrate, 1 g fiber, 4 g protein.
***Diabetic Exchanges:** 1-1/2 starch, 1 fat.*

Multigrain Muffins

Low-sodium Meatless

(Pictured above)

My husband and I love including grains in our diet. The cornmeal and oats in these muffins give them an interesting texture, which I hope you'll enjoy as much as we do.
—Peggy Corcoran, Apex, North Carolina

1/2 cup all-purpose flour
1/2 cup cornmeal
1/2 cup quick-cooking oats
1/4 cup whole wheat flour
1/4 cup packed brown sugar
3 tablespoons toasted wheat germ
2 teaspoons baking powder
1/4 teaspoon salt
1 egg, lightly beaten
1 cup fat-free milk
1/4 cup canola oil
1/4 cup chopped walnuts
1/4 cup raisins

In a bowl, combine the first eight ingredients. In another bowl, combine the egg, milk and oil; stir into dry ingredients just until moistened. Fold in walnuts and raisins.

Coat muffin cups with nonstick cooking spray; fill two-thirds full with batter. Bake at 375° for 15-18 minutes or until a toothpick comes out clean. Cool for 5 minutes before removing from pan to a wire rack. **Yield:** 1 dozen.

Nutritional Analysis: One muffin equals 166 calories, 7 g fat (1 g saturated fat), 18 mg cholesterol, 107 mg sodium, 22 g carbohydrate, 2 g fiber, 4 g protein.
Diabetic Exchanges: 1-1/2 starch, 1 fat.

Cinnamon Buns

Meatless

(Pictured at right)

With a yummy cinnamon-raisin flavor and a drizzle of vanilla glaze, these tender sweet rolls are a real taste treat.
—Susan Corpman, Newhall, Iowa

1 package (1/4 ounce) active dry yeast
1 cup warm fat-free milk (110° to 115°), *divided*
3 tablespoons canola oil
1 tablespoon sugar
1 teaspoon salt
2-1/2 to 2-3/4 cups all-purpose flour
3 tablespoons dark corn syrup
3 tablespoons packed brown sugar
2 teaspoons ground cinnamon
1/8 teaspoon ground nutmeg
1/4 cup raisins
GLAZE:
1/2 cup confectioners' sugar
1/4 teaspoon vanilla extract
1 to 2 teaspoons fat-free milk

In a large mixing bowl, dissolve yeast in 1/4 cup warm milk. Add the oil, sugar, salt, 1-1/2 cups flour and remaining milk. Beat on medium speed for 3 minutes. Stir in enough remaining flour to form a soft dough.

Turn onto a lightly floured surface; knead until smooth and elastic, about 6-8 minutes. Place in a bowl coated with nonstick cooking spray, turning once to coat top. Cover and let rise in a warm place until doubled, about 1 hour.

Punch dough down. Turn onto a lightly floured surface; roll into a 12-in. x 10-in. rectangle. Carefully spread corn syrup over dough to within 1/2 in. of edges. In a bowl, combine the brown sugar, cinnamon and nutmeg; sprinkle over corn syrup. Sprinkle with raisins. Roll up jelly-roll style, starting with a long side; pinch seam to seal. Cut into 12 slices. Place cut side down in a 9-in. round baking pan coated with nonstick cooking spray. Cover and let rise in a warm place until doubled, about 40 minutes.

Bake at 350° for 25-30 minutes or until golden brown. Cool on a wire rack. For glaze, in a bowl, combine confectioners' sugar, vanilla and enough milk to achieve drizzling consistency. Drizzle over cinnamon buns. **Yield:** 1 dozen.

Nutritional Analysis: One bun equals 193 calories, 4 g fat (trace saturated fat), trace cholesterol, 218 mg sodium, 36 g carbohydrate, 1 g fiber, 4 g protein.
Diabetic Exchanges: 2-1/2 starch, 1/2 fat.

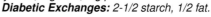

Sour Cream Blueberry Coffee Cake

Meatless

Oozing with blueberry flavor, this coffee cake from our home economists is tender and moist with a topping of brown sugar, cinnamon and oats.

- 2 cups all-purpose flour
- 3/4 cup sugar
- 1 teaspoon baking powder
- 1/2 teaspoon salt
- 1/4 teaspoon baking soda
- 1 egg
- 1 cup (8 ounces) reduced-fat sour cream
- 1/4 cup unsweetened applesauce
- 3 tablespoons canola oil
- 1 teaspoon vanilla extract
- 1-1/2 cups fresh *or* frozen blueberries

TOPPING:
- 1/4 cup packed brown sugar
- 1/4 cup quick-cooking oats
- 1/2 teaspoon ground cinnamon
- 2 tablespoons cold butter

In a large bowl, combine the flour, sugar, baking powder, salt and baking soda. In another bowl, combine the egg, sour cream, applesauce, oil and vanilla. Stir into dry ingredients just until moistened. Fold in blueberries.

Pour into 9-in. square baking pan coated with nonstick cooking spray. Combine the brown sugar, oats and cinnamon; cut in butter until mixture resembles coarse crumbs. Sprinkle over the batter. Bake at 350° for 40-45 minutes or until a toothpick inserted near the center comes out clean. Cool on a wire rack. **Yield:** 12 servings.

Editor's Note: If using frozen blueberries, do not thaw before adding to batter.

Nutritional Analysis: One piece equals 242 calories, 9 g fat (3 g saturated fat), 31 mg cholesterol, 201 mg sodium, 38 g carbohydrate, 1 g fiber, 4 g protein.
Diabetic Exchanges: 2-1/2 starch, 1-1/2 fat.

Country Corn Bread

Meatless

For my family's traditional Christmas Eve gathering, I'm always asked to bring this corn bread, the lightest and fluffiest I've ever tasted.
—Burdell Fossum, Plymouth, Minnesota

- 1 cup all-purpose flour
- 1 cup cornmeal
- 1/4 cup sugar
- 1/2 teaspoon baking soda
- 1/2 teaspoon salt
- 1 egg
- 1 cup (8 ounces) reduced-fat plain yogurt
- 1/4 cup canola oil

In a large bowl, combine the flour, cornmeal, sugar, baking soda and salt. Whisk together the egg, yogurt and oil.

Stir into the dry ingredients just until combined.

Transfer to an 8-in. square baking dish coated with nonstick cooking spray. Bake at 375° for 20-25 minutes or until top is lightly browned and a toothpick inserted near the center comes out clean. Serve warm. **Yield:** 9 servings.

Nutritional Analysis: One piece equals 207 calories, 8 g fat (1 g saturated fat), 25 mg cholesterol, 226 mg sodium, 30 g carbohydrate, 2 g fiber, 5 g protein.
Diabetic Exchanges: 2 starch, 1 fat.

Onion Herb Biscuits

Meatless

(Pictured below)

These fluffy well-seasoned biscuits developed in our Test Kitchen make a pleasant accompaniment to almost any meal.

- 2 cups all-purpose flour
- 1 tablespoon baking powder
- 1 tablespoon minced fresh thyme *or* 1 teaspoon dried thyme
- 1 teaspoon dried savory
- 1/2 teaspoon salt
- 1/4 teaspoon baking soda
- 1/4 teaspoon pepper
- 1-1/2 cups reduced-fat sour cream
- 2 tablespoons olive oil
- 1/4 cup thinly sliced green onions
- 1 tablespoon butter, melted

Combine the flour, baking powder, thyme, savory, salt, baking soda and pepper. Combine sour cream and oil. With a fork, stir sour cream mixture into dry ingredients just until

blended and mixture holds together. Stir in green onions. Turn onto a lightly floured surface; gently knead three or four times. Roll dough to 3/4-in. thickness; cut with a floured 2-1/2-in. biscuit cutter.

Place 1 in. apart on ungreased baking sheet. Brush lightly with butter. Bake at 400° for 14-18 minutes or until lightly browned. Serve warm. **Yield:** 1 dozen.

Nutritional Analysis: One biscuit equals 144 calories, 6 g fat (3 g saturated fat), 13 mg cholesterol, 277 mg sodium, 18 g carbohydrate, 1 g fiber, 4 g protein.
Diabetic Exchanges: 1 starch, 1 fat.

Chocolate Chip Banana Muffins

Meatless

I often bake these yummy treats with lots of banana flavor. Plenty of chocolate chips "disguise" the whole wheat taste in these moist muffins. They're perfect for breakfast or an anytime snack.
—Lauren Heyn, Oak Creek, Wisconsin

3/4 cup all-purpose flour
3/4 cup whole wheat flour
1/2 cup wheat bran
1/2 cup packed brown sugar
1 teaspoon baking powder
3/4 teaspoon baking soda
1/2 teaspoon salt
2 eggs, lightly beaten
1/4 cup fat-free milk
1-1/3 cups mashed ripe bananas (2 to 3 medium)
1/3 cup unsweetened applesauce
1 teaspoon vanilla extract
1/2 cup miniature chocolate chips
1/3 cup chopped pecans

In a large bowl, combine the first seven ingredients. Combine the eggs and milk; stir in the bananas, applesauce and vanilla. Stir into dry ingredients just until moistened. Stir in chocolate chips.

Coat muffin cups with nonstick cooking spray or use paper liners; fill three-fourths full with batter. Sprinkle with pecans. Bake at 375° for 18-22 minutes or until a toothpick comes out clean. Cool for 5 minutes before removing from pan to a wire rack. **Yield:** 1 dozen.

Nutritional Analysis: One muffin equals 191 calories, 6 g fat (2 g saturated fat), 36 mg cholesterol, 236 mg sodium, 33 g carbohydrate, 4 g fiber, 4 g protein.
Diabetic Exchanges: 2 starch, 1/2 fat.

Lemon Ginger Muffins

Meatless

(Pictured above)

These quick muffins are tender and have a lovely aroma while they're baking. Fat-free yogurt keeps them moist. If you like lemon and ginger, you're sure to enjoy their fresh flavor.
—Joyce Baker Mabry, Hamilton, Montana

1/3 cup butter, softened
1/2 cup sugar
Sugar substitute equivalent to 1/2 cup sugar
4 egg whites
2 tablespoons minced fresh gingerroot
2 tablespoons grated lemon peel
2 cups all-purpose flour
1 teaspoon baking soda
1 cup fat-free plain yogurt

In a large mixing bowl, beat butter, sugar and sugar substitute until crumbly. Add egg whites; beat well. Stir in ginger and lemon peel. Combine flour and baking soda; add to butter mixture alternately with yogurt.

Coat muffin cups with nonstick cooking spray; fill three-fourths full. Bake at 375° for 18-20 minutes or until a toothpick comes out clean. Cool for 5 minutes before removing from pan to a wire rack. Serve warm. **Yield:** 1 dozen.

Editor's Note: This recipe was tested with Splenda No Calorie Sweetener. Look for it in the baking aisle of your grocery store.

Nutritional Analysis: One muffin equals 171 calories, 5 g fat (3 g saturated fat), 14 mg cholesterol, 186 mg sodium, 27 g carbohydrate, 1 g fiber, 4 g protein.
Diabetic Exchanges: 2 starch, 1/2 fat.

ing spray. Using fingertips, make indentations 1 in. apart on dough; cover. In a small skillet, saute the onion, rosemary and thyme in the remaining oil for 3-4 minutes or until tender. Spread evenly on dough. Cover and let rise in a warm place until doubled, about 30 minutes.

Bake at 375° for 14-18 minutes or until golden brown. Remove from pans to wire racks. **Yield:** 2 breads (10 wedges each).

Nutritional Analysis: *One wedge equals 104 calories, 3 g fat (trace saturated fat), 11 mg cholesterol, 154 mg sodium, 16 g carbohydrate, 1 g fiber, 3 g protein.*
Diabetic Exchanges: *1 starch, 1/2 fat.*

Potato Refrigerator Rolls

Low-fat **Low-sodium** *Meatless*

I started making these rolls in the 1960s because my children liked their meat or cheese separate from their bread. Sometimes I add poppy seeds or use rye flour instead of wheat flour and add caraway seeds.
—Ruthelaine Hoolsema, Grand Rapids, Michigan

- 1 package (1/4 ounce) active dry yeast
- 3/4 cup warm water (110° to 115°)
- 1/2 cup warm mashed potatoes (made with fat-free milk)
- 3 tablespoons butter, softened
- 1/4 cup sugar
- 2 tablespoons molasses
- 1 egg, lightly beaten
- 3/4 teaspoon salt
- 1-1/2 cups whole wheat flour
- 2 cups all-purpose flour
- 1 tablespoon cornmeal
- 4 teaspoons fat-free milk
- 4 teaspoons toasted wheat germ

In a large mixing bowl, dissolve yeast in warm water. Add the mashed potatoes, butter, sugar, molasses, egg, salt and whole wheat flour; beat until smooth. Stir in enough all-purpose flour to form a soft dough.

Turn onto a floured surface; knead until smooth and elastic, about 6-8 minutes. Place in a greased bowl, turning once to grease top. Cover and refrigerate for 2 hours.

Coat baking sheets with nonstick cooking spray and sprinkle with cornmeal; set aside. Punch down dough. Turn onto a lightly floured surface; divide into 18 pieces. Shape each into a ball. Place 2 in. apart on prepared baking sheets. Cover and let rise in a warm place until doubled, about 45 minutes.

Brush rolls with milk; sprinkle with wheat germ. Bake at 375° for 12-15 minutes or until golden brown. Remove from pans to wire racks to cool. **Yield:** 1-1/2 dozen.

Nutritional Analysis: *One roll equals 129 calories, 2 g fat (1 g saturated fat), 16 mg cholesterol, 139 mg sodium, 24 g carbohydrate, 2 g fiber, 4 g protein.*
Diabetic Exchange: *1-1/2 starch.*

Herb Focaccia Bread

Low-fat *Meatless*

(Pictured above)

This well-seasoned yeast bread from our Test Kitchen adds an attractive accent to any Italian meal…and the aroma while it's baking is scrumptious. The wedges also go great with soup, stew or chili.

- 1 package (16 ounces) hot roll mix
- 1 cup warm water (120° to 130°)
- 1 egg, lightly beaten
- 2 tablespoons plus 2 teaspoons olive oil, *divided*
- 1 cup finely chopped onion
- 1 teaspoon dried rosemary, crushed
- 1 teaspoon dried thyme

In a large mixing bowl, combine the hot roll mix and contents of yeast packet; mix well. Stir in the warm water, egg and 2 tablespoons oil; beat for 2 minutes or until dough pulls away from sides of bowl. Turn onto a floured surface; knead until smooth and elastic, about 5 minutes. Place in a bowl coated with nonstick cooking spray, turning once to grease top. Let rest for 5 minutes.

Divide dough in half. Roll each half into a 12-in. circle. Transfer to two 12-in. pizza pans coated with nonstick cook-

Favorite Recipe Made Lighter

SINCE SHE began watching her diet more closely, Shirley Wilder of Marietta, Georgia has avoided preparing Blueberries 'n' Cheese Coffee Cake.

Shirley asked our home economists to work their magic so she could enjoy it again.

The result? The fat was reduced by more than 40%, saturated fat and cholesterol were cut in half and calories were reduced by a quarter.

Blueberries 'n' Cheese Coffee Cake

Meatless

1/2 cup butter, softened
1-1/4 cups sugar
2 eggs
1 teaspoon grated lemon peel
2-1/4 cups all-purpose flour, *divided*
3 teaspoons baking powder
1 teaspoon salt
3/4 cup milk
1/4 cup water
2 cups fresh *or* frozen blueberries
1 package (8 ounces) cream cheese, diced
TOPPING:
1/4 cup all-purpose flour
1/4 cup sugar
1 teaspoon grated lemon peel
2 tablespoons cold butter

In a large mixing bowl, cream butter and sugar. Add eggs, one at a time, beating well after each addition. Beat in lemon peel. Combine 2 cups flour, baking powder and salt; add to the creamed mixture alternately with milk and water. In a bowl, toss blueberries with remaining flour; fold into batter along with cream cheese. Pour into a greased 13-in. x 9-in. x 2-in. baking pan.

For topping, combine the flour, sugar and lemon peel in a bowl; cut in butter until mixture is crumbly. Sprinkle over batter. Bake at 375° for 35-40 minutes or until a toothpick inserted near the center comes out clean. Cool completely on a wire rack. **Yield:** 15 servings.

Editor's Note: If using frozen blueberries, do not thaw before adding to batter.

Nutritional Analysis: One piece equals 300 calories, 14 g fat (8 g saturated fat), 66 mg cholesterol, 396 mg sodium, 40 g carbohydrate, 1 g fiber, 5 g protein.

Makeover Blueberries 'n' Cheese Coffee Cake

Meatless

(Pictured at right)

2 tablespoons butter, softened
3/4 cup sugar

1 egg
2 egg whites
1/4 cup unsweetened applesauce
2 tablespoons canola oil
1 teaspoon grated lemon peel
2-1/4 cups all-purpose flour, *divided*
1-1/4 teaspoons baking powder
1 teaspoon salt
1/2 teaspoon baking soda
1 cup 1% buttermilk
2 cups fresh *or* frozen blueberries
1 package (8 ounces) reduced-fat cream cheese, diced
TOPPING:
1/4 cup all-purpose flour
1/4 cup sugar
1 teaspoon grated lemon peel
2 tablespoons cold butter

In a large mixing bowl, beat the butter and sugar until light and crumbly. Beat in the egg, egg whites, applesauce, oil and lemon peel. Combine 2 cups flour, baking powder, salt and baking soda; add to the sugar mixture alternately with buttermilk. In a bowl, toss blueberries with remaining flour; fold into batter along with cream cheese. Pour into a 13-in. x 9-in. x 2-in. baking dish coated with nonstick cooking spray.

For topping, combine the flour, sugar and lemon peel in a bowl; cut in butter until mixture is crumbly. Sprinkle over batter. Bake at 375° for 30-35 minutes or until a toothpick inserted near the center comes out clean. Cool completely on a wire rack. **Yield:** 15 servings.

Editor's Note: If using frozen blueberries, do not thaw before adding to batter.

Nutritional Analysis: One piece equals 224 calories, 8 g fat (4 g saturated fat), 31 mg cholesterol, 346 mg sodium, 34 g carbohydrate, 1 g fiber, 5 g protein.
Diabetic Exchanges: 2 starch, 1-1/2 fat.

In a large mixing bowl, dissolve yeast in 1/2 cup warm water. Add the whole wheat flour, oil, honey, cornmeal, rosemary, salt, 1 cup bread flour and remaining water. Beat until smooth. Stir in enough remaining bread flour to form a soft dough. Turn onto a floured surface; add pecans. Knead until smooth and elastic, about 6-8 minutes. Place in a bowl coated with nonstick cooking spray, turning once to coat top. Cover and let rise in a warm place until doubled, about 1 hour.

Punch dough down. Divide in half; shape into two loaves. Place in two 9-in. x 5-in. x 3-in. loaf pans coated with nonstick cooking spray. Cover and let rise until doubled, about 30 minutes.

Brush egg over loaves. Bake at 350° for 35-40 minutes or until bread sounds hollow when tapped. Remove from pans to wire racks. **Yield:** 2 loaves (16 slices each).

Nutritional Analysis: One slice equals 150 calories, 5 g fat (trace saturated fat), 7 mg cholesterol, 76 mg sodium, 23 g carbohydrate, 1 g fiber, 4 g protein.
Diabetic Exchanges: 1-1/2 starch, 1 fat.

Nutty Rosemary Bread

Low-sodium Meatless

(Pictured above)

This tender golden loaf has a mild rosemary and pecan flavor. A doctor who came to our office regularly made bread for us every year. I wanted the recipe, and he knew it by heart. Now I make it to give as gifts and for our hospital fair.
—*Naomi Knobloch, Lester, Iowa*

    2 packages (1/4 ounce *each*) active dry yeast
2-1/2 cups warm water (110° to 115°), *divided*
   3/4 cup whole wheat flour
   1/4 cup canola oil
   1/4 cup honey
     3 tablespoons cornmeal
     1 tablespoon dried rosemary, crushed
     1 teaspoon salt
     5 to 6 cups bread flour
     1 cup chopped pecans
     1 egg, beaten

🍎 Flour Power

MANY RECIPES for pizza crust and bread (especially bread machine recipes) call for bread flour, which has more gluten and protein than all-purpose flour plus a little malted barley flour.

The barley flour helps the yeast work. The extra gluten results in a tall loaf that's nicely textured.

You can substitute all-purpose flour for bread flour, although the results will not be the same. It's not recommended, however, to use bread flour where all-purpose flour is called for because the end product may be tough and chewy.

Dazzling Desserts

It used to be the words "rich", "creamy" and "yummy" were never spoken in the same sentence as "low fat", especially when the conversation turned to desserts. But now you can have your cake and eat it, too!

Fruit Pizza (page 211)

Cranberry Apple Crisp

Low-sodium

My mother was a great cook who loved to entertain. This warm and comforting crisp was one of her best recipes. With a buttery golden topping, it's an irresistible ending to a holiday dinner or informal gathering.
—Mary Bachman Foltz, Wolcottville, Indiana

- 3 cups chopped peeled tart apples
- 2 cups fresh *or* frozen cranberries
- 1 cup sugar
- 3 tablespoons all-purpose flour
- 1 cup crushed cornflakes
- 1/2 cup chopped pecans
- 1/2 cup packed light brown sugar
- 3 tablespoons butter, melted

In a large bowl, combine the apples, cranberries, sugar and flour; spoon into a 2-qt. baking dish coated with nonstick cooking spray. Combine the cornflakes, pecans, brown sugar and butter; sprinkle over apple mixture. Bake at 350° for 35-40 minutes or until top is golden brown and filling is bubbly. **Yield:** 10 servings.

Nutritional Analysis: One serving (1/2 cup) equals 260 calories, 8 g fat (3 g saturated fat), 9 mg cholesterol, 136 mg sodium, 48 g carbohydrate, 2 g fiber, 2 g protein.

Hawaiian Wedding Cake

(Pictured above right)

I got this wonderful recipe from a cousin whose husband was Hawaiian. I've changed it some to reduce the fat and calories, but it still tastes as rich as the original. It's very simple to make... and guests will love it. Enjoy!
—JoAnn Desmond, Madison Heights, Virginia

- 1 package (18-1/4 ounces) yellow cake mix
- 1-1/4 cups 1% buttermilk
- 4 egg whites
- 1 egg
- 1 package (8 ounces) reduced-fat cream cheese, cubed
- 1 cup cold 2% milk
- 1 package (1 ounce) sugar-free instant vanilla pudding mix
- 2 cans (one 20 ounces, one 8 ounces) unsweetened crushed pineapple, drained
- 1 carton (8 ounces) frozen fat-free whipped topping, thawed
- 1/2 cup flaked coconut, toasted

In a mixing bowl, beat the dry cake mix, buttermilk, egg whites and egg on low speed until moistened. Beat on high for 2 minutes. Transfer to a 13-in. x 9-in. x 2-in. baking pan coated with nonstick cooking spray. Bake at 350° for 25-30 minutes or until a toothpick inserted near the center comes out clean. Cool on a wire rack.

In another mixing bowl, beat cream cheese until fluffy. Gradually beat in milk. Gradually add pudding mix. Spread over cake. Spoon pineapple over pudding mixture. Top with whipped topping. Sprinkle with coconut. Store in the refrigerator. **Yield:** 18 servings.

Nutritional Analysis: One piece equals 221 calories, 5 g fat (2 g saturated fat), 17 mg cholesterol, 378 mg sodium, 38 g carbohydrate, 1 g fiber, 6 g protein.
Diabetic Exchanges: 2 starch, 1 fat, 1/2 fruit.

Orange Pineapple Delight

Low-fat

A spoonful of pudding, with its pineapple and coconut flavor and sunny orange color, is a sweet reminder of warmer climates. This is especially good in summer because it's so refreshing.
—Pat Coauette, Crookston, Minnesota

- 1 can (8 ounces) unsweetened crushed pineapple
- 1 package (0.8 ounce) sugar-free cook-and-serve vanilla pudding mix
- 2/3 cup nonfat dry milk powder
- 1 cup orange juice
- 1/2 teaspoon coconut extract
- 1/2 cup miniature marshmallows
- 1/2 cup reduced-fat whipped topping
- 4 teaspoons flaked coconut, toasted

Drain pineapple, reserving juice; set pineapple aside. Add enough water to reserved juice to equal 3/4 cup. In a saucepan, combine the pudding mix, milk powder, orange juice and juice mixture. Cook and stir until mixture comes to a full boil. Remove from the heat; stir in coconut extract. Cool for 5 minutes. Stir in marshmallows until melted. Fold in pineapple. Transfer to four individual serving dishes. Cover and refrigerate for 2 hours. Garnish with whipped topping and coconut. **Yield:** 4 servings.

Sweetheart Red Cake

(Pictured below)

In North Smithfield, Rhode Island, red velvet cake is a favorite of Jeannette Beauchemin's family. But she asked our home economists to lighten up the recipe so her family can enjoy it without feeling too much guilt.

6 tablespoons butter, softened
1-3/4 cups sugar
1 egg
2 egg whites
1/4 cup unsweetened applesauce
1 bottle (1 ounce) red food coloring
1 teaspoon white vinegar
1 teaspoon vanilla extract
2-1/2 cups cake flour

1 teaspoon salt
1 teaspoon baking soda
1 teaspoon baking cocoa
1-1/4 cups 1% buttermilk
FROSTING:
1-1/2 cups sugar
4 egg whites
1/4 cup water
1/2 teaspoon cream of tartar
1 teaspoon vanilla extract
Pink gel food coloring

Coat two 9-in. round baking pans with nonstick cooking spray and flour. In a mixing bowl, cream the butter and sugar for 2 minutes or until crumbly. Add egg and egg whites, one at a time, beating well after each addition. Beat in the applesauce, food coloring, vinegar and vanilla. Combine the flour, salt, baking soda and cocoa; add to the creamed mixture alternately with buttermilk.

Pour into prepared pans. Bake at 350° for 25-30 minutes or until a toothpick inserted near the center comes out clean. Cool for 10 minutes before removing from pans to wire racks to cool completely.

For frosting, in a heavy saucepan, combine the sugar, egg whites, water and cream of tartar. With a portable mixer, beat mixture on low speed for 1 minute. Continue beating on low speed over low heat until frosting reaches 160°, about 8-10 minutes. Pour into a large mixing bowl; add vanilla. Beat on high speed until frosting forms stiff peaks, about 7 minutes. Remove 1/2 cup frosting; tint pink. Spread remaining frosting between layers and over top and sides of cake. Pipe pink hearts over top of cake. **Yield:** 12 servings.

Editor's Note: A stand mixer is recommended for beating the frosting after it reaches 160°.

Cherry Chocolate Cake

I've had the recipe for this cake for years—it's a chocolate lover's delight! It's so easy to make and is perfect for cupcakes and bake sale treats, too. I get many requests for the recipe.
—Ann Purchase, Panama City, Florida

1 package (18-1/4 ounces) chocolate cake mix
3 eggs, lightly beaten
1 teaspoon almond extract
2 cans (20 ounces *each*) reduced-sugar cherry pie filling, *divided*
3/4 teaspoon confectioners' sugar

In a mixing bowl, combine the dry cake mix, eggs and almond extract. Stir in one can of pie filling until blended. Transfer to a 13-in. x 9-in. x 2-in. baking pan coated with nonstick cooking spray. Bake at 350° for 30-35 minutes or until a toothpick inserted near the center comes out clean. Cool completely. Dust with confectioners' sugar. Top individual servings with remaining pie filling. **Yield:** 18 servings.

white; gradually stir 1/2 cup hot filling into egg mixture; return all to the pan, stirring constantly. Bring to a gentle boil; cook and stir for 2 minutes. Remove from the heat; stir in grapefruit peel and food coloring if desired. Pour hot filling into crust. Spread meringue evenly over hot filling, sealing edges to crust. Broil for 30-60 seconds or until meringue is golden brown. Cool on a wire rack. Refrigerate for at least 3 hours before serving. Store leftovers in the refrigerator. **Yield:** 8 servings.

Nutritional Analysis: One piece equals 254 calories, 8 g fat (3 g saturated fat), 32 mg cholesterol, 173 mg sodium, 42 g carbohydrate, trace fiber, 4 g protein.
Diabetic Exchanges: 2 starch, 1-1/2 fat, 1/2 fruit.

Citrus Meringue Pie

(Pictured at right)

This pretty meringue pie stars grapefruit, orange and lemon juices. I made several changes to lighten up the original recipe. This pie has a very fresh citrus flavor and the filling tastes nice and rich.
—Donna Schweighofer, Pickerington, Ohio

    3 egg whites
    6 tablespoons sugar
    1 tablespoon water
    1/4 teaspoon plus 1/8 teaspoon cream of tartar
1-1/2 teaspoons cornstarch
    2 tablespoons plus 1-1/2 teaspoons cold water
    1/2 teaspoon vanilla extract
    1/8 teaspoon salt
FILLING:
    2/3 cup sugar
    3 tablespoons cornstarch
    1 cup grapefruit juice
    1/2 cup water
    1/4 cup orange juice
    1 tablespoon lemon juice
    1 egg
    1 egg white
    1 teaspoon grated grapefruit peel
    7 drops yellow food coloring, optional
    1 pastry shell (9 inches), baked

In a heavy saucepan or double boiler, combine the egg whites, sugar, water and cream of tartar; mix well. Heat over low heat or simmering water while beating with a portable mixer on low speed for 1 minute, scraping down sides of pan. Continue beating until mixture reaches 160°. Remove from the heat. In a small saucepan, combine cornstarch and cold water until smooth. Bring to a boil; cook and stir for 1-2 minutes or until thickened. Remove from the heat; cool for 1 minute. Whisk into egg white mixture; add vanilla and salt. Beat on high until stiff peaks form. Set meringue aside.

In a saucepan, combine sugar and cornstarch. Gradually add the grapefruit juice, water, orange juice and lemon juice until smooth. Bring to a boil over medium-high heat; cook and stir for 2 minutes or until thickened. Remove from the heat. In a small bowl, whisk together egg and egg

Fortune Cookies

Low-sodium

(Pictured at right)

Our Test Kitchen staff came up with these sweet treats. Tuck a written sentiment inside... and share the tasty homemade fortune cookies with your loved ones on a special day.

    6 tablespoons butter, softened
    1/3 cup sugar
    2 egg whites
    1/2 teaspoon almond extract
    1/2 teaspoon vanilla extract
    2/3 cup all-purpose flour
    1/4 cup semisweet chocolate chips
    2 ounces white candy coating
Red sprinkles, optional

Write fortunes on 10 strips of paper (5-in. x 3/4-in.); fold in half. Set aside. Line a baking sheet with parchment paper. Draw two 5-in. circles on the parchment paper. Set aside.

In a mixing bowl, beat the butter, sugar, egg whites and extracts. Add flour; mix well. Spread 2 tablespoons of batter over each circle. Bake at 400° for 6-7 minutes or until lightly browned.

Working with one cookie at a time, remove carefully from pan using a thin spatula (cover other cookie with clean kitchen towel to keep warm). Place a fortune in the center of cookie; fold cookie in half over fortune strip so that the edges meet. Press edges together for 3 seconds. Place center of cookie over rim of a glass; gently press ends down to bend cookie in half. Let cookie cool on glass for 1 minute, then remove to a wire rack. Repeat with remaining cookie. If cookies become too cool to fold, return to oven to soften for 1 minute. Repeat with remaining batter.

In a microwave, melt chocolate chips; stir until smooth. Drizzle over cookies. Melt candy coating; stir until smooth. Drizzle over cookies. Top with sprinkles if desired. **Yield:** 10 cookies.

Nutritional Analysis: One cookie equals 172 calories, 10 g fat (6 g saturated fat), 20 mg cholesterol, 87 mg sodium, 19 g carbohydrate, 1 g fiber, 2 g protein.
Diabetic Exchanges: 2 fat, 1 starch.

Coffee Mousse

Low-carb Low-sodium

(Pictured below)

The recipe for this very low-sugar dessert comes from my daughter. Its texture is light as a cloud and its taste is perfect for coffee lovers.
—*Vernette Dechaine, Pittsfield, Maine*

  1 envelope unflavored gelatin
1/4 cup cold water
  2 teaspoons instant coffee granules
1/4 cup boiling water
Sugar substitute equivalent to 2 teaspoons sugar
  2 ice cubes
  2 cups plus 4 tablespoons reduced-fat whipped topping
Crushed coffee granules

In a small bowl, sprinkle gelatin over cold water; let stand for 2 minutes. In a small saucepan, dissolve coffee in boiling water; add gelatin mixture. Cook and stir coffee just until gelatin is dissolved (do not boil). Remove from the heat; stir in sugar substitute. Add ice cubes; stir until ice cubes are melted and mixture begins to thicken.

In a mixing bowl, beat the coffee mixture and about 2/3 cup whipped topping until blended. Fold in 1-1/3 cups topping by hand. Transfer to four individual serving dishes. Top each with 1 tablespoon whipped topping. Refrigerate for at least 2 hours. Dust with the crushed coffee granules. **Yield:** 4 servings.

Editor's Note: This recipe was tested with Splenda No Calorie Sweetener. Look for it in the baking aisle of your grocery store.

Nutritional Analysis: One serving (1/2 cup) equals 101 calories, 5 g fat (5 g saturated fat), 0 cholesterol, 4 mg sodium, 10 g carbohydrate, 0 fiber, 2 g protein.
Diabetic Exchanges: 1 starch, 1/2 fat.

Apple-Raisin Rice Dessert

Low-sodium

This recipe combines apples, cinnamon, raisins and leftover rice in a warm and satisfying dessert. No one can resist the down-home flavor.
—*Marjorie Grunewald, Weimar, Texas*

2-1/4 cups water
  1 cup sugar
  3 cups sliced peeled tart apples
  3 tablespoons lemon juice
  1 teaspoon ground cinnamon
1/2 teaspoon ground nutmeg
  3 cups cooked long grain rice
1/2 cup raisins
  2 tablespoons plus 1-1/2 teaspoons butter
  2 teaspoons vanilla extract
1/2 cup plus 2 tablespoons reduced-fat whipped topping

In a large saucepan, bring water to a boil; add sugar. Cook and stir until sugar is dissolved. Stir in the apples, lemon juice and spices. Reduce heat; simmer for 3-5 minutes or until apples are tender. Stir in the rice, raisins, butter and vanilla.

Pour into a 2-qt. baking dish coated with nonstick cooking spray. Bake, uncovered, at 350° for 50-55 minutes or until liquid is absorbed. Let stand for 10 minutes before serving. Garnish each serving with whipped topping. Serve warm. **Yield:** 10 servings.

Nutritional Analysis: One serving (2/3 cup with 1 tablespoon whipped topping) equals 218 calories, 4 g fat (2 g saturated fat), 8 mg cholesterol, 32 mg sodium, 46 g carbohydrate, 1 g fiber, 2 g protein.
Diabetic Exchanges: 2 fruit, 1 starch, 1/2 fat.

Layered Banana Dessert

No-cook banana dessert is old-fashioned comfort food that tastes like you fussed. This recipe is a real winner at our house. Not only is it lighter in fat and calories, but it's light on your time, too. Plus, it's a great way to use up bananas.
—*Trish Schoofs, West Bend, Wisconsin*

1-1/2 cups cold fat-free milk
  1 package (3.4 ounces) instant vanilla pudding mix
  1 carton (8 ounces) frozen reduced-fat whipped topping, thawed

18 cinnamon graham cracker squares (about 2-1/2
   inches x 2-1/2 inches *each*)
2 medium firm bananas, cut into 1/4-inch slices

In a bowl, whisk milk and pudding mix for 2 minutes. Let
stand for 2 minutes or until soft-set. Fold in half of the
whipped topping. Place nine graham cracker squares in
an ungreased 8-in. square dish. Top with half of the pudding
mixture and half of the banana slices. Repeat layers. Spread
with remaining whipped topping. Cover and refrigerate for
at least 1 hour before serving. **Yield:** 9 servings.

Nutritional Analysis: *One serving equals 194 calories, 4 g
fat (3 g saturated fat), 1 mg cholesterol, 261 mg sodium, 35 g
carbohydrate, 1 g fiber, 3 g protein.*
Diabetic Exchanges: *1-1/2 starch, 1 fat, 1/2 fruit.*

Strawberry Yogurt Pie

(Pictured above)

*Pretty enough for a party or shower, this yummy
pink pie is covered with fluffy whipped topping and
garnished with fresh strawberries. It's easy to prepare, too.*
—Onieda Brummett, Wilber, Nebraska

1 refrigerated pie pastry (9 inches)
1 package (.3 ounce) sugar-free strawberry
   gelatin
3/4 cup boiling water
3 ounces reduced-fat cream cheese, softened

3/4 cup cold water
1 carton (6 ounces) fat-free reduced-sugar
   strawberry yogurt
2 cups reduced-fat whipped topping
1 cup halved fresh strawberries

Place pastry in a 9-in. pie plate; prick with a fork. Bake according to package directions. Cool completely on a wire
rack. In a bowl, dissolve gelatin in boiling water. Whisk in
cream cheese until smooth. Whisk in cold water and yogurt.
Refrigerate until mixture begins to thicken, about 50 minutes. Pour into cooled crust. Refrigerate until firm, about 1
hour. Spread with whipped topping and garnish with strawberries. **Yield:** 8 servings.

Nutritional Analysis: *One piece equals 209 calories, 12 g fat
(7 g saturated fat), 14 mg cholesterol, 187 mg sodium, 21 g carbohydrate, trace fiber, 3 g protein.*
Diabetic Exchanges: *2 fat, 1-1/2 starch.*

Cut Calories from Cake

FOR A light moist cake, try this trick. Use any flavor cake mix and beat in a 12-ounce can of diet soda. Try diet lemon-lime soda with white or yellow
cake mix and diet cola with a chocolate cake mix.
Do not add any other ingredients. Then just pour the
batter into cake pans and bake as usual. Top each
piece with 2 tablespoons of fat-free whipped topping instead of icing.   —Debbie McBride
                              Owensboro, Kentucky

Apricot Delight

Low-fat

(Pictured above)

My mother sent me the original recipe for this delightful dessert 45 years ago, and I lightened it up. With bits of angel food cake and a cream cheese-like texture, this refreshing treat tastes so rich that no one will guess it's light.
—Alice Case, Carrollton, Texas

 2 cans (5-1/2 ounces *each*) apricot nectar, *divided*
 1 package (.3 ounce) sugar-free orange gelatin
 1 package (1 ounce) sugar-free instant vanilla pudding mix
 2/3 cup nonfat dry milk powder
 1 carton (8 ounces) frozen reduced-fat whipped topping, thawed
 1 loaf (5 ounces) angel food cake, cubed
 1 can (15 ounces) unsweetened apricot halves, drained and sliced

In a microwave-safe bowl, microwave 1 cup apricot nectar on high for 50-60 seconds or until hot. Dissolve gelatin in hot nectar. Set aside to cool.

In a large bowl, combine remaining apricot nectar and enough water to measure 1-1/4 cups; whisk in pudding mix and milk powder for 1-2 minutes. Let stand for 2 minutes or until soft-set. Whisk in cooled gelatin; fold in whipped topping and cake. Pour into an 11-in. x 7-in. x 2-in. dish. Refrigerate for 2-4 hours. Garnish with apricot slices. **Yield:** 8 servings.

Nutritional Analysis: One serving equals 178 calories, 3 g fat (3 g saturated fat), 1 mg cholesterol, 303 mg sodium, 31 g carbohydrate, 1 g fiber, 4 g protein.
Diabetic Exchanges: 1 starch, 1 fruit, 1/2 fat.

Raspberry Cream Pie

I found the inspiration for this praiseworthy pie in my abundant raspberry patch. Fresh-picked berries are luscious, but frozen unsweetened ones will do. Combine plain and chocolate graham crackers to form the delicious crust.
—Julie Yuswak, Savanna, Illinois

 3 graham crackers (about 5 inches x 2-1/2 inches *each*), crushed
 3 chocolate graham crackers (about 5 inches x 2-1/2 inches *each*), crushed
 1 tablespoon sugar
 1/4 cup reduced-fat stick margarine, melted
 1 package (.3 ounce) sugar-free raspberry gelatin
 1/3 cup boiling water
 1 package (8 ounces) reduced-fat cream cheese
 1 teaspoon vanilla extract
 2 cups reduced-fat whipped topping
 2-1/2 cups fresh raspberries *or* blackberries

In a bowl, combine the graham cracker crumbs, sugar and margarine. Press onto the bottom and up the sides of an ungreased 9-in. pie plate. Bake at 375° for 8-10 minutes or until set. Cool on a wire rack.

In a bowl, dissolve gelatin in boiling water. Cool to room temperature.

In a mixing bowl, combine the cream cheese and vanilla until well blended. Gradually beat gelatin mixture into cream cheese mixture. Fold in whipped topping. Transfer to crust. Top with raspberries. Refrigerate for at least 2 hours. **Yield:** 8 servings.

Editor's Note: This recipe was tested with Parkay Light stick margarine.

Nutritional Analysis: One piece equals 209 calories, 11 g fat (6 g saturated fat), 16 mg cholesterol, 196 mg sodium, 20 g carbohydrate, 3 g fiber, 5 g protein.
Diabetic Exchanges: 2 fat, 1 starch, 1/2 fruit.

🍎 Berry Briefly Speaking

HERE ARE some fruitful tips for handling and storing fresh raspberries, courtesy of the Oregon Raspberry and Blackberry Commission.

- When shopping, choose unblemished berries in dry, unstained containers. Raspberries should be medium to bright red in color, depending on the variety. They should be free of surface moisture, which hastens decay.
- Store berries uncovered in the fridge as soon as possible after purchase. Arrange unwashed berries in a shallow pan lined with paper towels. Top them with a paper towel to absorb additional moisture.
- Shelf life is short…raspberries should be consumed within 2 to 3 days of purchase.
- Wash berries just prior to use. For fullest flavor, eat them at room temperature.

Favorite Recipe Made Lighter

WHEN LaVerne Yeager is looking to satisfy a chocolate craving, she turns to her recipe for Moist Fudgy Brownies. "These brownies taste so good, but I know they're bad for me. Can you lighten them up?" writes the St. Thomas, Pennsylvania cook.

While the rich treats are packed with chocolate flavor, they're also loaded with fat.

To trim them down, the home economists in our Test Kitchen replaced the cup of butter originally called for with 1/4 cup of butter, 1/4 cup of canola oil and 2 jars of prune baby food. With this combination, they were able to retain the fudgy texture of the original brownies with only a fraction of the fat.

They also substituted baking cocoa for some of the chocolate chips and reduced the number of eggs and amount of nuts to further lower the fat.

The Test Kitchen's changes cut calories by more than a quarter, fat by nearly half and saturated fat and cholesterol by about 60%.

But the makeover brownies are still rich and moist and full of the chocolaty goodness of the original recipe.

Moist Fudgy Brownies

Low-sodium

    2 cups (12 ounces) semisweet chocolate
      chips
    1 cup butter
    4 eggs
    1 cup sugar
    1 teaspoon vanilla extract
1-1/4 cups all-purpose flour
    1 cup chopped pecans
    1 teaspoon confectioners' sugar

Melt chocolate chips and butter; stir until smooth. In a mixing bowl, combine eggs, sugar, vanilla and chocolate mixture. Add flour; mix well. Stir in nuts. Pour into a greased 13-in. x 9-in. x 2-in. baking pan. Bake at 350° for 25-30 minutes or until a toothpick inserted near the center comes out clean. Cool on a wire rack. Sprinkle with confectioners' sugar. **Yield:** 1-1/2 dozen.

Nutritional Analysis: *One piece equals 307 calories, 21 g fat (10 g saturated fat), 75 mg cholesterol, 118 mg sodium, 31 g carbohydrate, 2 g fiber, 4 g protein.*

Makeover Moist Fudgy Brownies

Low-sodium

(Pictured at right)

1-1/4 cups semisweet chocolate chips
    1/4 cup butter
      2 eggs
    3/4 cup sugar
    1/2 cup packed brown sugar
      2 jars (2-1/2 ounces *each*) prune baby food
    1/4 cup canola oil
      2 teaspoons vanilla extract
      1 cup all-purpose flour
    1/2 cup baking cocoa
    1/4 teaspoon baking soda
    1/4 teaspoon salt
    1/3 cup chopped pecans, toasted
      1 teaspoon confectioners' sugar

Melt chocolate chips and butter; stir until smooth. In a mixing bowl, combine eggs, sugars, baby food, oil, vanilla and chocolate mixture. Combine the flour, cocoa, baking soda and salt. Add to the chocolate mixture; mix well. Stir in nuts. Spread into a 13-in. x 9-in. x 2-in. baking pan coated with nonstick cooking spray. Bake at 350° for 25-30 minutes or until a toothpick inserted near the center comes out clean. Cool on a wire rack. Sprinkle with confectioners' sugar. **Yield:** 1-1/2 dozen.

Nutritional Analysis: *One piece equals 221 calories, 11 g fat (4 g saturated fat), 31 mg cholesterol, 86 mg sodium, 31 g carbohydrate, 2 g fiber, 3 g protein.*
Diabetic Exchanges: *2 starch, 1-1/2 fat.*

Double Peanut Bars

Low-sodium

*These sweet no-bake snacks are great energy bars.
Any dried fruit works well, but I prefer cranberries.
Grain cereals, plus honey, peanuts and peanut
butter make the bars popular at my house.*
—Kim Rocker, LaGrange, Georgia

1-1/2 cups Wheaties
  1 cup Multi Grain Cheerios
1/2 cup unsalted dry roasted peanuts
1/2 cup chopped dried mixed fruit
1/3 cup packed brown sugar
1/3 cup honey
  3 tablespoons peanut butter

In a bowl, combine the cereals, peanuts and mixed fruit. In
a small saucepan, combine the brown sugar, honey and
peanut butter. Cook and stir until brown sugar and peanut
butter are melted and mixture is smooth. Pour over cereal
mixture; gently stir to coat evenly. Transfer to an 8-in. square
dish coated with nonstick cooking spray; gently press down.
Cool and cut into bars. Store in the refrigerator. **Yield:** 9
servings.

*Nutritional Analysis: One bar equals 201 calories, 7 g fat
(1 g saturated fat), 0 cholesterol, 65 mg sodium, 34 g carbohydrate,
3 g fiber, 5 g protein.*
Diabetic Exchanges: 2 starch, 1 fat.

Popover Apple Pie

*This is a family favorite that's perfect for cozy
winter nights. The golden brown crust bakes in the
oven, and the apple and cranberry filling cooks in
the microwave, then is spooned into the crust.*
—Beki Kosydar-Krantz, Clarks Summit, Pennsylvania

3/4 cup all-purpose flour
1/2 teaspoon salt
  2 eggs
  2 egg whites
3/4 cup 1% milk
  1 cup cold orange juice
  1 package (.8 ounce) sugar-free cook-and-serve
    vanilla pudding mix
3/4 teaspoon apple pie spice
  6 large peeled tart apples, sliced
1/2 cup dried cranberries

1/4 cup chopped walnuts
  1 teaspoon confectioners' sugar

In a bowl, combine flour and salt. Combine the eggs, egg
whites and milk; whisk into the dry ingredients just until
blended. Pour into a 10-in. ovenproof skillet coated with butter-flavored nonstick cooking spray. Bake at 450° for 20 minutes. Reduce heat to 350° (do not open oven door). Bake
10-15 minutes longer or until deep golden brown (do not
underbake).

In a microwave-safe bowl, whisk the orange juice, pudding mix and apple pie spice. Stir in apples and cranberries.
Cover and microwave on high for 5 minutes, stirring once.
Cover and cook 3-4 minutes longer or until apples are tender, stirring once. Spoon hot apple mixture into crust. Sprinkle with walnuts. Dust with confectioners' sugar and serve
immediately. **Yield:** 8 servings.

Editor's Note: This recipe was tested in a 1,100-watt
microwave.

*Nutritional Analysis: One serving (1 slice with 2/3 cup apple
mixture) equals 202 calories, 4 g fat (1 g saturated fat), 55 mg cholesterol, 307 mg sodium, 37 g carbohydrate, 3 g fiber, 5 g protein.*
Diabetic Exchanges: 1-1/2 fruit, 1 starch, 1 fat.

Fresh Strawberry Pie

Low-sodium

(Pictured below)

*This attractive fruit pie is almost too pretty to eat, but no
one will be able to resist the juicy whole strawberries
and delightfully sweet glaze that fill the tender pie crust.*
—Judy Watson, Newmarket, Ontario

  3 pints plus 1 cup fresh strawberries
  1 pastry shell (9 inches), baked
2/3 cup sugar
1/2 cup water
  2 tablespoons cornstarch
  2 tablespoons cold water
  2 to 3 drops red food coloring, optional
  8 tablespoons reduced-fat whipped topping

Set aside 1 cup strawberries. Arrange remaining berries in pie shell. With a fork, mash reserved 1 cup strawberries; set aside.

In a saucepan, combine sugar and water; cook and stir until sugar is dissolved. Add mashed strawberries and bring to a boil. Combine cornstarch and cold water until smooth. Gradually stir into strawberry mixture. Bring to a boil; cook and stir for 2 minutes or until thickened. Stir in food coloring if desired. Cool for 15-20 minutes, stirring occasionally. Spoon over strawberries in crust. Refrigerate for at least 2 hours. Garnish with whipped topping. **Yield:** 8 servings.

Nutritional Analysis: One piece equals 234 calories, 8 g fat (4 g saturated fat), 5 mg cholesterol, 101 mg sodium, 40 g carbohydrate, 3 g fiber, 2 g protein.
Diabetic Exchanges: 1-1/2 fruit, 1-1/2 fat, 1 starch.

Fruit Pizza

(Pictured on page 201)

For an easy showstopper, give eye-popping fruit pizza a try. Like everyone else, I enjoy desserts…but not the calories that come with them. My roommates and I don't feel guilty about gobbling down a pizza with good-for-you toppings like strawberries, kiwifruit and pineapple.
—Julie Meyer, Madison, Wisconsin

1 sheet refrigerated pie pastry
1 cup water
1 package (.8 ounce) sugar-free cook-and-serve vanilla pudding mix
1 package (.3 ounce) sugar-free lemon gelatin
1 package (8 ounces) fat-free cream cheese, cubed
Sugar substitute equivalent to 2 tablespoons sugar
1/2 cup reduced-fat whipped topping
1-1/2 cups quartered fresh strawberries
1-1/2 cups sliced halved peeled kiwifruit
1 can (8 ounces) unsweetened pineapple chunks, drained

On a lightly floured surface, roll out pastry to a 12-in. circle. Transfer to a 14-in. pizza pan; prick with a fork. Bake at 450° for 6-8 minutes or until golden brown. Cool on a wire rack.

In a saucepan, combine the water and pudding mix until smooth. Bring to a boil over medium heat, stirring constantly. Whisk in gelatin; cook and stir 1 minute longer or until thickened. Remove from the heat and let cool.

In a small mixing bowl, beat cream cheese and sugar substitute until smooth; fold in whipped topping. Spread cream cheese mixture over crust to within 1/2 in. of edges. Spread gelatin mixture evenly over cream cheese mixture. Arrange fruit over top. Refrigerate for 1 hour or until chilled. Refrigerate leftovers. **Yield:** 8 servings.

Editor's Note: This recipe was tested with Splenda No Calorie Sweetener. Look for it in the baking aisle of your grocery store.

Nutritional Analysis: One piece equals 212 calories, 8 g fat (4 g saturated fat), 7 mg cholesterol, 400 mg sodium, 28 g carbohydrate, 2 g fiber, 6 g protein.
Diabetic Exchanges: 1-1/2 starch, 1-1/2 fat, 1/2 fruit.

Lemon Yogurt Cream Pie

Low-sodium

(Pictured above)

Creamy lemon yogurt and grated lemon peel provide the lively flavor in this tempting dessert. It's handy to make the night before you need it.
—Susan Kostecke, St. Louis, Missouri

1 envelope unflavored gelatin
1/4 cup cold water
Sugar substitute equivalent to 1/3 cup sugar
1/3 cup lemon juice
2 cartons (6 ounces *each*) fat-free lemon yogurt
1 teaspoon grated lemon peel
1 carton (8 ounces) frozen reduced-fat whipped topping, thawed
1 reduced-fat graham cracker crust (8 inches)
Lemon slices and mint, optional

In a microwave-safe bowl, sprinkle gelatin over cold water; let stand for 1 minute. Microwave, uncovered, on high for 20 seconds. Stir in sugar substitute and lemon juice. Add yogurt and lemon peel; mix well. Fold in whipped topping; spoon into crust. Cover and refrigerate for 8 hours or overnight. Garnish with lemon slices and mint if desired. **Yield:** 8 servings.

Editor's Note: This recipe was tested with Splenda No Calorie Sweetener. Look for it in the baking aisle of your grocery store.

Nutritional Analysis: One piece equals 226 calories, 6 g fat (4 g saturated fat), 1 mg cholesterol, 130 mg sodium, 33 g carbohydrate, trace fiber, 7 g protein.
Diabetic Exchanges: 2 starch, 1/2 fat-free milk, 1/2 fat.

Sweeten the Holidays

HOLIDAYS can be troubling times for folks on a diabetic diet. So the American Diabetes Association offers these suggestions to make your celebrations a little sweeter.

- You can enjoy an occasional sugar-containing food, but it must be substituted for other carbohydrates already in your diet. If you want a small slice of pumpkin pie, for instance, give up the baked potato and toppings at dinner.
- When you are making a festive dessert, try cutting the sugar by one-third to one-half and increasing the cinnamon, nutmeg, vanilla and any other sweet-tasting spices and flavorings.
- Decide ahead of time what and how much you will eat and how you will handle social pressure to indulge in foods that are not normally in your diet.
- Take a smaller serving size of dessert or scrape off the high-fat whipped cream topping.
- Volunteer to bring a favorite low-sugar dish such as baked apples or sugar-free puddings to social functions.
- Don't take a holiday from your daily exercise routine. Continue your normal workouts in addition to extra activities such as power walking while shopping.

Rustic Peach Tart

(Pictured at right and on back cover)

Our Test Kitchen staff came up with this peachy change of pace from a traditional baked fruit pie. Great for company, it's sure to impress guests—especially when it's served warm from the oven. For a pretty presentation, serve slices with a dollop of reduced-fat whipped topping or a scoop of low-fat frozen yogurt.

3/4 cup cake flour
1/2 cup whole wheat flour
6 tablespoons sugar, *divided*
1/2 teaspoon salt
4 tablespoons cold butter
1 tablespoon canola oil
3 tablespoons cold water
2 tablespoons 1% buttermilk
2 tablespoons all-purpose flour
4 cups fresh *or* frozen sliced peaches, thawed
1 tablespoon fat-free milk

In a bowl, combine the cake flour, whole wheat flour, 2 tablespoons sugar and salt. Cut in butter until crumbly. Add oil and toss with a fork. Gradually add water and buttermilk, tossing with a fork until mixture sticks together. Shape dough into a ball; flatten dough. Wrap in plastic wrap and refrigerate for at least 1 hour.

On a lightly floured surface, roll out dough into a 14-in. circle. Transfer to a parchment-lined baking sheet. In a bowl, combine 3 tablespoons sugar and all-purpose flour; add

peaches and toss to coat. Spoon over pastry to within 2 in. of edges. Fold edges of pastry over peaches, leaving center uncovered. Brush folded edge with milk; sprinkle with remaining sugar. Bake at 400° for 25-30 minutes or until crust is golden and filling is bubbly. Use parchment paper to slide tart onto a wire rack to cool completely. Discard parchment paper. **Yield:** 8 servings.

Nutritional Analysis: *One piece equals 215 calories, 8 g fat (4 g saturated fat), 16 mg cholesterol, 210 mg sodium, 35 g carbohydrate, 3 g fiber, 3 g protein.*
Diabetic Exchanges: *1-1/2 starch, 1 fruit, 1 fat.*

Light Chocolate Cheesecake

(Pictured at right and on back cover)

I created this easy reduced-fat take on cheesecake for my mom, who loves chocolate but not the calories. People can't believe it's light. Just one small slice will satisfy your sweet tooth!
—Theresa McEndree, Hall, Montana

2 chocolate graham crackers (about 5 inches x 2-1/2 inches *each*), crushed
1/4 cup fat-free half-and-half
12 ounces reduced-fat cream cheese
1 cup (8 ounces) fat-free cottage cheese
1 cup sugar
6 tablespoons baking cocoa
1/4 cup all-purpose flour
1 teaspoon vanilla extract
1/4 cup egg substitute
1/4 cup miniature semisweet chocolate chips
1/2 square white baking chocolate, shaved
1/2 square semisweet chocolate, shaved

Coat a 9-in. springform pan with nonstick cooking spray. Sprinkle with crumbs; set aside. Place the half-and-half, cream cheese, cottage cheese, sugar, cocoa, flour and vanilla in a food processor or blender; cover and process until smooth. Transfer to a bowl; stir in egg substitute. Fold in chocolate chips.

Pour into prepared pan. Place pan on a baking sheet. Bake at 325° for 25-30 minutes or until almost set. Cool on a wire rack for 10 minutes. Carefully run a knife around the edge of pan to loosen and cool 1 hour longer. Refrigerate overnight. Remove sides of pan. Sprinkle with shaved chocolate. Refrigerate leftovers. **Yield:** 10 servings.

Nutritional Analysis: *One piece equals 243 calories, 9 g fat (5 g saturated fat), 20 mg cholesterol, 238 mg sodium, 35 g carbohydrate, 2 g fiber, 9 g protein.*
Diabetic Exchanges: *2 starch, 1 lean meat, 1 fat.*

Creme Brulee

Low-fat

This lightened-up classic from our Test Kitchen is smooth and creamy with a pleasant vanilla flavor. Instead of broiling the sugary sauce on top, we used a foolproof stovetop method so the custard is evenly coated.

- **2/3 cup sugar,** *divided*
- **2 eggs**
- **2 egg whites**
- **1-1/2 cups 2% milk**
- **1 teaspoon vanilla extract**
- **1/8 teaspoon salt**
- **3 tablespoons water**

In a bowl, whisk together 1/3 cup sugar, eggs, egg whites, milk, vanilla and salt; pour into five 6-oz. custard cups. Place cups in a baking pan. Fill pan with boiling water to a depth of 1 in. Bake, uncovered, at 325° for 25-30 minutes or until a knife inserted near the center comes out clean. Remove from water bath. Cool for 10 minutes and refrigerate.

Before serving, in a heavy saucepan over medium heat, heat water and remaining sugar until sugar is melted. Do not stir. When sugar is melted, continue to cook until syrup is golden, about 5 minutes, swirling pan occasionally. With a spoon, quickly pour over custards, tilting cups to coat custard with syrup. Serve immediately. Refrigerate leftovers. **Yield:** 5 servings.

Nutritional Analysis: *One serving equals 183 calories, 3 g fat (2 g saturated fat), 91 mg cholesterol, 150 mg sodium, 31 g carbohydrate, 0 fiber, 7 g protein.*
Diabetic Exchanges: *2 starch, 1 lean meat.*

No-Bake Lemon Cheesecake

Low-carb

(Pictured above right)

This dazzling dessert is a dieter's delight. A light and refreshing alternative to classic cheesecake, the slim sweet calls for gelatin and lower-fat cheeses. Vary the gelatin and pie filling flavors to suit your family's taste.
—Eva Wright, Grant, Alabama

- **1 reduced-fat honey graham cracker (5 inches x 2-1/2 inches), crushed**
- **1 package (.3 ounce) sugar-free lemon gelatin**
- **2/3 cup boiling water**
- **1 package (8 ounces) reduced-fat cream cheese, cubed**
- **1 cup (8 ounces) 1% cottage cheese**
- **2 cups reduced-fat whipped topping**
- **1 cup reduced-sugar cherry pie filling**

Coat a 9-in. springform pan with nonstick cooking spray. Sprinkle half of graham cracker crumbs on the bottom and 1 in. up the sides of pan; set aside. Dissolve gelatin in boiling water; cool to room temperature.

In a blender, combine the gelatin mixture, cream cheese and cottage cheese; cover and process until smooth. Transfer mixture to a bowl; fold in whipped topping. Pour into prepared pan.

Sprinkle with remaining graham cracker crumbs. Cover and refrigerate for at least 4 hours or until set. Carefully run a knife around edge of pan to loosen, then remove sides of pan. Garnish with pie filling. **Yield:** 8 servings.

Nutritional Analysis: *One piece equals 163 calories, 8 g fat (5 g saturated fat), 17 mg cholesterol, 240 mg sodium, 15 g carbohydrate, trace fiber, 7 g protein.*
Diabetic Exchanges: *1 lean meat, 1 fat, 1/2 starch, 1/2 fruit.*

🍎 Crumb Crust Capers

HERE'S one of the tricks I use when making a crumb crust for a dessert. I reduce the amount of butter or margarine by one tablespoon and press the crumb mixture into the pan.

Then I spray the crust with nonstick cooking spray. This gives it an extra crispness without adding fat. Plus, I found it keeps the crust from getting soggy from the filling.
—Vera Kina
Foster City, California

Favorite Recipe Made Lighter

WHO wouldn't like a treat that combines the best of chocolate chip, oatmeal and peanut butter cookies—all in one? That's just what you get in Out-on-the-Range Cookies from Sharon Weaver of Fort Collins, Colorado.

"I bake these cookies for our two nephews when they make their annual trip to visit us," she explains. "They love them. The problem is that the recipe has far too much fat and sugar in it, so we only make it for this one visit—never just for us. I would love a makeover version of this recipe."

The staff in our Test Kitchen was happy to lend a hand. To reduce the fat, they replaced the shortening with about half the amount of butter, substituted two egg whites for one of the eggs and used only half the peanut butter, substituting the reduced-fat variety.

They cut back on the amount of sugar in the original recipe, too. And finally, they added a bit of cornstarch to keep the cookie's wonderful melt-in-your-mouth texture.

The revised recipe makes a smaller batch, but yields cookies the same size as the original. The fat in each cookie was reduced by 40% and the calories by about 15%. Yet they remain sweet, crunchy and a terrific treat for kids of any age.

Out-on-the-Range Cookies

Low-carb   Low-sodium

3/4 cup shortening
1-1/4 cups packed brown sugar
1 cup sugar
2 eggs
1 cup peanut butter
1 teaspoon vanilla extract
1-3/4 cups all-purpose flour
1 cup quick-cooking oats
2 teaspoons baking soda
1/2 teaspoon salt
1 cup (6 ounces) semisweet chocolate chips

In a mixing bowl, cream shortening and sugars. Add eggs, one at a time, beating well after each addition. Beat in peanut butter and vanilla. Combine the flour, oats, baking soda and salt; gradually add to the creamed mixture. Stir in chips.

Drop by rounded tablespoonfuls 2 in. apart onto greased baking sheets. Bake at 325° for 12-14 minutes or until golden brown. Remove to wire racks to cool. **Yield:** 4-1/2 dozen.

Nutritional Analysis: One cookie equals 122 calories, 7 g fat (2 g saturated fat), 8 mg cholesterol, 96 mg sodium, 15 g carbohydrate, 1 g fiber, 2 g protein.

Makeover Out-on-the-Range Cookies

Low-sodium

(Pictured below)

6 tablespoons butter, softened
3/4 cup sugar
3/4 cup packed brown sugar
1 egg
2 egg whites
1/2 cup reduced-fat peanut butter
1 teaspoon vanilla extract
1/2 teaspoon butter flavoring, optional
1-1/2 cups all-purpose flour
1 cup quick-cooking oats
1/4 cup cornstarch
1/2 teaspoon baking soda
1/2 teaspoon baking powder
1/2 teaspoon salt
1/2 cup miniature semisweet chocolate chips

In a mixing bowl, beat butter and sugars until crumbly, about 2 minutes. Add the next five ingredients; mix well. Combine dry ingredients; gradually add to the creamed mixture. Stir in chips.

Drop by rounded tablespoonfuls 2 in. apart onto ungreased baking sheets. Bake at 325° for 12-14 minutes or until golden brown. Remove to wire racks to cool. **Yield:** 3-1/2 dozen.

Nutritional Analysis: One cookie equals 103 calories, 4 g fat (2 g saturated fat), 10 mg cholesterol, 93 mg sodium, 16 g carbohydrate, 1 g fiber, 2 g protein.
Diabetic Exchanges: 1 starch, 1/2 fat.

Orange Angel Food Cake Dessert

Low-fat

With just one bite of light-as-air angel food, even dieters will be on cloud nine! Cutting back on the fat and sugar doesn't squeeze the flavor from the sunny citrus cake I make frequently.
—Janet Springer, St. Petersburg, Florida

1 package (16 ounces) angel food cake mix
1 package (.3 ounce) sugar-free orange gelatin
3/4 cup boiling water
1/2 cup cold water
1-1/2 cups cold fat-free milk
1 package (1 ounce) sugar-free instant vanilla pudding mix
1 teaspoon orange extract
1 carton (8 ounces) frozen reduced-fat whipped topping, thawed
1 small navel orange, halved and sliced
1/2 cup sliced almonds, toasted

Prepare and bake cake according to package directions, using an ungreased 10-in. tube pan. Immediately invert tube pan; cool completely.

In a small bowl, dissolve gelatin in boiling water; stir in cold water and set aside. Cut cake into 2-in. slices; arrange cake slices in an ungreased 13-in. x 9-in. x 2-in. dish. With a meat fork, poke holes about 2 in. apart into the cake. Slowly pour gelatin over cake; refrigerate.

In a bowl, whisk milk and pudding mix for 2 minutes. Whisk in extract. Let stand for 2 minutes or until soft-set. Fold in whipped topping. Spread over cake. Garnish with orange slices and almonds. Cover and refrigerate until serving. **Yield:** 15 servings.

Nutritional Analysis: One piece equals 184 calories, 3 g fat (2 g saturated fat), trace cholesterol, 285 mg sodium, 32 g carbohydrate, 1 g fiber, 5 g protein.
Diabetic Exchanges: 2 starch, 1/2 fat.

Lemon Raspberry-Filled Cake

(Pictured at right)

This attractive layer cake tastes as good as it looks. It's special enough for company...but you'll have to convince your guests it's light.
—Heidi Scott, Appleton, Wisconsin

1 package (18-1/4 ounces) lemon cake mix
2 eggs

1 egg white
1-1/4 cups water
1/4 cup baking fat replacement
FROSTING:
2 cups confectioners' sugar
2 tablespoons butter, softened
1 teaspoon vanilla extract
1/8 teaspoon salt
2 to 3 tablespoons fat-free milk
1/2 cup 100% raspberry spreadable fruit

Coat two 9-in. round baking pans with nonstick cooking spray and line with waxed paper. Coat the waxed paper with nonstick spray and flour; set aside. In a large mixing bowl, combine the cake mix, eggs, egg white, water and baking fat replacement; beat on low speed for 30 seconds. Beat on medium for 2 minutes. Pour into prepared pans. Bake at 350° for 30-35 minutes or until a toothpick inserted near the center comes out clean. Cool on wire racks for 10 minutes; remove from pans to cool.

In a mixing bowl, beat first five frosting ingredients until smooth. Place a cake layer on a serving plate. Spread with spreadable fruit. Top with second layer; frost top of cake. **Yield:** 12 servings.

Editor's Note: This recipe was tested with Smucker's Baking Healthy. Look for it in the baking aisle of your grocery store.

Nutritional Analysis: One piece equals 299 calories, 6 g fat (3 g saturated fat), 41 mg cholesterol, 338 mg sodium, 59 g carbohydrate, 1 g fiber, 3 g protein.

Blackberry Frozen Yogurt

Low-fat   Low-sodium

(Pictured at right)

I pair sweet blackberries with tangy vanilla yogurt to churn out this purple delight. You could also use boysenberries, raspberries or strawberries.
—Rebecca Baird, Salt Lake City, Utah

5 cups fresh *or* frozen blackberries
1/3 cup water
2 tablespoons lemon juice
1 cup sugar
2 teaspoons vanilla extract
4 cups (32 ounces) fat-free vanilla yogurt

In a food processor or blender, puree blackberries, water and lemon juice. Strain blackberries, reserving juice and pulp. Discard seeds. Return pureed blackberries to food processor; add sugar and vanilla. Cover and process until smooth.

In a bowl, combine yogurt and blackberry mixture; mix well. Freeze in an ice cream freezer according to manufacturer's instructions. Allow to ripen in ice cream freezer or firm up in your refrigerator freezer 2-4 hours before serving. **Yield:** 8 servings.

Nutritional Analysis: One serving (3/4 cup) equals 248 calories, 1 g fat (trace saturated fat), 2 mg cholesterol, 78 mg sodium, 57 g carbohydrate, 5 g fiber, 6 g protein.

White Chocolate Cranberry Granola Bars

Low-fat   Low-sodium

I created these chewy granola bars while searching for a healthy snack for my family. Now, wherever we go, folks request these bars—and the recipe.
—Janis Loomis, Madison, Virginia

1/4 cup sugar
1/4 cup maple syrup
1/4 cup honey
  2 tablespoons reduced-fat peanut butter
  1 egg white
  1 tablespoon fat-free evaporated milk
  1 teaspoon vanilla extract
  1 cup whole wheat flour
1/2 teaspoon baking soda
1/2 teaspoon ground cinnamon
1/4 teaspoon ground allspice
  2 cups old-fashioned oats
1-1/2 cups crisp rice cereal
1/3 cup vanilla *or* white chips
1/4 cup dried cranberries
1/4 cup chopped walnuts

In a large bowl, combine the first seven ingredients; mix well. Combine the flour, baking soda, cinnamon and all-spice; add to the sugar mixture. Stir in remaining ingredients.

Press into a 13-in. x 9-in. x 2-in. baking pan coated with nonstick cooking spray. Bake at 350° for 18-20 minutes or until golden brown. Score the surface with shallow cuts, making rectangular bars. Cool completely on a wire rack. Cut along score lines. **Yield:** 2 dozen.

Nutritional Analysis: One bar equals 109 calories, 3 g fat (1 g saturated fat), 1 mg cholesterol, 57 mg sodium, 20 g carbo-hydrate, 2 g fiber, 3 g protein.
Diabetic Exchange: 1-1/2 starch.

Lime Honeydew Sorbet

Low-fat   Low-sodium

(Pictured above and on front cover)

This frosty dessert that relies on an ice cream freezer is a refreshing end to a spring or summer meal. The burst of lime in each spoonful is complemented by a pleasant hint of honeydew. Our Test Kitchen created the recipe.

  3 cups cubed honeydew
1/2 cup sugar
1/2 cup lime juice
  1 tablespoon sweet white wine *or* water
  2 teaspoons grated lime peel
  2 to 3 drops green food coloring, optional

In a food processor or blender, combine honeydew and sug-ar; cover and process until sugar is dissolved. Add the re-maining ingredients; cover and process until blended.

Freeze in an ice cream freezer according to manufac-turer's directions. Spoon mixture into a freezer-safe con-tainer; cover and freeze in the refrigerator freezer 2-4 hours before serving. **Yield:** 4 servings.

Nutritional Analysis: One serving (3/4 cup) equals 154 calo-ries, trace fat (trace saturated fat), 0 cholesterol, 14 mg sodium, 40 g carbohydrate, 1 g fiber, 1 g protein.
Diabetic Exchanges: 1-1/2 fruit, 1 starch.

Blondies with Chips

Low-sodium

My friends and family love this pared-down version of the classic snack and never suspect that I use whole wheat flour.
—Kai Skupinski, Canton, Michigan

1/3 cup all-purpose flour
1/3 cup whole wheat flour
1/4 cup packed brown sugar
1/2 teaspoon baking powder
1/4 teaspoon salt
  1 egg
1/4 cup canola oil
  2 tablespoons honey
  1 teaspoon vanilla extract
1/2 cup semisweet chocolate chips

In a small bowl, combine the first five ingredients. Whisk the egg, oil, honey and vanilla; stir into dry ingredients until blended. Stir in chocolate chips. (Batter will be thick.)

Spread into an 8-in. square baking dish coated with non-stick cooking spray. Bake at 350° for 20-22 minutes or until a toothpick inserted near the center comes out clean. Cool on a wire rack. Cut into bars. **Yield:** 12 servings.

Nutritional Analysis: One bar equals 133 calories, 7 g fat (2 g saturated fat), 18 mg cholesterol, 67 mg sodium, 17 g carbohydrate, 1 g fiber, 2 g protein.
Diabetic Exchanges: 1 starch, 1 fat.

🍎 Low-Fat Brownies

A FRIEND told me about this neat baking trick for lowering the fat in brownies, and it really works! I prepared a deluxe brownie mix according to the package directions, but did not add the oil called for.

I didn't substitute anything for it...I eliminated it altogether. The brownies were as moist and tasty as usual. Even my husband, Jim, who can tell when I change anything, could not tell the difference!
—*LaDonna Reed, Ponca City, Oklahoma*

Strawberry Cream Dessert

This "berry" light and creamy dessert is a fantastic finale to a special meal. For a fun variation, use instant lemon pudding with mandarin oranges and pineapple tidbits mixed in.
—*Nancy Haigh, Philip, South Dakota*

1 package (8 ounces) reduced-fat cream cheese, softened
1 carton (8 ounces) reduced-fat whipped topping, thawed
3 cups cold fat-free milk
2 packages (1 ounce *each*) sugar-free instant vanilla pudding mix
2 pints fresh strawberries, halved

In a large mixing bowl, beat cream cheese until smooth. Beat in whipped topping on low speed until smooth; set aside. In another large mixing bowl, combine milk and pudding mixes. Beat on low speed for 2 minutes. Let stand for 5 minutes. Stir in cream cheese mixture until smooth. Set aside 1 cup of strawberries. Fold remaining strawberries into pudding mixture. Transfer to a serving bowl or individual dessert dishes. Cover and refrigerate for at least 2 hours. Arrange remaining strawberries on top. **Yield:** 8 servings.

Nutritional Analysis: One serving (about 3/4 cup) equals 216 calories, 9 g fat (7 g saturated fat), 18 mg cholesterol, 428 mg sodium, 25 g carbohydrate, 2 g fiber, 7 g protein.
Diabetic Exchanges: 1-1/2 starch, 1-1/2 fat, 1/2 fruit.

Walnut Raisin Apple Cookies

(Pictured below)

These chunky cookies are jam-packed with goodies...from apples and raisins to oats and nuts. They're perfect for taking to potlucks.
—*Amber Gregoire, Monterey, Tennessee*

1/4 cup butter, softened
1 cup packed brown sugar
2 eggs
1/4 cup unsweetened apple juice
1/4 teaspoon lemon extract
1-1/2 cups all-purpose flour
1 cup quick-cooking oats
1 teaspoon ground cinnamon
3/4 teaspoon baking soda
3/4 teaspoon salt
1/4 teaspoon ground nutmeg
1/8 teaspoon ground cloves
1-1/2 cups chopped peeled tart apples (about 2 medium)
1 cup raisins
1/2 cup chopped walnuts

In a mixing bowl, cream butter and brown sugar until crumbly, about 2 minutes. Add eggs, one at a time, beating well after each addition. Add apple juice and lemon extract. Combine the flour, oats, cinnamon, baking soda, salt, nutmeg and cloves. Gradually add to creamed mixture. Stir in the apples, raisins and walnuts.

Drop by rounded tablespoonfuls 2 in. apart onto ungreased baking sheets. Bake at 350° for 11-13 minutes or until lightly browned. Remove to wire racks. **Yield:** 4 dozen.

Nutritional Analysis: One serving (2 cookies) equals 139 calories, 4 g fat (2 g saturated fat), 23 mg cholesterol, 143 mg sodium, 24 g carbohydrate, 1 g fiber, 2 g protein.
Diabetic Exchanges: 1 starch, 1 fat, 1/2 fruit.

Orange Parfaits

Low-sodium

The first time my son's fiancee tried this citrus parfait, she wanted the recipe. The next time, she wanted the leftovers!
—Deborah Greenwood, Elmer, New Jersey

    2 envelopes unflavored gelatin
1/2 cup orange juice
    1 cup fat-free milk
    1 package (8 ounces) reduced-fat cream cheese
1/3 cup sugar
    1 teaspoon vanilla extract
1/2 teaspoon grated orange peel
    1 can (11 ounces) mandarin oranges, undrained
    1 can (20 ounces) unsweetened crushed pineapple, undrained
    1 carton (8 ounces) reduced-fat frozen whipped topping, thawed
1/2 cup chocolate graham cracker crumbs (about 12 crackers), *divided*

In a bowl, combine gelatin and orange juice; let stand for 5 minutes. Heat milk until boiling. Add milk to gelatin. Let stand to cool slightly. Place in a blender; cover and process for 30 seconds or until blended. Add the cream cheese, sugar, vanilla and orange peel; process until blended.

Drain oranges; reserve juice. Add pineapple and reserved juice to gelatin mixture. Process until smooth; fold in whipped topping. Set aside 2 tablespoons crumbs for topping. Place half the oranges into eight parfait glasses. Layer with half the gelatin mixture and half the remaining crumbs. Repeat gelatin and crumb layers; top with remaining oranges. Chill for 4 hours. Top with reserved crumbs. **Yield:** 8 servings.

Nutritional Analysis: One parfait equals 277 calories, 10 g fat (7 g saturated fat), 17 mg cholesterol, 130 mg sodium, 39 g carbohydrate, 1 g fiber, 6 g protein.
Diabetic Exchanges: 2 fat, 1-1/2 starch, 1 fruit.

Double Blueberry Pie

(Pictured at right)

Blueberry lovers are sure to enjoy this mouth-watering deep-dish pie. The cream cheese layer is a nice surprise.
—Jay Holzworth, Murray, Utah

6 ounces reduced-fat cream cheese
2 tablespoons fat-free milk

1/2 teaspoon lemon extract
    1 pastry shell (9 inches), baked
    2 tablespoons cornstarch
1/4 cup water
    1 tablespoon lemon juice
    4 cups fresh *or* frozen blueberries, *divided*
Sugar substitute equivalent to 1/2 cup sugar

In a small mixing bowl, beat the cream cheese, milk and extract until smooth; spread onto bottom of pastry shell.

In a saucepan, combine the cornstarch, water and lemon juice until smooth. Mash 2 cups blueberries and add to the pan. Bring to a boil; cook and stir for 1-2 minutes or until thickened. Remove from the heat; cool for 15 minutes.

Stir in sugar substitute. Spoon over cream cheese mixture. Top with remaining blueberries. Refrigerate for 3 hours or until set. Refrigerate leftovers. **Yield:** 8 servings.

Editor's Note: This recipe was tested with Splenda No Calorie Sweetener. Look for it in the baking aisle of your grocery store.

Nutritional Analysis: One piece equals 231 calories, 12 g fat (6 g saturated fat), 21 mg cholesterol, 191 mg sodium, 28 g carbohydrate, 2 g fiber, 4 g protein.
Diabetic Exchanges: 2 fat, 1 fruit, 1 starch.

Strawberry-Lemon Angel Cake

(Pictured at right)

I couldn't decide how to use the lemon curd a friend had given me, so I tried spreading it between layers of angel food cake. I topped each piece with strawberries. We loved it! Now I make my own lemon curd just for this dessert.
—Marietta Eklund, Pittsburgh, Pennsylvania

    1 package (16 ounces) angel food cake mix
    3 eggs
    1 cup sugar
1/2 cup lemon juice
    6 tablespoons butter, melted
    2 tablespoons grated lemon peel
    4 to 5 drops yellow food coloring, optional
    1 quart fresh strawberries, sliced

Prepare cake batter according to package directions. For lemon curd, in the top of a double boiler, beat eggs and sugar. Stir in the lemon juice, butter and lemon peel. Cook over simmering water for 15 minutes or until mixture has thickened and a thermometer reads 160°. Strain to remove peel and stir in food coloring if desired. Refrigerate.

Split cake horizontally into three layers. Place bottom layer on a serving plate; top with a third of the lemon curd. Repeat layers twice. Refrigerate until serving. Garnish with strawberries. **Yield:** 14 servings.

Nutritional Analysis: One serving (1 piece with strawberries) equals 248 calories, 6 g fat (3 g saturated fat), 59 mg cholesterol, 256 mg sodium, 45 g carbohydrate, 1 g fiber, 5 g protein.
Diabetic Exchanges: 2-1/2 starch, 1 fat, 1/2 fruit.

Candy Chip Bar Cookies

Low-sodium

(Pictured below)

I try to cut back on the saturated fats and trans fats my family consumes. So I fix these sweet homemade bars, which have less fat than commercial baked goods.
— *Wendy Budlong, Acton, Massachusetts*

1/2 cup canola oil
1/2 cup packed brown sugar
Sugar substitute equal to 1/2 cup sugar
1/4 cup reduced-fat peanut butter
1 egg
1 teaspoon vanilla extract
2 cups all-purpose flour
1/2 teaspoon baking soda
1/4 teaspoon salt
3/4 cup miniature semisweet M&M baking bits

In a bowl, combine the oil, brown sugar, sugar substitute, peanut butter, egg and vanilla. Combine the flour, baking soda and salt; stir into the peanut butter mixture. Stir in baking bits.

Spread in a 13-in. x 9-in. x 2-in. baking pan coated with nonstick cooking spray. Bake at 350° for 12-15 minutes or until lightly browned. Cool on a wire rack. **Yield:** 1-1/2 dozen.

*Editor's Note: This recipe was tested with Splenda No Calorie Sweetener. Look for it in the baking aisle of your grocery store.

Nutritional Analysis: One piece equals 204 calories, 10 g fat (2 g saturated fat), 13 mg cholesterol, 108 mg sodium, 25 g carbohydrate, 1 g fiber, 3 g protein.
Diabetic Exchanges: *2 fat, 1-1/2 starch.*

Oat Berry Squares

Low-sodium

Spreadable fruit and a crumb topping flavor these popular snack bars. I found the original recipe in an old children's book, but I pared down the sugar and added more fruit for sweetness. I'm always asked for the recipe.
— *Jennifer Robinson, Clover, South Carolina*

1 cup whole wheat flour
1 cup quick-cooking oats
2/3 cup packed brown sugar
1/2 teaspoon baking soda
1/4 teaspoon salt
1/3 cup butter, melted
1 jar (10 ounces) 100% cherry, strawberry *or* raspberry spreadable fruit

In a large bowl, combine the flour, oats, brown sugar, baking soda and salt; stir in butter. Reserve 3/4 cup for topping. Pat remaining oat mixture into a 9-in. square baking pan coated with nonstick cooking spray. Bake at 350° for 5-7 minutes. Spread with fruit spread. Sprinkle with the reserved crumb mixture. Bake 25-30 minutes or until edges are lightly browned. Cool on a wire rack. **Yield:** 16 servings.

Nutritional Analysis: One piece equals 150 calories, 4 g fat (2 g saturated fat), 10 mg cholesterol, 118 mg sodium, 27 g carbohydrate, 1 g fiber, 2 g protein.
Diabetic Exchanges: *1 starch, 1/2 fruit, 1/2 fat.*

Banana Anna Surprise

Low-fat

This quick-to-fix layered dessert looks so pretty spooned into dessert glasses. You can also make this recipe in an 8-inch square glass dish and replace the strawberry gelatin with your favorite flavor.
— *Eva Wright, Grant, Alabama*

1 package (.3 ounce) sugar-free strawberry gelatin
3/4 cup boiling water
1/2 cup cold water
3/4 cup ice cubes
2 medium firm bananas, sliced
4 ounces fat-free cream cheese, cubed
1/2 cup fat-free whipped topping
1 teaspoon grated lemon peel

In a bowl, dissolve gelatin in boiling water. Combine cold water and ice cubes; add to gelatin. Stir until slightly thickened; remove any unmelted ice. Add bananas. Spoon half of the gelatin into four dessert glasses. Refrigerate for 30 minutes or until firm.

In a blender or food processor, combine the cream cheese, whipped topping and lemon peel; cover and process until smooth. Spoon into glasses. Top with remaining gelatin. Refrigerate for 3 hours or until firm. **Yield:** 4 servings.

Nutritional Analysis: One serving equals 103 calories, trace fat (trace saturated fat), 3 mg cholesterol, 202 mg sodium, 19 g carbohydrate, 1 g fiber, 6 g protein.
Diabetic Exchanges: 1 fruit, 1 very lean meat.

Low-Calorie Pumpkin Pie

Low-fat

(Pictured above)

I've brought this crustless pie to the office, and no one knows it's sugar-free. Even the fellow who says he doesn't eat anything healthy likes its traditional pumpkin pie flavor.
—Diane Jessen, Roeland Park, Kansas

1 egg
2 egg whites
1 can (15 ounces) solid-pack pumpkin
Sugar substitute equivalent to 3/4 cup sugar
1/2 cup reduced-fat biscuit/baking mix
1 teaspoon vanilla extract
1 teaspoon ground cinnamon
1/2 teaspoon ground ginger
1/4 teaspoon ground cloves
1 can (12 ounces) fat-free evaporated milk
1 cup reduced-fat whipped topping

In a large mixing bowl, combine the egg, egg whites, pumpkin, sugar substitute, biscuit mix, vanilla and spices until smooth. Gradually stir in evaporated milk.

Pour into a 9-in. pie plate coated with nonstick cooking spray. Bake at 350° for 35-40 minutes or until a knife inserted near the center comes out clean. Cool on a wire rack. Dollop with whipped topping before serving. Refrigerate leftovers. **Yield:** 8 servings.

Editor's Note: This recipe was tested with Splenda No Calorie Sweetener. Look for it in the baking aisle of your grocery store.

Nutritional Analysis: One piece with 2 tablespoons topping equals 124 calories, 2 g fat (1 g saturated fat), 28 mg cholesterol, 160 mg sodium, 19 g carbohydrate, 3 g fiber, 6 g protein.
Diabetic Exchange: 1-1/2 starch.

Cocoa Chip Cookies

Low-carb   Low-fat   Low-sodium

Our Test Kitchen staff whipped up these soft airy cookies using a double dose of chocolate flavor from baking cocoa and semisweet chips. The lower-in-sugar treats are sure to please the chocoholic in your family!

- 2 tablespoons butter, softened
- 2 ounces reduced-fat cream cheese, cubed
- 6 tablespoons sugar
- 6 tablespoons brown sugar
- 1 egg
- 1 egg white
- 1 cup all-purpose flour
- 3 tablespoons baking cocoa
- 1/2 teaspoon baking soda
- 1/2 teaspoon salt
- 1/2 cup semisweet miniature chocolate chips

In a mixing bowl, cream the butter, cream cheese and sugars. Add the egg and egg white; mix well. Combine the flour, cocoa, baking soda and salt; gradually add to the creamed mixture. Stir in chocolate chips.

Drop by rounded tablespoonfuls 2 in. apart onto baking sheets coated with nonstick spray. Bake at 375° for 7-10 minutes or until edges are set. Cool for 2 minutes before removing to wire racks. Store in an airtight container. **Yield:** 2-1/2 dozen.

Nutritional Analysis: One cookie equals 64 calories, 2 g fat (1 g saturated fat), 10 mg cholesterol, 79 mg sodium, 11 g carbohydrate, trace fiber, 1 g protein.
Diabetic Exchange: 1 starch.

Blueberry Oat Dessert

(Pictured above)

I've been preparing these blueberry squares for more than 10 years now, and everyone looks forward to them. The recipe looks time-consuming, but it's not difficult at all.
—Mary Arkoette, Huntington, Massachusetts

- 1/4 cup sugar
- 2 tablespoons cornstarch
- 1/3 cup water
- 1 teaspoon lemon juice
- 2-1/2 cups fresh *or* frozen blueberries
- 1 package (18-1/4 ounces) yellow cake mix
- 1-1/2 cups quick-cooking oats, *divided*
- 8 tablespoons cold butter, *divided*
- 1/4 cup egg substitute
- 1/4 cup packed brown sugar

In a saucepan, combine sugar and cornstarch. Gradually whisk in water and lemon juice until smooth. Bring to a boil, stirring constantly. Stir in blueberries. Cook and stir for 2 minutes longer or until thickened and bubbly. Remove from the heat; set aside.

In a bowl, combine the dry cake mix and 1 cup oats. Cut in 6 tablespoons butter until crumbly. Set aside 1 cup crumb mixture for topping. Stir egg substitute into remaining crumb mixture. Press into a 13-in. x 9-in. x 2-in. baking dish coated with nonstick cooking spray. Spread blueberry mixture to within 1/4 in. of edges. Combine the brown sugar, remaining oats and reserved crumb mixture. Cut in remaining butter until crumbly. Sprinkle over top. Bake at 350° for 30-35 minutes or until golden brown. Serve warm. **Yield:** 18 servings.

Nutritional Analysis: One piece equals 232 calories, 8 g fat (4 g saturated fat), 14 mg cholesterol, 261 mg sodium, 37 g carbohydrate, 1 g fiber, 3 g protein.
Diabetic Exchanges: 2 starch, 1 fat , 1/2 fruit.

Marinated Oranges

Low-fat   Low-sodium

This flavorful fruit was actually the topping in a cake recipe. But I didn't want all the calories or fat from the cake—and the oranges are a good dessert all by themselves! The dash of vanilla extract brings out the fruit's sweetness.
—Carol Poindexter, Norridge, Illinois

- 4 medium oranges, peeled and thinly sliced (about 3 cups)
- 1 cup orange juice
- 1 tablespoon sugar
- 1 tablespoon lemon juice
- 1 tablespoon grated orange peel
- 1 teaspoon grated lemon peel
- 1 teaspoon vanilla extract

Reduced-fat vanilla yogurt, optional

Place the orange slices in an 8-in. square baking dish; set aside. In a bowl, combine the orange juice, sugar, lemon juice, peels and vanilla; pour over the oranges. Cover and refrigerate for 2-3 hours. Serve with a slotted spoon. Top with vanilla yogurt if desired. **Yield:** 4 servings.

Nutritional Analysis: One serving (3/4 cup fruit, calculated without yogurt) equals 88 calories, trace fat (trace saturated fat), 0 cholesterol, 2 mg sodium, 22 g carbohydrate, 4 g fiber, 1 g protein.
Diabetic Exchange: 1-1/2 fruit.

Favorite Recipe Made Lighter

KATHLEEN Hackford of West Seneca, New York is sweet on her yummy Cherry Coconut Bars. The crumbly treats have a shortbread-like crust and a gooey cherry, coconut and chopped nut filling that makes them a favorite with family and friends. Unfortunately, they're also rich in fat and calories.

"I would love to see these delicious bars lightened up," says Kathleen.

Our Test Kitchen staff was eager to help out. They began by reducing the 1/2 cup of butter in the shortbread crust to just 3 tablespoons. To ensure a crispy crust, they cut the cold butter into the flour and confectioners' sugar using a food processor. Merely minimizing the butter helped to significantly reduce the calories, fat, saturated fat, cholesterol and sodium in the revamped recipe.

To cut even more calories, our staff reduced the amount of walnuts and coconut. They also substituted 1 egg and 2 egg whites for the 2 eggs in the original recipe to bring down the cholesterol count.

Makeover Cherry Coconut Bars have less than half of the fat, saturated fat and cholesterol of the original recipe...plus 32% fewer calories. Yet the thin crust retains its buttery taste and the fruity filling is still sweet and gooey.

Cherry Coconut Bars

1 cup all-purpose flour
3 tablespoons confectioners' sugar
1/2 cup cold butter
FILLING:
2 eggs
1 cup sugar
1 teaspoon vanilla extract
1/4 cup all-purpose flour
1/2 teaspoon baking powder
1/4 teaspoon salt
3/4 cup chopped walnuts
1/2 cup flaked coconut
1/2 cup quartered maraschino cherries

In a bowl, combine flour and confectioners' sugar; cut in butter until crumbly. Press into an ungreased 9-in. square baking pan. Bake at 350° for 15-20 minutes or until lightly browned. Cool on a wire rack.

For filling, combine the eggs, sugar and vanilla in a bowl. Combine the flour, baking powder and salt; add the egg mixture. Stir in nuts, coconut and cherries. Spread over crust. Bake for 20-25 minutes or until firm. Cool on a wire rack. Cut into bars. Refrigerate leftovers. **Yield:** 1 dozen.

Nutritional Analysis: One bar equals 284 calories, 15 g fat (7 g saturated fat), 56 mg cholesterol, 178 mg sodium, 35 g carbohydrate, 1 g fiber, 4 g protein.

Makeover Cherry Coconut Bars

Low-sodium

(Pictured below)

3/4 cup all-purpose flour
3 tablespoons confectioners' sugar
3 tablespoons cold butter
FILLING:
1 egg
2 egg whites
1 cup sugar
1 teaspoon vanilla extract
1/4 cup all-purpose flour
1/2 teaspoon baking powder
1/4 teaspoon salt
1/2 cup quartered maraschino cherries
1/3 cup chopped walnuts
1/3 cup flaked coconut

In a food processor, place flour and confectioners' sugar; cover and process until blended. Add butter; cover and pulse 15 times or until mixture resembles fine crumbs. Press into a 9-in. square baking pan coated with nonstick cooking spray. Bake at 350° for 12-15 minutes or until lightly browned. Cool on a wire rack.

For filling, combine the egg, egg whites, sugar and vanilla in a bowl. Combine the flour, baking powder and salt; add the egg mixture. Stir in the cherries, nuts and coconut. Spread over crust. Bake for 20-25 minutes or until firm. Cool on a wire rack. Cut into bars. Refrigerate leftovers. **Yield:** 1 dozen.

Nutritional Analysis: One bar equals 194 calories, 7 g fat (3 g saturated fat), 25 mg cholesterol, 128 mg sodium, 31 g carbohydrate, 1 g fiber, 3 g protein.
Diabetic Exchanges: 2 starch, 1 fat.

Cheery Cherry Crisp

Low-sodium

I love the aroma and flavor of basil! So when I found a recipe that called for basil in a strawberry-rhubarb crisp, I couldn't wait to try it. I reduced the fat in the recipe and changed the strawberries to cherries since I had a tree loaded with them. The tart fruit flavor goes perfectly with the tangy basil.
—Beth Rice, Springfield, Oregon

3-1/2 cups frozen pitted dark sweet cherries, thawed
3/4 cup sugar, *divided*
2 tablespoons cornstarch
1 cup chopped fresh *or* frozen rhubarb, thawed
2 tablespoons minced fresh basil
TOPPING:
1/2 cup all-purpose flour
1/2 cup quick-cooking oats
1/4 cup packed brown sugar
1/4 teaspoon salt
1/4 cup cold reduced-fat stick margarine

Drain cherries, reserving juice. Add enough water to measure 1/2 cup. Set cherries aside. In a microwave-safe 8-in. square dish, combine 1/2 cup sugar, cornstarch and reserved juice until smooth. Microwave, uncovered, on high for 3-4 minutes or until thickened, stirring occasionally. Gently stir in the rhubarb, basil, reserved cherries and remaining sugar.

In a bowl, combine flour, oats, brown sugar and salt. Cut in margarine until mixture resembles coarse crumbs. Sprinkle over cherry mixture. Bake, uncovered, at 350° for 30-35 minutes or until golden brown. **Yield:** 8 servings.

Editor's Note: If using frozen rhubarb, measure rhubarb while still frozen, then thaw completely. Drain in a colander, but do not press liquid out.

Nutritional Analysis: One serving (1/2 cup) equals 229 calories, 4 g fat (1 g saturated fat), 0 cholesterol, 115 mg sodium, 50 g carbohydrate, 1 g fiber, 2 g protein.

🍎 It's a Cherry Jubilee

CHERRIES have been a favorite fruit since the Stone Age. Archaeologists have found pits piled in prehistoric caves from Europe to America.

It's believed that cherries were first cultivated around 300 B.C. in the Turkish town of Cerasus, which they may have been named after.

Two main groups—sweet and tart—make up the cherry family. Sweet cherries are large, firm and heart-shaped and include varieties such as burgundy Bing and Lambert and golden-pink Royal Ann and Rainier.

Tart cherries are smaller, softer and more globular and feature types such as bright-red Montmorency and Early Richmond.

When selecting fresh cherries, look for fruit that is large, glossy, plump and firm. Those with green stems last longer.

Frozen Mousse Brownie Sandwiches

(Pictured above)

Try this tempting take on store-bought ice cream sandwiches that relies on convenient brownie and pudding mixes. The frosty hand-held treats from our Test Kitchen have a sweet filling tucked between fudgy brownie layers.

1 package reduced-fat brownie mix (13-inch x 9-inch pan size)
2 cups cold fat-free milk
2 packages (1 ounce *each*) sugar-free instant vanilla pudding mix
3 tablespoons vanilla *or* white chips, melted and cooled
1/2 cup reduced-fat whipped topping

Line the bottom and sides of two 13-in. x 9-in. x 2-in. baking pans with parchment paper. Coat the paper with nonstick cooking spray. Prepare brownie mix according to package directions; divide batter evenly between the pans.

Bake at 350° for 15-18 minutes or until edges just begin to pull away from sides of pan and a toothpick inserted near the center comes out with moist crumbs. Cool on wire racks.

For mousse, in a bowl, whisk together the milk and pudding mixes for 2 minutes. Stir a small amount of the pudding into the melted chips, then return all to the pudding. Fold in whipped topping.

Cover two large cutting boards or inverted 15-in. x 10-in. x 1-in. baking pans with plastic wrap. Invert one pan of brownies onto prepared board or pan. Gently peel off the parchment paper. Spread the mousse to within 1/2 in. of edges. Carefully invert second brownie layer onto second board or pan. Gently peel off parchment paper, then place right side up over mousse filling.

Cover and freeze for about 4 hours or until the filling is firm. Remove from the freezer 10 minutes before cutting into sandwiches. Individually wrap leftover sandwiches; store in the freezer. **Yield:** 15 servings.

Nutritional Analysis: One sandwich equals 206 calories, 5 g fat (2 g saturated fat), 1 mg cholesterol, 199 mg sodium, 40 g carbohydrate, 1 g fiber, 4 g protein.
Diabetic Exchange: 2-1/2 starch.

Lemon Berry Pie

(Pictured below)

This refreshing dessert makes a beautiful presentation and tastes delicious! To cut a few calories, I use Splenda sugar substitute instead of sugar.
—Ann Flores, Seneca, Kansas

    4 ounces reduced-fat cream cheese
    1 tablespoon plus 1 cup cold fat-free milk
    1 tablespoon sugar
    1 tablespoon lemon juice
    2 teaspoons grated lemon peel
2-1/4 cups reduced-fat whipped topping, *divided*
    1 reduced-fat graham cracker crust (8 inches)
    1 pint fresh strawberries
    1 package (3.4 ounces) instant lemon
      pudding mix

In a small mixing bowl, combine cream cheese, 1 table-spoon milk and sugar until blended. Add lemon juice and peel; mix well. Fold in 1-1/2 cups whipped topping. Carefully spread into crust. Set aside 4 strawberries. Cut remaining strawberries in half; place over cream cheese mixture.

In a bowl, place the remaining milk; whisk in pudding mix for 2 minutes or until thickened. Fold in 1/2 cup whipped topping. Spoon over strawberries. Cover and refrigerate for at least 2 hours. Garnish with remaining whipped topping and reserved strawberries. **Yield:** 8 servings.

Nutritional Analysis: One piece equals 260 calories, 9 g fat (6 g saturated fat), 13 mg cholesterol, 330 mg sodium, 38 g carbohydrate, 1 g fiber, 4 g protein.
Diabetic Exchanges: 2 starch, 1-1/2 fat, 1/2 fruit.

Baked Apple Pudding

This moist, nutty pudding seasoned with cinnamon and nutmeg is a favorite at our house.
—Margery Bryan, Moses Lake, Washington

    1/4 cup butter, softened
      1 cup sugar
      1 egg
      1 cup all-purpose flour
      1 teaspoon baking soda
    1/4 teaspoon salt
    1/4 teaspoon ground nutmeg
    1/4 teaspoon ground cinnamon
      2 cups grated peeled tart apples
    1/4 cup chopped walnuts
      1 teaspoon vanilla extract
      4 cups reduced-fat frozen vanilla yogurt

In a mixing bowl, beat together the butter, sugar and egg until blended. In a bowl, combine the flour, baking soda, salt, nutmeg and cinnamon; gradually add to the sugar mixture and mix well. Stir in the apples, walnuts and vanilla until well combined.

Spread mixture into an 8-in. square baking dish coated with nonstick cooking spray. Bake at 350° for 35-40 minutes or until pudding is lightly browned and springs back when lightly touched. Serve warm with frozen yogurt. **Yield:** 12 servings.

Nutritional Analysis: One serving (1 serving of pudding with 1/3 cup frozen yogurt) equals 243 calories, 7 g fat (3 g saturated fat), 31 mg cholesterol, 238 mg sodium, 41 g carbohydrate, 1 g fiber, 5 g protein.
Diabetic Exchanges: 2 starch, 1 low-fat milk, 1/2 fat.

Rosy Pear Compote

Low-fat   Low-sodium

Pears and cranberries bring down-home flair to this comforting compote.
—Lorraine Darocha, Mountain City, Tennessee

    6 firm ripe pears, peeled, cored and cut into
      quarters
    1 can (16 ounces) whole-berry cranberry sauce
1/4 cup sugar
    1 tablespoon lemon juice
1/4 teaspoon ground cinnamon
1/4 teaspoon ground ginger
    2 medium navel oranges, peeled, cut into
      8 slices and halved
Cinnamon sticks, optional

In a 13-in. x 9-in. x 2-in. baking dish coated with nonstick cooking spray, arrange pears. In a saucepan, combine the cranberry sauce, sugar, lemon juice, cinnamon and ginger. Cook and stir until mixture comes to a boil; pour over pears. Top with oranges.

Cover and bake at 350° for 30-35 minutes or until pears are tender. Serve warm. Garnish with cinnamon sticks if desired. **Yield:** 8 servings.

Nutritional Analysis: One serving (3 pear quarters, 4 orange pieces with 2 tablespoons sauce) equals 195 calories, 1 g fat (trace saturated fat), 0 cholesterol, 12 mg sodium, 50 g carbohydrate, 5 g fiber, 1 g protein.

Coconut Custard Pie

My husband and I are both diabetic. We really appreciate desserts such as this creamy custard pie. Coconut extract in the filling and a toasted coconut topping flavor the tasty low-sugar creation.
—Eva Wright, Grant, Alabama

1/2 cup flaked coconut
1 refrigerated pastry shell (9 inches)
4 eggs
1/2 teaspoon salt
1-3/4 cups fat-free milk
Sugar substitute equivalent to 1/2 cup sugar
1-1/2 teaspoons coconut extract
1/2 teaspoon vanilla extract

Place coconut in an ungreased 9-in. pie plate. Bake at 350° for 4 minutes, stirring several times; set aside. (Coconut will not be fully toasted.)

Line unpricked pastry shell with a double thickness of heavy-duty foil. Bake at 450° for 8 minutes. Remove foil; bake 4-6 minutes longer. Cool.

In a mixing bowl, beat the eggs and salt for 5 minutes. (Mixture will be lemon-colored and slightly thickened.) Add the milk, sugar substitute, coconut extract and vanilla. Transfer to crust. (Crust with be full.)

Bake at 350° for 30 minutes. Sprinkle with coconut. Bake 8-10 minutes longer or until a knife inserted near center comes out clean and coconut is lightly browned. Cool on wire rack for 1 hour. Cover and refrigerate. **Yield:** 8 servings.

Editor's Note: This recipe was tested with Splenda No Calorie Sweetener. Look for it in the baking aisle of your grocery store.

Nutritional Analysis: One piece equals 214 calories, 12 g fat (6 g saturated fat), 112 mg cholesterol, 322 mg sodium, 20 g carbohydrate, trace fiber, 6 g protein.
Diabetic Exchanges: 2 fat, 1-1/2 starch.

Poppy Seed Lemon Cake

(Pictured at right)

I made this moist bundt cake one Sunday for a brunch after church, and no one believed it was light.
—Marcia Fuller, Sheridan, Montana

1/4 cup butter, softened
1 cup packed brown sugar
2 eggs
4 egg whites
1 cup (8 ounces) fat-free plain yogurt
1/4 cup canola oil
2 tablespoons lemon juice
3-1/2 cups all-purpose flour
2 tablespoons grated lemon peel
4 teaspoons poppy seeds
2 teaspoons baking powder
1 teaspoon baking soda
1/2 teaspoon salt
1 cup fat-free milk

GLAZE:
1 cup confectioners' sugar
2 tablespoons plus 1-1/2 teaspoons lemon juice
1/2 teaspoon poppy seeds

Coat a 10-in. fluted tube pan with nonstick cooking spray and dust with flour; set aside. In a large mixing bowl, beat butter and brown sugar until crumbly, about 2 minutes. Add eggs and egg whites, one at a time, beating well after each addition. Beat in the yogurt, oil and lemon juice. Combine the flour, lemon peel, poppy seeds, baking powder, baking soda and salt; add to the creamed mixture alternately with milk. Pour into prepared pan.

Bake at 350° for 50-55 minutes or until a toothpick inserted near the center comes out clean. Cool for 10 minutes before inverting onto a wire rack. Cool 10 minutes longer. Place rack on waxed paper. For glaze, combine confectioners' sugar and lemon juice; brush over warm cake. Sprinkle with poppy seeds. Cool completely before cutting. **Yield:** 14 servings.

Nutritional Analysis: One piece equals 302 calories, 9 g fat (3 g saturated fat), 40 mg cholesterol, 327 mg sodium, 50 g carbohydrate, 1 g fiber, 6 g protein.

Frozen Cranberry Pie

Low-sodium

(Pictured at right)

Like everyone else, I love desserts but don't need the calories. I make this pie for my roommates, and they never complain...they just gobble it up! No one misses the calorie-laden pastry crust.
—Julie Meyer, Madison, Wisconsin

1 cup whole-berry cranberry sauce
3/4 teaspoon grated orange peel
5 cups reduced-fat vanilla ice cream, softened
4 to 5 drops red food coloring, optional
1/2 cup crushed chocolate wafers (about 9 wafers)
16 fresh *or* frozen cranberries, thawed
8 orange peel strips
2 tablespoons sugar

In a bowl, whisk cranberry sauce and orange peel until blended. Fold in ice cream and food coloring if desired. Cover and freeze for 15 minutes.

Meanwhile, sprinkle crushed wafers in a 9-in. pie plate coated with nonstick cooking spray. Freeze for 10 minutes. Spoon ice cream mixture into pie plate. Cover and freeze 4 hours or until firm. Toss cranberries and orange peel in sugar. Remove pie from freezer 10-15 minutes before cutting. Garnish with sugared cranberries and orange peel. **Yield:** 8 servings.

Nutritional Analysis: One piece equals 209 calories, 5 g fat (2 g saturated fat), 12 mg cholesterol, 117 mg sodium, 41 g carbohydrate, 1 g fiber, 4 g protein.

Lemon Meringue Desserts

Low-sodium

(Pictured below)

These pretty individual dessert cups from our Test Kitchen are cute as can be...and yummy, too. A sweet and fluffy golden meringue tops the pudding that's rich with lemony flavor.

2 egg whites
2/3 cup plus 2 tablespoons sugar, *divided*
2 tablespoons cornstarch
1 cup cold water
1 egg, lightly beaten
1/2 cup lemon juice
1 tablespoon butter
1 teaspoon grated lemon peel
1/8 teaspoon cream of tartar

Let egg whites stand at room temperature for 30 minutes. In a small saucepan, combine 2/3 cup sugar and cornstarch. Stir in water until smooth. Cook and stir over medium-high heat until thickened and bubbly. Reduce heat; cook and stir 2 minutes longer.

Remove from the heat. Stir a small amount of hot filling into egg; return all to pan, stirring constantly. Bring to a gentle boil; cook and stir 2 minutes longer. Remove from the heat. Gently stir in lemon juice, butter and peel. Pour into four 6-oz. custard cups; set aside.

In a mixing bowl, beat egg whites and cream of tartar on medium speed until soft peaks form. Gradually beat in remaining sugar, 1 tablespoon at a time, on high until stiff glossy peaks form and sugar is dissolved. Immediately spread meringue over lemon mixture, sealing edges to sides of cups. Bake at 375° for 5-7 minutes or until golden brown. **Yield:** 4 servings.

Nutritional Analysis: One dessert equals 227 calories, 4 g fat (2 g saturated fat), 61 mg cholesterol, 73 mg sodium, 46 g carbohydrate, trace fiber, 3 g protein.

Vanilla Yogurt Ambrosia

Low-sodium

This simple fruit salad is so yummy. I have served it many times, and it's always one of the first dishes to go. Fat-free vanilla yogurt also works very well as the dressing.
—Sherry Hulsman, Louisville, Kentucky

1 can (20 ounces) pineapple tidbits, drained
1 can (11 ounces) mandarin oranges, drained
1-1/2 cups green grapes
1 cup miniature marshmallows
1/2 cup flaked coconut
1 carton (6 ounces) reduced-fat vanilla yogurt
1/4 cup chopped pecans, toasted

In a serving bowl, combine the pineapple, oranges, grapes, marshmallows and coconut. Fold in the yogurt. Cover and refrigerate for at least 1 hour. Just before serving, stir in pecans. **Yield:** 6 servings.

Nutritional Analysis: One serving (3/4 cup) equals 202 calories, 7 g fat (3 g saturated fat), 1 mg cholesterol, 50 mg sodium, 34 g carbohydrate, 3 g fiber, 3 g protein.
Diabetic Exchanges: 2 fruit, 1 fat.

Apple Oat Snack Cake

Apples and oats make up one of my favorite flavor combinations, and they are delicious in this snack cake.
—Julie Dometrovich, Aliquippa, Pennsylvania

1 cup boiling water
1/2 cup old-fashioned oats
1-3/4 cups all-purpose flour
1 teaspoon baking soda
1 teaspoon ground cinnamon
1/4 teaspoon salt
3/4 cup sugar
3/4 cup packed brown sugar
1/3 cup unsweetened applesauce
1 egg
1-1/2 teaspoons vanilla extract
1 medium apple, peeled and chopped
TOPPING:
1/2 cup old-fashioned oats
1/4 cup all-purpose flour
1/4 cup packed brown sugar
1 teaspoon ground cinnamon
3 tablespoons cold butter

In a bowl, combine boiling water and oats; set aside. In a large bowl, combine the flour, baking soda, cinnamon and salt. In a mixing bowl, combine the sugars and applesauce; beat well. Add the egg, vanilla and oat mixture; mix well. Stir into dry ingredients just until combined. Fold in apple.

Pour into an 8-in. square baking dish coated with nonstick cooking spray. For the topping, combine the oats, flour, brown sugar and cinnamon. Cut in butter until mixture resembles coarse crumbs; sprinkle over batter. Bake at 350° for 40-45 minutes or until a toothpick inserted near the center comes out clean. Cool on a wire rack. **Yield:** 12 servings.

Nutritional Analysis: One piece equals 286 calories, 4 g fat (2 g saturated fat), 25 mg cholesterol, 196 mg sodium, 58 g carbohydrate, 3 g fiber, 5 g protein.

Favorite Recipe Made Lighter

IF YOU know a chocolate lover, here's a delectable way to make his or her dreams come true. Set one of these yummy oh-so-chocolaty cakes in front of them. "I recently came across this wonderful recipe for Molten Chocolate Cakes," says Deanna Kymer of Broomfield, Colorado.

"The whole family loves the rich syrupy center inside these cakes, but I'm concerned about the fat content and calories. Is there any way to create a healthier version?"

Deanna's dessert is unbelievably rich, with a cup of butter, a half pound of chocolate and nine egg yolks.

To lighten up the cakes, our home economists reduced the butter by two-thirds, replaced over half the chocolate with baking cocoa and used egg whites for some of the egg yolks.

Brown sugar was used in place of some of the confectioners' sugar for its richer taste and moistness. Vanilla, an ingredient in semisweet chocolate, was added to round out the flavor.

The makeover recipe makes one less cake than the original, but the size of the cakes is the same.

So if you want to indulge in an irresistible dessert for a special dinner or the holidays, try these trimmer treats. They have 40% fewer calories and about 60% less fat and cholesterol than the originals. Yet they are still full of chocolaty flavor.

Molten Chocolate Cakes

8 squares (1 ounce *each*) semisweet chocolate, coarsely chopped
1 cup butter, cubed
5 eggs
4 egg yolks
2 cups confectioners' sugar
3/4 cup all-purpose flour

Place chocolate and butter in a microwave safe-bowl. Microwave, uncovered, at 50% power for 1 minute; stir. Microwave at 50% power 1 minute longer; stir until smooth. Add the eggs, egg yolks and sugar; mix well. Add flour; stir until blended. Pour into eight greased 6-oz. custard cups.

Place custard cups on a baking sheet. Bake at 425° for 15-16 minutes or until a thermometer inserted near the center reads 160°. Remove from the oven and let stand for 1 minute. Run a knife around edge of custard cups; invert onto individual dessert plates. Serve immediately. **Yield:** 8 servings.

Editor's Note: This recipe was tested in a 1,100-watt microwave.

Nutritional Analysis: One cake equals 578 calories, 38 g fat (21 g saturated fat), 300 mg cholesterol, 275 mg sodium, 56 g carbohydrate, 2 g fiber, 9 g protein.

Makeover Molten Chocolate Cakes

(Pictured below)

1/3 cup butter, cubed
1/3 cup baking cocoa
3 squares (1 ounce *each*) semisweet chocolate, coarsely chopped
3 eggs
7 egg whites
1 cup confectioners' sugar
1/2 cup packed brown sugar
1-1/2 teaspoons vanilla extract
1/3 cup all-purpose flour
1/8 teaspoon salt

Place the butter, cocoa and chocolate in a microwave safe-bowl. Microwave, uncovered, at 50% power for 20 seconds; stir. Microwave at 50% power 20 seconds longer; stir until smooth. Add the eggs, egg whites, confectioners' sugar, brown sugar and vanilla; mix well. Stir in flour and salt until blended. Pour into seven 6-oz. custard cups coated with nonstick cooking spray.

Place custard cups on a baking sheet. Bake at 450° for 10-12 minutes or until a thermometer inserted near the center reads 160°. Remove from the oven and let stand for 1 minute. Run a knife around edge of custard cups; invert onto individual dessert plates. Serve immediately. **Yield:** 7 servings.

Editor's Note: This recipe was tested in a 1,100-watt microwave.

Nutritional Analysis: One cake equals 346 calories, 14 g fat (9 g saturated fat), 114 mg cholesterol, 196 mg sodium, 47 g carbohydrate, 2 g fiber, 8 g protein.

Marshmallow Fruit Kabobs

Low-fat **Low-sodium**

Both kids and adults love these fun grilled fruit kabobs. I like the fact that the sauce can be made ahead of time. Kids will have a great time helping to assemble the kabobs, too.
—Claudia Ruiss, Massapequa, New York

1-1/2 cups fresh *or* frozen raspberries, thawed
1/3 cup orange juice
1 tablespoon confectioners' sugar
2 medium firm bananas, cut into 3/4-inch slices
2 cups cubed fresh pineapple
2 large fresh plums, cut into 3/4-inch pieces
24 large marshmallows
1 tablespoon lemon juice
1 tablespoon honey

Mash and strain raspberries, reserving juice. Discard seeds. In a bowl, combine the orange juice, sugar and raspberry juice. Set aside.

Coat grill rack with nonstick cooking spray before starting the grill. On 12 metal or soaked wooden skewers, alternately thread fruit and marshmallows. Combine lemon juice and honey; brush over fruit. Grill kabobs over indirect medium heat for 1-2 minutes on each side or until marshmallows are golden. Serve kabobs with raspberry sauce. **Yield:** 6 servings.

Nutritional Analysis: *One serving (2 kabobs with 3 tablespoons raspberry sauce) equals 204 calories, 1 g fat (trace saturated fat), 0 cholesterol, 15 mg sodium, 52 g carbohydrate, 4 g fiber, 2 g protein.*

Chewy Coconut Macaroons

Low-carb *Low-fat* **Low-sodium**

(Pictured above right)

These chewy cookies are my husband's favorites, so he requests them often. I like to make the macaroons on cold winter days and keep them in an airtight bowl on the kitchen counter. They never last long!
—Peggy Key, Grant, Alabama

2-1/2 cups flaked coconut
3/4 cup all-purpose flour
1/8 teaspoon salt
1 can (14 ounces) fat-free sweetened condensed milk
1-1/2 teaspoons almond extract

In a bowl, toss together the coconut, flour and salt. Stir in sweetened condensed milk and almond extract until blended. (Mixture will be thick and sticky.)

Drop by rounded teaspoonfuls 3 in. apart on baking sheets lightly coated with nonstick cooking spray. Bake at 300° for 18-22 minutes or until edges are lightly browned. Cool for 2 minutes before removing to wire racks. **Yield:** 32 cookies.

Nutritional Analysis: *One cookie equals 83 calories, 3 g fat (2 g saturated fat), 1 mg cholesterol, 41 mg sodium, 13 g carbohydrate, trace fiber, 2 g protein.*
Diabetic Exchange: *1 starch.*

Apple Gingerbread Cobbler

Nicely spiced with cinnamon, nutmeg and ginger, this delicious cobbler is one of my family's favorites. It is easy to prepare…and the recipe has been in my family for years.
—Edie DeSpain, Logan, Utah

4 medium tart apples, peeled and sliced
1 cup water
1/2 cup packed brown sugar
1 tablespoon lemon juice
1/4 teaspoon ground cinnamon
1 egg
1/4 cup sugar
1/2 cup 1% buttermilk
1/4 cup molasses
2 tablespoons canola oil
1 cup all-purpose flour
1/2 teaspoon *each* baking powder, baking soda and ground ginger
1/4 teaspoon *each* salt and ground nutmeg
2 teaspoons cornstarch
1 tablespoon cold water

🍎 Fruit Favorite

LIKE TO enjoy apple pie a la mode for dessert, but can't afford the calories? Try this trick. Heat up some applesauce in the microwave and pour it over a scoop of low-fat frozen yogurt. Then sprinkle it with a little cinnamon and granola.
—Martha Pollock, Oregonia, Ohio

In a saucepan, combine the apples, water, brown sugar, lemon juice and cinnamon. Bring to a boil. Reduce heat; cover and simmer for 8-10 minutes or until apples are tender. Remove from the heat and set aside.

In a bowl, beat the egg, sugar, buttermilk, molasses and oil. Combine the flour, baking powder, baking soda, ginger, salt and nutmeg; stir into buttermilk just until combined. Combine cornstarch and cold water until smooth; stir into apple mixture. Pour apple mixture into 8-in. square baking dish coated with nonstick cooking spray. Spread gingerbread mixture over apples. Bake at 350° for 25-30 minutes or until a toothpick inserted into the topping comes out clean. **Yield:** 8 servings.

Nutritional Analysis: One piece equals 247 calories, 5 g fat (1 g saturated fat), 27 mg cholesterol, 200 mg sodium, 50 g carbohydrate, 2 g fiber, 3 g protein.

Cherry-Almond Snack Cake

(Pictured below)

Dried cherries and almond flavoring give this tender golden cake from our Test Kitchen a sweet-tart flavor, and crushed almonds lend a nice crunch to each tasty square. It's great for snacking or afternoon tea.

2/3 cup reduced-fat stick margarine, softened
Sugar substitute equivalent to 3/4 cup sugar
1/4 cup honey
1 egg
1 teaspoon almond extract
2 cups all-purpose flour
2 teaspoons baking powder

1/2 teaspoon baking soda
1/2 teaspoon salt
3/4 cup fat-free milk
2/3 cup ground almonds
1/2 cup dried cherries, finely chopped

In a large mixing bowl, beat the margarine, sugar substitute and honey. Beat in the egg and almond extract (mixture will appear curdled). Combine the flour, baking powder, baking soda and salt; add to the creamed mixture alternately with milk. Stir in almonds and cherries.

Spread into a 13-in. x 9-in. x 2-in. baking pan coated with nonstick cooking spray. Bake at 325° for 25-30 minutes or until a toothpick inserted near the center comes out clean. Cool on a wire rack. **Yield:** 15 servings.

Editor's Note: This recipe was tested with Parkay Light stick margarine and Splenda No Calorie Sweetener.

Nutritional Analysis: One piece equals 169 calories, 7 g fat (1 g saturated fat), 14 mg cholesterol, 248 mg sodium, 24 g carbohydrate, 1 g fiber, 4 g protein.
Diabetic Exchanges: 1-1/2 starch, 1 fat.

Pear Cranberry Crumble

Low-sodium

Our Test Kitchen cooks got creative with this crumble. Pears provide a tasty change of pace from apples and other fruits that are more commonly used in pies and desserts. Cranberries add color, and spiced-up oats top off this old-fashioned dessert with a yummy crunch.

1/2 cup unsweetened apple juice
1/3 cup dried cranberries
1/2 teaspoon vanilla extract
4 firm ripe pears, *each* peeled, cored and cut into 12 slices
3 tablespoons sugar
1/3 cup quick-cooking oats
1/4 cup packed brown sugar
3 tablespoons all-purpose flour
3 tablespoons whole wheat flour
1 teaspoon ground cinnamon
1/8 teaspoon ground nutmeg
2 tablespoons cold butter

In a small bowl, combine the apple juice, cranberries and vanilla; let stand for 15 minutes. Arrange pear slices in an 11-in. x 7-in. x 2-in. baking dish coated with nonstick cooking spray. Sprinkle with sugar. Pour apple juice mixture over pears.

In a bowl, combine the oats, brown sugar, all-purpose flour, whole wheat flour, cinnamon and nutmeg. Cut in butter until crumbly. Sprinkle over pears. Bake, uncovered, at 350° for 40-45 minutes or until pears are tender and topping is golden brown. Serve warm. **Yield:** 6 servings.

Nutritional Analysis: One serving equals 234 calories, 5 g fat (2 g saturated fat), 10 mg cholesterol, 43 mg sodium, 49 g carbohydrate, 4 g fiber, 2 g protein.
Diabetic Exchanges: 1-1/2 starch, 1-1/2 fruit, 1 fat.

Cream Cheese Bonbons

Low-carb   Low-sodium

(Pictured above)

These pretty coconut-speckled candies are rolled in grated chocolate, but you could also coat them in finely chopped nuts, chocolate sprinkles or jimmies. For variety, substitute almond extract for the vanilla and chopped toasted almonds for the coconut.
—Beverly Coyde, Gasport, New York

1 package (8 ounces) reduced-fat cream cheese
Sugar substitute equivalent to 1/3 cup sugar
1 tablespoon sugar
1/2 teaspoon vanilla extract
1 cup flaked coconut
1 square (1 ounce) unsweetened chocolate, grated

In a small mixing bowl, beat the cream cheese, sugar substitute, sugar and vanilla until smooth. Stir in the coconut until combined. Refrigerate for 30 minutes or until easy to handle.

Shape into 1-in. balls, then roll in grated chocolate. Refrigerate for at least 1 hour. Store in an airtight container in the refrigerator. **Yield:** 1-1/2 dozen.

Editor's Note: This recipe was tested with Splenda No Calorie Sweetener. Look for it in the baking aisle of your grocery store.

Nutritional Analysis: *One bonbon equals 73 calories, 6 g fat (4 g saturated fat), 10 mg cholesterol, 64 mg sodium, 5 g carbohydrate, trace fiber, 2 g protein.*
Diabetic Exchanges: *1 fat, 1/2 starch.*

Gingerbread Biscotti

Low-carb   Low-fat   Low-sodium

Friends love it when I put the dry ingredients in a jar, attach the biscotti recipe and give it as a gift.
—Linda James, Greenfield, Wisconsin

2-1/4 cups all-purpose flour
2 teaspoons ground cinnamon
1 teaspoon baking powder
3/4 teaspoon ground ginger
1/2 teaspoon baking soda
1/4 teaspoon ground nutmeg
1/4 teaspoon ground allspice
1 egg, lightly beaten
2 egg whites, lightly beaten
2/3 cup packed brown sugar
1/4 cup molasses
2 teaspoons vanilla extract
1/4 cup chopped pecans
1/4 cup dried currants

In a large bowl, combine the first seven ingredients. In another bowl, combine the egg and egg whites, brown sugar, molasses and vanilla until smooth. Stir into dry ingredients just until moistened. Fold in pecans and currants. Cover and refrigerate for 30 minutes.

Divide dough in half; shape each half into a ball. On a baking sheet coated with nonstick cooking spray, roll each ball into a 14-in. x 1-1/2-in. rectangle. Bake at 325° for 24-28 minutes or until firm to the touch. Remove from the oven and reduce the heat to 300°. Cool for 5 minutes.

Transfer to a cutting board; cut diagonally with a serrated knife into 1/2-in. slices. Place cut side down on baking sheets coated with nonstick cooking spray. Bake for 15-20 minutes or until lightly browned, turning once. Remove to wire racks to cool. Store in an airtight container. **Yield:** 2-1/2 dozen.

Nutritional Analysis: *One cookie equals 74 calories, 1 g fat (trace saturated fat), 7 mg cholesterol, 38 mg sodium, 15 g carbohydrate, 1 g fiber, 2 g protein.*
Diabetic Exchange: *1 starch.*

Chock-full of Fruit Snackin' Cake

Low-sodium

This wholesome treat is loaded with healthy ingredients, including apples, raisins, cranberries and walnuts. There's plenty of flavor in every moist bite, and it comes together in minutes.
—Sami Taylor, Hermiston, Oregon

2 cups all-purpose flour
2 cups quick-cooking oats
Sugar substitute equivalent to 1-1/2 cups sugar
2-3/4 teaspoons baking powder
1/4 teaspoon baking soda
1/8 teaspoon salt
3 eggs
1 cup orange juice
1/3 cup canola oil
2 large carrots, shredded
2 medium apples, peeled and shredded
1 cup raisins
1 cup dried cranberries
1 cup chopped walnuts

In a large bowl, combine the first six ingredients. Whisk the eggs, orange juice and oil; stir into dry ingredients just until moistened. Fold in the remaining ingredients.

Pour into a 13-in. x 9-in. x 2-in. baking dish coated with nonstick cooking spray. Bake at 350° for 40-45 minutes or until a toothpick inserted near the center comes out clean. Cool on a wire rack. Cut into squares. **Yield:** 18 servings.

Editor's Note: This recipe was tested with Splenda No Calorie Sweetener. Look for it in the baking aisle of your grocery store.

Nutritional Analysis: *One piece equals 248 calories, 10 g fat (1 g saturated fat), 35 mg cholesterol, 84 mg sodium, 36 g carbohydrate, 3 g fiber, 5 g protein.*
Diabetic Exchanges: *1-1/2 starch, 1-1/2 fat, 1 fruit.*

Nutty Chocolate Fudge

Low-carb Low-sodium

I've trimmed down this recipe over the years, and now my family likes it better than ever. They don't even miss all of the sugar that I used to add. Try it with peanut butter or butterscotch chips.
—A.J. Ristow, Tucson, Arizona

1 jar (7 ounces) marshmallow creme
2/3 cup fat-free evaporated milk
1/2 cup butter, cubed
2 teaspoons vanilla extract
3 cups (18 ounces) semisweet chocolate chips
2 cups chopped pecans *or* walnuts, toasted

Line a 9-in. square pan with foil and coat foil with nonstick cooking spray; set aside. In a large saucepan, combine the marshmallow creme, evaporated milk and butter. Cook and stir over medium heat until smooth. Bring to a boil; boil for 5 minutes, stirring constantly. Remove from the heat; add vanilla. Stir in chocolate chips until melted. Add pecans. Pour into prepared pan. Refrigerate for 2 hours or until firm.

Using foil, remove fudge from pan; carefully remove foil. Cut into 1-in. squares. Store in the refrigerator. **Yield:** 2-2/3 pounds (81 pieces).

Nutritional Analysis: *One piece equals 70 calories, 5 g fat (2 g saturated fat), 3 mg cholesterol, 16 mg sodium, 7 g carbohydrate, 1 g fiber, 1 g protein.*
Diabetic Exchanges: *1 fat, 1/2 starch.*

Almond Cookie Cutouts

(Pictured below)

Colored sugar and sprinkles create the festive look for these easy-to-decorate cookies from our home economists. A little almond extract gives them pleasant flavor. They're a nice addition to a Christmas cookie tray.

6 tablespoons butter, softened
1/2 cup sugar
1/2 cup packed brown sugar
1 egg
3/4 teaspoon almond extract
1/2 teaspoon vanilla extract
1-1/4 cups all-purpose flour
1/4 cup cornstarch
3 tablespoons ground almonds
1/2 teaspoon baking powder
1/2 teaspoon salt
Red and green colored sugar *and/or* sprinkles, optional

In a small mixing bowl, cream butter and sugars. Add egg and extracts; mix well. Combine the flour, cornstarch, almonds, baking powder and salt. Add to creamed mixture just until blended. Shape into two balls. Cover and refrigerate for at least 2 hours.

On a lightly floured surface, roll out dough to 1/4-in. thickness. Cut with lightly floured 2-1/2-in. cutters. Transfer to baking sheets coated with nonstick cooking spray. Sprinkle with colored sugar and/or sprinkles if desired.

Bake at 350° for 7-9 minutes or until set and bottoms are lightly browned. Cool for 2 minutes before removing to wire racks. **Yield:** 28 cookies.

Nutritional Analysis: *One serving (2 cookies) equals 163 calories, 6 g fat (3 g saturated fat), 28 mg cholesterol, 159 mg sodium, 25 g carbohydrate, 1 g fiber, 2 g protein.*
Diabetic Exchanges: *1-1/2 starch, 1 fat.*

Frosty Peanut Butter Cups

*With their creamy smooth texture and peanut
butter flavor, these cups are addictive!*
—Kimberly Rendino, Cicero, New York

9 reduced-fat graham crackers, crushed
2 tablespoons reduced-fat spreadable margarine
1 cup cold 1% milk
1/2 cup reduced-fat creamy peanut butter
**1 package (3.4 ounces) instant vanilla pudding
    mix**
2 cups fat-free whipped topping

In a small bowl, combine the cracker crumbs and margarine. Press about 1 tablespoon each into 12 paper-lined muffin cups.

In a large bowl, whisk milk and peanut butter until blended. Whisk in pudding mix until smooth. Fold in whipped topping. Spoon into cups. Freeze until firm. Remove liners and let stand at room temperature for 5 minutes before serving. **Yield:** 1 dozen.

Editor's Note: This recipe was tested with Parkay reduced-fat tub margarine.

*Nutritional Analysis: One serving equals 154 calories, 6 g
fat (1 g saturated fat), 1 mg cholesterol, 277 mg sodium, 23 g
carbohydrate, 1 g fiber, 4 g protein.*
Diabetic Exchanges: 1-1/2 starch, 1 fat.

Miracle Baklava

*Always asked to bring baklava to special
occasions, I created this lighter version.*
—Sue Klima, Northlake, Illinois

1 package (12 ounces) vanilla wafers, crushed
2 tablespoons sugar
1 teaspoon ground cinnamon
Refrigerated butter-flavored spray (about 4 ounces)
**1 package (16 ounces, 14-inch x 9-inch sheet
    size) frozen phyllo dough, thawed**
SYRUP:
1 cup sugar
1 cup water
1/2 cup honey
1 teaspoon grated lemon peel
1 teaspoon vanilla extract

In a large bowl, combine the wafer crumbs, sugar and cinnamon; set aside. Spritz a 13-in. x 9-in. x 2-in. baking pan with refrigerated butter-flavored spray. Unroll phyllo sheets. Place one sheet of phyllo in pan; spritz with butter-flavored spray and brush to coat evenly. Repeat seven times, spritzing and brushing each layer. Keep remaining phyllo dough covered with plastic wrap to avoid drying out.

Sprinkle 1/4 cup wafer crumb mixture over phyllo in pan. Layer with two sheets of phyllo, spritzing and brushing with butter-flavored spray between each. Sprinkle with 1/4 cup wafer crumb mixture; repeat 11 times. Top with one phyllo sheet; spritz and brush with butter-flavored spray. Repeat seven more times, spritzing and brushing each layer.

Cut into 15 squares; cut each square in half diagonally. Bake at 350° for 40-45 minutes or until golden brown.

Meanwhile, in a saucepan, bring the sugar, water, honey and lemon peel to a boil. Reduce heat; simmer, uncov-

ered, for 20 minutes. Remove from the heat. Stir in vanilla and cool to lukewarm. Pour syrup over warm baklava. **Yield:** 30 servings.

Editor's Note: This recipe was tested with I Can't Believe It's Not Butter Spray.

*Nutritional Analysis: One piece equals 154 calories, 4 g fat
(1 g saturated fat), 1 mg cholesterol, 154 mg sodium, 30 g carbohydrate, 1 g fiber, 2 g protein.*
Diabetic Exchange: 2 starch.

Martha Washington Pies

Low-sodium

(Pictured below)

*I like topping the nutty meringues with strawberries at
Christmas, and I use peaches during the summer.*
—Ginger Clark, Hinesville, Georgia

4 egg whites
1/4 teaspoon cream of tartar
1 cup plus 1 tablespoon sugar, *divided*
1 cup finely chopped pecans
1/2 cup crushed saltines (about 12 crackers)
1 teaspoon vanilla extract
6 cups sliced fresh strawberries
2/3 cup reduced-fat whipped topping

In a large mixing bowl, beat egg whites and cream of tartar on medium speed until soft peaks form. Gradually beat in 1 cup sugar, 2 tablespoons at a time, on high until stiff glossy peaks form and sugar is dissolved.

Fold in nuts, crackers and vanilla. Drop by rounded 1/3 cupfuls onto parchment-lined baking sheets. Shape into 3-1/2-in. rounds with the back of a spoon.

Bake at 300° for 25-30 minutes or until set. Turn oven off; leave in oven with door closed for 2 hours. Toss strawberries with the remaining sugar; spoon 2/3 cup into each shell. Dollop each with whipped topping. **Yield:** 9 servings.

*Nutritional Analysis: One serving equals 253 calories, 11 g
fat (2 g saturated fat), 0 cholesterol, 78 mg sodium, 38 g carbohydrate, 4 g fiber, 4 g protein.*

Fine Dining Pared Down

A special occasion calls for candles, fine
china and a marvelous meal. But there's
no need to add to your guests' waistlines at
the same time. Pamper friends and family
with these elegant but light menus.

Berry Barbecued Pork Roast, Swiss Scalloped Potatoes
and Orange Poppy Seed Dressing (page 248)

Go Out on a Limb with Lamb

Lamb Marsala

Low-carb

Lamb was a special treat for my family when I was growing up. I've had this recipe for more than 30 years.
—*Bonnie Silverstein, Denver, Colorado*

3/4 cup marsala wine *or* **1/2 cup chicken broth, 1/4 cup white grape juice and 1 tablespoon white wine vinegar**
1 garlic clove, minced
1 tablespoon dried oregano
1 tablespoon olive oil
1 boneless leg of lamb (2-1/2 pounds), rolled and tied
1/2 teaspoon salt
1/4 teaspoon pepper
1 pound fresh mushrooms, quartered

In a small bowl, combine the wine, garlic and oregano; set aside. Rub oil over lamb, then sprinkle with salt and pepper. Place roast on a rack in shallow roasting pan; spoon some of wine mixture over roast. Set aside remaining wine mixture.

Bake, uncovered, at 325° for 1 to 1-1/2 hours or until meat reaches desired doneness (for rare, a meat thermometer should read 140°; medium, 160°; well-done, 170°), basting occasionally with some of reserved wine mixture. Remove from the oven; cover loosely with foil for 10-15 minutes.

Meanwhile, pour pan drippings into a measuring cup; skim fat. In a large nonstick skillet coated with nonstick cooking spray, saute mushrooms until tender. Add pan drippings and any remaining wine mixture; heat through. Slice lamb and serve with mushroom sauce. **Yield:** 6 servings.

Nutritional Analysis: *One serving (4 ounces cooked lamb with 1/4 cup mushroom sauce) equals 299 calories, 13 g fat (4 g saturated fat), 106 mg cholesterol, 283 mg sodium, 6 g carbohydrate, 1 g fiber, 34 g protein.*
Diabetic Exchanges: *4 lean meat, 1 vegetable.*

Orange-Glazed Asparagus

Low-carb   Meatless

My family loves it when I use a tangy orange glaze to perk up fresh asparagus from my garden. It's an easy dish for entertaining.
—*Gloria Bisek, Deerwood, Minnesota*

3 pounds fresh asparagus, trimmed
1/2 cup orange juice
2 tablespoons olive oil
1/2 teaspoon salt
1 teaspoon grated orange peel

Place asparagus in a large nonstick skillet; add 1/2 in. of water. Bring to a boil. Reduce heat; cover and simmer for 10-12 minutes or until crisp-tender. Drain. Remove asparagus and keep warm. Add the remaining ingredients to the pan; bring to a boil. Cook, uncovered, over medium-high heat until juices are slightly thickened. Drizzle over asparagus. **Yield:** 8 servings.

Nutritional Analysis: *One serving equals 59 calories, 4 g fat (1 g saturated fat), 0 cholesterol, 155 mg sodium, 5 g carbohydrate, 1 g fiber, 2 g protein.*
Diabetic Exchanges: *1 vegetable, 1/2 fat.*

Make-Ahead Lemon Bombe

My neighbor gave me the recipe for this refreshing dessert, but it was made with sugar and lots of whipped cream. I lightened it up for my diabetic husband, and it's difficult to taste the difference.
—*Nadine Johnson, Clackamas, Oregon*

1 package (16 ounces) angel food cake mix
2 envelopes unflavored gelatin
1/4 cup cold water
1 cup boiling water
1 can (12 ounces) frozen orange juice concentrate, thawed
Sugar substitute equivalent to 1 cup sugar
2 tablespoons lemon juice
1/4 teaspoon grated lemon peel
1/8 teaspoon salt
3 cartons (8 ounces *each***) frozen reduced-fat whipped topping, thawed,** *divided*
1/2 cup flaked coconut, toasted
Mint leaves, maraschino cherries and lemon and orange slices, optional

Prepare and bake cake according to package directions, using an ungreased 10-in. tube pan. Cut cooled cake into 1-1/2-in. cubes. Set aside.

In a bowl, sprinkle gelatin over cold water; let stand for 1 minute. Add boiling water; stir until gelatin is dissolved. Add the orange juice concentrate, sugar substitute, lemon juice, lemon peel and salt; mix well. Refrigerate for 30 minutes or until partially set. Fold in 2 cartons of whipped topping.

Line a 5-1/2-qt. bowl with two overlapping pieces of plastic wrap, letting plastic wrap hang over edge of bowl. In another large bowl, gently combine the cake cubes and whipped topping mixture. Spoon into prepared bowl, gently pushing against side to prevent holes. Cover and refrigerate for at least 24 hours.

Just before serving, uncover bombe. Invert onto a cake plate. Remove bowl and plastic wrap. Frost with remaining carton of whipped topping; sprinkle with coconut. Garnish with mint, cherries and lemon and orange slices if desired. **Yield:** 14 servings.

Editor's Note: This recipe was tested with Splenda No Calorie Sweetener. Look for it in the baking aisle of your grocery store.

Nutritional Analysis: *One serving equals 301 calories, 7 g fat (7 g saturated fat), 0 cholesterol, 225 mg sodium, 52 g carbohydrate, trace fiber, 4 g protein.*

Simply Elegant Stir-Fry

Zippy Shrimp Linguine

I won a community recipe contest several years ago with this spicy dish. I make it often for my family, but it's pretty enough to serve guests. Red pepper flakes put a little zing in the shrimp, and the lightly sauteed veggies are crisp-tender and colorful.
—Jackie Selover, Sidney, Ohio

> 1 package (16 ounces) linguine
> 1 pound uncooked large shrimp, peeled and deveined
> 2 garlic cloves, minced
> 1/2 to 1 teaspoon crushed red pepper flakes
> 2 tablespoons olive oil
> 1 teaspoon butter
> 1-1/2 cups sliced zucchini
> 1 cup sliced yellow summer squash
> 1 cup julienned carrots
> 1 cup fresh broccoli florets
> 1 tablespoon minced fresh parsley
> 1 tablespoon minced fresh basil
> 3/4 teaspoon salt
> 1/2 cup shredded Parmesan cheese

Cook pasta according to package directions. Meanwhile, in a large nonstick skillet, stir-fry the shrimp, garlic and pepper flakes in oil and butter for 3-5 minutes or until shrimp turn pink. Remove shrimp; keep warm.

Add the zucchini, summer squash, carrots and broccoli to same skillet; stir-fry for 8-10 minutes or until crisp-tender. Return shrimp to skillet. Drain the pasta; add to skillet along with the parsley, basil and salt. Heat through. Sprinkle with Parmesan cheese. **Yield:** 8 servings.

Nutritional Analysis: One serving (1-1/2 cups) equals 312 calories, 7 g fat (2 g saturated fat), 73 mg cholesterol, 407 mg sodium, 45 g carbohydrate, 3 g fiber, 18 g protein.
Diabetic Exchanges: 2-1/2 starch, 1 vegetable, 1 lean meat, 1 fat.

Berries in a Nest

Low-fat   Low-sodium

I enhance a medley of fresh berries with sugar, pepper and balsamic vinegar. Serve the berries on lettuce, for a fun summer salad...or showcase them in pretty phyllo cups, for an impressive dinner finale.
—Iola Egle, Bella Vista, Arkansas

> 4 cups halved fresh strawberries
> 1 cup fresh blackberries
> 1 cup fresh raspberries
> 1/3 cup sugar
> 3 tablespoons balsamic vinegar
> 1/4 to 1/2 teaspoon coarsely ground pepper

PHYLLO NESTS:
> 8 sheets phyllo dough (18 inches x 14 inches)
> 2 teaspoons sugar
> 1/4 teaspoon ground cinnamon

In a large bowl, combine the strawberries, blackberries and raspberries. Sprinkle with sugar; gently toss to coat. Let stand for 20 minutes. Pour vinegar over berries; sprinkle with pepper. Gently toss to coat. Cover and refrigerate for 2 hours.

For phyllo nests, coat giant nonstick muffin cups with a nonstick cooking spray; set aside. Unroll phyllo dough sheets; remove one sheet. (While assembling, keep remaining dough covered with plastic wrap and a damp cloth.)

For each nest, cut one sheet in half lengthwise and cut in thirds widthwise. Stack three sections and place in a prepared cup; spray with nonstick cooking spray. Stack remaining three sections and place in cup, alternating points. Spray with nonstick cooking spray. Combine the sugar and cinnamon; sprinkle about 1/4 teaspoon cinnamon-sugar over dough. Repeat with remaining sheets of dough.

Bake at 375° for 7-8 minutes or until golden brown. Cool for 5 minutes before carefully removing to a wire rack to cool completely. Using a slotted spoon, fill each nest with about 3/4 cup berry mixture. Drizzle with a small amount of juice. Serve immediately. **Yield:** 8 servings.

Nutritional Analysis: One filled nest equals 142 calories, 1 g fat (trace saturated fat), 0 cholesterol, 92 mg sodium, 33 g carbohydrate, 4 g fiber, 3 g protein.
Diabetic Exchanges: 1 fruit, 1 starch.

Cran-Raspberry Iced Tea

Low-carb   Low-fat   Low-sodium

The fruity flavor of this refreshing ruby-red beverage from our Test Kitchen has just the right touch of sweetness. It's sure to brighten up any warm weather get-together.

> 4 cups water
> 1 cup frozen unsweetened raspberries
> 4 teaspoons sugar
> 8 individual raspberry-flavored tea bags
> 4 cups reduced-sugar cranberry-raspberry juice

In a large saucepan, bring the water, raspberries and sugar to a boil. Reduce heat; cover and simmer for 10 minutes. Remove from the heat; strain and discard raspberry seeds. Add tea bags. Let stand for 4 minutes. Discard tea bags. Stir in cranberry-raspberry juice. Serve over ice. **Yield:** 8 servings.

Nutritional Analysis: One serving (1 cup) equals 38 calories, trace fat (0 saturated fat), 0 cholesterol, 48 mg sodium, 8 g carbohydrate, 1 g fiber, trace protein.
Diabetic Exchange: 1/2 fruit.

A Little Italy at the Table

Chicken Piccata

Low-carb

Once you've tried this tangy yet delicate entree, you won't hesitate to make it for company. Seasoned with Parmesan and parsley, the chicken cooks up golden brown, then is drizzled with a light lemon sauce.
—*Susan Pursell, Fountain City, California*

8 boneless skinless chicken breast halves (4 ounces *each*)
1/2 cup egg substitute
2 tablespoons plus 1/4 cup dry white wine *or* chicken broth, *divided*
5 tablespoons lemon juice, *divided*
3 garlic cloves, minced
1/8 teaspoon hot pepper sauce
1/2 cup all-purpose flour
1/2 cup grated Parmesan cheese
1/4 cup minced fresh parsley
1/2 teaspoon salt
3 teaspoons olive oil, *divided*
2 tablespoons butter

Flatten chicken to 1/4-in. thickness. In a shallow dish, combine the egg substitute, 2 tablespoons wine or broth, 2 tablespoons lemon juice, garlic and hot pepper sauce. In another shallow dish, combine the flour, Parmesan cheese, parsley and salt. Coat chicken with flour mixture, dip in egg substitute mixture, then coat again with flour mixture.

In a large nonstick skillet, brown half of the chicken breasts in 1-1/2 teaspoons oil for 3-5 minutes on each side or until juices run clear. Remove chicken and keep warm. Drain drippings. Repeat with remaining chicken and oil. Remove chicken and keep warm.

In the same pan, melt butter. Add remaining wine or broth and lemon juice. Bring to a boil. Boil, uncovered, until reduced by a fourth. Drizzle over chicken. **Yield:** 8 servings.

Nutritional Analysis: One chicken breast half equals 246 calories, 8 g fat (4 g saturated fat), 79 mg cholesterol, 398 mg sodium, 8 g carbohydrate, trace fiber, 32 g protein.
Diabetic Exchanges: 4 lean meat, 1/2 starch.

Garlicky Green Beans With Mushrooms

Low-carb   Low-fat   Meatless

We love green beans at our house and enjoy them at least once a week. I'm always experimenting with new ways to fix them. Garlic cloves and mushrooms lend them delicious flavor in this quick-and-easy dish. I like to steam the beans so they keep most of their nutrients.
—*Sue Haviland, Lake Mills, Wisconsin*

2-1/2 pounds fresh green beans, trimmed
2 cups sliced fresh mushrooms
2 to 3 garlic cloves, minced

4 teaspoons butter
1/2 teaspoon salt
1/2 teaspoon onion powder
1/4 teaspoon pepper

Place beans in a large saucepan and cover with water; bring to a boil. Reduce heat; cover and simmer for 8-10 minutes or until crisp-tender. Meanwhile, in a large nonstick skillet, saute mushrooms and garlic in butter until tender. Drain beans; add to skillet. Stir in the salt, onion powder and pepper; heat through. **Yield:** 8 servings.

Nutritional Analysis: One serving (2/3 cup) equals 61 calories, 2 g fat (1 g saturated fat), 5 mg cholesterol, 175 mg sodium, 10 g carbohydrate, 4 g fiber, 3 g protein.
Diabetic Exchanges: 2 vegetable, 1/2 fat.

🍎 Garlic Leads to Healthy Living

LOADED with good scents and flavor, garlic is proving potent in promoting health.

Modern research supports garlic's effectiveness in lowering cholesterol and reducing the formation of blood clots. Studies also indicate garlic may be helpful in preventing cancer by stimulating the immune system.

Garlic seems to be most beneficial when eaten raw and in large amounts.

Chilled Red Wine Fruit Dressing

Low-carb   Low-fat   Low-sodium

The fruit bowl will be the first to empty when this elegant dressing is tossed into the mix. It's wonderful with melon balls, sliced oranges, strawberries, bananas and most any type of fruit. Use it to dress either a salad or a light dessert.
—*Donna Warner, Tavares, Florida*

1 cup dry red wine *or* 1/2 cup grape juice plus 1 tablespoon red wine vinegar
1/2 cup sugar
2 tablespoons red wine vinegar
1 cinnamon stick (3 inches)
8 whole cloves

In a saucepan, combine the wine or grape juice plus vinegar, sugar, red wine vinegar, cinnamon stick and cloves. Bring to a boil. Reduce heat; simmer, uncovered, for 10 minutes. Strain liquid; discard cinnamon sticks and cloves. Cover and refrigerate until serving. **Yield:** 8 servings.

Editor's Note: If using grape juice instead of wine, reduce sugar to 1/3 cup.

Nutritional Analysis: One serving (4 teaspoons dressing) equals 60 calories, trace fat (0 saturated fat), 0 cholesterol, 1 mg sodium, 13 g carbohydrate, trace fiber, trace protein.
Diabetic Exchange: 1 fruit.

Dress Up Dinner with Beef

Roasted Beef Tenderloin

Low-carb

A marinade provides a savory seasoning for tenderloin. I serve this simple, elegant roast often.
—Schelby Thompson, Dover, Delaware

- **1 beef tenderloin (3 pounds)**
- **1/2 cup port wine *or* 1/2 cup beef broth and 1 tablespoon balsamic vinegar**
- **1/2 cup reduced-sodium soy sauce**
- **2 tablespoons olive oil**
- **4 to 5 garlic cloves, minced**
- **1 bay leaf**
- **1 teaspoon dried thyme**
- **1 teaspoon pepper**
- **1/2 teaspoon hot pepper sauce**

Tie roast at 2-in. intervals with kitchen string. In a bowl, combine the remaining ingredients; mix well. Pour 3/4 cup marinade into a large resealable plastic bag; add the tenderloin. Seal the bag and turn to coat; refrigerate for 8 hours or overnight. Cover and refrigerate remaining marinade.

Drain and discard marinade from beef. Place tenderloin on a rack in a shallow roasting pan. Bake, uncovered, at 425° for 45-60 minutes or until roast reaches desired doneness (for rare, a meat thermometer should read 140°; medium, 160°; well-done, 170°), basting occasionally with reserved marinade. Transfer to warm platter. Let stand 10 minutes before slicing. Serve with remaining reserved marinade. **Yield:** 12 servings.

Nutritional Analysis: One serving (3 ounces cooked beef) equals 328 calories, 16 g fat (7 g saturated fat), 122 mg cholesterol, 391 mg sodium, 2 g carbohydrate, trace fiber, 40 g protein.
Diabetic Exchange: 5 lean meat.

Herb-Dressed Asparagus Orange Salad

Meatless

This unique salad combines the goodness of greens and the refreshing flavor of oranges.
—Sue Dannahower, Denver, Colorado

- **2/3 cup fat-free mayonnaise**
- **1/2 cup 1% buttermilk**
- **2 tablespoons olive oil**
- **2 tablespoons white wine vinegar**
- **4 tablespoons minced fresh basil, *divided***
- **2 tablespoons minced fresh tarragon, *divided***
- **24 fresh asparagus spears, trimmed**
- **12 cups torn mixed salad greens**
- **4 medium navel oranges, peeled and sliced**
- **1 small red onion, thinly sliced and separated into rings**

In a bowl, whisk the mayonnaise, buttermilk, oil and vinegar. Stir in 3 tablespoons basil and 1 tablespoon tarragon. Cover and refrigerate.

Place asparagus in a large skillet. Cover with water. Bring to a boil. Reduce heat; cover and simmer for 2-3 minutes or until crisp-tender. Drain and immediately place asparagus in ice water; drain.

Place three asparagus spears on an individual serving plate. Top with 1-1/2 cups salad greens. Drizzle with 2 tablespoons of dressing. Arrange oranges and onions over salad greens. Sprinkle with remaining basil and tarragon. **Yield:** 8 servings.

Nutritional Analysis: One serving (1 salad with 2 tablespoons dressing) equals 115 calories, 4 g fat (1 g saturated fat), 3 mg cholesterol, 198 mg sodium, 17 g carbohydrate, 5 g fiber, 4 g protein.
Diabetic Exchanges: 1 vegetable, 1 fat, 1/2 starch.

Caramel Apple Cheesecake

In my opinion, cheesecake is the ultimate dessert! This delicious version has less fat and calories.
—Kylene Owen, Jermyn, Pennsylvania

- **1-1/4 cups crushed reduced-fat cinnamon graham crackers (about 14 squares)**
- **1/4 cup finely chopped walnuts**
- **2 tablespoons brown sugar**
- **2 tablespoons butter, melted**
- **FILLING:**
- **2 large tart apples, peeled and sliced**
- **1/2 teaspoon ground cinnamon**
- **1/2 teaspoon ground nutmeg**
- **2 packages (8 ounces *each*) reduced-fat cream cheese**
- **2 packages (8 ounces *each*) fat-free cream cheese**
- **1 cup sugar**
- **1-1/4 cups egg substitute**
- **1/2 cup reduced-fat sour cream**
- **1/4 cup chopped walnuts, toasted**
- **3/4 cup fat-free caramel ice cream topping**

In a bowl, combine the crumbs, nuts, brown sugar and butter. Press onto the bottom and up the sides of a 9-in. springform pan coated with nonstick cooking spray. Place on a baking sheet. Bake at 350° for 8-10 minutes or until lightly browned. Cool on a wire rack.

In a small nonstick skillet coated with nonstick cooking spray, cook apples over medium heat for 6-8 minutes or until tender. Stir in cinnamon and nutmeg; set aside.

In a mixing bowl, beat cream cheese and sugar until smooth. Add egg substitute and sour cream just until blended. Stir in apple mixture and walnuts. Pour into crust. Place pan on a baking sheet. Bake at 350° for 45-55 minutes or until center is almost set. Turn oven off; leave cheesecake in oven with door ajar for 30 minutes.

Remove from oven. Carefully run a knife around edge of pan to loosen. Cool 1 hour longer. Refrigerate overnight. Remove sides of pan. Before serving, drizzle with caramel topping. Refrigerate leftovers. **Yield:** 12 servings.

Nutritional Analysis: One piece equals 351 calories, 14 g fat (7 g saturated fat), 33 mg cholesterol, 466 mg sodium, 43 g carbohydrate, 2 g fiber, 14 g protein.
Diabetic Exchanges: 2 starch, 2 fat, 1 lean meat, 1 fruit.

Delightful Holiday Dinner

Apple-Glazed Pork Loin

An impressive main dish for any special occasion, this succulent pork roast has a sweet, tangy flavor. I found this easy recipe in a church cookbook. Friends constantly request it.
—Jean Graf-Joyce, Albany, Oregon

1-1/8 teaspoons salt, *divided*
1/4 teaspoon plus 1/8 teaspoon pepper, *divided*
1 boneless rolled pork loin roast (about 3 pounds)
1 jar (12 ounces) apple jelly
4 teaspoons Dijon mustard
3 teaspoons lemon juice, *divided*

Rub 1 teaspoon salt and 1/4 teaspoon pepper over roast. Place on a rack in a shallow roasting pan. Bake, uncovered, at 350° for 45 minutes. Meanwhile, in a saucepan, melt jelly over low heat. Whisk in mustard and 1 teaspoon lemon juice. Brush roast lightly with jelly mixture. Bake 60-75 minutes longer or until a meat thermometer reads 160°, basting once with jelly mixture. Let roast stand for 10-15 minutes before slicing.

Stir drippings in pan to loosen browned bits. Pour into a measuring cup; skim fat. Stir the remaining jelly mixture, lemon juice, salt and pepper into drippings; heat through. Serve with the roast. **Yield:** 12 servings.

Nutritional Analysis: *One serving (3 ounces cooked pork with 1 tablespoon sauce) equals 256 calories, 8 g fat (3 g saturated fat), 67 mg cholesterol, 330 mg sodium, 20 g carbohydrate, trace fiber, 23 g protein.*
Diabetic Exchanges: *3 lean meat, 1-1/2 fruit.*

Green Bean Bundles

Low-carb *Low-fat* **Low-sodium** *Meatless*

The presentation for fresh green beans is so pretty, it could serve as the centerpiece for your dinner table! Bundled in yellow squash rings, the beans are seasoned with a drizzle of garlic and tarragon.
—Joyce Turley, Slaughters, Kentucky

1 pound fresh green beans
2 yellow summer squash (1-1/2-inch diameter)
1 garlic clove, minced
1/4 teaspoon dried tarragon, crushed
4 teaspoons olive oil
1/4 teaspoon salt
1/4 teaspoon coarsely ground pepper

Trim stem end from beans and arrange in eight bundles. Slice squash into 1/2-in. slices; hollow squash slices to within 1/4 in. of edges. Place beans through squash rings.

Place bean bundles in a steamer basket. Place in a saucepan over 1 in. of water; bring to a boil. Cover and steam for 8-10 minutes or until crisp-tender. Meanwhile, in a small nonstick skillet, saute garlic and tarragon in oil for 1 minute. Remove from the heat. Arrange bean bundles on a serving platter; drizzle with garlic mixture. Sprinkle with salt and pepper. **Yield:** 8 servings.

Nutritional Analysis: *One bundle equals 43 calories, 2 g fat (trace saturated fat), 0 cholesterol, 78 mg sodium, 5 g carbohydrate, 2 g fiber, 1 g protein.*
Diabetic Exchanges: *1 vegetable, 1/2 fat.*

Cream of Vegetable Soup

Meatless

I belong to an RV club and have passed on this recipe to 30 other women. The creamy soup is comforting on a cool day.
—Vicki Kamstra, Spokane, Washington

2 cups chopped sweet onions
1-1/2 cups chopped carrots
1 cup chopped celery
2 tablespoons canola oil
4 cups cubed peeled potatoes
1 large head cauliflower, broken into florets
3 cans (14-1/2 ounces *each***) reduced-sodium chicken broth** *or* **vegetable broth**
2 teaspoons salt
1/2 teaspoon white pepper
1/2 cup half-and-half cream
Fresh basil

In a large kettle or Dutch oven, saute onions, carrots and celery in oil until onions are tender. Add potatoes and cauliflower; saute 5-6 minutes longer. Add the broth, salt and pepper. Bring to a boil. Reduce heat; cover and simmer for 10-12 minutes or until vegetables are tender. Let stand until cool.

Puree vegetable mixture in a blender or food processor in batches. Return to pan. Stir in cream; heat through. (Do not boil.) Garnish with fresh basil. **Yield:** 11 servings.

Nutritional Analysis: *One serving (1 cup) equals 132 calories, 4 g fat (1 g saturated fat), 5 mg cholesterol, 773 mg sodium, 21 g carbohydrate, 4 g fiber, 5 g protein.*
Diabetic Exchanges: *1 starch, 1 vegetable, 1/2 fat.*

🍎 Cauliflower Power

TO MAKE mealtime bloom with good nutrition, call on cauliflower.

Low in sodium, calories and carbohydrates, cauliflower is a good source of fiber, folate and vitamins C, B6 and B5. It is also fat- and cholesterol-free.

A member of the cruciferous family (along with cabbage and kale) cauliflower is rich in compounds which may help prevent cancer.

Acids in cauliflower form strong-smelling sulfur compounds when heated…so don't overcook it.

Menu Features Pleasing Pork

Berry Barbecued Pork Roast

(Also pictured on page 237)

Moist and tender, this elegant pork roast topped with a thick ruby-red cranberry barbecue sauce is sure to please dinner guests!
—Doris Heath, Franklin, North Carolina

    1 boneless rolled pork loin roast (3 pounds)
1/4 teaspoon salt
1/4 teaspoon pepper
    4 cups fresh *or* frozen cranberries
    1 cup sugar
1/2 cup orange juice
1/2 cup barbecue sauce

Sprinkle roast with salt and pepper. Place roast fat side up on a rack in a shallow roasting pan. Bake, uncovered, at 350° for 45 minutes.

Meanwhile, in a saucepan, combine the cranberries, sugar, orange juice and barbecue sauce. Bring to a boil. Reduce heat; cook and stir over medium-low for 10-12 minutes or until cranberries pop and sauce is thickened. Brush over roast. Bake 15-20 minutes longer or until a meat thermometer reads 160°, brushing often with sauce. Let stand for 10 minutes before slicing. Serve with remaining sauce. **Yield:** 12 servings.

Nutritional Analysis: One serving (3 ounces cooked pork with 1/4 cup sauce) equals 262 calories, 8 g fat (3 g saturated fat), 67 mg cholesterol, 190 mg sodium, 23 g carbohydrate, 1 g fiber, 24 g protein.
Diabetic Exchanges: 3 lean meat, 1 starch, 1/2 fruit.

Swiss Scalloped Potatoes

Meatless

(Also pictured on page 237)

Our Test Kitchen came up with this ultimate comfort food that even calorie-counters can feel comfortable eating.

    9 cups sliced peeled potatoes (2-1/2 pounds)
    4 cups 2% milk
    2 teaspoons salt
    1 garlic clove, minced
1/4 teaspoon white pepper
    1 fresh rosemary sprig
    1 bay leaf
    4 teaspoons cornstarch
    2 tablespoons cold water
    4 ounces reduced-fat Swiss cheese, shredded
1-1/2 cups soft bread crumbs
    2 tablespoons butter, melted

In a large saucepan or Dutch oven, combine the potatoes, milk, salt, garlic, pepper, rosemary and bay leaf. Bring to a boil. Reduce heat to low; cover and cook for 6-8 minutes or until almost tender. Discard rosemary sprig and bay leaf.

In a small bowl, combine cornstarch and cold water until smooth; stir into potato mixture. Bring to a boil. Reduce heat; cook and stir for 2 minutes. Remove from the heat; gently stir in cheese.

Transfer to a 13-in. x 9-in. x 2-in. baking dish coated with nonstick cooking spray. Combine bread crumbs and butter; sprinkle over potato mixture. Bake, uncovered, at 350° for 25-30 minutes or until bubbly and crumbs are golden brown. **Yield:** 12 servings.

Nutritional Analysis: One serving (2/3 cup) equals 190 calories, 6 g fat (4 g saturated fat), 17 mg cholesterol, 511 mg sodium, 27 g carbohydrate, 2 g fiber, 8 g protein.
Diabetic Exchanges: 1-1/2 starch, 1/2 fat-free milk, 1/2 fat.

Orange Poppy Seed Dressing

Low-carb Low-fat Low-sodium

(Also pictured on page 237)

This light, refreshing dressing is yummy over spinach and other types of salad greens. The sweet-tart combination of honey, mustard, vinegar and citrus also accompanies fresh fruit nicely.
—Sue Dannahower, Denver, Colorado

    4 teaspoons cornstarch
    6 tablespoons cold water
1-1/3 cups orange juice
1/4 cup white vinegar
    4 teaspoons honey Dijon mustard
    4 teaspoons honey
1-1/2 teaspoons poppy seeds
1/2 teaspoon salt

In a small saucepan, combine cornstarch and cold water until smooth. Stir in the orange juice, vinegar, mustard and honey. Bring to a boil; cook and stir for 1 minute or until thickened. Stir in poppy seeds and salt. Cover and refrigerate until chilled. **Yield:** 1-1/2 cups.

Editor's Note: As a substitute for honey Dijon mustard, combine 2 teaspoons Dijon mustard and 2 teaspoons honey.

Nutritional Analysis: One serving (2 tablespoons) equals 26 calories, trace fat (trace saturated fat), 0 cholesterol, 88 mg sodium, 6 g carbohydrate, trace fiber, trace protein.
Diabetic Exchange: 1/2 fruit.

🍎 Poppy Seed Primer

POPULAR as a topping and all-purpose ingredient, poppy seeds are among the oldest of spices. These nutlike flecks of flavor have been cultivated for over 3,000 years and were used as a condiment as early as the first century A.D.

Poppy plants yield seeds ranging from white to black. There are about 900,000 tiny poppy seeds per pound!

Family-Style Suppers

In this chapter, you'll "meet" cooks
who share how they prepare good-for-you
fare for their families' tables. You'll
also find three dinners that don't
break your household budget.

Baked Vegetable Beef Stew, Cheesy Onion Quick Bread
and Pineapple Buttermilk Sherbet (page 253)

A Meal for Just $1.69 a Plate!

Raspberry Corn Muffins

Low-fat **Meatless**

I don't recall where I got this recipe, but these golden muffins have been a hit whenever I make them.
—*Jane Bray, Temple Terrace, Florida*

1 cup all-purpose flour
1 cup cornmeal
1/2 cup sugar
1 teaspoon baking powder
1/2 teaspoon baking soda
1/4 teaspoon salt
2 eggs, lightly beaten
2 cartons (6 ounces *each*) fat-free plain yogurt
2 tablespoons butter, melted
1 cup fresh raspberries

In a bowl, combine the flour, cornmeal, sugar, baking powder, baking soda and salt. In a small bowl, combine the eggs, yogurt and butter until smooth. Stir in dry ingredients just until moistened. Fold in raspberries.

Coat muffin cups with nonstick cooking spray; fill three-fourths full. Bake at 375° for 18-22 minutes or until a toothpick comes out clean. Cool for 5 minutes before removing from pan to wire rack. Serve warm. **Yield:** 1 dozen.

Nutritional Analysis: One muffin equals 164 calories, 3 g fat (2 g saturated fat), 41 mg cholesterol, 175 mg sodium, 29 g carbohydrate, 2 g fiber, 5 g protein.
Diabetic Exchange: *2 starch.*

Nutritional Analysis: One serving (1 cup) equals 227 calories, 4 g fat (1 g saturated fat), 65 mg cholesterol, 259 mg sodium, 25 g carbohydrate, 2 g fiber, 23 g protein.
Diabetic Exchanges: *3 lean meat, 1-1/2 fruit.*

Fruited Chicken Salad

This fresh-tasting chicken salad is sweetened with pineapple, dates and golden raisins. I often serve this salad on lettuce, but you could stuff a tomato with it or spoon it into pita bread as well.
—*Audrey Moser, Drummond Island, Michigan*

4 cups cubed cooked chicken breast
1 can (8 ounces) unsweetened crushed pineapple, drained
1/2 cup diced celery
1/2 cup diced red onion
1/2 cup golden raisins
1/2 cup chopped dates
DRESSING:
3/4 cup fat-free salad dressing *or* mayonnaise
1/2 cup reduced-fat sour cream
2 teaspoons lemon juice
1 teaspoon ground mustard
1/4 teaspoon garlic powder
1/8 teaspoon pepper
6 lettuce leaves

In a large bowl, combine the chicken, pineapple, celery, onion, raisins and dates. In another bowl, combine the salad dressing, sour cream, lemon juice, mustard, garlic powder and pepper; mix well. Pour over chicken mixture; toss to coat. Serve on lettuce leaf. **Yield:** 6 servings.

Lime Parfaits

Low-sodium

You don't need to give up delicious treats just because you are eating lighter! This refreshing four-ingredient dessert is easy to prepare and pretty to serve.
—*Mitzi Sentiff, Alexandria, Virginia*

1/2 cup plus 2 tablespoons chocolate wafer cookie crumbs, *divided*
1/4 cup finely chopped macadamia nuts, toasted
3 cups lime sherbet, softened
1 tablespoon grated lime peel

In a bowl, combine 1/2 cup cookie crumbs and nuts. In another bowl, combine sherbet and lime peel. Spoon 1 tablespoon cookie mixture into six parfait glasses; top with 1/4 cup sherbet mixture. Repeat layers. Sprinkle with remaining cookie crumbs. Cover and freeze until firm. **Yield:** 6 servings.

Nutritional Analysis: One parfait equals 193 calories, 7 g fat (2 g saturated fat), 5 mg cholesterol, 102 mg sodium, 32 g carbohydrate, 1 g fiber, 2 g protein.
Diabetic Exchanges: *1 starch, 1 fruit, 1 fat.*

A Meal for Just $1.15 a Plate!

Oriental Oven Omelet

Meatless

A great source of low-cost protein, eggs are an ideal way to liven up any meal on a budget. If you enjoy egg foo yong, you're sure to like this recipe.
—Edna Hoffman, Hebron, Indiana

2 packages (3 ounces *each***) ramen noodles**
1/2 cup thinly sliced celery
2 teaspoons canola oil
1 package (8 ounces) sliced fresh mushrooms
4 tablespoons green onions, thinly sliced, *divided*
2 tablespoons minced fresh gingerroot
3 eggs
6 egg whites
1 teaspoon sesame oil
1/2 teaspoon sugar
1/2 teaspoon salt
2 tablespoons reduced-sodium soy sauce

Discard seasoning packet from ramen noodles or save for another use. Cook noodles according to package directions. Drain and rinse in cold water; transfer to a bowl and set aside.

Meanwhile, in a large nonstick ovenproof skillet over medium heat, cook celery in canola oil for 1 minute. Stir in the mushrooms, 2 tablespoons green onions and ginger; cook and stir for 7 minutes or until mushrooms are lightly browned. Stir into noodles. Whisk the eggs, egg whites, sesame oil, sugar and salt. Stir into noodle mixture; spread into an even layer in the skillet. Cook on medium for 2 minutes. Bake, uncovered, at 350° for 10-12 minutes or until set. Cut into wedges. Sprinkle with remaining green onions. Drizzle with soy sauce. **Yield:** 6 servings.

Nutritional Analysis: One wedge equals 221 calories, 10 g fat (4 g saturated fat), 106 mg cholesterol, 597 mg sodium, 21 g carbohydrate, 1 g fiber, 11 g protein.
Diabetic Exchanges: 1-1/2 starch, 1 lean meat, 1 fat.

Sunflower Broccoli Salad

Low-carb   Meatless

The unique crunch of sunflower kernels and a zesty tang from a vinegar and sesame oil dressing turn basic broccoli into a sensational salad. We're on a low-carb diet, and this is one of our favorite dishes.
—Rick and Sheila Ellison, Prattville, Alabama

6 cups fresh broccoli florets
3 tablespoons rice vinegar
3 tablespoons reduced-sodium soy sauce
3 tablespoons sesame oil
Sugar substitute equivalent to 1 tablespoon sugar
1/4 cup unsalted sunflower kernels

In a large saucepan, bring 8 cups water to a boil. Add broccoli; cover and cook for 3 minutes. Drain and immediately place broccoli in ice water. Drain and pat dry.

In a small bowl, whisk the vinegar, soy sauce, oil and sugar substitute. Pour over broccoli; toss to coat evenly.

Cover and refrigerate for at least 1 hour, stirring several times. Just before serving, stir in sunflower kernels. **Yield:** 6 servings.

Editor's Note: This recipe was tested with Splenda No Calorie Sweetener. Look for it in the baking aisle of your grocery store.

Nutritional Analysis: One serving (3/4 cup) equals 121 calories, 10 g fat (1 g saturated fat), 0 mg cholesterol, 322 mg sodium, 6 g carbohydrate, 3 g fiber, 4 g protein.
Diabetic Exchanges: 2 fat, 1 vegetable.

Vegetable Fried Rice

Low-fat   Meatless

Our Test Kitchen stirred up this pleasing, low-fat combination of rice, vegetables and seasonings.

1/4 cup finely chopped onion
2 teaspoons canola oil
2 teaspoons minced fresh gingerroot
2 garlic cloves, minced
3 tablespoons reduced-sodium teriyaki sauce
2 tablespoons lime juice
1 teaspoon brown sugar
1/4 teaspoon salt
1/4 teaspoon hot pepper sauce
3 cups cold cooked rice
2 cups frozen mixed vegetables, thawed

In a nonstick skillet, saute onion in oil until tender. Add ginger and garlic; saute 1 minute longer. Add the teriyaki sauce, lime juice, brown sugar, salt and hot pepper sauce; bring to a boil. Reduce heat; cook and stir for 2 minutes. Add rice and mixed vegetables; cook and stir over medium heat until vegetables are tender. **Yield:** 6 servings.

Nutritional Analysis: One serving (3/4 cup) equals 169 calories, 2 g fat (trace saturated fat), 0 cholesterol, 286 mg sodium, 34 g carbohydrate, 3 g fiber, 5 g protein.
Diabetic Exchanges: 2 vegetable, 1-1/2 starch.

A Meal for Just $1.57 a Plate!

Baked Vegetable Beef Stew

When my granddaughter was 3, she had a bear that sang a song about "root stew". She thought he was talking about tree roots, so I took her to the store to buy root veggies, and we made this stew.
—*Alice McCabe, Climax, New York*

1-1/2 pounds boneless beef sirloin tip roast, cut
   into 1-inch cubes
   3 cups cubed peeled potatoes
   3 celery ribs, cut into 1-inch pieces
1-1/2 cups cubed peeled sweet potatoes
   3 large carrots, cut into 1-inch pieces
   1 large onion, cut into 12 wedges
   1 cup cubed peeled rutabaga
   1 envelope reduced-sodium onion soup mix
   2 teaspoons dried basil
   1/2 teaspoon salt
   1/4 teaspoon pepper
   1/2 cup water
   1 can (14-1/2 ounces) stewed tomatoes

In a large resealable plastic bag, combine the beef, vegetables, soup mix and seasonings. Seal bag; shake to coat evenly.

Transfer to a Dutch oven or 13-in. x 9-in. x 2-in. baking dish coated with nonstick cooking spray (pan will be very full). Pour water over beef mixture. Cover and bake at 325° for 1-1/2 hours. Stir in tomatoes. Bake, uncovered, for 30-40 minutes, stirring after 15 minutes, or until beef and vegetables are tender. **Yield:** 6 servings.

Nutritional Analysis: One serving (1-1/3 cups) equals 343 calories, 6 g fat (2 g saturated fat), 71 mg cholesterol, 699 mg sodium, 42 g carbohydrate, 5 g fiber, 29 g protein.
Diabetic Exchanges: 3 lean meat, 3 vegetable, 1-1/2 starch.

Cheesy Onion Quick Bread

Low-carb   Meatless

I make this bread ahead, then slice, wrap and freeze it. Then I heat up slices at the last minute.
—*Davona Henderson, Bountiful, Utah*

   1 medium onion, chopped
   1 teaspoon olive oil
1-1/2 cups reduced-fat biscuit/baking mix
   1 egg, lightly beaten
   1/2 cup fat-free milk
   1 cup (4 ounces) shredded reduced-fat cheddar
     cheese, *divided*
   2 teaspoons poppy seeds
   1 tablespoon butter, melted

In a small nonstick skillet, saute onion in oil until tender; set aside. Place biscuit mix in a bowl. Combine egg and milk; mix well. Stir into the biscuit mix just until moistened. Stir in the onion mixture, 1/2 cup cheese and poppy seeds.

Transfer to an 8-in. x 4-in. x 2-in. loaf pan coated with nonstick cooking spray. Sprinkle with the remaining cheese. Drizzle with butter. Bake at 400° for 20-25 minutes or until a toothpick inserted near the center comes out clean and loaf is golden brown. Cool for 10 minutes before removing from pan to a wire rack. Store in the refrigerator. **Yield:** 1 loaf (12 slices).

Nutritional Analysis: One slice equals 115 calories, 5 g fat (2 g saturated fat), 27 mg cholesterol, 275 mg sodium, 12 g carbohydrate, trace fiber, 5 g protein.
Diabetic Exchanges: 1 starch, 1 fat.

Pineapple Buttermilk Sherbet

Low-fat   Low-sodium

This icy sweet sherbet stirs up easily for freezing in a jiffy. It's a great dessert to have on hand.
—*Dolores Kastello, Waukesha, Wisconsin*

   2 cups 1% buttermilk
   1 can (20 ounces) unsweetened crushed
     pineapple, undrained
   3/4 cup sugar

In a bowl, combine all ingredients; stir until sugar is dissolved. Pour into a 9-in. square dish. Cover and freeze for 1 to 1-1/2 hours or until mixture begins to harden. Stir and return to freezer. Freeze 3-4 hours longer, stirring occasionally until firm. Remove from the freezer 20-25 minutes before serving. **Yield:** 10 servings.

Nutritional Analysis: One serving (1/2 cup) equals 113 calories, trace fat (trace saturated fat), 3 mg cholesterol, 57 mg sodium, 26 g carbohydrate, trace fiber, 2 g protein.
Diabetic Exchanges: 1 starch, 1/2 fruit.

No-Stress, Simple Supper

FAMILY comes first for Vickie Madrigal. Ten years ago, she married her high-school sweetheart, Tim. The couple bought a home in Shreveport, Louisiana, where they are raising two children, Tyler and Abby.

"Tim works as a machinist," Vickie explains, "and I'm a stay-at-home mom who occasionally substitute teaches. I love spending time with our children. And by teaching, I can keep up with what goes on with other kids today."

Vickie and Tim also raise chickens and hunting dogs. And she is the treasurer of a local parent-teacher association and updates the group's Web site in her free time.

"I like to play baseball and go swimming with our kids," she adds. "I also love to cook and lighten up family favorites, making them as healthy as possible."

Vickie's interest in cooking light started a few years back. "I was gaining weight, and I was tired of being tired," she shares. "I didn't want my children to follow the same path. I wanted them to learn about nutrition now so they would eat right in the future."

Cooking healthy became Vickie's goal. "I started incorporating reduced-fat products and sugar substitutes into my recipes," she says. "Much to my surprise, the dishes tasted nearly the same as their full-fat counterparts. My family usually didn't even notice that our meals were lighter."

While experimenting with seasonings, Vickie also discovered a few tricks to getting her children to eat their vegetables. "For example, I found that if I tossed steamed veggies with a little chicken broth and low-sodium soy sauce, the kids ate them right up," she says.

In addition, cooking healthier led Vickie to dust off some cookware and appliances that weren't getting much attention. "With my nonstick skillet and stovetop grill, I found that I could decrease the amount of butter and oil I previously used to prepare foods," she says.

"By using my slow cooker and experimenting with herbs and seasonings, I learned how to turn tough cuts of meat into tender, flavorful entrees without adding much fat and without much effort on my part.

"I knew these changes were working when I began to feel healthier," relates Vickie. "I must admit that trying to lose weight is the hardest thing I've ever done, but I don't dwell on the pounds I lose. Instead, I focus on making nutritious choices in the family meals I prepare."

One of the delicious dinners Vickie and her gang look forward to is the one she offers here. The no-stress supper kicks off with a marvelous Mushroom Chicken Pizza.

"Who doesn't like pizza?" asks Vickie. "This is a great alternative to the greasy variety, and its crispy crust and fresh toppings are always a hit." She adds that it's the perfect way to use up leftover chicken or veggies.

Vickie pairs the pizza with refreshing Pineapple Salad, but its mildly tangy dressing would complement most any entree. "After enjoying a similar salad at a restaurant, I tried to re-create it at home," she notes. "Adding sliced grilled chicken makes it a meal in itself.

"And while I don't prepare dessert very often, Creamy Peanut Butter Pie is a terrific way to top off any dinner," suggests Vickie. "Sugar-free pudding, a reduced-fat graham cracker crust and a few other items keep the fat and calories down, but no one guesses that this sweet treat is lighter than other desserts."

Mushroom Chicken Pizza

    1 tube (10 ounces) refrigerated pizza crust
    1 can (6 ounces) Italian tomato paste
1-1/2 cups cubed cooked chicken breast
    2 cups grape *or* cherry tomatoes, halved
  1/2 cup sliced fresh mushrooms
  1/4 cup sliced ripe olives
  1/8 teaspoon garlic salt
  1/8 teaspoon salt
  1/8 teaspoon pepper
    1 tablespoon olive oil
1-1/2 cups (6 ounces) shredded part-skim mozzarella cheese

Spread pizza dough in a 15-in. x 10-in. x 1-in. baking pan coated with nonstick cooking spray. Prick crust with a fork. Bake at 400° for 5 minutes. Spread with tomato paste. Sprinkle with the chicken, tomato halves, mushrooms, olives, garlic salt, salt and pepper. Drizzle with oil. Sprinkle with cheese. Bake 13-16 minutes longer or until cheese is melted. **Yield:** 6 servings.

    Nutritional Analysis: One piece equals 319 calories, 10 g fat (4 g saturated fat), 46 mg cholesterol, 618 mg sodium, 32 g carbohydrate, 3 g fiber, 23 g protein.
    Diabetic Exchanges: 2 lean meat, 1-1/2 starch, 1 vegetable, 1/2 fat.

Pineapple Salad

Low-carb *Low-fat* *Low-sodium* *Meatless*

    1 can (8 ounces) unsweetened pineapple slices
    1 tablespoon olive oil
    1 tablespoon honey
1-1/2 teaspoons cider vinegar
1-1/2 teaspoons reduced-sodium soy sauce
    6 cups torn romaine
  1/2 cup thinly sliced red onion

Drain pineapple, reserving juice. Cut slices in half; set aside. In a jar with a tight-fitting lid, combine the oil, honey, vinegar, soy sauce and reserved pineapple juice; shake well. Refrigerate for at least 30 minutes. Combine the romaine, onion slices and pineapple slices in a serving dish. Drizzle with dressing; toss to coat. **Yield:** 6 servings.

Nutritional Analysis: One serving (1 cup dressed salad) equals 64 calories, 2 g fat (trace saturated fat), 0 cholesterol, 59 mg sodium, 11 g carbohydrate, 1 g fiber, 1 g protein.
Diabetic Exchanges: 1 vegetable, 1/2 fruit.

Creamy Peanut Butter Pie

1-3/4 cups cold 2% milk
   1 package (1 ounce) sugar-free instant vanilla
     pudding mix
1/3 cup reduced-fat creamy peanut butter
   1 reduced-fat graham cracker crust (8 inches)
   2 cups reduced-fat whipped topping
   8 teaspoons chocolate syrup

In a bowl, whisk milk and pudding mix for 2 minutes. Stir in peanut butter. Transfer to crust. Cover and chill for at least 3 hours. Just before serving, spread with whipped topping. Drizzle servings with chocolate syrup. **Yield:** 8 servings.

Nutritional Analysis: One piece equals 258 calories, 12 g fat (5 g saturated fat), 5 mg cholesterol, 180 mg sodium, 30 g carbohydrate, 1 g fiber, 6 g protein.
Diabetic Exchanges: 2 starch, 2 fat.

Hands-on Helpers

TEACHING her little ones about eating right is important to Vickie Madrigal. "Every week I help each of my two children plan a healthy meal," she reports.

"They choose from their favorite family recipes or they look through a cooking magazine for new ideas. We discuss the items they selected and make any necessary adjustments together. Once their meals are set, I add them to the weekly menu plan I create, and then we hit the supermarket.

"The kids love to help out in the kitchen, preparing the meals they planned," explains Vickie. "More importantly, I get the opportunity to provide them with hands-on learning about working in the kitchen and making healthy food choices."

A From-the-Sea Favorite

CREATING succulent recipes is a family tradition for Kara De la vega. "My grandmother was a talented chef at a restaurant many years ago," shares this cook from her Somerset, California home.

"My mother also prepared wonderful meals for our family while I was growing up. One of my brothers became a chef, and I made cooking my favorite hobby."

After Kara married her husband, Jubencio, she discovered a wealth of new recipes and ingredients that she wasn't accustomed to using.

"Jubencio is from Mexico, and I wanted to fix him the traditional meals that his family served," Kara explains. "Many of these dishes called for lard or other high-fat items, which became staples in our kitchen."

As the years passed, Kara didn't think much about the heavy ingredients used in the meals she prepared for her husband and sons—Jon and Steven.

"But when both of my parents needed to have serious heart surgery, I realized that it was time to change my cooking style significantly," she says.

Kara immediately made several adjustments to her family's dinners. "No one was happy with the changes because I made too many too quickly," she admits. "I knew I had to take things much slower.

"So I began baking with honey, applesauce and egg whites or egg substitute instead of sugar, oil and whole eggs," says Kara. "And because Jubencio loves cheesecake, I experimented with reduced-fat cream cheese when preparing his favorite dessert. He didn't notice any difference."

"I gradually worked other light products, such as reduced-fat sour cream, into my recipes," she continues. "Soon, none of us could tell the difference between these items and the high-fat versions."

In addition to paring down dishes, Kara regularly introduced her family to healthier items, including exotic produce. "I admit that the boys aren't always crazy about the new foods I set in front of them," she shares.

"Like many kids, they say they don't like something before they even try it. I ask them to take at least one bite, and they often end up finishing their serving and asking for seconds."

The stay-at-home mom continues to invent delicious and nutritious meals. "I like experimenting with recipes," Kara says. "I think it's fun to see how close I can get to a dish's original flavor while slimming it down. Best of all, my family usually doesn't realize they're eating a healthy dinner."

One of the scrumptious suppers Kara is likely to serve is the one she shares here. Fiery Skewered Shrimp kick off the mouth-watering meal.

"This easy-to-make entree gets its great taste from a simple yet spicy marinade," she notes. "You can broil the kabobs or throw them on the grill outside. We like the shrimp served on a bed of greens or with Vegetable Rice Medley."

In this no-fuss side dish, green peppers, cauliflower and broccoli share the stage with brown rice that's mildly flavored with soy sauce. "We eat a lot of fresh vegetables, so this versatile combination is always well received," Kara says.

Another popular side dish is her colorful Broiled Parmesan Tomatoes. Basil and garlic deliver plenty of flavor while a bread crumb topping offers a slight crunch to each serving. "I hope you make these tasty tomatoes an addition to your menu soon," Kara concludes.

Fiery Skewered Shrimp
Low-carb

- 1 tablespoon olive oil
- 2 garlic cloves, minced
- 1/2 to 1 teaspoon crushed red pepper flakes
- 1/4 teaspoon ground ginger *or* 1 teaspoon minced fresh gingerroot
- 1-1/2 pounds uncooked large shrimp, peeled and deveined
- 2 small green peppers, cut into 1-inch squares
- 1 medium lemon, sliced

In a shallow bowl, combine the oil, garlic, pepper flakes and ginger. Add shrimp; stir to coat evenly. Cover and refrigerate for 2 hours.

Thread shrimp and green pepper alternately on metal or soaked wooden skewers. Place on a broiler pan coated with nonstick cooking spray. Broil 4-6 in. from the heat for 3 minutes. Turn shrimp; broil 2-3 minutes longer or until shrimp turn pink. Garnish with lemon slices. **Yield:** 4 servings.

Nutritional Analysis: *One serving equals 173 calories, 5 g fat (1 g saturated fat), 252 mg cholesterol, 291 mg sodium, 4 g carbohydrate, 1 g fiber, 28 g protein.*
Diabetic Exchanges: *4 very lean meat, 1/2 fat.*

Vegetable Rice Medley
Low-fat   Meatless

- 3 cups water
- 3 tablespoons reduced-sodium soy sauce
- 1 tablespoon reduced-sodium chicken bouillon granules *or* 1 vegetable bouillon cube
- 1-1/2 cups uncooked brown rice
- 2 medium green peppers, julienned
- 2 cups chopped fresh cauliflower
- 2 cups chopped fresh broccoli
- 3/4 cup chopped onion
- 2 garlic cloves, minced
- 2 teaspoons canola oil
- 1/2 teaspoon dried thyme

In a large saucepan, bring the water, soy sauce and bouillon to a boil. Stir in rice. Reduce heat; cover and simmer for 45-50 minutes or until liquid is absorbed. In a large nonstick skillet, saute the green peppers, cauliflower, broccoli, onion and garlic in oil until crisp-tender. Stir vegetables and thyme into rice mixture. **Yield:** 7 servings.

Nutritional Analysis: One serving (1 cup) equals 199 calories, 3 g fat (trace saturated fat), 0 cholesterol, 457 mg sodium, 38 g carbohydrate, 5 g fiber, 6 g protein.
Diabetic Exchanges: 2 starch, 1 vegetable.

Broiled Parmesan Tomatoes

Low-carb *Low-fat* *Low-sodium* *Meatless*

> 3 large tomatoes
> 1 tablespoon olive oil
> 1 garlic clove, minced
> 1/4 teaspoon coarsely ground pepper
> 1 tablespoon minced fresh basil *or* 1 teaspoon dried basil
> 3/4 cup soft bread crumbs
> 2 tablespoons grated Parmesan cheese

Slice tomatoes in half. Using a small spoon, remove seeds. Place tomato halves on a broiler pan coated with nonstick cooking spray. Combine the oil, garlic and pepper. Brush over tomatoes. Sprinkle with basil.

Broil about 6 in. from heat for 3-4 minutes or until heated through. In a small bowl, combine bread crumbs and Parmesan cheese. Sprinkle over tomatoes. Broil 1-2 minutes longer or until crumbs are lightly browned. Serve immediately. **Yield:** 6 servings.

Nutritional Analysis: One tomato half equals 55 calories, 3 g fat (1 g saturated fat), 1 mg cholesterol, 64 mg sodium, 6 g carbohydrate, 1 g fiber, 2 g protein.
Diabetic Exchanges: 1 vegetable, 1/2 fat.

A No-Soda Solution

MANY parents are finding refreshing good-for-you alternatives to sugary sodas and popular pops. "Soda is reserved for an occasional treat at our house," says Kara De la vega. "Instead of giving our children soda, we make our own fruit juice.

"We always have freshly squeezed grapefruit and orange juice in the refrigerator as well as homemade lemonade. Our youngest son loves picking fresh fruit from the trees in our yard," she adds.

"Because he's involved in making the fruit juice, he's happy to drink it instead of soda."

Saucy Chicken Is Choice

KEEPING fit isn't an option for Joy and Corey Cochran—it's an order! "We have to stay in shape to meet the physical fitness standards of the military," Joy says from Roy, Washington.

"Corey is an engineer for the Army, and I'm a sergeant in the Army Reserves, in addition to working as a government contractor."

To keep in step with her demanding lifestyle, Joy relies on simple exercises such as running and biking. "I also love taking walks with my children, Timothy and Alice, and my step-daughter, Nichole."

But working out isn't the only way Joy keeps in shape. Putting nutritious meals on the table is paramount in the Cochran home. "We hardly ever buy boxed dinners from the supermarket," she says. "In the time it takes to put a packaged meal on the table, I can prepare a well-rounded supper myself.

"Cooking from scratch also gives me the chance to make extra. For example, if I'm preparing a casserole, I'll make an additional one to store in the freezer for a busy night," she explains. "Then, when I'm in a hurry, I'm less likely to pick up fast food because the freezer is stocked with homemade meals."

Joy makes nutritious foods fun by adding color with fruits and vegetables. "The children love fresh salad, and they'll usually eat it without salad dressing if I toss the greens with baby carrots and cherry tomatoes," she says. "And if I add black olives, they think of it as a treat. Pizza topped with colorful veggies is another of their favorites."

When it comes to desserts, Joy has some kid-friendly solutions, too. "I rely on yogurt and fruit parfaits. I layer the ingredients in pretty glasses, and the kids love it.

"We make a lot of Popsicles as well. The children like to freeze fruit juice in small containers and shave it for snow cones," confirms Joy, who likes to get her little ones involved in the kitchen.

"They're excited to eat a dinner they helped prepare," she shares. "That's what I like about the following menu. I can spend time with the children because they help with each recipe."

Aspiring cooks will have no trouble stirring together the sweet-tangy sauce for Joy's Apricot-Glazed Chicken. "Rather than frying chicken in a lot of oil, I prefer to cook it in this simple sauce—it's tasty and so much better for us," she says.

When chicken is on her table, Home-Style Coleslaw usually makes an appearance, too. "It's a staple at our house," Joy notes. "The colors get the kids' attention, especially when I use red and green cabbage.

"Another one of their favorites is Ham 'n' Cheese Muffins. "They measure the ingredients and grease the muffin tins. The muffins not only round out most meals, but they also make great grab-and-go snacks on busy mornings."

Joy completes the dinner by coating bananas with chocolate, rolling them in nuts and freezing them. "Frozen Banana Pops make a nice dessert after a casual meal," she suggests. "The kids love rolling the bananas in various toppings, and I like keeping the frosty treats in the freezer for healthy snacks."

Apricot-Glazed Chicken

- 1/2 cup ketchup
- 1/2 cup 100% apricot spreadable fruit
- 1 tablespoon canola oil
- 2 teaspoons lemon juice
- 2 teaspoons minced garlic
- 1 to 2 teaspoons hot pepper sauce
- 1 teaspoon coarsely ground pepper
- 3/4 teaspoon salt
- 6 bone-in skinless chicken breast halves (7 ounces *each*)

Line a shallow roasting pan with foil; spray foil with non-stick cooking spray and set aside. In a large microwave-safe bowl, combine the first eight ingredients. Microwave, uncovered, on high for 90 seconds, stirring once.

Dip chicken into sauce. Arrange in prepared pan. Pour remaining sauce over chicken. Bake, uncovered, at 350° for 45-55 minutes or until a meat thermometer reads 170°, basting once. **Yield:** 6 servings.

Nutritional Analysis: One chicken breast half equals 273 calories, 6 g fat (1 g saturated fat), 89 mg cholesterol, 615 mg sodium, 20 g carbohydrate, 1 g fiber, 33 g protein.
Diabetic Exchanges: 4 lean meat, 1/2 fruit, 1/2 starch.

Ham 'n' Cheese Muffins

Low-carb

- 1/3 cup finely chopped onion
- 1 tablespoon butter
- 2 cups (8 ounces) shredded reduced-fat cheddar cheese
- 1-1/2 cups reduced-fat biscuit/baking mix
- 1/2 cup fat-free milk
- 1 egg, beaten
- 1 cup finely chopped fully cooked ham

In a nonstick skillet, saute onion in butter until tender; set aside. In a bowl, combine cheese and biscuit mix. Stir in milk and egg just until moistened. Fold in ham and onion mixture.

Coat muffin cups with nonstick cooking spray or use paper liners; fill three-fourths full. Bake at 425° for 13-15 minutes or until a toothpick inserted near the center comes out clean. Cool for 5 minutes before removing from pan to a wire rack. Serve warm. **Yield:** 1 dozen.

Nutritional Analysis: One muffin equals 146 calories, 7 g fat (4 g saturated fat), 37 mg cholesterol, 327 mg sodium, 12 g carbohydrate, trace fiber, 9 g protein.
Diabetic Exchanges: 1 starch, 1 lean meat, 1/2 fat.

Home-Style Coleslaw

Low-carb Meatless

    8 cups finely shredded cabbage
    1/2 cup shredded carrot
DRESSING:
    1/3 cup reduced-fat mayonnaise
    1/3 cup fat-free sour cream
    1 tablespoon sugar
    2 teaspoons cider vinegar
    1/2 teaspoon salt
    1/4 teaspoon pepper

In a large bowl, combine cabbage and carrot. In a small bowl, combine the dressing ingredients. Pour over cabbage mixture and toss to coat. Cover and refrigerate for 6-8 hours or overnight. **Yield:** 7 servings.

Nutritional Analysis: One serving (2/3 cup) equals 88 calories, 4 g fat (1 g saturated fat), 5 mg cholesterol, 292 mg sodium, 12 g carbohydrate, 3 g fiber, 2 g protein.
Diabetic Exchanges: *2 vegetable, 1 fat.*

Frozen Banana Pops

Low-sodium

(Not pictured)

    1/2 cup semisweet chocolate chips
    3 tablespoons honey
    1/4 cup reduced-fat peanut butter

    2 tablespoons fat-free milk
    4 medium firm bananas, halved
    1/3 cup finely chopped nuts

In a small heavy saucepan, melt chocolate chips and honey over low heat, stirring constantly. Add peanut butter; stir until smooth. Remove from the heat and stir in milk.

Peel bananas and insert wooden sticks into one end. Spoon chocolate mixture over bananas to coat. Sprinkle with nuts. Place on a waxed paper-lined baking sheet. Freeze for at least 30 minutes. Serve frozen. **Yield:** 8 servings.

Nutritional Analysis: One pop equals 213 calories, 9 g fat (3 g saturated fat), trace cholesterol, 67 mg sodium, 32 g carbohydrate, 3 g fiber, 5 g protein.
Diabetic Exchanges: *1-1/2 fat, 1 fruit, 1 starch.*

🍎 Fixing Company Fare

HOSTING drop-in guests doesn't have to hinder healthy-eating goals. Just follow Joy Cochran's lead.

"I keep light frozen yogurt and low-fat brownie mix on hand for unexpected company," she says. "I top the baked brownies with yogurt."

Not interested in slimmed-down sweets? Try Joy's savory party starter. "Guacamole dip is always a hit, but I substitute pureed peas for half of the avocado. Thanks to the dip's seasonings, no one ever notices they're getting an extra serving of veggies."

Mouth-Watering Mexican Meal

FEELING FIT is a family priority for Sandy Shortt and her gang. "We always try to eat healthy and keep active," notes the Cedarville, Ohio mom. "My mother set a good example for me. She taught me how to cook delicious and nutritious foods...and that's what I serve to my children and husband."

Sandy's husband, Jeff, teaches at Cedarville University, the same university where Sandy works part time. "I coordinate a wellness center and teach health-education courses," she says.

"I love helping people make positive changes through the weight management groups and fitness seminars that I set up. I sometimes plan health-related events at my church, too."

Staying active is also important to Sandy. "I walk, hike and bike," she says. "I'm also learning Royal Scottish dancing, which is a fun way to exercise."

When she's not working out, you'll find Sandy sewing, gardening or tending to four of the couple's five children—Joel, Glen, Cindy and Libby. Daughter Celia lives in Tennessee.

Sandy admits that having a toddler, teenagers and adults all living under one roof can cause some meal-planning challenges. "The biggest one is meeting everyone's tastes and nutritional needs," she confirms.

"Because the kids are still growing, I believe they need to eat differently than adults do. Plus, I try to teach the children about choosing the right foods. Luckily, I learned how to do all of this from the way my mother raised my siblings and me."

Sandy says that her interest in nutrition was fostered from an early age. "My mother encouraged us to eat healthy snacks, and she included carrot sticks in most of our bagged lunches.

"Mom has always cooked healthy, serving a variety of vegetables and watching the amount of salt in our diets. In addition, she's adventurous with ethnic foods. She knows that these dishes can be as light as they are tasty," shares Sandy.

"Now that I have my own family, I've simply expanded Mom's ideas. I keep fresh produce available for snacking, and in packed lunches I include fruit, veggies or plain yogurt that I sweeten with homemade jam."

Sandy also follows her mother's lead at dinnertime. "I usually serve at least one cooked vegetable and one raw vegetable with our suppers," she explains. "And I don't cook with much salt. In fact, I mix up my own seasoning blends.

"Like Mom did, I also taught my family to be open to trying ethnic foods. We particularly like Indian, Chinese and Mexican recipes."

Big on taste and lower on fat and sodium, the meal Sandy shares here features a south-of-the-border entree that's sure to be popular at your home. Southwest Summer Pork Chops get their zesty appeal from a simple combination of herbs and seasonings.

"We love the seasoning blend on pork, but you can also use it on chicken," shares Sandy. "It gives foods a terrific taste without added salt."

Red, yellow and green peppers lend a pleasant sweetness to Sandy's suggested side dish, Three-Pepper Pasta Toss. Ideal alongside the savory chops, this lightly coated medley complements most any meal. "It's simple, looks good and tastes wonderful," she says. "Jeff likes it as a meatless main course."

Cap off the succulent dinner with frosty Frozen Fruit Delight. Four ingredients are all you'll need to fix the berry-filled favorite. "It's a refreshing way to end a summer meal," Sandy promises.

Southwest Summer Pork Chops

Low-carb

    4 teaspoons dried minced onion
    2 teaspoons ground cumin
    1 teaspoon cornstarch
    1 teaspoon chili powder
    1 teaspoon dried minced garlic
1/2 teaspoon dried oregano
1/2 teaspoon paprika
1/4 teaspoon cayenne pepper
    6 bone-in pork loin chops (about 3/4 inch thick
      and 7 ounces *each*)
1/4 cup barbecue sauce
    2 tablespoons lemon juice

In a small bowl, combine the first eight ingredients; rub over pork chops. Place pork chops in a large resealable plastic bag. In a bowl, combine barbecue sauce and lemon juice. Pour over pork chops. Gently rub bag to distribute sauce. Refrigerate 1-2 hours.

If grilling the pork chops, coat grill rack with nonstick cooking spray before starting the grill. Grill chops, covered, over medium heat or broil 6 in. from the heat for 6-8 minutes on each side or until a meat thermometer reads 160°. **Yield:** 6 servings.

Nutritional Analysis: One serving (1 pork chop) equals 234 calories, 8 g fat (3 g saturated fat), 81 mg cholesterol, 202 mg sodium, 8 g carbohydrate, 1 g fiber, 30 g protein.
Diabetic Exchanges: *4 lean meat, 1/2 starch.*

Three-Pepper Pasta Toss

Low-fat   Meatless

    8 ounces uncooked penne *or* medium tube pasta
    1 *each* large sweet red, yellow and green pepper,
      chopped
    1 large red onion, cut into wedges
    1 tablespoon olive oil

3 tablespoons red wine vinegar
1 tablespoon sugar
3/4 teaspoon salt
3/4 teaspoon dried basil
1/2 teaspoon coarsely ground pepper

Cook pasta according to package directions. Meanwhile, in a large nonstick skillet, cook peppers and onion in oil until crisp-tender. Drain pasta; add to vegetable mixture. Stir in the vinegar, sugar, salt, basil and pepper. Cook and stir for 1-2 minutes or until heated through. **Yield:** 6 servings.

Nutritional Analysis: One serving (1 cup) equals 165 calories, 3 g fat (trace saturated fat), 0 cholesterol, 300 mg sodium, 31 g carbohydrate, 3 g fiber, 5 g protein.
Diabetic Exchanges: 2 vegetable, 1-1/2 starch.

Frozen Fruit Delight

Low-fat   Low-sodium

2 packages (16 ounces *each*) frozen
   unsweetened mixed fruit
2 cartons (6 ounces *each*) reduced-fat vanilla
   yogurt
1 medium ripe banana, cut into 1/4-inch slices
   and frozen
2 tablespoons sugar

Place contents of one frozen mixed fruit package in a microwave-safe dish. Microwave, uncovered, at 50% power for 1 minute. Repeat with remaining mixed fruit.

In a blender or food processor, place half the fruit, yogurt, banana and sugar; cover and process until smooth (mixture will be thick). Transfer to serving dishes. Repeat. Serve immediately or freeze up to 4 hours. **Yield:** 8 servings.

Nutritional Analysis: One serving (3/4 cup) equals 107 calories, 1 g fat (trace saturated fat), 4 mg cholesterol, 37 mg sodium, 23 g carbohydrate, 1 g fiber, 3 g protein.
Diabetic Exchange: 1-1/2 fruit.

🍎 Festive Family Foods

LIKE most moms, Sandy Shortt doesn't have time to fix separate entrees for the different tastes at her table. There are some entrees, however, that everyone takes to.

"I slice chicken breasts, onions and peppers and cook it all on my tabletop grill," she says. "Everyone rolls up the items they like in tortillas with their favorite taco fixings.

"Pizza is also great because you can put different toppings on different parts of the pizza...and please everyone's tastes.

"Mixing Parmesan and Asiago cheeses with a low-fat variety gives pizza more flavor with less fat."

Baked Fish Reels in Raves

WHEN IT COMES to feeding her family right, Sondra Ostheimer gets straight A's. And good grades are important to Sondra and her husband, Jeff, since they're both teachers.

"Jeff is an agriculture and science teacher at a local high school," Sondra says from Boscobel, Wisconsin. "I teach communication and business at a nearby technical college.

"Maybe it's because of my profession, but I'm always anxious to learn new things. That's why I read up on nutrition, looking for information and tips on how to prepare good-for-you foods for my family," she says.

"I know that educating myself, Jeff and our daughter, Casey, about making the right food choices will help keep us all healthy."

Sondra's interest in staying fit began a few years ago. "I was concerned about my risk for heart disease because I knew it ran in the family," she reports. "So I attended a wellness seminar. Surprisingly, it changed my life for good.

"Learning about the impact of food on our bodies made me reevaluate what I was eating. Before I knew it, I had purchased a grain mill so I could grind wheat myself. I bought 50 pounds of wheat and used it to bake my own bread. Since then, I've made bread for my family nearly every week.

"Casey absolutely loves 'Mommy's yummy bread' and looks for it at suppertime," adds Sondra. "The extra work is worth it, knowing that on any given day my toddler is eating healthier than many adults do."

Sondra tries to prepare recipes that are as nutrient-rich as possible while keeping fat to a minimum. "We eat a lot of whole wheat pastas and brown rice instead of their white counterparts," she explains. "The difference in taste may be subtle...but the health benefits are great.

"I also read food labels carefully. I buy fat-free everything—milk, sour cream, cream cheese, etc. I stay away from foods that are high in sodium, saturated fat, calories and overall fat.

"I also try not to saute foods in butter or oil. I bought a set of pots and pans a few years ago that were especially designed for sauteing vegetables in water instead of butter. Now, if I need a little more liquid in the skillet, I just add water. This way I'm cutting down on fat but letting the natural flavors of the food come through.

"Plus, I use my microwave for cooking vegetables because they lose fewer nutrients than on the stovetop." A dinner that satisfies both appetites and good-eating goals is exactly the sort of menu Sondra shares here.

Low in carbohydrates but pleasing in taste, Baked Walleye with Vegetables makes for a moist and tender main course. Parmesan cheese flavors a medley of zucchini, mushrooms and onions that tops the fish fillets.

"Sometimes, I stuff the fish with the cooked vegetables," Sondra suggests, "and other times we grill the fillets."

Colorful Cranberry Applesauce, spiced with cinnamon and ginger, is a nice complement to the walleye. "While searching the Internet for bread recipes, I happened upon one that used cranberries and apples," says Sondra. "I adapted some of the ingredients and created this sweet-tart applesauce.

"And when I found a recipe for Tomato Pea Couscous in a magazine, I revised it, keeping good nutrition in mind."

With a hint of cumin and other mellow flavors, the quick-to-fix couscous is an ideal accompaniment with most any entree. Serve it with Sondra's walleye fillets...or prepare it the next time you serve chicken or even pork.

Baked Walleye with Vegetables

Low-carb

1 small onion, thinly sliced
1 tablespoon olive oil
2 small zucchini, julienned
1 cup sliced fresh mushrooms
1/4 teaspoon pepper
1/8 teaspoon garlic powder
2 tablespoons lemon juice
2 tablespoons grated Parmesan cheese, *divided*
4 walleye fillets (about 6 ounces *each*)
1 tablespoon butter, melted

In a nonstick skillet, cook onion in oil over medium heat for about 2 minutes. Stir in zucchini and mushrooms; cook and stir 2 minutes longer. Sprinkle with pepper and garlic powder; stir in lemon juice. Cook and stir 30 seconds longer. Remove from the heat; stir in 1 tablespoon Parmesan cheese.

Place fillets in a 13-in. x 9-in. x 2-in. baking dish coated with nonstick cooking spray. Top each fillet with about 1/4 cup onion mixture. Drizzle with butter and sprinkle with remaining Parmesan cheese. Bake, uncovered, at 375° for 18-22 minutes or until fish flakes easily with a fork. **Yield:** 4 servings.

Nutritional Analysis: One fillet equals 250 calories, 9 g fat (3 g saturated fat), 156 mg cholesterol, 166 mg sodium, 6 g carbohydrate, 2 g fiber, 35 g protein.
Diabetic Exchanges: 4 lean meat, 1 vegetable.

Cranberry Applesauce

Low-fat   Low-sodium   Meatless

1/2 cup sugar
2 tablespoons water
4 medium Rome Beauty apples, peeled and chopped
1-1/2 cups fresh *or* frozen cranberries
1/2 teaspoon ground cinnamon
1/2 teaspoon ground ginger
1/2 teaspoon grated lemon peel

In a large saucepan, heat sugar and water over medium heat until sugar is dissolved, stirring occasionally. Stir in apples; cover and cook for 5 minutes, stirring several times. Stir in cranberries; cook and stir for about 8 minutes or until cranberries begin to pop. Cover and cook 5 minutes longer or until apples are tender, stirring several times.

Add cinnamon, ginger and lemon peel. Cook and stir for about 5 minutes. Remove from the heat; mash until mixture reaches desired consistency. **Yield:** 6 servings.

Nutritional Analysis: One serving (1/3 cup) equals 126 calories, trace fat (trace saturated fat), 0 cholesterol, trace sodium, 33 g carbohydrate, 3 g fiber, trace protein.
Diabetic Exchanges: 1 fruit, 1 starch.

Tomato Pea Couscous

Meatless

1/2 cup chopped onion
  2 garlic cloves, minced
  1 tablespoon olive oil
1/2 teaspoon ground cumin
  1 cup reduced-sodium chicken broth *or*
    vegetable broth
1/2 cup frozen peas
1/2 cup coarsely chopped seeded tomato
3/4 cup uncooked couscous

In a saucepan, saute onion and garlic in oil until tender. Stir in cumin; cook and stir for 30 seconds. Stir in the broth, peas and tomato. Cook for 1-2 minutes or until peas are almost tender. Stir in couscous; cover. Remove from the heat; let stand for 5 minutes. Fluff with fork. **Yield:** 4 servings.

Nutritional Analysis: One serving (3/4 cup) equals 184 calories, 4 g fat (1 g saturated fat), 0 cholesterol, 182 mg sodium, 31 g carbohydrate, 3 g fiber, 6 g protein.
Diabetic Exchanges: 2 starch, 1/2 fat.

🍎 Giving Tips a Try

EXPERIMENTING in the kitchen is key for Sondra Ostheimer. "It's important to be open-minded about trying healthy-cooking tips, even though they might seem unusual," she advises.

"I refused to rinse cooked meats to get rid of additional fat—the idea just sounded odd. I didn't think I'd ever try it," shares Sondra.

"After I gave it a shot, however, I quickly realized just how much more fat that step really does eliminate. Now, I can't imagine serving ground beef or sausage without giving it a quick rinse after cooking and draining it."

Tasty Soup and Salad Dinner

PREPARING nutritious meals is how Linda Kees practices what she preaches. "As a registered dietitian, I'm always looking to reduce fat yet add flavor to my family's meals," she says. "We eat red meat and fish only occasionally, so being creative in the kitchen is a necessity." Linda and her husband, Steve, a financial analyst, live in Boise, Idaho with their three young children—Lauren, Mitchell and Ella.

"Before I became a stay-at-home mom, I worked as a dietitian in an intensive care unit," explains Linda. "I continue to keep updated on nutrition research and trends by thoroughly reading professional journals."

In her free time, Linda searches for bargains at garage sales, sells items on the Internet and exercises. "I like to run, hike, ski and swim," she adds. "And I love spending time in the kitchen, creating good-for-you recipes."

Jumping aboard the healthy-eating bandwagon didn't happen overnight for Linda…or Steve, for that matter. "While I was in college, I found that a meatless diet was not only healthy but less expensive," she says, "and I gradually began eating more vegetarian foods.

"I was already dating Steve at this point, so he was aware of the sort of recipes I'd prepare for him once we were married. He grew up eating meat and drinking whole milk at nearly every meal, but he was willing to give my cooking a try.

"I found that a great way to get others accustomed to new food items is to hide them in dishes that they like," Linda recommends. "For instance, I would put tofu in Steve's favorite lasagna recipe instead of all the meat, and I'd stir a little flaxseed into things such as muffin batter or cookie dough."

Soon, beans, grains, pasta and tofu became regular substitutions for meat at the couple's dinner table. "Chicken enchiladas were replaced with black bean enchiladas, giving us the protein we needed as well as adding fiber to our diets," she notes. "It wasn't long before Steve was used to my meatless meals, and I'm happy to say that fat-free milk is now a staple in our house."

It should come as no surprise that the comforting meal Linda offers here is not only mouth-watering but meatless as well. "Your family won't even miss the meat in my Garlic-Basil Tortellini Soup," she assures.

"I created the recipe through trial and error. I make it with vegetable broth, but feel free to use chicken broth if you prefer."

A quick fix with frozen pasta and canned beans, it's sure to heat up the chilliest of winter nights.

For an easy accompaniment, toss together Linda's Asian Crunch Salad. The medley of fresh veggies is lightly coated with a dressing of soy sauce, cider vinegar and sesame oil. "I don't care much for broccoli, but I gladly eat it in this salad," she writes. "Consider adding carrots for more color, crunch and nutrition."

Loaded with nutty flavor, down-home Toasted Walnut Bread is sure to be another hit with your gang. "I received the recipe from a co-worker and simply substituted some of the all-purpose flour with the whole wheat variety," Linda explains.

Whether you serve it as part of Linda's meal or pair it with a long-standing family favorite, the hearty golden loaf is sure to be requested time and again.

Garlic-Basil Tortellini Soup

Meatless

    2 garlic cloves, minced
    1 teaspoon butter
    2 cans (14-1/2 ounces *each*) reduced-sodium chicken broth *or* vegetable broth
  1/2 cup water
  1/3 cup minced fresh basil
  1/4 teaspoon pepper
2-1/2 cups frozen cheese tortellini
    1 can (19 ounces) white kidney *or* cannellini beans, rinsed and drained
    2 tablespoons balsamic vinegar
  1/4 cup shredded Parmesan cheese

In a large saucepan, saute garlic in butter until tender. Stir in the broth, water, basil and pepper. Bring to a boil. Stir in tortellini. Reduce heat; simmer, uncovered, for about 3 minutes or until tortellini begins to float. Stir in beans and vinegar; heat through. Sprinkle with Parmesan cheese. **Yield:** 4 servings.

Nutritional Analysis: One serving (1-1/4 cups soup with 1 tablespoon Parmesan cheese) equals 284 calories, 8 g fat (4 g saturated fat), 20 mg cholesterol, 953 mg sodium, 37 g carbohydrate, 6 g fiber, 15 g protein.
Diabetic Exchanges: 2-1/2 starch, 2 lean meat.

Asian Crunch Salad

Low-carb **Meatless**

    1 cup broccoli florets
    1 cup cauliflowerets
    1 cup cherry tomatoes
  1/2 cup fresh snow peas
    2 green onions, thinly sliced
  1/2 cup sliced water chestnuts, drained
4-1/2 teaspoons reduced-sodium soy sauce
    1 tablespoon cider vinegar
    1 tablespoon sesame oil
  3/4 teaspoon sugar
  1/2 teaspoon sesame seeds, toasted
  1/2 teaspoon olive oil
Dash pepper

In a large bowl, combine the broccoli, cauliflowerets, tomatoes, snow peas and green onions. Stir in water chestnuts.

In a small bowl, whisk the soy sauce, vinegar, sesame oil, sugar, sesame seeds, olive oil and pepper. Pour over broccoli mixture; stir to coat. Cover and refrigerate until chilled. **Yield:** 4 servings.

Nutritional Analysis: One serving (1 cup) equals 82 calories, 4 g fat (1 g saturated fat), 0 cholesterol, 246 mg sodium, 10 g carbohydrate, 3 g fiber, 2 g protein.
Diabetic Exchanges: *2 vegetable, 1 fat.*

nonstick cooking spray. Bake at 350° for 50-55 minutes or until a toothpick inserted near the center comes out clean. Cool for 10 minutes before removing from pan to a wire rack to cool completely. **Yield:** 1 loaf (12 slices).

Nutritional Analysis: One slice equals 202 calories, 11 g fat (1 g saturated fat), 18 mg cholesterol, 237 mg sodium, 23 g carbohydrate, 2 g fiber, 5 g protein.
Diabetic Exchanges: *2 fat, 1-1/2 starch.*

Toasted Walnut Bread

Meatless

    1 cup all-purpose flour
    1 cup whole wheat flour
  1/3 cup sugar
    3 teaspoons baking powder
  1/2 teaspoon salt
    1 egg, lightly beaten
    1 cup fat-free milk
  1/4 cup canola oil
  1/2 teaspoon vanilla extract
    1 cup coarsely chopped walnuts, toasted

In a large bowl, combine the flours, sugar, baking powder and salt. Combine the egg, milk, oil and vanilla. Stir into dry ingredients just until moistened. Fold in walnuts.
　Transfer to an 8-in. x 4-in. x 2-in. loaf pan coated with

🍎 Light Baking Basics

WHEN IT COMES to whipping up a better-for-you treat, Linda Kees keeps a few tricks up her apron sleeve. "I puree prunes or use baby food as a replacement for some of the fat in my brownies and cookies," she explains.

　"I have also found that light sour cream and cream cheese perform well in many baked goods and desserts," she adds. "They often offer the same flavor and creaminess as their heavier counterparts, without the high fat and calorie content."

　Similarly, Linda uses sugar substitute in some of her goodies. "I've recently experimented with low-calorie sweeteners," she says. "So far, things have been coming out of the oven perfectly!"

Trimmed-Down Dishes for Two

Turn to this chapter if you're cooking
for just two and neither of you
cares to eat leftovers. These lighter
recipes yield smaller quantities
without sacrificing flavor.

Thyme-Marinated Pork Chops, Macaroni Green Salad
and Snappy Individual Peach Crisps (page 268)

Shrimp with Vegetables

Low-carb

Colorful sweet pepper, zucchini and yellow summer squash team up with tender shrimp in this delightful main dish. If you clean the shrimp and slice the vegetables the night before, it makes a quick weeknight meal. It's my husband's favorite stir-fry.
—Beth Woodard, Jamestown, North Carolina

1 teaspoon cornstarch
1/2 cup cold water
2 tablespoons reduced-sodium soy sauce
1 medium onion, halved and sliced
1/2 medium sweet red pepper, cut into strips
1/2 medium zucchini, sliced
1/2 medium yellow summer squash, sliced
1 tablespoon canola oil
3/4 pound uncooked medium shrimp, peeled and deveined
1/2 teaspoon dried tarragon
1/4 teaspoon grated lemon peel
1/8 to 1/4 teaspoon crushed red pepper flakes
Hot cooked rice, optional

In a bowl, combine the cornstarch, water and soy sauce until smooth; set aside. In a nonstick skillet or wok, stir-fry the onion, red pepper, zucchini and summer squash in hot oil for 2 minutes. Add the shrimp, tarragon, lemon peel and crushed pepper flakes. Stir-fry until shrimp turns pink and vegetables are tender, about 2 minutes. Stir soy sauce mixture; stir into skillet. Bring to a boil; cook and stir for 2 minutes or until thickened. Serve over rice if desired. **Yield:** 2 servings.

Nutritional Analysis: One serving (1-1/2 cups shrimp mixture, calculated without rice) equals 302 calories, 10 g fat (1 g saturated fat), 259 mg cholesterol, 862 mg sodium, 14 g carbohydrate, 3 g fiber, 38 g protein.
Diabetic Exchanges: 5 lean meat, 2 vegetable.

Carrots and Onions

Low-carb   Low-fat   Meatless

I buy a box of Vidalia onions every year, and this is one of my favorite ways to fix them. Rosemary and thyme season the veggies in the quick-to-fix side dish that's great for a holiday meal or every day.
—Norma Essex, Porthill, Idaho

1/4 cup sliced sweet onion
1-1/2 cups sliced carrots
1/4 teaspoon dried rosemary
1/4 teaspoon dried thyme
2 teaspoons minced fresh parsley
1 teaspoon butter
1/8 teaspoon salt
Dash pepper

Cut onion slices in half. Place onions and carrots in a steamer basket. Sprinkle with rosemary and thyme. Place in a saucepan over 1 in. of water; bring to a boil. Cover and steam for 8-10 minutes or until crisp-tender. Remove to a serving bowl. Toss with parsley, butter, salt and pepper. **Yield:** 2 servings.

Nutritional Analysis: One serving (1 cup) equals 69 calories, 2 g fat (1 g saturated fat), 5 mg cholesterol, 201 mg sodium, 12 g carbohydrate, 4 g fiber, 1 g protein.
Diabetic Exchanges: 2 vegetable, 1/2 fat.

Strawberry Banana Cups

Low-fat   Low-sodium

My husband and I like Jell-O salad now and then, but if I make a whole package, it goes to waste. This recipe makes just enough for two. You can substitute other gelatin flavors for variety.
—Evelyn Savage, Belfair, Washington

1-1/2 teaspoons sugar-free strawberry gelatin powder
1/2 cup boiling water
1/2 cup unsweetened apple juice
3 strawberries, sliced
1 small firm banana, cut into 1/4-inch slices
2 strawberries, halved for garnish

Dissolve gelatin in boiling water. Stir in apple juice. Refrigerate for 30 minutes. Place sliced strawberries in the bottom of two individual serving dishes or 10-oz. custard cups. Stir bananas into gelatin mixture. Pour over strawberries. Refrigerate for at least 2 hours or until firm. Garnish with strawberry halves. **Yield:** 2 servings.

Nutritional Analysis: One serving equals 107 calories, 1 g fat (trace saturated fat), 0 cholesterol, 5 mg sodium, 27 g carbohydrate, 3 g fiber, 1 g protein.
Diabetic Exchange: 2 fruit.

Quick Marinara

Meatless

My husband and I love garlic, so we enjoy this pasta dish often. Crushed red pepper flakes give this meatless fast-to-fix sauce a little kick, but you can adjust the "heat level" to your liking.
—Donna Yarbam, Springfield, Missouri

3 garlic cloves, minced
1 teaspoon olive oil
1 can (14-1/2 ounces) Italian diced tomatoes, undrained
1 teaspoon dried basil
1/8 teaspoon pepper
1/8 teaspoon crushed red pepper flakes
Hot cooked linguine
2 tablespoons grated Parmesan cheese

In a small nonstick skillet, saute garlic in oil for 1 minute. Add the tomatoes, basil, pepper and red pepper flakes; bring to a boil. Reduce heat; simmer, uncovered, for 10 minutes or until liquid is reduced. Serve over linguine. Sprinkle with cheese. **Yield:** 2 servings.

Nutritional Analysis: One serving (2/3 cup marinara sauce, calculated without linguine) equals 128 calories, 4 g fat (1 g saturated fat), 4 mg cholesterol, 886 mg sodium, 19 g carbohydrate, 2 g fiber, 4 g protein.
Diabetic Exchanges: 3 vegetable, 1 fat.

Thyme-Marinated Pork Chops

Low-carb

(Pictured on page 266)

A garlic and thyme marinade and a crisp bread-crumb coating enhance these juicy chops. They're great for an everyday dinner or special occasion.
—Allyson Harms, Edmond, Oklahoma

1/2 cup white wine *or* chicken broth
2 tablespoons fresh thyme leaves, *divided*
2 garlic cloves, minced
2 bone-in pork loin chops (7 ounces *each*)
1/2 cup soft bread crumbs
1/8 teaspoon salt
1/8 teaspoon pepper
2 teaspoons olive oil

In a resealable plastic bag, combine the wine or broth, 1 tablespoon thyme and garlic; add pork. Seal bag and shake to coat; refrigerate for 30 minutes. Turn and refrigerate 30 minutes longer.

Drain and discard marinade. In a shallow bowl, combine the bread crumbs, salt, pepper and remaining thyme. Coat pork chops on both sides with crumb mixture. In a nonstick skillet over medium heat, cook pork in oil for 8 minutes on each side or until golden brown and a meat thermometer reads 160°. **Yield:** 2 servings.

Nutritional Analysis: One pork chop equals 287 calories, 13 g fat (4 g saturated fat), 81 mg cholesterol, 269 mg sodium, 7 g carbohydrate, trace fiber, 31 g protein.
Diabetic Exchanges: 4 lean meat, 1/2 starch.

Macaroni Garden Salad

Meatless

(Pictured on page 266)

I enjoy making this delightful salad in summer. Tomato, cucumber and sweet red pepper are tossed with macaroni and herbs, then coated in a creamy fat-free mayonnaise dressing. Serve it as a light lunch or as a side dish with your favorite meat for supper.
—Bonnie Sturgeon, Berwick, New Brunswick

1 cup cooked elbow macaroni
1 medium tomato, seeded and chopped
1/2 cup chopped seeded cucumber
1/2 cup chopped sweet red pepper
2 tablespoons minced fresh basil
1 tablespoon minced fresh parsley
2 tablespoons fat-free mayonnaise
2 teaspoons olive oil
1 teaspoon balsamic vinegar
1 garlic clove, minced
1/4 teaspoon salt
1/8 teaspoon pepper

In a bowl, combine the macaroni, tomato, cucumber, red pepper, basil and parsley. In a small bowl, whisk together the mayonnaise, oil, vinegar, garlic, salt and pepper until blended. Stir into macaroni mixture until coated. Cover and refrigerate for at least 2 hours. **Yield:** 2 servings.

Nutritional Analysis: One serving (1-1/4 cups) equals 181 calories, 6 g fat (1 g saturated fat), 2 mg cholesterol, 426 mg sodium, 29 g carbohydrate, 3 g fiber, 5 g protein.
Diabetic Exchanges: 1-1/2 starch, 1 vegetable, 1 fat.

Snappy Individual Peach Crisps

(Pictured on page 266)

Crushed gingersnaps spice up the warm sweet peaches in this down-home dessert from our Test Kitchen. It's so yummy, you won't think you're eating light!

2 teaspoons cornstarch
3 teaspoons sugar, *divided*
1 teaspoon lemon juice
1/8 teaspoon salt
1/8 teaspoon ground nutmeg
2 cups fresh *or* frozen sliced peeled peaches, thawed
1/4 cup crushed gingersnap cookies (about 4 cookies)
1/4 teaspoon ground cinnamon
1 tablespoon cold butter

In a bowl, combine the cornstarch, 2 teaspoons sugar, lemon juice, salt, nutmeg and peaches. Set aside for 30 minutes. Divide peaches between two 10-oz. baking dishes. In a bowl, combine cookie crumbs, cinnamon and remaining sugar. Cut in butter until crumbly. Sprinkle over peaches. Bake, uncovered, at 350° for 20-30 minutes or until the peaches are tender. **Yield:** 2 servings.

Nutritional Analysis: One serving equals 219 calories, 7 g fat (4 g saturated fat), 15 mg cholesterol, 291 mg sodium, 39 g carbohydrate, 4 g fiber, 2 g protein.
Diabetic Exchanges: 1-1/2 starch, 1 fruit, 1 fat.

Stovetop Latte

Low-carb   Low-fat   Low-sodium

Skip the trip to the trendy coffee shop and brew this good-for-you version of latte in the comfort of your own home. It's a great winter warm-up!
—Delores Ward, Decatur, Indiana

1-1/3 cups fat-free milk
Sugar substitute equivalent to 2 teaspoons sugar
2/3 cup hot strong brewed coffee
Ground cinnamon *or* baking cocoa, optional

In a small saucepan, combine the milk and sugar substitute. Whisk over medium heat until foamy and steaming (do not boil). Slowly pour into a mug. Pour coffee through the foam. Sprinkle with cinnamon or cocoa if desired. **Yield:** 2 servings.

Editor's Note: This recipe was tested with Splenda No Calorie Sweetener. Look for it in the baking aisle of your grocery store.

Nutritional Analysis: One serving (1 cup) equals 61 calories, trace fat (trace saturated fat), 3 mg cholesterol, 86 mg sodium, 9 g carbohydrate, 0 fiber, 6 g protein.
Diabetic Exchange: 1/2 fat-free milk.

Turkey Noodle Soup

Low-fat

(Pictured above)

*My husband must eat a very low-fat diet,
so I'm always experimenting to find things that will
agree with his stomach, too. This recipe is a hit.*
—*Doris Nehoda, Coos Bay, Oregon*

  2 cups water
3/4 cup cubed cooked turkey breast
  1 celery rib with leaves, sliced
1/4 cup chopped onion
  2 garlic cloves, minced
1/2 teaspoon salt
1/8 teaspoon dried marjoram
1/8 teaspoon pepper
  1 bay leaf
1/2 cup cubed peeled potato
1/4 cup frozen peas
1/4 cup uncooked yolk-free wide noodles
Dash browning sauce, optional

In a large saucepan, combine the first nine ingredients;
bring to a boil. Reduce heat; cover and simmer for 10 minutes or until celery is tender. Add the potato, peas and
noodles; cover and simmer 15 minutes longer or until potatoes are tender. Discard bay leaf. Stir in browning sauce
if desired. **Yield:** 2 servings.

   *Nutritional Analysis: One serving (1-1/2 cups) equals 156
calories, 1 g fat (trace saturated fat), 45 mg cholesterol, 659 mg
sodium, 18 g carbohydrate, 3 g fiber, 19 g protein.*
   Diabetic Exchanges: *2 very lean meat, 1 starch.*

Herbed Tuna Salad

Low-carb *Low-fat*

(Pictured above)

*Cooking for two is such a challenge for us,
since my husband and I do not care for leftovers.
We enjoy this well-seasoned salad, with its
distinctive dill flavor. It's my favorite lunch recipe.*
—*Rebecca Schweizer, Chesapeake, Virginia*

  1 can (6 ounces) light water-packed tuna,
    drained and flaked
  2 tablespoons finely chopped red onion
  1 tablespoon minced fresh parsley
1-1/2 teaspoons dill weed
1/8 teaspoon garlic salt
1/8 teaspoon dried thyme
1/8 teaspoon pepper
Pinch cayenne pepper
  2 tablespoons fat-free mayonnaise
  1 tablespoon reduced-fat sour cream
  3 cups spring mix salad greens
  1 medium tomato, cut into wedges

In a small bowl, combine the first eight ingredients. Combine the mayonnaise and sour cream; stir into tuna mixture.
Divide salad greens between two plates. Top with tuna
mixture and tomato wedges. **Yield:** 2 servings.

   *Nutritional Analysis: One salad equals 170 calories, 2 g fat
(1 g saturated fat), 30 mg cholesterol, 452 mg sodium, 14 g carbohydrate, 4 g fiber, 25 g protein.*
   Diabetic Exchanges: *3 very lean meat, 2 vegetable.*

Ramen Noodle Stir-Fry

(Pictured above)

This mildly flavored stir-fry combines tender strips of chicken with vegetables and popular ramen noodles. I came up with this recipe when I wanted a quick meal for myself. Sometimes I change the vegetables or substitute ground turkey for the chicken.
—Dawn Boothe, Lynn Haven, Florida

　1　package (3 ounces) ramen noodles
1-1/2　cups hot water
　8　ounces boneless skinless chicken breasts,
　　　cut into 2-inch strips
　2　teaspoons canola oil, *divided*
　1　large green pepper, cubed
2/3　cup chopped onion
　1　garlic clove, minced
1/2　cup reduced-sodium chicken broth
　2　teaspoons reduced-sodium soy sauce
　1　teaspoon salt-free seasoning blend
　1　small tomato, cut into wedges

In a bowl, place noodles in hot water for 2 minutes; drain and set aside. Discard seasoning package or save for another use. In a large nonstick skillet, stir-fry chicken in 1 teaspoon oil until no longer pink. Remove and keep warm. Stir-fry the green pepper, onion and garlic in remaining oil until crisp-tender. Add the chicken, broth, soy sauce, seasoning blend and noodles; toss gently. Add tomato; heat through. **Yield:** 2 servings.

Nutritional Analysis: One serving (2 cups) equals 419 calories, 14 g fat (5 g saturated fat), 66 mg cholesterol, 590 mg sodium, 39 g carbohydrate, 3 g fiber, 33 g protein.
Diabetic Exchanges: 3 lean meat, 3 vegetable, 1-1/2 starch, 1 fat.

Waffled French Toast

Meatless

Are waffles too much trouble for the two of you? You'll want to try this quick and clever alternative. I drizzle crispy slices of whole wheat bread with a yummy sauce that combines pancake syrup and fresh sliced strawberries. It's sure to become a breakfast favorite at your house, too!
—Martha Osborne, Jackson, Michigan

　1　egg
　1　egg white
1/4　cup fat-free milk
　4　slices whole wheat *or* white bread
　1　cup sliced fresh strawberries
1/4　cup reduced-calorie pancake syrup

In a shallow dish, beat the egg, egg white and milk. Dip bread into egg mixture, coating both sides. Bake in a preheated waffle iron according to manufacturer's directions until golden brown.

For sauce, in a bowl, crush the strawberries; stir in the pancake syrup. Serve French toast with the strawberry sauce. **Yield:** 2 servings.

Nutritional Analysis: One serving (2 pieces French toast with 6 tablespoons sauce) equals 261 calories, 5 g fat (1 g saturated fat), 107 mg cholesterol, 401 mg sodium, 45 g carbohydrate, 4 g fiber, 11 g protein.
Diabetic Exchanges: 2-1/2 starch, 1 lean meat, 1/2 fruit.

Seasoned Scrambled Eggs

Low-carb　Meatless

Whip up this fluffy egg dish for two in your kitchen. The addition of ranch dressing, brown mustard and mozzarella cheese makes these fast-to-fix scrambled eggs something special.
—Charlotte Wiley, New York City, New York

　4　egg whites
　3　eggs
　2　tablespoons reduced-fat ranch salad dressing
　2　teaspoons spicy brown mustard
　1　teaspoon minced fresh parsley
1/2　teaspoon garlic powder
　1　teaspoon canola oil
1/4　cup shredded part-skim mozzarella cheese

In a bowl, whisk together the egg whites and eggs. Stir in the salad dressing, mustard, parsley and garlic powder. In a nonstick skillet, cook egg mixture in oil over medium heat for 2 minutes or until eggs are almost set. Stir in cheese. Cook 1 minute longer or until eggs are set and cheese is melted. Serve immediately. **Yield:** 2 servings.

Nutritional Analysis: One serving (1 cup) equals 251 calories, 16 g fat (4 g saturated fat), 331 mg cholesterol, 496 mg sodium, 4 g carbohydrate, trace fiber, 21 g protein.
Diabetic Exchanges: 3 lean meat, 1-1/2 fat.

Braised Autumn Pork Chops

Low-carb

My husband found this recipe in a cookbook of healthy recipes. A braising liquid keeps the pork tender and juicy.
—Sarah Susanka, Ventura, California

   2 bone-in pork loin chops (7 ounces *each*)
   1/4 teaspoon salt
Dash pepper
   1 teaspoon canola oil
   3/4 cup thinly sliced onion
   1 celery rib, thinly chopped
   1/2 cup apple cider *or* unsweetened apple juice
   2 teaspoons cider vinegar
   1 tablespoon minced fresh sage *or* 1 teaspoon rubbed sage

Sprinkle pork with salt and pepper. In a nonstick skillet, cook meat in oil for about 3 minutes on each side or until browned; drain. Remove meat; keep warm.

In same skillet, cook onion and celery for about 4 minutes or until tender. Stir in the apple cider, vinegar and sage. Return meat to skillet. Bring to a boil. Reduce heat; cover and simmer for 15-20 minutes or until meat is tender. **Yield:** 2 servings.

Nutritional Analysis: One pork chop equals 277 calories, 11 g fat (3 g saturated fat), 86 mg cholesterol, 383 mg sodium, 12 g carbohydrate, 1 g fiber, 31 g protein.
Diabetic Exchanges: 4 lean meat, 1 vegetable, 1/2 fruit.

Eggnog Shakes

Low-sodium

This easy-to-fix recipe retains the thick creamy consistency of the classic Christmas beverage.
—Dale Hartman, Coventry, Rhode Island

1-1/2 cups fat-free sugar-free vanilla ice cream
   1/2 cup fat-free milk
   1 tablespoon fat-free whipped topping
Sugar substitute equivalent to 1/2 teaspoon sugar
   1/8 teaspoon rum extract
   1/8 teaspoon brandy extract *or* vanilla extract
Dash ground nutmeg

In a blender, combine the first six ingredients; cover and process until smooth. Pour into chilled glasses; sprinkle with nutmeg. **Yield:** 2 servings.

Editor's Note: This recipe was tested with Splenda No Calorie Sweetener. Look for it in the baking aisle of your grocery store.

Nutritional Analysis: One serving (3/4 cup) equals 163 calories, 7 g fat (4 g saturated fat), 39 mg cholesterol, 109 mg sodium, 21 g carbohydrate, 0 fiber, 7 g protein.
Diabetic Exchanges: 1 starch, 1/2 milk, 1 fat.

Spicy Sweet-Sour Pork

(Pictured below)

I combine tender strips of pork with pineapple and sweet peppers in this colorful entree that's not too sweet and not too sour. It gets a little zip from red pepper flakes and is sure to perk up any meal.
—Shannon Talmage, Alexandria, Indiana

   1 can (8 ounces) pineapple chunks
   1 tablespoon cornstarch
   2 tablespoons reduced-sodium soy sauce
   1 teaspoon brown sugar
   1/8 to 1/4 teaspoon crushed red pepper flakes
   1/2 pound pork tenderloin, cut into 2-inch strips
   2 teaspoons canola oil
   1/2 cup green pepper strips
   1/2 cup sweet red pepper strips
Hot cooked rice, optional

Drain pineapple, reserving juice in a 1-cup measuring cup; set pineapple aside. Add enough water to pineapple juice to measure 1/2 cup. In a small bowl, combine the cornstarch, soy sauce, brown sugar, pepper flakes and reserved juice until smooth. Set aside.

In a nonstick skillet or wok, stir-fry pork in hot oil until meat is no longer pink. Remove and keep warm. In the same skillet, stir-fry peppers for 3-4 minutes or until just crisp-tender. Return meat to the skillet; add reserved pineapple. Stir pineapple juice mixture; add to skillet. Bring to a boil; cook and stir for 2 minutes or until thickened. Serve over rice if desired. **Yield:** 2 servings.

Nutritional Analysis: One serving (1 cup pork mixture, calculated without rice) equals 277 calories, 9 g fat (2 g saturated fat), 63 mg cholesterol, 661 mg sodium, 24 g carbohydrate, 2 g fiber, 24 g protein.
Diabetic Exchanges: 3 lean meat, 1 vegetable, 1 fruit, 1/2 starch.

General Recipe Index

This handy index lists every recipe by food category, major ingredient and/or cooking method, so you can easily locate recipes to suit your needs.

SANDWICHES

SAUSAGE *(also see Turkey Sausage)*

SEAFOOD *(see Fish & Seafood)*

SKILLET & STOVETOP SUPPERS

Alphabetical Index

*This handy index lists every recipe in alphabetical order
so you can easily find your favorite dish.*

Reference Index

Use this index to locate the many healthy cooking hints located throughout the book.